· THE JEWS IN THE GREEK AGE ·

Published in cooperation with
The Jewish Theological Seminary of America

THE JEWS

IN THE

GREEK AGE

Elias J. Bickerman

HARVARD UNIVERSITY PRESS

CAMBRIDGE, MASSACHUSETTS

LONDON, ENGLAND

1988

Copyright © 1988 by The Jewish Theological Seminary of America
All rights reserved
Printed in the United States of America
Fourth printing, 1997

Library of Congress Cataloging-in-Publication Data

Bickerman, E. J. (Elias Joseph), 1897–
    The Jews in the Greek Age.

"Published in cooperation with the
Jewish Theological Seminary of America"—Half t.p.
Bibliography: p.
Includes index.
1. Jews—History—586 B.C.–70 A.D.
2. Judaism—History—Post-exilic period, 586 B.C.–210 A.D.
3. Jews—Civilization—Greek influences.
4. Hellenism.
I. Jewish Theological Seminary of America.
II. Title.
DS121.65.B53   1988   909'.04924   87-23771
        ISBN 0-674-47490-2 (alk. paper) (cloth)
            ISBN 0-674-47491-0 (paper)

PARENTUM MEMORIAE

S.

Foreword

I N THE latter part of the 1950s, Professor Louis Finkelstein, chancellor of The Jewish Theological Seminary of America, invited several scholars, each a leading authority in his area of research in Jewish history, to compose a book-length work on "the state of the field" in his area. Of those invited by Dr. Finkelstein, only the late Professor Elias Bickerman submitted a manuscript, and it is his work, edited with diligence and acumen by Shari Friedman, a member of the Seminary research staff, that constitutes this book. Dr. Albert Baumgarten of the Department of Jewish History of Bar-Ilan University, a former student of Professor Bickerman, assisted with the final preparation of the manuscript and compiled a bibliography for the book, a project that Professor Bickerman had not yet begun before his death.

Bickerman was a familiar face at the Seminary. He had been given a fellowship there in 1943 by Dr. Finkelstein, and he had become a warm friend of several faculty members and students. He conducted occasional seminars in Hellenistic texts and freely gave scholarly aid and advice when asked. Some of his seminal monographs were composed in his office on the sixth floor of the Unterberg building at the Seminary. On occasion he traveled to the West Coast branch of the Seminary, the University of Judaism, where he also conducted seminars. In 1952 he accepted the invitation of the Department of History of Columbia University to fill the professorship of ancient Greek and Roman history, a post he held until his retirement in 1967.

Bickerman was a formidable scholar whose knowledge of history generally, and of ancient history especially, was staggering. His self-discipline was such that he would not express himself on any matter in which he had not read the primary sources. Although essentially a specialist in Greek and Roman history, his critical competence enabled him to be more fluent in ancient Jewish history, biblical as well as rabbinic, than many who worked specifically in those areas. Indeed, the subject in which he had the greatest impact was Hellenistic Jewish history. Bickerman's treatment of the text in which Antiochus the Great assures the Jews that Jerusalem would be religiously autonomous elucidated the concept of Jewish religious freedom in the ancient world. It was a vital study not only in and of itself but also because it became the basis for his epoch-making *Der Gott der Makkabäer* (1939). Here Bickerman proclaimed that the Epiphanian persecutions required explanation in view of the fact that—Jewish notions to the contrary notwithstanding—Antiochus IV Epiphanes was not given to religious intolerance. Bickerman's solution of this problem and his meticulous survey of each step of the conflict for Jewish religious freedom generated much discussion on the place of the Jews in the Hellenistic world. In his shorter survey, *Die Makkabäer,* Bickerman proposed that the Maccabees should be perceived not as enemies of Hellenism and its encroachments on Jewish society, but as a native Jewish group that succeeded in achieving and maintaining power precisely because it knew how to come to terms with Hellenism—indeed, as the embodiment of a successful encounter with ancient Hellenism.

Now that we are privileged to have his final statement of the encounter between Judaism and Hellenism, we have a worthy colophon to the works of a scholar who will continue to speak with authority to generations of students.

Gerson D. Cohen

The Jewish Theological Seminary of America

February 1987

Preface

THE THEME of this volume is stability and change in Jewish society during the first centuries of the Greek Age, from the fourth century until approximately 175 B.C.E. As a Hellenist, the writer sees the men and events he describes not as a link between the Hebrew Scriptures and the rabbinic period, but as a part of universal history, the final meaning of which only He knows, before Whom a thousand years are like one day.

Because place and time are the dimensions of history, the author has avoided the use of data from later periods and other areas for his reconstruction. Accordingly, the volume contains no information on many important matters for which we lack contemporary evidence.

The author has labored to evade the two worst pitfalls of historiography: nationalism and anachronism. He is conscious, however, of the sin of ignorance. Although Boaz Cohen, H. L. Ginsberg, Saul Lieberman, and Morton Smith gave freely to him out of the treasures of their knowledge, the author does not doubt that this volume contains its just share of mistakes and errors. In truth, without both ignorance and arrogance, who would dare to publish a historical work?

Yet the purpose of a historical work is not merely to pour out accumulated knowledge. A historical work should be, rather, a ferment which excites the reader's own thinking. The author hopes that his book offers enough questionable opinions to stimulate disagreement and enough facts to help the reader in forming his or her own judgment.

This volume could not have been written or published without the generous aid of The Jewish Theological Seminary of America. I hope that Chancellor Louis Finkelstein, who sustained the work through the years of its preparation, and the other officers of the Seminary will be gratified by their faith and interest in this book. With all its shortcomings, it retrieves a hundred and sixty years of the Jewish past, from Alexander the Great to the Maccabees.

E. J. B.

Columbia University

Contents

III · PERMANENCE AND INNOVATION

PART I

BEFORE
AND AFTER
ALEXANDER

ONE

Alexander and Jerusalem

I N THE third year of the reign of the last Babylonian king, Daniel the prophet was transported in a vision to the citadel of Susa, the future seat of the coming Persian Empire. There he saw a ram, which "magnified" itself. But a he-goat came from the west and smote the ram, "and there was none who could deliver the ram out of his hand."

This myth became history on a November day in 333 B.C.E., when Alexander of Macedon, the he-goat of Daniel's vision, met and put to rout Darius III of Persia and his host at Issus, the plain by the bay of Alexandretta in Cilicia, the historic gateway from Asia Minor to Syria and Egypt. Four days after the victory Alexander's cavalry crossed over the passes of Mount Amanus and entered Damascus, the capital of the Persian satrapy of Syria, while the Macedonian himself moved down the coast toward Egypt.

The first rumors of Darius' defeat must have been received at Jerusalem with incredulity and misgiving. There was no quarrel between the Temple of the Lord and the house of Darius. Since the days of Cyrus, six generations of God-fearing Jews had been brought up under the protection of Persian archers. An oath of fealty bound Jerusalem to its pagan sovereign. Every day since the year 520 the priests of Jerusalem had sacrificed to the Lord of Zion, praying for the life and prosperity of the King of Kings.

Of course, there were in circulation old prophecies predicting doom for the nations and promising grandeur for the Chosen People, but the ruling men of Jerusalem, the aristocracy of land and of altar, hardly longed for "the great and terrible day of the Lord." The failure of the messianic hopes aroused by Haggai and Zechariah during the general insurrection of subject peoples against Darius I (521 B.C.E.) was probably not forgotten. The Temple scribe who, some decades before Alexander's conquest, had written a new history of the elected nation from Adam to

Nehemiah (preserved in the Bible as Chronicles and Ezra-Nehemiah), certainly believed in a coming restoration of David's throne, but for the present he remained a faithful subject of the Great King and regarded the Persian dominion as everlasting. From among the evildoings of the last king of Judah, this pious writer had singled out his rebellion against Nebuchadnezzar, "who had made him swear by God" an oath of loyalty. This condemnation was taken from Ezekiel, but it was also salutary advice for the readers of Chronicles. Besides, only ten years before Alexander's campaign, Artaxerxes III had taught a lesson of prudence to hotheads eager to speculate on the fall of the Persian monarchy. In 351, when he had failed to reconquer Egypt, Phoenicia had also broken away from him; but in 343 he had come back to capture and destroy Sidon, the leading city of the Phoenicians, and then to subdue Egypt again. In October 345, Sidonian prisoners had already begun to arrive in Babylonia. To that country, and to Hyrcania (Mazanderan) on the south shore of the Caspian Sea, were transferred those Jews who had sided with the rebels.

As for "the sons of Yavan," the Greeks, they were servants of the King of Kings, just like the Phoenicians and the Jews. They fought his battles as mercenaries, worked as stonecutters at his palace at Susa, and traded in his ports. According to royal bulletins, even the Greeks dwelling beyond the sea had been conquered in the days of Xerxes. The population of Syria, therefore, at first regarded the Macedonian conquerors with contempt, for Darius still lived and ruled the whole East beyond the Syrian desert.

The fall of Damascus, however, had deprived the satrapy of its government. Now each city and each tribe had to make a choice between the present anger of Alexander and the future retaliation of Darius. Some Phoenician cities (Aradus, Tripolis, Byblus) hastened to welcome the conqueror; Sidon, ruined by Artaxerxes III, received Alexander with open arms. The Tyrians, however, traditional rivals of Sidon, refused to submit. Because their city was the base of Persian sea power, the capture of Tyre was imperative for Alexander, and he began his siege toward the end of 333. Seven months later Tyre was taken and cruelly punished.

In the meantime the Macedonians were also subjugating the interior of Syria. Alexander needed money, supplies, and men for the siege of Tyre, which had never before been taken by force; Jerusalem, among other cities, was ordered to furnish men, supplies, and tribute in the amount that had previously been paid to Darius. According to a later Jewish fictional account of this incident used by Josephus, the High Priest refused to violate his oath to Darius; but the motif of fealty is introduced only to prepare us for the unexpected denouement of the story: an angry Alexander, meeting the High Priest on the road to Jerusalem, suddenly makes obeisance upon seeing the ineffable Name on the mitre of the Pontiff. He recognizes in the High Priest the man he saw in his sleep in Macedonia urging him to conquer Persia. Thankfully, Alexander sacrifices to the Lord and grants privileges to the Jews.

This silly story judaizes Greek tales of a similar nature. It was told, for instance, that about 400 B.C.E. the Celtic king Catumundus besieged Marseilles. In his sleep he saw a goddess commanding him to raise the siege; he obeyed, made peace with the city, and recognized in the idol of Athena, which he saw in Marseilles, the woman of his vision. He offered a golden necklace to the goddess, praised the Massaliotes for their piety, and made a treaty of eternal friendship with them. In reality, since Persian rule in Palestine had rested on military colonies outside Jewish territory (such as Samaria, Gerar, and Lachish), and since the Persian governor of Samaria, who was commander in chief of the region, had himself readily submitted to the Macedonian, Jerusalem could hardly have been expected to brave Alexander's battering rams alone.

After the fall of Tyre the resistance of Gaza, the great Persian stronghold controlling the approaches to Egypt, checked Alexander's southward advance for two months, but after its capture the Persian satrap of Egypt handed his province to Alexander, in November 332. In the spring the conqueror returned to Tyre and from there set forth to conquer the eastern part of the Persian Empire.

The Jewish account discussed above places Alexander's visit to Jerusalem after the capture of Gaza, that is, in the fall of 332. A variant of the same story preserved in talmudic tradition states that the king came up to Jerusalem from the Phoenician coast—that is, in the previous summer of 333. When and whether Alexander entered Jerusalem we cannot say; the entire story of his visit is probably fictitious, invented to flatter Jewish self-esteem. But if Alexander did go to Jerusalem, he surely "sacrificed to God under the guidance of the High Priest," as the Jewish tale says. In the pagan world the conqueror generally respected the deities of the defeated enemy on the grounds that it would be foolish to offend any supernatural power.

When Alexander led his army out of Tyre against Darius, he had among his troops some Jewish auxiliaries. On the first of October 331, he encountered and defeated Darius for the second time, this time decisively. After this victory, at Gaugamela (in the vicinity of modern Mosul), the Babylonians opened their gates to him and as their legitimate ruler, Alexander ordered the restoration of Esagila, the cathedral of the city. On this occasion the Greeks learned for the first time of the strength of the Jewish aversion to idolatry; neither corporal punishment nor heavy fines could compel Alexander's Jewish soldiers to work on rebuilding a heathen temple.

From Babylon, Alexander advanced to Susa (December 331) and then, in pursuit of Darius, to the Caspian Sea. After Darius was murdered by his own officers (July 330), Alexander continued the subjugation of the East, from the Aral Sea to the Indus. In the Indus valley, however, his army rebelled, refusing to go any farther, and the conqueror was compelled to turn back. He died of fever at Babylon on the evening of June 10, 323 B.C.E.

The encounter of this heir of Hercules with the seed of Abraham stirs our imagination. We might expect that the opening of a new age would have been heralded by Greeks and Jews alike. But Alexander's Greek historians did not even mention Jerusalem, the obscure abode of an insignificant tribe; nor did any Jewish folktale of the time garland the name of the Macedonian. In Alexandria, on the other hand, Hellenized Egyptians appropriated Alexander for themselves by pretending that he was a son of Nectanebus II, the last Pharaoh, and in Persia he became an offspring of Artaxerxes III. The Persian priests saw "the evil-destined villain Alexander" as having been sent by the Devil (Ariman) to extirpate the Persian aristocracy and destroy the true religion. Even before the conquest vaticinations against Alexander, the enemy of the Persians, had circulated in Asia; we can still read some of these prophecies in Greek in the collection of the Sibylline Oracles.

The Jews neither cursed nor appropriated the conqueror. If there were Hebrew oracles that referred to him, none has been preserved. It is significant that for Daniel, the ram, the zodiacal sign for Persia, is smitten by the he-goat, the zodiacal sign for Syria. Here, as elsewhere in Palestinian tradition, Alexander is viewed as the ancestor of the Seleucid kings of Syria. It was not until the posthumous renown of Alexander among the Greeks sufficiently impressed the Jews that they began to speak of his (presumed) visit to Jerusalem and his (imaginary) journey to the "mountain of darkness." As a matter of fact the stories of Alexander in rabbinic tradition are drawn from the Greek Alexander Romance and testify only to the popularity of this fabulous work in Roman times.

The reason for this Jewish indifference to Alexander is easy to discover. Alexander's arrival did not change anything in Jerusalem except the name of the pagan sovereign. The rulers of the people, the tribute, the status of the Temple, all remained as they had been under the Persian kings. Except for some months in 320 and some weeks in 312, when Palestine was governed from Alexandria, until 301 the overlord of Jerusalem continued to dwell at Babylon or elsewhere in the East, while the satrap of Syria resided, as before, in Damascus. It did not matter much to the men and women of Jerusalem and Judea whether the heathen in command of the citadel in the Holy City had taken his oath of allegiance to a Macedonian or a Persian master. The idea of a sharp separation between the "Persian" and the "Greek" periods in Jewish history derives from Daniel, who, trying to understand the origin of the persecution under Antiochus IV, and following the traditional scheme of the succession of kings and dynasties, used the (originally Persian) idea of successive world empires. For Daniel, these were Babylonia, Media, Persia, and Macedonia. It was the nationalist delirium of post-Napoleonic Europe that transformed Daniel's purely political arrangement into a succession of ethnic and cultural units: the Orientals, the Greeks, and then the Romans. But even Daniel's political schema is inappropriate for the history of the Jews (or, say, the Tyrians) under Persian and then Macedonian and Roman domination. Ancient empires were neither willing nor able to change the traditional structures of subject cities, villages, and tribes. Thus the privileges obtained from the Persian kings remained essentially in force under Macedonian rulers and Roman emperors alike. For six centuries (539 B.C.E.–70 C.E.), from Cyrus to the destruction of the Temple by Titus—except for some three years of Antiochus' persecution and the Hasmonean-Herodian period of Jewish independence and semi-independence—the political history of Jerusalem and Judea operated within the same framework.

Alexander and Samaria

Alexander did make history in Jerusalem, however, by his treatment of Samaria. Throughout its existence the royal city of the kingdom of Israel had overshadowed the fortunes of the older capital of Judah. When Sargon the Assyrian conquered Samaria in 721, he not only removed the Jewish population of the city to northern Mesopotamia and Media but also repeopled the city with Assyrian military colonists—"making Samaria greater than before," as he proudly stated. The successors of Sargon, from Assyrian kings to Roman emperors, took over the great military camp, "the army of Samaria," one from the other and used this "place of watch" to secure their domination over Palestine. The two main defensive walls around the summit of the hill of Samaria, as well as the works on the lower slopes, had been so solidly built by Israelite engineers of the ninth century B.C.E. that the fortifications, patched and from time to time reinforced, rendered the city impregnable for eight centuries. Like Sargon, the Maccabean king John Hyrcanus was unable to take Samaria by assault, eventually starving the Seleucid garrison out around 109 B.C.E.

After Persian authority in Syria collapsed following the rout of Darius' army at Issus, Samaria (toward the end of 333 B.C.E.) submitted to Alexander. The next winter, however, while Alexander remained in Egypt, Samaria revolted. Darius was preparing a new army for his decisive battle with Alexander and it would have been a great advantage for him had the Macedonian been compelled to lay a long siege to the Palestinian fortress. Unfortunately for Darius, upon Alexander's arrival in the north in the spring of 331, the rebels were handed over to him and the other supporters of the Persian cause fled. A group of them, seeking refuge in a desert cave fourteen kilometers north of ancient Jericho were discovered by their Macedonian pursuers and slaughtered. Their skeletons, some two hundred of them, including men, women, and children, were found in the cave, along with legal documents written in Aramaic concerning properties in Samaria. The victims had clearly expected to return home after the hoped-for defeat of Alexander and had optimistically carried their legal papyri with them.

Alexander, too, attached great military importance to Samaria and placed his own military colonists—Macedonians, of course—there in order to secure the fortress. In doing so he set in motion a chain of historical events that eventually provoked a religious schism and created a new people, whose last remnant, perhaps two hundred souls, still dwells in the ghetto of Nablus, close to ancient Shechem. We call these people "Samaritans," but in order to understand this name, as well as the origins of the people, we must go back again to Sargon the Assyrian.

The people who were transferred to Samaria from Elam in Babylonia and from northern Syria by Sargon and his successors brought with them their ancestral gods, Adamilki and Nergal; the latter was the demon of pestilence and the patron saint of Cutha (situated between Babylon and the Tigris), who was also worshipped at Sidon, another city resettled by the Assyrians. Of course, the Israelites who had not been deported by the Assyrians continued to worship the God of their ancestors and of their land, while the newcomers, being polytheists, worshipped the gods they had brought with them and in due course also accepted the heavenly Lord of the land in which they now dwelled—just as the Assyrians at Sidon learned to worship Sidonian gods.

A famous passage in II Kings (17:25 ff.) describes why the Assyrian colonists in Samaria felt it was necessary to learn the law of the God of their new land. As they themselves declared to the Jews of Jerusalem in 520 B.C.E. (Ezra 4:2), they had sacrificed to the Lord since the days of Esarhaddon, king of Assyria; that is, they had been combining their ancestral idolatry with worship of the Lord at the traditional high places and shrines of Israel for a long time. The question of how and when they became monotheists and came to recognize only the God of Jerusalem is still unanswerable, but in 520 B.C.E. they offered their help in rebuilding his Temple, saying to the leaders of the Jews, "We seek your God as you do." Their offer was refused on the legal pretext that Cyrus' order to restore the Temple was addressed to the Jews alone (Ezra 4:3), but there was no mention of idolatry. A century later Sanballat, the governor of Samaria, gives his sons names that invoke the Lord of Jerusalem, and two generations after that, on the eve of Alexander's conquest, a descendant of Sanballat, who also bears a name invoking the Lord of Jerusalem and who, like his ancestor, was "governor of Samaria," uses a seal inscribed in Hebrew in the Old Hebrew script.

When Alexander settled his Macedonians in Samaria, however, he unwittingly destroyed the religious harmony that had existed between

Samaria and Jerusalem. The new masters of the northern stronghold did not know anything about the God of Israel. The new "Samarians" looked across the sea to the west: at Athens a Greek cult association crowned a "Samarian" as its benefactor and temples of Hellenic gods (such as the Athenian Kore), altars of Isis and Osiris, and monuments of the Dioscuri were now to be seen in Samaria. The Macedonian settlers, like their Assyrian predecessors, would probably have accepted the God of Israel into their pantheon eventually, but such syncretism was no longer possible for the Jews. God's people had been kept in exile for purposes of discipline and the experience had taught the worshippers of the Lord to abandon the harlotry of heathen cults forever. No one could follow both the Lord and Baal. Thus, when Samaria again became a city of numerous gods, the believers of the unique Deity, rejecting the Olympians, withdrew to Shechem.

With the Macedonians settled in Samaria, the former upper class of the city, the officers and officials who "ate the salt of the palace" under the Persian kings, lost their status. As monotheists they could no longer worship in Samaria, now defiled by Greek idols, but although they believed in the same Deity as the people of Jerusalem, in the eyes of the Jerusalemites they were second-class Jews because they lacked the right of priesthood and a place of worship on their own territory. They therefore boldly challenged Jerusalem's claim to be the sole rightful place of sacrificial worship of the Lord and built a temple to Him on their own holy mountain, Gerizim, a place sacred from time immemorial: the Chosen People had been enjoined by the Lawgiver to "set the blessing upon Mount Gerizim" after entering the Promised Land (Deut. 11:20 and Josh. 8:33).

Josephus tells us that the shrine on Gerizim was built by Sanballat, the last Persian governor of Samaria, with the authorization of Alexander the Great. This item must stem from Samaritan tradition; no Jew would have invented a link between the schismatic altar and the glorious Macedonian. On the contrary, the Jews insisted that no "king of Asia" had shown any favor to Gerizim. Although Josephus himself confuses this Sanballat with the homonymous adversary of Nehemiah, the Samaritan tradition is indirectly confirmed by the legal papyri mentioned above. The mere fact that the new temple was erected on Mount Gerizim, adjoining Shechem, and not at Samaria, the seat of Nehemiah's rival, is conclusive evidence of the correctness of the Samaritan chronology. It often happened that when an interloping Greek colony was established, the natives under its control banded together around a common sanctuary. Following the same pattern, the monotheist population of Macedonian Samaria formed a new community whose members worshipped at the new temple on Gerizim and whose political center was established at the foot of the sacred mountain, on the site of the Israelite Shechem, destroyed by the Assyrians about 724 B.C.E.

The new city inherited the name of the ancient biblical city, but the community styled itself, in Greek, as "the Sidonians of Shechem." In Greek from Homer on, the term "Sidonians" was used to refer to the Phoenicians, that is, the Canaanites of Scripture, in which Sidon is designated as the firstborn son of Canaan (Gen. 10:15). Indeed, Canaan is called the father of the Phoenicians by a Samaritan author writing in Greek. Therefore, because Shechem had originally been a Canaanite city, its inhabitants were qualified to call themselves "Sidonians" in Greek. Place, no less than race, distinguished a people. In 677 B.C.E. the islet of Sidon was laid waste by Esarhaddon and its population deported. The new Assyrian colonists built their city on a new site on the mainland and gave it a new name, the "Fortress of Esarhaddon." Less than a century later, however, the Assyrian colony appropriated the proud old name of Sidon, and no one then or afterward questioned their right to call themselves Sidonians. Likewise, the citizens of Greek Ilion considered themselves, and were acknowledged to be, the legitimate heirs of Homer's Trojans.

The worshippers on Gerizim were badly in need of a distinguished name. "Samaria" now belonged to the Persian colonists and "Israel," the historical name of the northern kingdom, had in the meantime been taken over by the Jews of Judea, who now referred to the worshippers at Gerizim as "Cutheans" (after the Babylonian city from which many of the Assyrian settlers of Samaria had come), in order to stress their alien origin. The Jews regarded these converts as half-breeds and intruders in the Promised Land. By styling themselves "Sidonians," that is, "Canaanites," and therefore autochthonous, the descendants of the Assyrian settlers appropriated the ancient glory of Shechem and trumped both the Jews in Jerusalem, the older arrivals in Canaan, as well as the Greeks at Samaria, the more recent arrivals. The Shechemites now asserted, for instance, that Melchizedek, king of Salem (in the vicinity of Shechem) and priest of the Most High God, who according to the Torah had blessed Abraham and received tithes from the Patriarch, was one of their people, since he belonged to "the race of Sidon and Canaan." Moreover, proclaiming that Melchizedek had officiated at Gerizim, they claimed for their temple an antiquity far surpassing that of Zion. Accordingly, the Samaritan Torah says that God "has chosen" (not "shall choose," as the Hebrew text has it) the place of His worship in the Promised Land. Let us here restate that according to the Greek (and Roman) view, "Sidonian" lineage would not prevent the schismatics from pretending to be the authentic Israel. No wonder that, as Jewish polemic shows, the Samaritan claims made Jerusalem uneasy.

In any case, the schismatics of Gerizim were true sons of Abraham with regard to their faith: for them, too, the Torah was the sole foundation of life. In a later Jewish treatise on the "Cutheans," their readmission into the fold hinges only upon their recognition of Jerusalem and their acknowledgment of the Resurrection. Since the doctrine of resurrection was a late pharisaic innovation, it is apparent that historically the whole controversy between the two groups of Moses' followers was subordinated to the sole question of which place, Zion or Gerizim, had been chosen by God for His habitation. The schismatics were Jews without Zion, but with Gerizim.

The influence of the latter shrine extended over only a small strip of land. The Macedonian colony of Samaria was five miles northwest of Shechem; some ten miles south of Mount Gerizim ran a religious boundary beyond which people continued to turn toward Jerusalem. Nevertheless, the shrine at Gerizim remained a threat to Zion. Ben Sira contrasts the people "upon the mountain of Samaria" (that is, the Macedonian colony) and the Philistines—two nations who vex him—to "the fools who dwell in Sichem," who are to him no nation at all. The Jews destroyed the rival place of worship at the first opportunity, that is, at the time of Maccabean expansion, about 128 B.C.E. Some twenty years later they succeeded in capturing Samaria, too.

When the Romans restored Samaria, about 57 B.C.E., it received a new name in honor of the Roman general Gabinius. Later, under Herod, it was named Sebaste, in honor of Augustus. However, the district around the new city continued to be called Samaria, and because the schismatics were dispersed throughout the villages of this district, they were organized by Herod (or some Roman prefect of Palestine) as "the nation of the Samaritans." Samaritans, therefore, is the name by which the schismatics are still known to us today. The temple of the Lord on Gerizim was never restored. Alexander the Great, who authorized its construction, unwittingly separated Judah and Israel forever.

The Greeks Discover the Jews

SMALL tribe lost in the immensity of the Persian Empire, an agricultural people situated on an isolated tableland and averse to commercial activity, the Jews of Jerusalem and Judea, as Josephus explained, could not have been known to the Greeks before Alexander's conquest. Perhaps we may, with Josephus, find an allusion to the Jews in Herodotus' mention of the Syrians of Palestine among the peoples practicing circumcision; word of the wonders of the Dead Sea had already reached Aristotle before Alexander's campaign in Palestine. But even after Alexander's arrival no Greek scholar hastened to visit Jerusalem. With the whole of the fabulous Orient, from the cataracts of the Nile to the valley of the Ganges, suddenly open to his curiosity, why should he have concerned himself with a minuscule tribe in Palestine?

Still, long before Alexander, Greeks and Jews had encountered each other outside their homelands. In the Persian period the Jewish diaspora had spread from the Ethiopian frontier to the Caspian Sea. And almost everywhere these Jews had come across Greek traders, craftsmen, and mercenaries. At Babylon the Jews of the Captivity had rubbed shoulders with Ionians—Greek mercenaries in the army of Nebuchadnezzar—among whom, apparently, was a brother of the poet Alcaeus of Lesbos. The poet mentions not only the "holy city" of Babylon, but also Ascalon, captured by the Babylonians in 604. Appolonides of Cos, Greek physician to Artaxerxes I, could not have missed seeing Nehemiah, cupbearer of that Persian king. Tahpanhes in the Egyptian Delta is identical with, or at least in the neighborhood of, the place that the Greeks called Daphne. Shortly after Daphne was garrisoned by Greek mercenaries settled there by Psammetichus II (594–588 B.C.E.) Jews fled to Tahpanhes. Jeremiah delivered his last admonitions in this Egyptian town.

Plato, however, never sat at Jeremiah's feet. Augustine, who at first believed this tale (invented by some Christian apologist to counter the

Neoplatonic charge that the new religion had borrowed from Plato) later nicely demonstrated that this bold hypothesis must be ruled out by chronology. The Jewish philosopher Aristobulus (ca. 175 B.C.E.) also failed to substantiate his claim that Plato and Pythagoras had borrowed from Moses. Nor had the legendary Orpheus, the earliest Greek poet; nor did Phocylides of Miletus, a contemporary of Cyrus, borrow from Deuteronomy or speak of Abraham. The Jews, who as soon as they had learned the elements of Greek poetic language hastened to fabricate pious hexameters and publish them under the names of venerable Greek authorities, forgot that according to a prophet (Isa. 66:19), Yavan was among the nations that had not heard of the fame of the Lord. Nevertheless, these Jewish (and later Christian) forgers had more historical sense than those German professors who denied the possibility of biblical influence on classical Greece.

It is too often forgotten that the Jews in the Persian period were in their life, speech, and manners part of a universal Levantine civilization served by a common language, Aramaic. We shall have many more occasions to point out this essential fact. Here it suffices to note that Aramaic, as the common language of the whole Near East, from the Indus to the Nile, enormously facilitated the exchange of knowledge between Greece and the Orient. Greek, Indian, and Egyptian physicians did not need to know other languages in order to discover the ideas of those who spoke them; as soon as a thought was formulated in Aramaic it became international. Greeks trading in the East, or working there, either had to know this international language or had to use Aramaic dragomans. If, as has been conjectured, the Armenian Er, whom we find in a Platonic tale, is an authentic figure of Asian myth, the knowledge of this Asian figure must have come to Plato through Greeks who were in contact with the Aramaic Levant. So, too, Hebrew ideas and images could have reached Greece long before Alexander.

The fact remains, however, that the Chosen People and its heroes are never mentioned in classical Greek literature. No Greek traveler in the Orient, neither Herodotus nor Ctesias, paid any attention to Jerusalem or its Deity. The uniformity of Aramaic, the common language of the Persian Empire, concealed national distinctions; to a Greek visitor both the Jew and the Turkoman in Mesopotamia were equally Babylonian.

For a similar reason, because Greek was the international language of ancient Italy, Josephus notes that Rome was not mentioned by Greek writers until quite late. The first Greek historian outside Italy and Sicily to record a Roman event—the capture of Rome by the Gauls in 387 B.C.E.—was Theopompus, a contemporary of Alexander the Great. Plato speaks of the laws of the Celts, of the Iberians, and even of the rights and duties of Sauromatian women on the Don, but neither he nor Aristotle had ever heard of Roman institutions; the Greeks in Greece became interested in Rome only during and after the war between Rome and King Pyrrhus of Epirus (280–272 B.C.E.). According to Cicero, Theophrastus (Aristotle's successor at the Peripatetic School from 322 until his death, ca. 286) dealt with the laws of nearly all the Greek and "barbarian" states in his work *On Laws*. Nevertheless, he must never have spoken of Rome, since otherwise Cicero, his admirer and assiduous reader, would have quoted him on this subject; nor of Moses and the Torah, as the silence of Josephus proves, who elsewhere quotes Theophrastus on Tyrian oaths. Yet Theophrastus did write elsewhere on the religion of the Jews; seeking proof for one of his anthropological ideas, he turned to the Jews because of the respect for oriental wisdom among the intellectuals of his time.

Anxiety about the future of the Greek city-state, the *polis*, threatened by social upheaval and endangered by the new monarchies of Philip of Macedon, of his son Alexander, and of Alexander's successors, brought forth the idea that life must remain static in order to prevent the failure of civilization. Plato admired Egyptian art for its changeless patterns and even suggested that the rules of children's games be frozen forever. At such a moment the priestly wisdom of the Orient, supposedly eternal, seemed particularly attractive compared to ever-changing and ephemeral Greek theories. Conversations between a Greek intellectual and an oriental sage became a favorite theme of popular philosophy; Aristoxenus of Tarentum even invented a meeting between Socrates and an Indian. The Indian easily scored off the Athenian.

Clearchus of Soli, a pupil of Aristotle and a contemporary of Aristoxenus, writing some years after his master's death in 322, had Aristotle, as a speaker in a philosophical dialogue, *On Sleep,* tell about his meeting with a Jewish sage in Asia Minor at the time he was teaching at Assos (347 to 344). Clearchus' Jew, like Aristoxenus' Indian, tests Greek wisdom. By a hypnotic experiment he proves that the soul really leaves the body in sleep, a demonstration that was very valuable for the Platonic theory, accepted by the young Aristotle, that the soul is independent of the corruptible body and in consequence immortal. Clearchus' Aristotle admires the endurance and self-control of the Jew, who did works "wonderful as a dream," and praises him as one who not only spoke Greek, but "also in soul was Greek." Since Aristotle did write *On Philosophy,* in which he dealt with Zoroaster and the Persian Magi, during his sojourn at Assos, and since there were Jews in Asia Minor at that time, the story may well be true—or may just as well be Clearchus' invention. It is symbolic, however, that in the first reported (or imaginary) meeting between a Jew and a Greek, it is the Greek who is the greatest of all savants while the Jew is a miracle worker: "For the Jews require a sign, and the Greeks seek after wisdom" (I Cor. 1:22).

Theophrastus, in his (probably) youthful work *On Piety*, the publication of which may have preceded Clearchus' dialogue, found in Jewish ritual the ethnographic evidence for his thesis that in the state of nature men did not know bloody sacrifices, but were satisfied with bringing fruits of the soil to the altars. (The Egyptian worship of animals was another confirmation of his theory.) He mistakenly imagined that the daily burnt offering was made at night; and learning that it was not consumed by the faithful, he inferred that the "philosophical" race of the Jews, who at night prayed and observed the stars—the visible gods of Platonic theology—was ashamed of its animal sacrifices.

Theophrastus was not alone in regarding the Jews as "philosophers." Clearchus also believed that in Syria philosophers are called "Ioudaoi" because they inhabit the territory called "Ioudaia." These philosophers were for him descendants of Indian sages. A generation later, about 300 B.C.E., Megasthenes, a Greek traveler to India, discovered that all the doctrines of the earlier Greek sages about nature were also known to the wise men of the East, men like the Indian Brahmans and "the so-called Jews in Syria."

These views, held by the best Greek scholars in the last decades of the fourth century B.C.E., were in no way preposterous. The Greeks did not distinguish metaphysics from theology. Josephus still spoke of Jewish "philosophy" and could explain the Jewish sects to his Greek readers only in terms of philosophical schools. In the same way the Greeks compared the Egyptian priests, the Persian Magi, and later the Celtic Druids, to their own wise men. They also naturally fused the various priests of the Aramaic-speaking East into a sacerdotal brotherhood of sages; Clearchus, for instance, suggested that the Indian Brahmans were descendants of the Persian Magi. Because the Jews inhabited Syria, spoke the "Syrian" language (that is, Aramaic), and were subject to ritual obligations elsewhere observed by other priestly castes, they too were placed by the Greeks among the sacerdotal sages of the Orient.

Only when the Jewish diaspora grew larger did the Greeks learn the real identity of the Jews. The work of Hecataeus of Abdera, written at Alexandria toward the end of the fourth century, was an eye-opener. His book, which may have been part of a work on Egypt, became the standard text on the subject. Three centuries later Diodorus condensed it for his *Universal History*, and Jewish forgers even published their own products under the authoritative name of Hecataeus.

Although Hecataeus knew of a Jewish book relating "the establishment and the constitution" of the Jews (the Torah), he relied on the accounts of Egyptian priests for his report on Jewish origins. These priests, regarding their country as the fountainhead of civilization, presented the Jews, the Babylonian priesthood, and Danaus (who founded Argos, the oldest city in Greece) as emigrants from Egypt. Having heard of the Exodus and having learned the Greek story of how Danaus had fled from Egypt, the Egyptian priests simply combined these tidbits of foreign information with their own tradition of the expulsion of unholy aliens by pious pharaohs. According to their version of the Exodus, the expelled Jews, led by a certain Moses, occupied the land "now called Judea," where Moses founded Jerusalem.

For the part of his book dealing with Mosaic institutions, Hecataeus collected information from Jews he met in Egypt. However, like many anthropologists both ancient and modern, he often misunderstood his informants. Furthermore, like many sociologists, he endeavored to bring his data into agreement with his philosophical views. Because his views on the state followed the Platonic trend, this first occidental account of the Jewish way of life was to that extent distorted.

Plato had expressed the hope that his ideal changeless society, ruled by sages, might exist in some country "far beyond our present sight." The discovery of the Jewish polity seemed to realize this hope. Accordingly, Hecataeus believed that among the Jews, the priests, who had gained leadership because of their superior wisdom, were entrusted with the guidance of the nation and with the care of the unchangeable laws of Moses. The common citizens, busy at husbandry, had equal and inalienable plots of land, which prevented the formation of large estates and, therefore, revolution. Moses made the nation populous by forbidding the exposure of newborn children, and the hard training he imposed on young men developed the virtues of bravery, endurance, and perseverance. Like other clever lawgivers, such as Zoroaster the Persian, or Zalmoxis among the Getae on the lower Danube, Moses pretended to have received his laws from the Deity in order to secure the obedience of the multitude. Following his example, the High Priest, charged with the government of the nation, also presented his directives as divine revelations. Because they had been brought up in this way, there existed, at last, men who refused to change their laws and who preferred to suffer death rather than transgress their ancestral customs. Judaism illustrated the sociological thesis that a religious fiction is the indispensable foundation of the state.

Josephus, quite naively, interpreted Hecataeus' presentation of this ethnographic evidence of a sociological theory as a mark of Hecataeus' admiration for Judaism. Modern scholars, less naive, accept Josephus' interpretation of Hecataeus' account and for this reason deny the authenticity of the passages quoted by Josephus. Nobody, however, has ever explained why a Greek author who admired Egyptian wisdom could not have admired Jewish wisdom as well.

The ideal commonwealth conceived by the philosophers was based on a pure religion. Amid a decaying polytheism, Plato and Aristotle propagated the idea that the perfect order of the heavenly bodies proves the existence of a Supreme Being who governs the universe. Unfortunately, not only the corrupt Greeks but also the wise Egyptians and the virtuous Indians worshipped idols. It was a windfall to discover a people who rejected false gods and adored the God of Heaven alone. According to Hecataeus, Moses regarded the firmament as the sole divinity, for which reason he made no images of the gods. Hecataeus here agrees with Theophrastus.

Hecataeus was also compelled to note, however, that the Jewish way of life was "unsociable and hostile to strangers." Such a disharmonious feature he explained as an effect of the expulsion of the Jews from Egypt; Greek historians explained the Spartan antialien laws in a similar way. On the other hand, he also pointed out that the Jews, like the Egyptians, had changed many of their ancient customs under Persian and Macedonian rule as a result of their contact with foreigners. Indeed, since neither the Egyptians nor the Jews actually behaved in accordance with his sociological premises, Hecataeus concluded that they must have fallen from the state of grace. This sad conclusion agreed with another Greek idea, that of the inevitable decay of polities.

Soon after 300 B.C.E., however, Greek literati lost any special interest in this oriental tribe; it no longer constituted a novelty. For instance, Hieronymus of Cardia, in his history of Alexander's successors (published about 270), did not even mention the Chosen People—to Josephus' dismay. But he did give a long eyewitness report of the Nabateans, a newly discovered people in Palestine. When, about 230 B.C.E., the great Eratosthenes wanted to prove to his Greek readers that "barbarians" might be no less civilized than Hellenes, he discussed the Carthaginians and the Arians (in eastern Iran), but made no mention of the Jews. Josephus, it is true, named an array of early Greek writers who, "not cursorily," did mention the Jews, but they either wrote before the period around 300 B.C.E. or were obscure writers on such special subjects that we are unable to identify them. In fact, Josephus and his Jewish readers had to be satisfied with only incidental references to the Jews from the works of Greek authors of the early Hellenistic period.

Not before the Maccabean wars did the Jews again attract the attention of Greek intellectuals. After the time of Aristotle and until the rise of the

Roman Empire, Greek scholars showed a similar lack of interest in Persian religion and history. Nor did they obtain a reasonably exact knowledge of Brahmanism in India before the second century C.E. Greek businessmen in India or Palestine cared not for ideological niceties, and Greek savants, as scholars are wont to do, cared only for facts that seemed to confirm their favorite theories.

FOUR

The Jews Discover the Greeks

THE Table of Nations in Genesis mentions "Yavan," the name, as an ancient scholar observed, that all the "barbarians" gave to the Greeks; meaning "Ionians" and derived from this tribal name, the name is common to the Egyptian, Babylonian, Persian, Lycian, Sanskrit, and Hebrew-Aramaic tongues. In the Bible, Yavan is a son of Yaphet, that is, of Iapetus, the father of Prometheus in Greek mythology. Among the four sons of Yavan in the Table of Nations, two represent Cyprus ("Kittim" and "Elishah") and one Rhodes ("Rodanim").

Greek merchandise from Rhodes and Cyprus began to reach Palestine in the seventh century. In the fifth century, the age of Athenian hegemony, Attic ware predominated and Attic money was the preferred medium of exchange throughout the entire Levant. Nonetheless, the intermediaries between the Athenian exporters and the consumers in Jerusalem were Phoenician traders; in the time of Nehemiah it was the men of Tyre who brought foreign merchandise to the Holy City. A century later, around 350 B.C.E., the principal ports of Palestine were in Phoenician hands: Dora and Joppa belonged to the Sidonians, and Ascalon to the Tyrians. When Ezekiel or Joel speaks of "the sons of Yavan," they are described as trading with the Phoenicians. Jerusalem and Athens remained ignorant of one another until the coming of Alexander.

Modern historians imagine that the barbarians in Asia should have received the Greek traders and Macedonian soldiers with the respect and admiration due to the missionaries of a higher civilization. In point of fact, however, the orientals heartily disliked the newcomers from the beginning; Hellenization was actually a long and often painful process, accomplished only under the auspices of the Pax Romana. It took time, as Philo says, to learn that Hellas alone produced real men.

Rather, because of the difference in mental outlook, the Greeks at first appeared to the orientals as "powerful and wicked," to quote a Sanskrit writer. Displacing the native aristocracy, the conquerors naturally formed the new upper class and with the buoyant optimism and insatiable greed of self-made men stopped at nothing to secure a life of prosperity. In Judea the newcomers rushed to the balsam gardens of Engedi, where precious balm, worth twice its weight in silver, was produced.

Alexander enriched his army and thus, indirectly, Macedonia and Greece, but the wealth that poured into the hands of his soldiers was taken from the money boxes of the conquered peoples. Using the gold and silver reserves of the Persian kings, Alexander depreciated gold and reduced the purchasing power of silver. This devaluation was a blow to the orientals. Time, however, would have set things straight, had not Alexander's death on June 10, 323, plunged his empire into a civil war that lasted for thirty years.

Alexander's heirs were an infant (Alexander IV) and a simpleton (Philip IV Arrhidaeus), and the regents were generals. The first regent, Perdiccas, was murdered by his officers; the second, Antipater, with difficulty escaped the same fate in 321, but died in 319. When the army appointed Polysperchon as Antipater's successor, the powerful governors of the provinces refused to obey him, and the fighting between the fragments of Alexander's army spread over the entire empire. In the struggle both kings, and even Alexander's mother Olympias, were murdered by the rival generals. At last, in 311, the generals, except for Seleucus in Mesopotamia, made peace. Antigonus, who commanded in Asia, then attempted to subdue Seleucus in a war that ravaged Babylonia. It was in 306, however, when war again became widespread, that Antigonus assumed the royal title, followed in 305 by Ptolemy, the viceroy of Egypt, and in 304 by Seleucus. Alexander's empire had come to an end at last, although the new kings continued the internecine struggle for some ten more years.

"The Way of the Sea," the road trampled by the armies moving from Egypt to Asia and back, traversed the maritime plain outside Judea. Accompanied by endless baggage trains, by the women, children, and slaves of the soldiers, and by traffickers of all kinds, the armed hordes lived well off the country. In addition to capturing towns and requisitioning supplies, they pillaged the countryside. In 306, for example, Antigonus led eighty thousand foot soldiers and eight thousand horsemen against Egypt. That meant that three hundred thousand people and countless horses, asses, mules, and cattle had to be maintained by the population of Palestine for a number of weeks. And, as Antigonus said, he was only gleaning what Alexander had reaped.

Jerusalem, of course, was necessarily drawn into these military operations by her repeated changes of allegiance. After Alexander's death Laomedon became the satrap of Syria, but in 320 (or 319) Nicanor was sent by Ptolemy to occupy Syria. Then, in 318, Eumenes recovered the Phoenician coast, or at least a part of it, for the central government. Three years later Antigonus, having defeated Eumenes, occupied Palestine down to Gaza. In 312 Ptolemy won the battle at Gaza and again came into possession of Palestine. But when, in the same year, Antigonus moved with his main forces from Asia toward Syria, Ptolemy withdrew, snail-like, into his Egyptian shell, taking the opportunity to raze the fortifications of Joppa, Samaria, and Gaza.

For a decade Syria and Palestine obeyed Antigonus, but in 302 a new coalition was formed against him. Ptolemy reoccupied the Phoenician coast, retired on false reports that Antigonus was on his way into Syria, and then in the spring of 301 hastened to reenter Syria after Antigonus' death in the battle against Seleucus and Lysimachus at Ipsus. Demetrius, Antigonus' son, however, continued to hold Tyre and Sidon, and only some years later did Ptolemy succeed in regaining full control of the coast.

In twenty years Jerusalem had changed hands seven times: once in 320 (or 319), twice in 318, once in 315, twice in 312, and once in 302. On one occasion the city resisted Ptolemy, but fell on a Sabbath, when the Jews, praying with outstretched hands to Heaven for divine help, abstained from fighting the enemy on a day sacred to the Lord. The city on that occasion got a "harsh master," as the Greek historian of the episode tells us: large numbers were carried away as slaves, and others were settled by Ptolemy in Egypt, although as free men. The operations of Antigonus and Demetrius probably produced similar effects.

Not since the fall of Babylon in 539 had Jerusalem witnessed such evidence of the passing of heathen kingdoms. From Darius I to Darius III, two centuries of Persian peace had assured them of the stability of the universal monarchy. Rebellions had often occurred in the immense expanse of the Persian dominions, but they were only local and temporary disturbances. The Persian court had propagated the doctrine that the first world empire, that of the Assyrians, had been inherited by the Medes, and inherited from them, in turn, by Cyrus and his successors, whose rule would not end before the end of time. Thus a rebellion was more than an act of disobedience; it was also a lie, a negation of the eternal truth of the eternal empire.

This quietist ideology, however, was refuted by the events following Alexander's death. Alexander's race, which had been called "mistress of every land which the sun looks on," seemed to be perishing through a malign fate. The divisions among the Macedonians appeared eternal, their internecine warfare endless. It seemed as though, like the men born from the dragon's teeth in Greek myth, the Macedonian rulers would exterminate themselves in suicidal combat. The world was turned upside down, exactly as the dying Diogenes had predicted. Wild hopes again became reasonable. When the Egyptians learned that they had only exchanged the hated Medes for the viciously methodical Ionian exploiters, they again began to hope for an early end to all foreign devils. An old oracle promised that a savior from Heracleopolis (Hanes in the Bible; the modern Ahnas) would reign after the Persians. This prediction was now revised: the Messiah of the Egyptians would come after the Medes (Persians) *and* the Ionians (Macedonians). An oracle that identified the Greeks with the "Typhonians" (worshippers of Seth, enemy of the Egyptian god Osiris) and foresaw the destruction of Alexandria probably originated in the time of Alexander's successors.

The expulsion of pestilential foreigners, as we have noted, was a traditional theme of Egyptian historiography. Now, however, Egyptian priests began to identify these aliens as Greeks: Danaus and Cadmus, primeval colonizers of Greece and ancestors of Alexander, they said, had been forced out of Egypt, together with the Jews, as polluted aliens. In Babylonia the astrologers dared to indicate a wrong date when ordered by Seleucus to choose a lucky one for the founding of his new capital, Seleucia on the Tigris—a Greek city intended to supplant Babylon. In Jerusalem a seer discovered in an old tale the promise of a new age about to dawn.

An Aramaic story told that the great Babylonian king Nebuchadnezzar had dreamed of a statue made of four metals: gold, silver, brass, and iron. The series of four metals, which were of descending value but formed a unit, pointed to the meaning of the vision: Nebuchadnezzar's dynasty would end in the fourth generation. A soothsayer says to Nebuchadnezzar: "You, King, are the head of gold." Similarly, Jeremiah (27:6) announces that all nations shall serve Nebuchadnezzar, his son, and his grandson, "until the time of his own land comes."

In a world ruled by absolute monarchs such oracles were eagerly sought. Similar prophecies were made about Cheops, the builder of the Great Pyramid in Egypt and, according to a medieval text, about Ala-ed-Din of Persia (1199–1220) some four thousand years later. The Delphic Pythia allegedly predicted to the Lydian king Gyges, who had died some fifty years before the accession of Nebuchadnezzar in 605, that he would have only five successors in his dynasty.

Whether the vision of Nebuchadnezzar was invented by a Jew or by some other victim of Babylonian conquest or whether it was fabricated for Cyrus' propaganda we do not know. Of course, according to history, four, and not three, Babylonian kings reigned after Nebuchadnezzar. But the number three was a traditional one, and neither the narrator nor his hearers were pedantic enough to make the prophecy conform to the latest almanac. In II Chronicles (36:21), Jeremiah's prophecy of seventy years of desolation for Jerusalem (29:10) is said to have been fulfilled with the establishment of the kingdom of Persia, although less than fifty years had passed between the Exile in 586 and the Return in 539. If, during the heyday of Nebuchadnezzar, a diviner predicted (or was believed to have predicted) that after three more reigns the Babylonian kingdom would collapse, his words would have comforted the victims of the "splendor and pride of the Chaldeans" (Isa. 13:19)—just as the Jews found comfort in Jeremiah's prediction (51:37) that Babylon would become a heap of ruins.

A similar tale made Nebuchadnezzar himself, before his death, predict to the Babylonians that a "Persian mule" (Cyrus was half-Persian, half-Median) would come and, aided by Babylonian gods, bring slavery upon the Babylonians. Such oracles were used for propaganda against Nabonidus, the last king of Babylon. Josephus tells us that the Jews had shown Cyrus Isaiah's prophecy (Isa. 45) about him.

The story of Nebuchadnezzar's dream has come down to us in the Book of Daniel (chap. 2), but with a different interpretation. The Jews identified the wise soothsayer of the story with a Jewish seer named Daniel. Daniel may or may not have been a real person, but the fulfillment of his prophecy about the end of Nebuchadnezzar's dynasty and the resultant end of the Babylonian Empire preserved the oracle from oblivion and established his fame among the Jews, for whom Nebuchadnezzar, the first heathen master of Jerusalem, remained the archetype of world ruler. Later, in Daniel's name and using the theory of successive empires, an exegete interpreted the four metals of Nebuchadnezzar's colossus as four successive world empires—the Persian being the third and the Macedonian the fourth—and interpreted the king's prophetic dream as pointing to the end of the dominion of the nations over the Chosen People. The new interpretation rendered the allegory of the descending value of the metals senseless; having conquered his predecessor, the ruler of each succeeding empire, should, rather, have proved his superior value. But absurdity is no disadvantage to an oracle. What was important was that heathen rule would be destroyed forever (Dan. 2:44).

The date of this reinterpretation of the ancient vision is clearly given in Daniel 2:41: when the Fourth Monarchy "shall become a divided kingdom." Now there was only one period when Macedonian dominion, as seen from Jerusalem, was a house divided against itself, that is, during the last two decades of the fourth century B.C.E. To an observer in Jerusalem in these decades, the Fourth Monarchy, like the feet of the colossus in Nebuchadnezzar's dream, now appeared to be made of "clay and iron." And, indeed, between 321 and 301 Alexander's universal empire shattered into pieces.

This bold interpretation, invented during the reign of Alexander's suc-

cessors, impressed later generations; under the Caesars, the Fourth Monarchy was identified with Rome, as Josephus attests. The division of
history into four empires dominated political theology until the sixteenth
century. The charm of this scheme was first broken by Jean Bodin in
1566. But a century later, those people who, expecting the immediate
advent of Christ, repudiated secular government, were known as Fifth
Monarchy men.

Yet both the Jewish seer and the Egyptian priests were soon disappointed. The carnage among the Macedonians ended as suddenly as it
had begun. Before and after the battle at Ipsus (301) the confusion reached
its peak and when Ptolemy, after Ipsus, once again occupied Palestine,
everybody expected that Seleucus would begin a war against his erstwhile
ally. But declaring that for friendship's sake he would for the present
take no action, Seleucus acquiesced in Ptolemy's gain. A long century of
Ptolemaic rule in Palestine began, and the Egyptian priests had to correct
their calculations of the end: "It will happen," the new interpretation
announced, "that the Ionians shall rule Egypt for a long time."

FIVE

Jerusalem and Judea

W HEN the Fourth Monarchy succeeded the Persian kingdom, Jerusalem was the center of the minuscule district of Yehud, governed by a *pehah* under the control of the viceroy of the enormous region "across the river," which extended from the Euphrates to the Mediterranean Sea and had Damascus as its capital. Macedonian rule changed both the top personnel of the royal administration and some administrative terms: the Persian district of Yehud became "Ioudaia" in Greek, situated in the satrapy of "Syria"; and the viceroy, *xshathparvan* in Persian, bore the same (graecised) title of *satrapes*. The machinery of government, however, remained essentially the same.

In the Persian period, under Alexander and his successors, and, it seems, under the Ptolemies too, the district of Judea roughly corresponded to the extent of the Kingdom of Judah at the time of its annexation by Nebuchadnezzar in 605 B.C.E. In the south, however, the Edomites had seized a slice of Jewish territory, and an administrative district called Idumea now bordered Judea there, the frontier running south of Nebo and Keilah and roughly agreeing with the ancient boundary between Judah and Caleb. But the name Idumea soon became anachronistic when Arab nomads, in their turn, occupied the land. At the time of Nehemiah, "Geshem the Arabian" was the southern rival of the Jewish governor; as head of a tribal group, his authority was recognized from Hebron, in Palestine, to the border of Egypt. In Alexander's time, however, control of the country south of the Dead Sea had passed into the hands of the Nabateans, another nomadic group, whose center was at Petra.

On the east the Jordan and the Dead Sea formed a natural boundary for Judea; and on the west the border followed another natural barrier, the succession of gorges running north-south that separates the steep wall of Judah's mountain range from the low hills and flat valleys of the maritime plain. In the Persian and early Hellenistic periods this plain on the western border of Judah belonged to the cities of Gaza, Ascalon, and Ashdod.

To the north and northwest of Judea was the province of Samaria. The boundary between it and Judea could, however, shift according to circumstances, as for instance after the revolt of Samaria in 332. Hecataeus, quoted by Josephus, reports that at that time Alexander gave "the Samaritan land" to the Jews, "free of tribute"; but the alleged cession probably concerned only the southwestern portion of Samaritan territory, which was already mainly inhabited by the Jews.

On the whole, the territory of Yehud-Ioudaia formed a rough oval stretching some twenty-five miles (40 km.) from Beth-horon and Beth-el southward to Beth-zur; its breadth, from Gezer, Emmaus, Modin, and Keila to Jericho, Engedi, the river Jordan, and the Dead Sea, was about thirty-two miles (50 km.). This area of some eight hundred square miles (2800 sq. km.) amounted to about one-tenth of the territory of the modern State of Israel. There are no data about the population of postexilic and early Hellenistic Judea, but the resettlement of the land after the horrible devastation by Nebuchadnezzar was, as archeological evidence attests, a very slow process.

"The Jews," says Hecataeus, "have many strongholds and villages, but only one fortified city." A village such as Beth-zur, or Bethlehem, which depended politically upon Jerusalem, was called a "town" *(ir)* by the Jews and had its own territory, comprising hamlets and isolated farms. The sole city was, indeed, Jerusalem, but Hecataeus' Jewish informant exaggerated. His Jerusalem had a circumference of five and one-half miles (8.8 km.) and no fewer than 120,000 inhabitants. In fact, at this date toward the end of the fourth century B.C.E., Jerusalem squatted on a ridge, the "Eastern" hill, little more than three-quarters of a mile (about 1200 m.) long, between the valley of Kidron in the east and a ravine in the west. The ravine, the Tyropean valley of Josephus, has been filled in with rubble during the centuries since the destruction of Jerusalem in 70 C.E., but its line is still marked by a street that runs southward from the Damascus Gate in the Old City of Jerusalem. In the early Hellenistic period some people also settled on the eastern slopes of a "Western" hill, that is, a slope west of the Tyropean valley, but to Greek visitors Jerusalem appeared to be perched high up on a narrow rugged plateau between two ravines.

The Temple, defended by a stone wall, covered two acres on the northern summit of the eastern ridge. A fortress (the future Antonia) dominated the Temple esplanade from the northwest and was permanently occupied by the royal governor and his guard; but the governor, who could be either a Jew (as was the "Yhzkqyo" [Hezekiah] known to us from his coins) or a Persian, interfered little with the daily life of the population and his province was too poor to excite covetous inclinations. The single precious product of Judea was the balsam of Jericho, but the balsam gardens in all probability belonged to the crown. The inscription "YHD" (often with addition of a town name—Mizpah, for instance), found on numerous storage jars and jar handles distributed throughout Judea in the Persian and early Hellenistic periods, seems to indicate some control of trade by the government, although the purpose of these inscriptions and of the stamp "YRSLIM" that appears on other jars remains unknown.

The governor could, as did for instance the "Yhzkqyo, *pehah,* of Yehud" just mentioned (the geographical indication is in apposition to the title), issue tiny silver coins (0.25 to 0.40 grams) bearing his name and title in Old Hebrew script. These pieces imitate Attic coins, as do the coins of Gaza, for example, in having a male head on the obverse and the Attic owl on the reverse. Since these coins were not counted but only weighed, the obverse could be left blank or could be printed with the head (but without the personal name) of the governor. The Yehud coins are extremely rare. These minute pieces probably supplemented the so-called philisto-arab coins, much heavier coins issued by Gaza and the local rulers in the region between Suez and Judea for use in trading for frankincense, myrrh, and other aromatic substances from Arabia. It is hardly by chance that the Yehud pieces found in excavations come from the southern towns of Beth-zur and Gerar.

According to Jewish tradition, which is very plausible, Alexander did not raise the Jews' yearly tribute, requiring them to pay him only what they had paid the Persian king. There were also direct taxes assessed on land, flocks, and persons, which the Macedonians undoubtedly continued to levy. In addition, if necessary, the government could always requisition supplies, compulsory labor, and Jewish recruits for Alexander's army.

Outside Jerusalem the administration of local justice and other local affairs was in the hands of local "rulers," the native headmen. But even the poorest Jew was legally a free man and a member of the "congregation" of the Chosen People. The absence of gradations of legal rank among the Jews was a particular feature of their society, in which only the priesthood was officially set above the rest of the elect. This state of affairs dignified the common Jew and, in his own eyes, placed him above the gentiles.

SIX

The Law of the Jews

WHEN Cyrus conquered Babylon in 539, he quite naturally reversed the policy of his defeated enemy and permitted the gods and the men taken into Babylonian captivity to return home. At this moment the restoration of Jerusalem, burned fifty years before by Nebuchadnezzar, depended on an accidental conjunction.

The Assyrian military colony that had been settled in Samaria, the former capital of Israel, had deprived the Ten Tribes, deported to Assyria, of their ancestral home; they could never go back to Samaria and reestablish the kingdom of Israel. On the other hand, the existence of a military camp in Samaria had made the establishment of an alien colony in Jerusalem superfluous. The walls of the Holy City had been broken by Nebuchadnezzar and the ancient capital of Judah had become an open village (probably governed from Samaria) around which the Jews who had escaped deportation and the refugees who had drifted back had continued to dwell. The result was a political vacuum that the Restoration could fill. This difference between the destiny of Jerusalem and the fate of Samaria was already pointed out by Josephus.

The restoration of Jerusalem and Judah proceeded in two stages, linked by a belief in the Divine Presence at Zion but otherwise differing considerably. The first stage was the Restoration of the Temple, ordered by Cyrus in 538. In his own inscription, the so-called Cyrus Cylinder, the Persian king distinguished between two of his pious acts. One act involved returning the gods whom Nabonidus, the last Babylonian king, had evacuated from Sumer and Akkad, at the time of the Persian advance. Here Cyrus' task was simple; he had only to send the idols, together with their apparel and the utensils used in their worship, back to their cities. But Cyrus also desired to restore the gods, such as Ashur, of cities that had been destroyed by the Babylonians, and here it was not enough to return the idols to their cities and reestablish them in their ancient sanctuaries; these gods also needed worshippers. Therefore Cyrus "gathered all their peoples and returned [them to] their dwellings." It was in accordance with this second kind of action that Cyrus, in a Hebrew proclamation, announced first, his order to rebuild the Temple of the God of Jerusalem, and second, his invitation to the "people" of the God of Jerusalem to go up to the Holy City. Moreover, because religious renewal in this case also meant political restoration, Cyrus also charged "the Chief of Judah," Sheshbazzar (probably a son of the Jewish king Jehoiachin and the pretender to his throne), to bring the sacred vessels of the Temple back to Jerusalem.

The actual beginnings of the new political organization of Jerusalem are obscure. For us, however, the salient fact is that the Jews returned to Jerusalem, as the Assyrians returned to Ashur and others to their homes, not just as former residents of their respective cities, but as worshippers of their respective city gods. This distinction was of scant importance in a polytheist community, but in Jerusalem it meant the triumph of orthodoxy and, further, the establishment of the Temple and its priesthood as preeminent in the Holy City.

The second phase of the Restoration was the promulgation in 458 of the Torah as the authoritative code for the Jews. The meaning of this act is often misunderstood. Artaxerxes I of Persia, and Ezra, his commissioner, neither created the Law nor founded normative Judaism. Ezra brought to Jerusalem a collection of the ancestral laws of the Chosen People, gathered together by its learned men during the Exile: "When the Law had been forgotten, Ezra came up from Babylonia and restored it." This rabbinic formulation is indirectly confirmed by an Egyptian record. In the fourth year of his reign, that is, in 518, Darius I wrote to his satrap in Egypt to send him learned men from the military, the clergy, and the scribes of Egypt. They were to write "the former law of Egypt which was until the year 44 of the Pharaoh Amasis the law of the Pharaoh, of the temples, and of the military." They did so, and "wrote it on one roll."

The Egyptians had formulated no new codes after the last year of the last pharaoh before the Persian conquest, 526 or 525 B.C.E. That was natural, since from the spring of 525 on, it had been the Persian monarch who had legislated in Egypt. By the same token, the "Law of God" in the hand of Ezra (Ezra 7:25) could not include norms fabricated by crafty priests during the Exile, for from 539 on, the Persian king and not the God of the Jews had legislated in Jerusalem and Judea. The "Law of God" could therefore now mean only the "former law" of the Chosen People; that is, the laws that Ezra collected in his Torah must have been those in force before 539. Thus did the Torah become the final Law of Israel: after 530, Darius, Alexander, his successors, and then the Caesars legislated for God's people. As Darius I was reckoned the sixth and last lawgiver of Egypt, so Artaxerxes I became the final codifier of Mosaic law. Yet to Ezra, and then to the Chronicler, the royal gifts to beautify the House of the Lord appeared of much greater importance than the promulgation of Artaxerxes' code—this establishment of the "life under the Law" which looms so large to modern biblical critics. In fact, like the Egyptians before Darius, the Jews before Artaxerxes had already regulated their way of life in accordance with their ancestral laws. It is true that now these laws were collected and fixed in writing forever, but what was really important to the people of that time was that Artaxerxes had made Moses' word the law of the king in respect to the royal administration of the Jews. From now on the Torah that bound the Jew also constrained the royal officers. The Jews were compelled to observe the Sabbath rest, as they had already been doing, but the royal officers were now also obliged to respect the Mosaic commandment in dealing with the Jews.

When Nehemiah returned to Jerusalem sometime after 432 B.C.E. he found the Sabbath again being profaned. Of course there are always disobedient elements; we see them even under the ferule of the medieval rabbis. Yet in the century that separated Nehemiah from Alexander, and again during the 160 years from Alexander to Antiochus Epiphanes, eight generations of Jews were brought up under the discipline of the Torah, a discipline under which dissidents were seen both as heretics and as rebels. The Law and the Commonwealth had become inseparable in the Jewish mind. Indeed, the dominion of the Law in Jerusalem amazed even the first Greek visitors. According to Artaxerxes' edict, the Torah was to be the rule of life for a particular religious group, that is, for all who knew the Law of God. By definition, then, non-Jews in Jerusalem and Judah could not be coerced into complying with the provisions of the Torah; powerful as he was at the Persian court, Nehemiah could not forbid the Tyrians to trade on the Sabbath day in Jerusalem. Similarly, Jews and other foreign settlers in Persian and Ptolemaic Egypt were not subject to the Egyptian code.

Foreigners, of course, were obliged to respect the local gods and were punished for sacrilege; a Roman visitor who, around 50 B.C.E., killed a cat in that part of Egypt in which the cat was held sacred was lynched by a mob. But foreigners were not prevented from worshipping their own deities privately. Nevertheless, the sight of idolatrous chapels and altars erected in the Holy Land angered the Jews, who, moved by the spirit of holy intolerance, rioted and razed the offensive structures, provoking an understandable reaction among their polytheist neighbors and bringing themselves in to conflict with the pagan authorities. Yet, now paying fines for insubordination, now obtaining pardons from the satraps, the Jews of Jerusalem, through their intolerant obstinacy, extirpated idolatry from their territory. In this respect, pagan visitors to the Holy Land had now to accommodate themselves to Mosaic precepts.

According to a later Jewish tale, it was Alexander who gave the Jews permission to live according to their ancestral law. The authenticity of this story is doubtful, but there can be no doubt that Alexander and his successors, following Persian policy explicitly or implicitly, accepted the validity of the Law of Moses in Jerusalem and Judea. Divine law continued to reign in the Holy Land at the pleasure of the heathen overlord.

SEVEN

The Jewish Periphery

HE Jews in Judea—their own land by the grace of Cyrus—constituted a semiautonomous political unit, an *ethnos,* to use Greek terminology. However, their Lilliputian territory covered only a small portion of the Promised Land: the God of Heaven had charged Cyrus to rebuild the Temple of Jerusalem, not to reestablish the Kingdom of David. Thus, after 539, numerous men of the Jewish faith lived in the Holy Land but outside the Jewish territory. Many of them belonged to families that had never been carried away either by the Assyrians or by the Babylonians. Others had returned from exile, for the edicts of Cyrus and Artaxerxes expressly authorized the return from captivity to their former homes of worshippers of the God of Jerusalem. As a result, before the Hasmonean expansion the Jewish diaspora began almost at the gates of Jerusalem and encircled tiny postexilic Judea.

Although the hill country in the south of the former Davidic kingdom was now occupied by Edomites and Arabs, and what had been the southwest of David's kingdom had fallen to the coastal towns, nevertheless, Jewish (by religion) settlements south of Jerusalem extended "from Beersheba to the valley of Hinnom" at the southern flank of the city (Neh. 11:30). To the north of Jerusalem there were Jewish pockets in the hill country of Narbatha, northwest of the city of Samaria, and to the southeast of Shechem, in Accrobatene; a Seleucid document of 145 B.C.E. attests that many people living in Lydda, Ramathaim, and Aphairema, three southern districts of the province of Samaria, were "sacrificing in Jerusalem."

Beyond Samaria, the highlands of Galilee that were the ancient portion of Issachar, Zebulun, and Naphtali had always remained, on the whole, the land of Israel; the Assyrians had neither emptied the villages in 733 B.C.E. nor brought in alien colonists. The Chronicler, writing at the beginning of the fourth century, knows of many from Asher (north of

Carmel) and from Zebulun going as pilgrims to Jerusalem. The hero of
the Book of Tobit, a man from the tribe of Naphtali, is a pious worshipper
of the Lord of Zion; Enoch lives near the sources of the Jordan, in the
portion of Dan; and in the Testaments of the Twelve Patriarchs, composed in the early Hellenistic age, the consecration of Levi is placed at
Abel-mayim, in the portion of Naphtali.

Moreover, in the Persian and the early Hellenistic periods people of
the Jewish faith also migrated to the gentile cities on the Mediterranean
coast of Palestine. According to the Testaments of the Twelve Patriarchs,
Zebulun was a fisherman living on the seacoast "in the land of Canaan";
and in the Testament of Naphtali (6: 1–3), Jacob and his sons had a boat
at Jamnia, where they once saw a pilotless and unmanned boat called
the "Ship of Jacob," which they sailed to investigate in their own boat.
In point of fact, in pre-Maccabean times the Jews were well settled at
both Jamnia and Joppa. Farther south, an ostracon written in the mid-
fifth century attests to a "vineyard of Zebadiah" on the territory of
Ashdod. And last but not least, toward the end of the fourth century,
Theophrastus mentions a Tyrian law that lists among prohibited foreign
oaths an oath "by the Korban" (that is, by an offering to the Temple)—
a specifically Jewish formula, as Josephus observes.

There were also numerous Jewish settlements on the other side of the
Jordan, in the land of Gilead, the land that had been allotted to Gad and
Manasseh, but that had subsequently been depopulated by Tiglath-Pileser
of Assyria in 733. Of particular importance here was the "land of Tob,"
a large tract between Abel-shittim (Abila), opposite Jericho, Rabbath-
ammon (afterward Philadelphia, now Amman), at the headwaters of the
Jabbok, and Heshbon (Essebon, now Hesban), between the Arnon and
the Jabbok. The territory was the hereditary fief of the Tobiads, an old
aristocratic family from Jerusalem. At the time of Nehemiah, the head
of the clan was the royal governor of the Ammonite land east of the
Jordan (Neh. 2:19). A pre-Maccabean Jewish colony also existed at Scythopolis (Beth-shan), a Greek city that dominated the main passage between the west and Transjordan and that was obviously a link between
the Jews living on both sides of the river.

Thus, in the Hasmonean period, when the author of the legend about
the seventy-two translators who rendered the Torah into Greek assumed
the existence of all Twelve Tribes in the Holy Land in his time, or the
author of the Book of Judith supposed that this land was always and
everywhere inhabited by the Chosen People, these patriotic fictions were
not without a factual basis. It is noteworty that throughout Palestine,
except in the Greek cities and the coastal zone, the Hasmonean kings
did not have to use force to bring the population back under the yoke

of the Law, while in Idumea to the south and in Iturea to the north, beyond Galilee, such compulsion was required.

To the men and women of Jerusalem at this time, the whole country, from Lebanon to Egypt, appeared to be their lawful inheritance. When Ben Sira compares wisdom to a beautiful plant, he speaks not only of the palms of Engedi and the roses of Jericho, but also of the trees of the maritime plain, which did not belong to Jerusalem, and of the cedars of Lebanon and the cypresses on Mount Hermon. Yet while the Jews (by religion) continued to inhabit the country from Dan to Beersheba, in the greater part of the Promised Land, north of Beth-el and south of Beth-zur, they were now only sojourners.

This uncommon situation brought about two contrasting psychological reactions. Many irredentist Jews expressed their attachment to Jerusalem by exemplary piety. Judith and her generation, chastened by the destruction of the Solomonic Temple, no longer worship gods made by human hands, as their ancestors did, and know no other deity but the Lord. Judith herself observes even the minutiae of the Law with respect to the testamentary distribution of her property, for instance, and follows the dietary laws even in the tent of Holophernes. Still, although she lives and acts for the exaltation of Jerusalem, she lives in Bethulia, somewhere at the edge of the plain of Esdraelon, at a greater distance from Jerusalem than from Tyre. Nor was she the only one who remembered God in the Holy Land beyond the limits of the Judaic province. It cannot be a pure accident that in the second century B.C.E. three of the five "fathers" of the Jewish tradition between Simon the Just and Simeon ben Shetah hailed from areas outside the province of Ioudaia: Antigonus was from Socho, a place to the west of Judea, Jose ben Joezer was from Zeredah, in the territory of Samaria, and Nitai was a Galilean.

On the other hand, the Jews who lived in the Holy Land outside the territory of Ioudaia and who thus escaped the control of the high priestly authority in Jerusalem were both less coerced by ancestral law and more exposed to contact with "unclean" foreigners. The reduced coercion may be illustrated by two archeological finds. Whereas no sacrificial worship of the Lord outside the Temple was tolerated in the province of Judea, at Lachish, just beyond the Jewish frontier, a certain Ya'ush, son of Mahalia ("YH has renounced"), dedicated an incense altar to Him. Moreover, a shrine of the same type as the preexilic sanctuary of the Lord in Arad was built in early Hellenistic Lachish and had probably been preceded by another smaller temple, built in Persian times. The Jews of Lachish, like the Jews of Elephantine, obviously continued the pre-Deuteronomic cult of the Lord. As for contact with foreigners, we have seen that Palestine in the fifth and fourth centuries B.C.E. belonged to the

Levantine belt of an eclectic Greco-Egyptian-Phoenician civilization. Throughout the Levant, united first under Persian rule and later under Alexander's scepter, such things as kitchen pots, or the heavy bronze anklets worn by girls, or men's weapons, were stylistically similar; Greek painted pottery, Egyptian idols, and Phoenician amulets could be found in the same household.

This cosmopolitan civilization naturally penetrated into the Holy Land. An Attic black-figured cup decorated with a sphinx was found at Tell-en-Nasbeh (Mizpah), only six miles north of Jerusalem, and in a hamlet situated among the ruins of biblical Jericho people used jugs and cups imported from Athens. And with this foreign merchandise came foreign ideas, images, and customs that would have dismayed Jerusalemites, isolated on their high plateau, had they received them from uncircumcised foreigners, but that appeared less outlandish and heretical when transmitted by a fellow Jew from Jamnia or Galilee. Before Jerusalem saw the first Greek trader or the first Macedonian soldier, the Holy City had, by means of the periphery of pious Jews living throughout pagan Palestine, felt indirectly the impact of Greek civilization.

EIGHT

The Dispersion

B Y THE time of Alexander's arrival the Jews were already dispersed over the whole extent of the Persian Empire, from Sardis to Susa in the east, from the Delta to the first Nile cataract and beyond in Egypt. And they were numerous in Mesopotamia and northern Syria, too.

The diaspora had been created in part by forces external to the Jews: Sargon had transplanted the Ten Tribes to northern Mesopotamia and western Media; captives from Judea had been sent into Assyria by Sennacherib; the deportations from Jerusalem in 595 and 587 transferred Jews to Babylonia; and in approximately 350, Artaxerxes III sent Jews from Palestine into northern Persia. Deuteronomy 17:16 warns the future king of the Chosen People not to trade Jewish troops for horses from Egypt, indicating that even in preexilic times Jews had been sent to Egypt by one or more of their kings to help the pharaohs. Others had returned to the fleshpots voluntarily. The Book of Isaiah (19:18) speaks of five cities in Lower Egypt that on the Day of the Lord will speak the language of Canaan and swear to the Lord of Hosts. In the Persian period there were Jews in Egypt from Migdol to Syene.

The Jewish diaspora was by no means unique; it met a Greek dispersion everywhere, from Sardis to Elephantine. There were similarly an Aramaic and a Phoenician diaspora in Egypt and surely elsewhere; and long before Alexander the Great emigrants from Egypt and Sidonian merchants had settled at Athens. Nor were the Jews the only people transferred to new places by Assyrian, Babylonian, and Persian despots. The Eretrians, too, were carried off from Greece by Darius I in 490 B.C.E. and settled in the region of Susa. One hundred and fifty years later their descendants in Persia still spoke Greek and still remembered their ancestral home. Nor were the Jews alone in weeping for their native city: every people, or fragment of a people, thrown into a foreign land continued to worship its ancestral gods. Bel and Nabu, gods of Babylon, were brought by emigrants to Elephantine on the southern frontier of Egypt. A Phoenician woman living at Tahpanhes, in the Nile delta, asked on behalf of another woman not only the blessing of all the gods of her current place of sojourn, but also the blessing of Baal Zaphon, the god of her native land. Aramean immigrants living at Memphis in the fifth and fourth centuries B.C.E. had their own cemetery, where they depicted themselves on their gravestones in Syrian dress.

It could hardly be otherwise: the tribal organization of oriental peoples blocked the road to assimilation. Royal permission was required to reckon the children of a deported Greek nobleman and his Persian wife as Persians. True, as time went by, individual immigrants or their descendants were absorbed into the people among whom they lived, but legally immigrants remained "sojourners," and the various communities of immigrants never lost their original identities. Of the Paeonians, deported from Macedonia to Phrygia, Herodotus says that they lived in a village "by themselves." The descendants of the settlers transferred to Samaria by Assyrian kings remained "Urukians" and "Susians who are Elamites"; in the official language of the Persian government they only "resided" in Samaria.

Newcomers everywhere constituted separate communities. Mesopotamian colonists in Syria (near Aleppo) and Palestine (in Gezer and Samaria) continued, under Persian rule, to draw up cuneiform deeds according to the Babylonian legal system. A "ruler" (segan) of the Carians in Mesopotamia is mentioned in cuneiform tablets of the Persian period. Unfortunately, however, archeological finds have thus far cast light on only two communities of the pre-Hellenic Jewish diaspora, one on the Nile and the other on the Euphrates. More than one hundred Aramaic papyri and about three hundred and fifty Aramaic ostraca, written by or about Jews, have been discovered at Elephantine, at the southern end of Egypt. The earliest text is from 495 B.C.E. and a few are later than the fifth century B.C.E., placing these documents in the period of Persian rule in Egypt.

The size and unity of the group is explained by the fact that the Jews who lived on this narrow island in the Nile, near the First Cataract, were not isolated settlers but members of a "Jewish force" (haila yehudaya) stationed at Elephantine to guard the Nubian frontier. This "foreign legion" may have been established at Elephantine as early as the time of Psammetichus I (664–610). The pharaohs of his dynasty (XXVI) often used foreign mercenaries; in 591, for instance, Carians, Ionians, Rhodians, and Phoenicians participated in the campaign against Nubia. After Cambyses' conquest of Egypt (525 B.C.E.) the foreign regiments passed into Persian service, and toward the middle of the fifth century we find these troops stationed at the main entrances to Egypt: Daphne, on the east of the Delta; Marea, toward Libya; and Elephantine, the gate to the countries of the south.

In the fifth century the mercenaries of the Jewish regiment at Elephantine were hereditary soldiers. Each colonist was officially described as "A, son of B, Jew [sometimes Aramean], of the fortress of Elephantine, of the detachment of C." Each detachment (*degel;* literally, "standard") was named after its chief, who was either a Persian or a Babylonian. "The chief of the force" was a Persian. The colonists received monthly pay and rations (mostly barley, lentils, and beans) from the royal treasury, and their military duties, such as protecting caravans from the Bedouin or escorting Nile shipping, do not seem to have been very exacting.

These soldiers appear in the legal documents of Elephantine as sellers and buyers and untiring litigants—whether the object of the claim is a deposit or a stolen fish—but there are only a few references to commerce or industry. The transactions by which these men borrowed money or produce were accommodation loans, in consideration of which they transferred and pledged their military rations; a woman, for instance, could cede her allowance from the treasury to her sister. We may suppose that more often than not the transactions involved in ordering or buying a carpet or a pair of shoes in a bazaar went unrecorded; and although several documents deal with real estate, there is no clear reference to fields or to the cultivation of the ground. Native Egyptian soldiers received land on condition of fulfilling their military service; foreign mercenaries obtained houses in cities but, it seems, no fields to cultivate.

The bulk of the Elephantine papyri consists of legal documents from the archives of two families. When these texts were first discovered, scholars were primarily interested in the relationship of this new evidence to biblical and talmudic law. But in fact the legal records from Elephantine—usually written by professional scribes, drafted according to a fixed international style, and used as evidence before Persian judges—reveal features of Aramaic "common law." The documents demonstrate that this law was created case by case, by scribes of all nationalities, speaking and writing in Aramaic, and acting either as advisers to Persian judges or as notaries, drafting the documents. Among the scribes at Elephantine, a certain Nathan had as a fellow worker an Egyptian named Petisi, whose father bore the Babylonian name of Nabunathan. The Aramaic letters sent to Egypt by a Persian magnate were countersigned by his officers, who bore Persian names, but were drafted by a cadre of clerks, among whom were Persians, Babylonians, Egyptians, and a Jew called Anani. An Aramaic lease agreement of 515, entered into in Egypt by parties who were not Jewish, used exactly the same form as deeds drafted on behalf of the Elephantine Jews.

Built up partly by the Persian king's judges, who were advised by Aramaic scribes, and partly by means of private agreements, Aramaic law was used alongside the traditional legal systems of the various nationalities, at times as a supplement to them and at times as a substitute. It was international in language and nature, and, as such, particularly convenient for dispersed minorities, whether traders or military colonists.

The typical form of the Aramaic contract in Persian Egypt was a declaration made before witnesses by the party undertaking the obligation (the debtor or seller) to the other party (the creditor or buyer). The document was then handed over to the person in whose favor it had been drafted. For instance, in 441 B.C.E. the settlement of the claims of a certain Pi against his former wife Mibtahiah was recorded in a "deed [sefar] of renunciation which Pi wrote for Mibtahiah." The document was carefully preserved by the woman, her son, and her grandson for some fifty years.

The style of demotic Egyptian contracts in the same period is similar to that of the Aramaic documents from Elephantine, yet the Aramaic agreement, which was sealed, cannot be derived from the Egyptian agreement, which was never sealed. We may note, rather, that certain types of cuneiform contracts of the same period are also set out from the standpoint of the vendor, and stress his volition, although, again, the Aramaic form, which does not mention the assent of the other party to the transaction, cannot be derived from the bilateral Babylonian form where acceptance follows offer. The drafting of deeds in a subjective style expresses, rather, a new psychological attitude: the humble scribes of the Levant, like the fiery prophets of Judah and Israel, had become interested in the intention behind the action. On the other hand, the contract *a latere venditoris* also facilitated the further transfer of property and thus economic mobility.

On behalf of their clients the Aramaic scribes freely utilized clauses from a variety of national legal systems and in turn influenced the legal traditions of the indigenous scribes who were drafting documents in their own national languages. The result was that Aramaic business law, because it was drafted by individual scribes, could not of necessity be uniform. For instance, a type of conveyance widely used in the Levant—the "double document," in which the transaction was recorded twice on the same sheet, the first under seal and the second open for perusal—does not appear at Elephantine. This very flexibility of Aramaic case law, however, made the legal innovations of the scribes possible.

The nuptial agreements of the Jews at Elephantine illustrate the creative role of Aramaic scribe. Marriage in fifth-century B.C.E. Elephantine was still based upon an agreement between the bridegroom and the bride's father, the latter continuing to receive the bride-price, the *mohar* of the

Bible. But Aramaic scribes, in drafting the individual marriage contracts, changed the function of the payment. According to a talmudic antiquarian notice, there came a time when the bride-price was returned to the husband to be held in trust for his wife. This is the stage represented in the fifth-century documents from Elephantine. Moreover, as the bride's *mohar* is now returnable to her in full, "be it straw or string," at the time of the divorce, this new idea, as the rabbis noted, acted as a financial restraint on the husband's legal right to dismiss his spouse.

The nuptial agreement of Elephantine goes even further. The Deuteronomic law of divorce (24:1) requires that the husband deliver to the wife a bill of divorce, repudiating her and giving her the right to marry again; the wife apparently lacks the legal capacity to dissolve her marriage in a similar unilateral manner. The Elephantine scribes, however, do not even mention a bill of divorce and allow either party to terminate the union at will, merely by stating publicly that he or she "hates" the spouse, that is, refuses cohabitation, a principle that came to be accepted in marriage contracts drawn in Palestine as well. Jesus says (Mark 10:11–11:12) that both the man who repudiates his wife and the woman who repudiates her mate commit adultery by marrying another person; clearly he has in mind the contractual clauses that grant the power to dissolve the marriage to both the husband and the wife. Josephus accordingly relates that Salome, a Herodian princess, repudiated her husband, and fragments of a divorce declaration by a wife of Bar-Kokhba's time have also been discovered in a cave near Engedi. Of course, if the wife wished to exercise her right to repudiate her husband, she in turn had to compensate him financially, the amount to be paid having been fixed beforehand in the nuptial agreement.

The scribes secured the monogamous structure of the union in the same way, by inserting clauses in the marriage contract, sanctioned by pecuniary penalties, prohibiting concubinage. Moreover, they left the inheritance rights of a surviving spouse to the discretion of the parties; the usual stipulation having been until then that in the absence of issue the living spouse inherited from the dead one. Generally speaking, the Elephantine nuptial agreement neatly balanced clauses dealing with the husband's rights with stipulations defining the wife's.

It is important to emphasize that the newly created rights for women were not the product of legislation, but rather resulted from the development of the marriage contract. Moreover, since a general principle of ancient law maintained that a consensual contract between two parties was binding absolutely, any contractual stipulations favoring the bride were valid even outside the scope of the positive law. Josephus could rightly state that a divorce initiated by the wife disagreed with Jewish law, and the rabbis regarded such a wife as a "rebellious" person, but bowing to the authority of the contract they were obliged to recognize the validity of the clause according the power of divorce to either spouse.

It is interesting to note, further, that although the Elephantine marriage agreements do not consider any possible business activity on the part of the wife, Jewish women at Elephantine, married or not, conducted business, held property, and were parties to litigation. In this they were like the ideal wife of Proverbs (31:16), she who buys a field and plants a vineyard. Seals bearing the names of women and dating from biblical times show that then, too, women were entitled to execute documents in their own right. Even in early Hellenistic Jerusalem, property to a great extent was in the hands of women. It was only in the rabbinic period that Jewish jurisconsults, following the general trend of opinion, strictly limited a woman's right to conduct business because of her innate levity.

The disagreement between Mosaic statutes and case law with regard to divorce appears both in Jerusalem and at Elephantine with respect to other transactions as well. For instance, the biblical prohibition against charging interest was disregarded at both places. In Jerusalem, Nehemiah found fields, vineyards, and houses pledged by Jews to their brothers, and at Elephantine interest on loans between Jews reached sixty percent yearly. It is worthwhile stressing, however, that in contrast to Egyptian and Palestinian practice in the same period, Elephantine contracts denied to the creditor the right to seize either the children of the debtor or his cattle at default. In this respect the practice of the notaries at Elephantine agreed with neo-Babylonian usage. On the other hand, rabbinic jurisprudence, as we have just seen, does not necessarily follow the lines marked out by the Torah, either.

We should not forget that the Torah is not a legal code in the modern sense of the term. The Lawgiver did not try to regulate everything, but left untouched the wide field covered by customary practice. For instance, Mosaic law (Lev. 25:47) grants that a Hebrew slave who sells himself to a resident alien may be redeemed, but it does not treat the question of the redemption rights of a Hebrew who sells himself to another Hebrew.

Another group of documents from Elephantine, written between 451 and 402 and kept together by a woman called Yehoyishma, may illustrate this situation. In 449, Meshullam, a man of substance, gave a female slave in marriage to Ananiah, a sexton of the Lord's temple at Elephantine. As her name, spelled "Tmt" (or "Tpmt" in Aramaic script) shows, she was an Egyptian. Mosaic law does not deny *connubium* to foreigners generally, and mixed marriages were common in Jerusalem, too, in the middle of the fifth century. It is true that rabbinic jurisprudence, reflecting the trend in the Greco-Roman world, declared marriage between a Jew and a slave girl invalid, but the Torah is silent on this point and the common law of the Near East recognized such unions. Indeed, a prominent family in Jerusalem about 400 B.C.E. was believed to have been descended from an Egyptian slave who had married a Jewish heiress.

Marriage to a free man did not free a slave woman. Tmt remained a slave, and her daughter Yehoyishma, offspring of her marriage to Ananiah, became the property of Meshullam, the mother's master; the principle that a child receives the legal status of the mother was generally followed in the ancient Near East. Only in 427 were both women manumitted. The Torah contains no provision with regard to voluntary manumission, but its existence is implictly proven by the compulsory emancipation of a slave maimed by his master. Though freed, both women had still to provide for their masters until the death of Meshullam's son. This condition was not exceptional, as manumission did not automatically end the personal relationship between master and slave. So far as the slave was concerned, the real value of the manumission was expressed in the clause by which the master relinquished the right to sell the released slave. By this act the slave's new status was finally stabilized.

In 420, Yehoyishma married a military settler also called Ananiah. Though a free woman at this date, as a former slave she had no legal father. In the pedigree of a freed slave, however, the name of the former owner took the place of that of the father, and so Yehoyishma was given in marriage not by her real father, but by the son and heir of Meshullam. Yet all these legal and formal restrictions prevented neither the social rise of a slave woman branded with the mark of her owner, nor the rise of her daughter.

The Jews of Elephantine were not alone on the island, and Jews and gentiles served in the same military company. A certain Mahseiah had a Khorasmian from the Aral Sea, at the other end of the Persian Empire, living next to him, while an Egyptian boatman lived across the street; and in 434 two Persian Magi witnessed the deed of a gift made by a clergyman of "Yahu, the God who dwells in Elephantine," to his wife.

Persian command and the Aramaic language united all the aliens living in Egypt. The same man—for example, the just-mentioned Mahseiah— could be referred to officially as a Jew or as an Aramean; for as their private letters and notes, scribbled on potsherds, evidence, the Jews at Elephantine spoke Aramaic, enriched by some (mostly technical) Egyptian and Iranian words. Actually, except for a few legal terms, such as *edah*, in business documents, there is no trace of Hebrew in the records of this colony. The two literary texts that were found here are the Aramaic story of Ahikar and an Aramaic version of Darius' record of his victories.

On the other hand, it is worthwhile noting that Phoenician dealers at Memphis who sent oil and wine to Elephantine continued to use their native tongue and script.

The religious community of the Jews was independent of the military organization in which they served. The cult was financed by voluntary contributions and a list of subscribers has been preserved; everyone gave the sum of two shekels. But though the half-shekel tax imposed to provide for the expenses of the Temple in Jerusalem was levied on male Israelites only, at Elephantine payment was collected from both men and women. A headman and "his associates, the priests at Elephantine the fortress," represented the community, an arrangement most likely made in imitation of the Persian system of administrative boards. In Elephantine marriage contracts, as we have seen, it is stipulated that a divorce could be obtained by a declaration of intent "in an assembly," but it is difficult to say whether the term *edah* as used in these contracts meant a religious congregation or just any gathering of people.

The Elephantine community had a temple with an altar upon which the sacrifices prescribed in the Torah were offered. This "house of the Lord," with its roof of cedarwood and its five entrances built of carved stone, lay close to the Egyptian temple of the ram-headed god Khnum, the Lord of Elephantine. Like their pagan neighbors, the Jews of Elephantine, when far away and writing home to the people in their city, sometimes added to their greeting the salutation, "To the house of YHW in Elephantine."

The Jews of Elephantine observed the Sabbath and the Passover; an official message of 419 B.C.E. enjoined them to abstain from all leaven from the fifteenth to the twenty-first of Nisan, in accordance with Mosaic Law. Their sacrifices followed the rules of Scripture and they styled their priests *kohanim,* as the Torah does. Their faith may have been homely, but it was fervent. They did not doubt that expensive sacrifices obtained grace from the Deity; they stated in an official document that their enemy had been punished because of their prayer to the God of Heaven. They never suspected that their "house of the Lord" was a violation of the divine commandment in Deuteronomy that forbade altars and immolations outside Zion. They spoke of "YHW, the God who dwells in the fortress of Elephantine" as their coreligionists in Judea spoke of "God, Who is in Jerusalem." As a matter of fact, they remained in communion with the Jews of Jerusalem.

Yet, some expressions in their documents have a ring of heathenism. We can understand that their monotheist faith could not prevent these simple folk from recognizing the power of their neighbors' deities. For instance, they speak of "YHW, the God who dwells in the fortress of Elephantine," and of "the priests of the god Knub [Khnum] who dwells in the fortress of Elephantine," in the same document; in the epistolary greeting just mentioned they sometimes add the name of a pagan deity to that of the Lord. But when, even in exculpatory oaths between two Jews, they can be found invoking Egyptian and West Semitic gods alongside the Lord, and when, in the subscription list for their temple, we find a reference to 70 shekels for Eshembethel and 120 shekels for Anatbetel, in addition to the 126 shekels for the Lord, we become puzzled. In point of fact, the Jews of Elephantine practiced the same pre-Deuteronomic syncretist religion as their Palestinian ancestors. For these people, YHW was their own god and protector, but they would have considered it foolish to neglect the supernatural powers worshipped by their neighbors. Let us remember that Second Isaiah was the first prophet who, around 540 B.C.E., proclaimed the futility of the gods of the nations. But the fiery prophet spoke to the Jews in exile, seared by catastrophe, while the Jews in Elephantine constituted a privileged group in the Egyptian Empire.

The temple at Elephantine was destroyed in 411 at the instigation of the Egyptian priests of Khnum. The motives of the Egyptians do not need elaboration: they always stood ready to rid themselves of impure foreigners who sacrificed lambs. It is also easy to understand how they could have bribed the local Persian governor; it was his son, the commander of the garrison at Syene, who led the Egyptians, "with other troops," and destroyed the shrine. The Jewish troops either offered no resistance or else were subdued. The governor was punished afterward, but the Persian authorities did not permit the restoration of the sanctuary. The Jews at Elephantine appealed, quite naively, to their brethren in Jerusalem for help. Of course the schismatics received no answer. But in 408, with the help of the schismatics in Samaria, and, naturally, with their way smoothed by bribery, they obtained the right to reestablish the sanctuary, although not the right to resume animal sacrifices. The compromise must have pleased both the Egyptians, who worshipped the ram, the sacred animal of Khnum, and the authorities of Judea, who in this manner reduced the altar of Elephantine to a lower rank. Some years later, about 401, the Egyptian revolt brought about the end of Persian rule at Elephantine and the garrison passed into the service of the new pharaohs. At this point, for some unknown reason the evidence concerning Jewish and other military colonists comes to an end. The latest relevant document is from 399, although there were Jews at Elephantine a century later who may have been descendants of the military colonists of the Persian period.

Little is known of the life of the diaspora in Persia and Babylonia. Some ten thousand inscribed clay tablets from Chaldean and Persian Babylonia have been found, but with rare exceptions (like that of Daniel and his comrades) the Jews in Babylonia did not learn the cuneiform script of the priests and scribes. Written in Aramaic or Hebrew on leather or other perishable material, their letters, accounts, and other records have disappeared completely in the humid soil of Mesopotamia. Moreover, ethnic designations were used rarely and haphazardly in the cuneiform records, and the terms "Jew" or "Jews" are lacking altogether, except in an official list mentioning King Jehoiachin and his attendants in the Babylonian exile. Therefore, in order to identify a Jew or, for instance, an Egyptian in the cuneiform records we must rely on proper names. It is obvious that this device is fallible; there was no reason why a foreigner living in Persian Babylonia should not have given his son a Babylonian or a Persian name. Nevertheless, minorities very often preserved their distinct names for generations. Thus, just as the names glorifying the god Ashur in Babylonian documents indicate, at least to a great extent, descendants of Assyrians deported to Babylonia in 612, so a Shabbatai, son of Belabusur, would in all probability be a Jew.

The names of at least nineteen persons in Assyrian documents dated from 709 to 622 B.C.E. sound Hebrew—for instance, the name Iliau. These individuals in all probability were among the deportees from Samaria or their descendants. Jewish names appear in and around the city of Babylon from 623 B.C.E. on, but only in isolated documents and on a few seals. Some Jewish names, for instance that of Sabbatai, who was a clerk, also appear in the records of Persepolis, written under Darius I.

The exiles from Jerusalem and Judea, however, were in the main settled, as Josephus says, "in the most convenient districts of Babylonia." Here, "by the river Chebar," a canal of the river Euphrates upon which the very old, originally Sumerian, city of Nippur stood, Ezekiel saw his vision. During the excavation of Nippur some 730 cuneiform documents written between 455 and 403 B.C.E., that is, in the age of Ezra and Nehemiah, and belonging to the archives of the business house of Murashu were found. Among some twenty-five hundred individuals mentioned in these records, over one hundred are identifiable as Jews.

The house of Murashu dealt almost exclusively with the owners of estates or with the holders of lots on crown land around Nippur. We learn almost nothing about the city of Nippur from these documents. Crown land was held by tenants in consideration of services and payment of rent and taxes. The tenants cultivated their lots individually, but were organized in ethnic and professional groups called *hatru* (for example, those of the "Armenians" or the "Carpenters"), which were collectively responsible for payments due the crown. To our knowledge there was no specifically Jewish *hatru*, but Jews held lands in twenty-one villages and were members of a dozen different *hatru* organizations. A certain Sherebiah headed the *hatru* of the *"Shushanu"* (the meaning of this term is unclear) "of the royal treasury." Some Jews owned military fiefs, and in 422 a man named Gedaliah served as a cuirassed horseman. Jews were also rent collectors, business agents of great landlords, and managers of canals. One Hanani managed a royal poultry farm. A few Jews were slaves, but the majority of them were engaged in cultivation of the rich Mesopotamian soil, either as holders of fiefs or as tenant farmers. In 434 one Jedaiah mortgaged his land to the house of Murashu and rented it from his creditor for about thirty thousand liters of barley annually. Three years later he and his partners enlarged their holdings to such an extent that the rent for the fields more than tripled.

In most cases Jews have gentile co-owners or cotenants on the land and gentile coworkers as well. One Samuel, "cashier" of a landlord, has two Babylonian colleagues, and a certain Zabadiah, together with four Babylonians, leases five fishing nets for twenty days. Since the sons of the captivity in Babylonia did not live in separate settlements, and since many spoke the same (Aramaic) language as the Babylonians and worked together with them, they were well integrated into Babylonian society; and following the advice of Jeremiah they sought the welfare of the city whither their ancestors had been transplanted. A number of them named their sons Shulum-babli, that is, "Welfare of Babylon," and many bestowed Babylonian names on their children, some even placing their sons under the protection of Babylonian gods, with names such as Bel-iada-ah or Bau-etir (that is, "Bel protects" and "[the goddess] Bau has spared"). The Jews of Elephantine shunned Egyptian names for their children, but they were soldiers of a Persian overlord, while the Jews of Babylonia, like the natives, were servants of the Persian conqueror.

Legal and business documents in the Murashu archives offer no direct information about the religion of the Jews around Nippur, but the history of their given names reveals a significant change in their faith. Personal names constructed as statements indicate the hopes and beliefs of the parents and names that invoke a deity assert the latter's might. A Jew in the district of Nippur who named his son Shameshladin, "May [the god] Shamash judge," and the Jew who bestowed on his son the name Jedaiah, "the Lord protects," both affirmed their faith forcefully. The singularity of the religious situation in Nippur was that here Shameshladin named his son Jedaiah.

The Jews were defeated aliens in Babylonia and, as strangers, were desirous of worshipping the gods of the land. All strangers felt this way, even conquerors, as the example of the Assyrian colonists in Samaria shows; but in this case the fall of Jerusalem only emphasized the superiority of Babylon's gods. On the other hand, the devotees of other humbled deities could also serve them far from their destroyed temples (an Assyrian deported to Babylonia, for example, could continue to offer sacrifices to "the Lady [Belit] of Nineveh" in her shrine in Babylon); but after the religious revolution of King Josiah in 622, a faithful Jew could offer sacrifices only on Mount Zion. In desperation the exiles cried, "Our transgressions are upon us . . . How, then, can we live?" (Ezek. 33:10). None of this means that the Jews in exile were forced to abandon the Lord of Jerusalem, only that they were pressured into fearing the idols of Babylon as well. The biblical prediction was fulfilled: in a foreign land, the unfaithful Jews who had disobeyed the Lord served "gods of wood and stone" (Deut. 4:28). These idols were both terrible and merciful and were fervently revered by their worshippers. An inscription by the mother of King Nabonides (555–539) attests her pious and moving devotion to Sin, the god of Haran. As a matter of fact, the first generation born in exile was even inclined to explain the hoped-for Restoration of Jerusalem as the favor of a preferred false god: "My idol did it" (Isa. 48:5). It is indicative that two men who took a decisive part in the rebuilding of the Temple, Sheshbazzar and Zerubabel, bore names marking them as clients of Babylonian gods.

It would be expected, therefore, that in the century following the Restoration the descendants of the original exiles, born and brought up in the comfortable environment of Persian Babylonia, would have turned more and more to the gods of their new land for help and consolation, just as the Assyrian colonists in Samaria did; and at first sight the Murashu documents seem to confirm this expectation. In these records persons are generally identified by their given names and those of their fathers, and the number of individuals who bear patronymics referring to foreign gods is equal to the number who bear names glorifying the Lord. But this paganized generation, without exception, gives its own offspring either names honoring the Lord or names with some other kind of Jewish significance, like Sabbatai. Only ten percent of these names are secular and, except for one doubtful case, no son bears an idolatrous name.

It would appear, then, that about 475 B.C.E. Jews stopped bestowing idolatrous names on their children. We must suppose, of course, that the less pious Jews continued to pay respect to the Babylonian gods, just as it must be supposed that there were faithful Jews who never placed their children under the protection of Babylonian gods in the first place. At any rate, there are no non-Jewish names in the genealogy of Ezra (Ezra 7:1–5). In the absence of relevant information we cannot explain the end of religious laxity among the Jews of Nippur, but the fact that it did occur makes the piety of Ezra and Nehemiah more understandable.

The Jews mentioned in the business documents from Nippur belonged to the lower classes. For the life and manners of the well-to-do Jews in the Eastern dispersion toward the end of the Persian domination we have to look to the Book of Tobit. Tobit and his nephew Ahikar are royal purveyors, Ahikar even rising to the post of chief of the financial admin-istration. As in the case of Nehemiah, the road to success for them has been royal favor, but Raguel, Tobit's relative by marriage, is an opulent landowner, with a fortune in "slaves, oxen, sheep, asses, and camels, clothing, money, and utensils." Still, there is no hint in the book of any commercial activity on the part of these middle and upper class Jews. Such people deposit money for safekeeping, not for investment; and as the money is a reserve intended for times of need (like the gold and silver in the Persian treasury), it brings no interest. In a society where agricul-tural produce (dates in Mesopotamia, for instance) was the mainstay of the economy and coined money hardly circulated, it is clear that landed property must have been the basis of wealth. The fanciful idea that Jews became traders and moneylenders in the Babylonian captivity belongs to professorial mythology.

In the Book of Tobit the ordinary Jew, the Jew of the Murashu doc-uments, appears anonymously, as one among the brethren who receive succor from the aristocracy. Occasionally we catch a glimpse of a Jewish guide who is hired for a journey and we learn that he receives a daily wage in addition to his food, as well as a bounty at the end of the voyage. We also read that Jewish women spin goods at home and sell them to the sheepowner; as at Athens in the same period, this was the sole means of earning a living that befitted an impoverished lady.

The families of the Jewish aristocracy married within their own social group and, like Ezra and Nehemiah, made much of lineage. After an oral betrothal, a deed of marriage was written by the father of the bride as proof that he had given his daughter in marriage. It is noteworthy that Raguel, in giving his daughter away, already used the sacramental for-mula of the present Jewish nuptial ceremony: "according to the Law of Moses."

Although litigations between Jews and Babylonians were judged by Babylonian courts, such as the city "assembly" of Nippur, Jews and other foreign groups also possessed the advantages (or disadvantages) of self-government in certain, to us unknown, areas. For instance, in 529 B.C.E. "the Elders of the Egyptians" in the city of Babylon judged a dispute concerning co-ownership of a fief. The Jews also had their "Elders" (*zekenim*) in Babylonia, who preceded the priests (Jer. 29:1) in the Jewish hierarchy and who were the spokesmen for the community. The much later story of Susanna illustrates the judicial power and arrogance of these Jewish "Elders of the People" in the city of Babylon: they judge the case of an adulterous woman and, according to the law of Moses, condemn her to be stoned to death. We are unable to say whether the legal background of this novelette is reliable, but the crime in question belongs to the complex of domestic law in which the state frequently

permitted family or tribal justice to prevail. Two cuneiform tablets illustrate this point further. In 531 B.C.E. a marriage entered into without
an authorization of the father of the bridegroom is dissolved by a court
and the bride is threatened with enslavement should she meet her lover
again. In the same year a Jewish girl, the daughter of one Joshua, is
warned in the presence of her mother that she will be enslaved if she
continues to see her boyfriend.

Fragmentary and insufficient as it is, our present evidence about self-
government on the part of minorities in Persian Babylonia allows us to
understand the meaning of a clause in Artaxerxes' instructions to Ezra
(Ezra 7:25). The "Scribe of the Law of the God of Heaven" is empowered
to appoint heads and judges who may judge all His people "beyond the
river [Euphrates]" who know "the laws of [your] God," to teach those
laws to men who do not know them, and to punish transgressors. This
formula demonstrates that self-government in the Persian Empire was
established by royal decree; that it was valid only for the territory expressly named in the decree; that the authorities established by the decree
could punish transgressors and even put them to death (as in the story
of Susanna) as long as their decision did not conflict with the king's law;
and that, in the case of the Jews at least, nationality was defined by
religion. For Artaxerxes, Israel was synonymous with the people who
worshipped the God Who was in Jerusalem. We may surmise that the
Egyptians in Babylon would be men who worshipped the gods of Egypt
in that city. I would add that the reference to Petahiah, who "was at the
king's hand in all matters concerning the people" (Neh. 11:24), points
to some kind of overseer of Jewish affairs operating at the court of Susa.
We may suppose, too, that there were other officers assigned to deal with
the other minorities dispersed throughout the provinces of the empire
(the Egyptians in Babylonia or the Greeks in Egypt, for instance). We
are reminded of the *politeumata* in Ptolemaic Egypt, those self-governing
associations of minorities that existed alongside both the civic bodies of
the cities and the administrative structure of the native population.

Aramaic Literature

I N THE days of Alexander the Great and his successors the business language—and probably the mother tongue—of the Jewish diaspora was Aramaic. Without contemporary evidence it is impossible to say how far and in what manner Aramaic crowded out Hebrew in pre-Maccabean Jerusalem. It is noteworthy, however, that the funerary inscriptions of earlier Jewish settlers in Alexandria, who were frequently Palestinians, are in Aramaic or Greek. We may postulate that about 300 B.C.E. every Jew who could read was more or less proficient in Aramaic.

The peculiarity of the Aramaic language was the nonexistence of an Aramean state or nation, although cities and peoples speaking Aramaic did exist. Writing in this language, an author, like a writer of Greek, addressed himself from the outset to an international audience. He wrote for the reader on the Nile and for the reader on the Indus alike, and for this reason he was apt to produce a cosmopolitan book. Although the Ahikar story may descend from a cuneiform original, in its Aramaic form it is free of any nationalistic hue; except for the proper names of the kings of Assyria, the plot might just as well have occurred anywhere and at any time in the ancient East. The only deity referred to by name is Shamash, the sun-god, and he was worshipped under this name not only at Babylon but at Elephantine as well.

The famous story of the Three Pages, now a part of the Greek and Latin bibles, was originally an Aramaic tale. The three young men were bodyguards of Darius I of Persia, but the contest for the royal prize in eloquence in which they participated could have occurred in any scribal school; and the competing propositions, each defended by one of the three orators—namely, that wine, a king, or a woman is the most potent force in the world—could have been debated by young and old, at any time, in any absolute monarchy.

Aramaic storytellers created the Semiramis legend around the name of an Assyrian queen of Aramaic origin, but they made it into a cosmopolitan novel, complete with a love theme. In its Greek adaptation the romance came to be a source of entertainment for an endless succession of readers who would never have cared about Sammu-ramat, queen regent of Assyria from 809 to 804 B.C.E. Alexander himself wanted to outdo the military feats of Semiramis. Exploited by Persians and embellished by Greeks, her legend became so internationalized that Berossus, the precise Babylonian historian of around 280 B.C.E., felt compelled to attack Greek authors who wrote fables about her.

Compare, on the other hand, Egyptian historical fiction: the conquests of Sesostris or the cycle of Petubastis. These stories paint people and events in Egyptian colors and evidence overt Egyptian nationalism. The demotic Wisdom Book, though composed in the Persian or Ptolemaic period, still breathes the same spirit as the Instructions of Ptah-hotep, written in the third millennium B.C.E. No wonder that no one except readers of demotic has ever heard of these books. But the story of Ahikar became known throughout the ancient world, from Egypt to Roman Germany.

We have seen that the taste of Jewish readers, too, was internationalized in the dispersion, as evidenced by the fact that the Ahikar story and two copies of the autobiographical record of Darius I were found as far away as Elephantine. On the Nile, or beside the rivers of Babylon, no mountain of Judah limited the horizon; Jewish books in Aramaic had to be understood at the southern frontier of Egypt as well as at the southern end of the Caspian. The Book of Tobit is a specimen of this new outlook. Written with rare skill and showing the heritage of a long literary tradition, Tobit acquired such popularity with Greek-speaking readers that although the Semitic original has been lost (except for fragments among the Dead Sea Scrolls), three different Greek editions have come down to us. An Aramaic redaction of Tobit was still being read in Palestine around 400 C.E. When in the Middle Ages the Jews became reacquainted with the book, which by then had become part of the Christian Scriptures, its literary art and its ethics appealed to them, with the result that a medieval Aramaic edition and four medieval Hebrew adaptations of Tobit are also known to us.

The discovery of three Aramaic fragments and one Hebrew manuscript of the work among the Dead Sea Scrolls has settled the question of its original language. It was written in Aramaic, but a Hebrew edition of it circulated alongside the Aramaic. In the same way, in medieval and postmedieval Europe Latin and vernacular editions of the same learned treatise could appear, both versions sometimes written by the author himself, as was the case with Calvin's *Institutiones*.

The tale begins at Nineveh, in Assyria. Carried to this city by King

"Enemesar" (that is, Shalmaneser V [727–722 B.C.E.]), who had deported the tribe of Naphtali (to which Tobit belonged), Tobit prospered in exile. Nevertheless, when King Sennacherib, enraged over his failure at Jerusalem (701 B.C.E.), slays many Jews in Nineveh and gives orders that their bodies are not to be buried, Tobit risks his future and buries the cast-out bodies. Denounced, he is compelled to flee, returning only after the accession of Esarhaddon (681 B.C.E.). Soon afterward, he again hears that the corpse of a murdered Jew lies unburied. He inters it, but loses his eyesight in a strange accident; reduced to poverty and misery, he prays for death.

The narrative now shifts to Ecbatana (Hamadan) in Media, where, three hundred miles from Tobit, the demon Asmodeus has killed seven successive bridegrooms of Sarah, daughter of Raguel, on their respective wedding nights. Disheartened, she too asks God to take her life. The angel Raphael is sent to help both Tobit and Sarah. Tobit meanwhile remembers that he has left a deposit at Rhagae (near Teheran) and sends Tobias, his son, to claim the money. The guide hired for the journey, who is actually the angel, advises Tobias to carry with him the vitals of a fish caught in the Tigris.

On the way to Rhagae, the guide brings Tobias to Raguel's house in Ecbatana and advises him to marry Sarah because he is her next of kin. Burning the liver and the heart of the fish, Tobias causes the demon to flee. The angel retrieves the deposit from Rhagae and Tobias returns home with Sarah and with the fish's gall restores the sight of his father. The angel then reveals his identity, and Tobit, in a psalm, gives thanks to God. A note about his and Tobias' later life concludes the book.

As the basis for his story the author used two widely known folkloric themes. In the first of these, an outcast boy is buried by a passerby, after which the dead youth, reappearing in human form, gratefully helps his benefactor. The second theme is that of the Dangerous Bride and the Monster in the Bridal Chamber. To enhance the plot the author also used other motifs from folklore: the magic power of entrails, the contest between two wizards (Raphael fetters the defeated Asmodeus), and the acquisition of a treasure through supernatural help. Moreover, a dog whose glance, according to Iranian beliefs, drives away corpse-fiends, accompanies Tobias and the angel on their journey.

But these fairy-tale elements are merely instrumental. Substituting the immortal angel for the dead youth's ghost enabled the author to split the functions of his hero: the good deeds are performed by Tobit, the bride is bestowed on his son. This alteration caused some inconsistencies in the plot, but at the same time it transformed a ghost story into a family novel. Moreover, because of the historical details which the author introduces into the story, it also becomes an historical novel.

The author's primary historical source was the Book of Kings. Here he found the backsliding of the kingdom of Samaria, Jeroboam's worship of the calf, and the names of the Assyrian kings. But because his source does not mention Sargon, who reigned between Shalmaneser and Sennacherib, he imagined that the latter was the son and successor of the former. Moreover, because he limited his study of the Book of Kings to those columns he thought relevant to his subject, he overlooked the statement that the tribe of Naphtali had already been deported by Tiglath-Pileser III and had Tobit exiled instead by Shalmaneser V.

The author could not, however, find anything in the Bible about the destruction of Nineveh. The capital of Assyria had been captured in 612 B.C.E. by a Babylonian-Median coalition. The Babylonian chroniclers naturally attributed the victory to Nabopolassar of Babylon; the Persians, as we know from Greek historians, assigned the chief glory to the Medes. Ctesias, for example, a Greek physician at the Persian court at the beginning of the fourth century B.C.E., thought that the Median king, whom he calls Abraces, had brought the spoils of Nineveh to Ecbatana. The author of Tobit agrees with Ctesias; he says that Tobit saw in Ecbatana the captivity of Nineveh, which "Achiacharos [i.e., Cyaxares], king of Media, took captive and led into Media."

These historical facts lend an air of verisimilitude to his fiction, which is buttressed by the autobiographical form with which the narrative begins (the point of view changes to that of the third person in the story of Sarah and remains in the third person until the end, but such a change is often made for logistical reasons, in order to avoid cumbersome indirect discourse). Furthermore, since an autobiography must be related to history, the author freely inserts details that will authenticate the story. We are told, for instance, that Sennacherib's sons fled into the mountains of Ararat, and we learn Tobit's age at the time he became blind and the duration of his blindness, along with other such chronological information. Even more adroit are the incidental references to that most famous of Aramaic books, the story of Ahikar: Tobit parenthetically mentions that the famous vizier was his nephew; in the same casual manner he tells us that during his blindness Ahikar cared for him "until he went to Elymais"; and the depravity of Nineveh is illustrated by a reference to Ahikar's misfortune. Our author is a master of historical fiction.

Still, this historical romance never speaks of kings or warriors, or even of the destiny of the Chosen People. Like Ruth, it is the story of a family, although unlike Ruth, which points toward David, the first king of Israel, no heroes are descended from Tobit. Tobias exults over the fall of Nineveh, a city of depravity; but historical events, whether the expedition of Sennacherib or even the destruction of Nineveh, are seen from the standpoint of the average apolitical man. This is a bourgeois novel and the historical events that take place in it are seen only as disturbing influences in its bourgeois world. The blessings of life are peace and affluence.

Although prayers and moral admonitions are not lacking in the book, the main intention of the author is artistic rather than didactic. He delights in painting characters, allowing dialogue again and again to arrest the development of the action in order to engross his audience. While the young Tobias, his bride, and her father are the rather conventional figures of an obedient youth, a well-bred girl, and an anxious father, old Tobit and his wife are worthy of an Attic comedy of manners. From his opening words Tobit appears a paragon of respectability. Yet, in spite of his honorable intentions, his good deeds are separated from his reward by a catastrophe that reminded Jerome of Job's destiny. Job, however, falls from high estate independently of his own doings. The tragic irony of Tobit's sorrows is that his pious deeds are the very cause of his misfortune.

During the feast of Pentecost, in obedience to the Law (Deut. 16:11) he sends his son to invite a poor coreligionist to the table. On the way the son discovers a corpse in the marketplace and tells his father. Caring for the dead body, Tobit renders himself ritually unclean and for this reason remains outside for the night. When he lies down next to the garden wall to sleep, droppings from sparrows nesting in the wall above his head fall in his eyes and cause him to become blind. Thus Tobit's pious act serves to bring about his downfall. Unfortunate experience notwithstanding, however, he does not compromise his principles. In the darkness of his sightless life, he hears the bleating of a kid his wife has received as a gift. Suspecting that she has stolen it, despite her denials, he stubbornly orders her to return the animal, reminding her of the law prohibiting the eating of stolen food (Deut. 22:1). Such obduracy lends a touch of the comical to his character. In another instance, when the angel, in disguise, comes to be hired, Tobit questions him intently about his tribe and family. Raphael asks ironically whether Tobit wants a genealogy or a hired man. Still, in order to satisfy Tobit, the angel invents a human name, whereupon Tobit gravely tells him that he, the angel, is of good stock.

In point of fact, the force that moves Tobit, in addition to his religious devotion, is his conception of honor *(kabod)*. As patiently as Job he bears his sufferings, until his wife, irritated by his rebuke about the kid, reproaches him with the uselessness of his righteous deeds. It is then that he wants to die. The same is true of Sarah. Not the death of seven husbands, but rather the mockery she endures because of it, leads her to think of suicide (although she abandons the idea in order to save her father from reproach). Both Sarah and Tobit pray for death on the same day and the prayers of both are heard before the Glory of God at the same time—an esthetically satisfying moment. The crisis is over and deliverance is near. Yet the crisis was precipitated only by the fear of losing face.

Anna, Tobit's wife, is drawn with few but precise strokes. When Tobit becomes blind she takes to spinning for wages. She is opposed to sending her son on a long journey to retrieve the deposit. She bewails him when his return is delayed, spends every day watching by the road, and runs to him when he is back at last.

As depicted in the Book of Tobit, a couple and their children, not a clan or a community, constitute the framework of life in the dispersion. The father, of course, is the family's center, as well as its master; he welds the family into a unit. Tobias is afraid to die because of the sorrow his death will cause his parents, and he prays in the bridal chamber that he and his wife may grow old together. But marriage also links the couple to a larger group: the parents of the bride are now the "father" and "mother" of the bridegroom, too, and the newlyweds are now "brother" and "sister." For this reason, the bride must be chosen "from the house" of the bridegroom; she must be of the stock of his father. This rule elevates the position of the mother-in-law. Edna, the mother of Sarah, reminds Tobias that she (and not the father) has committed Sarah to him in trust only, as a "deposit" before the Lord: "So do not grieve her, ever." It is illustrative of the decline of civilization in Christian Rome that Jerome, in his version of the story, omitted these words of Edna's and substituted instructions to Sarah to honor her parents-in-law and love her husband.

Outside the tightly knit family group there is emptiness. Of course, in the absence of inns Tobias lodges at the house of a relative, and of course the pious Tobit, obeying the Torah and following his own code of honor, performs many acts of kindness for his Jewish "brothers"—particularly his distant relatives—even taking it upon himself to bury the unclaimed corpses of Jewish dead. But there is no mention of friendship in the book, or of any other kind of interdependent relationship. No Jewish collectivity, no prayer house, no occasion of common prayer is mentioned, even in Tobit's admonitions to his son. The didactic commonplaces directed at Tobias relate primarily to the welfare of the individual and are morally utilitarian: "Alms deliver from death." As for gentiles, except for those in government, they remain outside Tobit's and the author's experience, yet their conversion at the end of this age is clearly expected.

Tobit, of course, is a devotee of the Temple of Jerusalem. He observes the Law strictly, he quotes and refers to Scripture, and he firmly believes in the fulfillment of the prophecies. But the Promised Land is now behind him, and in his injunctions to his son he does not indicate any actual duty toward Jerusalem. His world stretches only from the Caspian to the Tigris.

The book offers no direct clue to the date of its composition, although an approximate date can be established. The *terminus ante quem* is indicated by the one Hebrew and three Aramaic manuscripts (all four fragmentary and not yet published) of the book found among the Dead Sea Scrolls. The book has to have been written, therefore, before approximately 100 B.C.E. at the latest. The *terminus post quem* is indicated by an anachronism in the book: Tobias' angelic guide is paid a drachma a day in addition to the provisions he receives for the journey. Whatever monetary term was used in the Aramaic (Hebrew) original, this sentence could not have been written before the fourth century B.C.E, when the daily use of small silver coins had become increasingly common in the Persian Empire. Indeed, the book must have been composed between approximately 400 and 336 B.C.E.

Moreover, on his deathbed Tobit tells his son and grandson of Nahum's prophecy of the doom of Nineveh and later Tobias' son witnesses the realization of the prophecy. Tobit also predicts the fall of Samaria and Jerusalem and the desolation and the reconstruction of the Temple. And he knows that in the distant future, at the appointed time, all the children of Israel will return to the land promised to Abraham, all the nations will abandon idolatry, all who love God will rejoice, and all sinners will disappear from the earth. Thus far, biblical prophecy and religious hope. But as a careful family man, Tobit also works out the practical consequences of these prophecies; he enjoins his son to leave Nineveh for Media because Media will have "real peace" until the appointed time. Thus, for the author, the fall of the Persian Empire will be followed by the establishment of the Kingdom of God. It is obvious, therefore, that the book must have been written before Alexander's conquest and the fall of the Fourth Monarchy.

The story of Tobit's adventures ends with a long hymn stating that the book is a record of God's "great doings." The angel Raphael himself twice admonishes Tobit that whereas the secrets of an earthly ruler must be kept close, the wondrous works of the heavenly King must be confessed and revealed. His last words to Tobit are: "Write all the things that have happened to you."

Thus the Book of Tobit is an *aretalogia,* to use the Greek term—a narrative proclaiming a god's power to help his devotees. The glorification of one's own, or preferred, deity was a popular literary theme in the Levant. In this case a common language (Aramaic) and the pell-mell of peoples under the Assyrian, neo-Babylonian, and Persian rulers activated this natural tendency. In Persian Egypt a Syrian, Anan, son of Elisha, became a priest of Isis, and an Aramaic ritual text was written in demotic characters. An Egyptian narrative of how the statue of the Theban god, Khons, had exorcised a Babylonian princess possessed by a demon was probably fabricated in the Persian period. In Babylon the worshipper of Belit, Marduk's spouse, was called upon to proclaim her miracles among the peoples. Tobit, too, admonished his brethren to declare God's greatness before the gentiles; God's deeds occurring here and now were His titles of nobility in the eyes of His worshippers. For many Jews, as for Tobit himself, praising the Lord in a foreign land gave providential meaning to the dispersion of the Chosen People: In the Lord's own day, a bright light will shine unto all the ends of the earth and many nations from afar will worship the Name of the Lord. Such a hope lightened the burden of exile.

There circulated many other Aramaic tales in which Jews were cast as the heroes, although owing to the character of our tradition, the stories that have been preserved are all religious and/or nationalist, or both. The sectarians of the Dead Sea, for example, read a story called "The Prayer of Nabonidus" about a Jewish exorcist who had cured Nabonidus, the last Babylonian king. Five similar Aramaic stories have been preserved in the first part of the Book of Daniel. Three, in which Daniel is portrayed as a better soothsayer than the Babylonian savants, probably descend from Babylonian court tales reworked by Jews to the glory of God and His faithful.

We have already discussed the story of Nebuchadnezzar's dream, in which the conqueror of Jerusalem learns of the doom of Babylon (Dan. 2). A similar Babylonian court tale, known only through a Greek source, describes how the same king, in a prophetic fit, shouts from the roof of his palace that a "Persian mule" (Cyrus was half-Persian, half-Mede) will, with the aid of the gods of the city, conquer Babylon. A third version of the same theme figures as the fourth chapter of the Book of Daniel: Nebuchadnezzar dreams of a tree cut down by celestial command. As the Church Father Hippolytus observed, this vision does not require an interpreter, since its meaning is obvious to everyone: the tree was a common symbol of life and power. Moreover, the author of this chapter intentionally uses the imagery of Ezekiel (31), who likens the pharaoh to the tallest cedar in Lebanon, which will be cut down by God because of its pride.

In his dream Nebuchadnezzar sees the stump of the tree being bound with bands of iron and bronze, just as such rings encircle the sacred trees on Mesopotamian monuments. Nevertheless, none of the king's numerous wizards is able to make sense of the vision, and the king calls upon Belshazzar, "the master of the magicians" (Dan. 4:6). This soothsayer must have been the hero of the original court tale, but in its Jewish redaction he was identified with Daniel. As for the vision, the inclusion of the idea that the "stump of the roots" remains after the tree is cut down indicates that in the original version the dream was meant to teach that the presumptuous monarch (or his arrogant city) would only lose preeminence, not be completely destroyed. The prophecy was borne out by the events of 539, for in that year Cyrus conquered Babylon. Yet even though the city lost its empire it was not destroyed. Nor did Cyrus destroy Nabonidus, the last Babylonian king; after his capture he was appointed governor of a Persian province. The proud tree was cut down, but not uprooted.

In the Jewish redaction the original meaning of the tale is changed. The author of the fourth chapter of the Book of Daniel adds another story about the dangers of pride, the fable of the man-beast, and, combining the two, both of which may have originally concerned King Nabonidus, he predicts that the king will receive "a beast's mind" and that "for seven times" he will live with the beasts of the field and eat grass like the ox. The incongruity between the parable of the tree and the fable of the man-beast clearly indicates literary contamination.

Nabonidus' problems began after he had placed his own deity, the moon-god Sin, "the king of gods," above Marduk, the celestial patron of Babylon. As the terrestrial order was believed to reflect the hierarchy above, this meant the elevation of Haran (a business center on a tributary of the Upper Euphrates), the city of Sin, over Babylon. Nabonidus' mother, also a devotee of Sin, had clothed herself in rags for many years, supplicating Sin and Sin's spouse to establish the glory of Haran and its gods. In early Mohammedan times the men of Haran still worshipped Sin and, like the Jews, prayed for the restoration of past glory.

Disliked by the clergy of Marduk, Nabonidus settled far from Babylon. He built a palace in Teima, a city of Sin in Arabia, and spent ten out of the seventeen years of his reign there—"and to my city of Babylon I did not go." No wonder that the gossips in Babylon ascribed his absence to some loathsome disease. In the Prayer of Nabonidus discovered among the Dead Sea Scrolls, the king admits that for seven of his years in Arabia he suffered from *shechin*, the same disease that afflicted Job, "from the sole of his foot to the crown of his head." The Jewish exorcist in the Prayer (whose name is not given in the extant fragment) advised the king to forsake idols if he would be cured. The prescription had, necessarily, to be sent in writing, since isolation was the usual fate of a chronically ill king (for example, Uzziah of Judah, struck with leprosy to punish his pride [II Chron. 26:16]). In the Greek version of Nebuchadnezzar's prophecy, Nebuchadnezzar curses Nabonidus: May he be drowned in the sea or driven into the desert to wander alone "where wild beasts have their pastures, and birds do roam."

The two tales in the fourth chapter of Daniel have been put together by the Jewish author as follows: The arrogant king receives advice from above to cease his sinning. Heedless, he boasts (as Nebuchadnezzar does in his inscriptions) that he built the great city of Babylon for his own glory. Immediately he becomes like a beast. Horrified, he humbles himself and is reestablished in his kingdom. The Jewish author inserted the story of the king's madness into the story of the tree cut down, because for the Jews it was not Nabonidus but Nebuchadnezzar, the conqueror of Jerusalem, who was the archetype of arrogance, and consequently it was he they identified with the story of the king's madness. Jewish readers were delighted to learn that the king who had burned the Temple had been compelled to proclaim the glory of the "Most High."

It was almost inevitable that Daniel, who had predicted the end of Babylon to Nebuchadnezzar in chapter 2, would be called upon to repeat the same warning to the last king of Babylon who, as the story is told in Daniel 5, was Belshazzar. From 553 this son of Nabonidus had governed Babylon while his father was in Arabia (returning to the capital city only about six months before Cyrus captured the city). It is understandable, therefore, that in the popular tradition of the Babylonian Jews Belshazzar should be remembered as the last king of Babylon. The future was announced this time at a feast in Belshazzar's palace by means of handwriting on the wall. After deciphering the written prediction, Daniel delivers a sermon on the dangers of pride, an admonition, as the Church Father John Chrysostom observes, that could be of no use to the king, whose fate had already been fixed, and must therefore have been meant by Daniel as a warning to his readers.

The use of the title "Most High" for God in Daniel 3, 4, and 5 indicates that these chapters in their present form were composed in the late third century B.C.E., since this title did not become popular before then. The dating of chapter 5, at least approximately, is of special importance because it presents for the first time a method of interpretation that later became important in Jewish thinking.

Daniel says to the king: "I shall make known the *peshar*." The term recurs in the Book of Daniel thirty-two times. This originally Akkadian word refers to "solving" dreams; a cognate term, *patar*, is used in the story of Joseph when the patriarch interprets Pharaoh's dream of seven fat and seven lean cows. In the story of Belshazzar, however, this technical term relating to the interpretation of dreams is used in opposition to the plain as well as the secret meaning of the text. Joseph says that seven lean cows symbolize seven years of hunger, but Daniel does not tell the king what the words on the wall—*mina* or *shekel*—signify. He substitutes the words, *mene, tekel,* and *peres* (not *parsin,* as in the writing, he explains) for the words actually written, and interprets the new text. Later, in the ninth chapter of Daniel, the seventy years of desolation predicted by Jeremiah become seventy weeks of years, and this new formula, too, becomes the basis for prediction.

In this new approach the text appears to the interpreter as a cipher. In the commentary of Habakkuk found among the Dead Sea Scrolls, when the prophet speaks of sacrifices to the "net" (1:16), the *pesher* is: sacrifices to the "[Roman] standards." Habakkuk also speaks of *"Kasdim,"* that is, Chaldeans (1:6), but for the new style of interpreter the word means *"Kittim,"* which is then interpreted as "Romans." The same method of interpretation was used in late Babylonian and Egyptian texts. For example, in the Egyptian priestly decree of 198 B.C.E. preserved on the Rosetta Stone, the traditional Egyptian emblems of the serpent and the vulture "indicate" that Ptolemy V "illuminates" Egypt.

This method of interpretation requires the atomization of the text. As Daniel uses it before Belshazzar, every word stands for something else and must (or may) be explained separately. The writers of the New Testament, the Church Fathers, and the rabbis applied this method to biblical texts, treating them as if they were reports of *omina* or dreams. No wonder that the haggadists borrowed their rules of interpretation from dream books.

Men used this approach because they believed that sacred words must be meaningful. According to their plain meaning, Scriptural stories belong to the past; but if the prophecies of Jeremiah and Habakkuk have already been fulfilled, why study these dusty pages? The sectarian author of the commentary on Habakkuk, however, was certain that God had told the prophet to write down that which was to come upon the latter age, and the rabbis explained that the prophetic oracles that had been preserved referred to the future. The Torah spoke to every age.

The interpretation of sacred oracles therefore became a matter of inspiration. Ben Sira speaks of sages who seek out the meanings of prophecies, parables, and proverbs, and through prayer obtain the revelation of truth. Daniel seeks the mercy of the God of Heaven concerning the meaning of Nebuchadnezzar's dream, and he supplicates and fasts in order to understand the meaning of Jeremiah's words. In both cases, the mysteries are revealed to him in visions. As Gregory the Miracle Worker stated in 238 C.E., understanding a prophecy requires the same divine interpretation that was vouchsafed to the prophet himself.

Two other stories in Daniel were also written primarily for Jewish audiences. They are tales that are essentially reports of martyrdom, stories that show their heroes in ideological conflict with heathen powers. In the same way, writers of novels about Christians in the Roman Empire never fail to include themes of persecution and martyrdom; otherwise the story would no longer have been considered "Christian" and the reader would have felt cheated of the most exciting part. In the first of the stories, in Daniel 3, three Jewish youths are cast into a fiery furnace for refusing to worship Nebuchadnezzar's golden idol. Similar stories are known: Semiramis, for example, ordered that no deity other than her own image should be worshipped, and Jehoiakim of Jerusalem (609–558) burned the prophet Jeremiah alive because he had rebuked the Jews for sacrifices to a golden image of Baal.

Refusal to bow before an idol was generally thought to be a good topic for edifying literature, and the tale of the three youths, composed in the third century B.C.E., is the earliest extant specimen of this genre. Yet at first sight the theme appears to be fictional. In the ancient polytheistic world no one was compelled to adore a foreign god. To a stranger sojourning among the Hebrews it was, rather, a privilege to be granted permission to partake of the blessings procured by worship of the Lord. Usually it was the foreigner himself who sought the protection of the deities of his new land. Even the rabbis make this point when they have Nebuchadnezzar say to the three youths: "The Lord will scatter you among the peoples . . . and there you will serve gods of wood and stone" (Deut. 4:27–28).

In reality, conflict between monotheist Jews and alien worship could arise only when, as happened to Daniel and his comrades, Jews became officers of a foreign ruler. Every king was also the head of a state religion, and every official action therefore had a cultic aspect. Elisha was forced to permit a convert, an officer of the king of Damascus, to bow before the idol when accompanying his master to the temple of Rimmon (II Kings 5:18).

Unlike the ancient prophet, the author of the tale in the third chapter of Daniel is intransigent. The rabbis understood the meaning of the parable very well: they have the three youths say to Nebuchadnezzar that in matters of government and taxation he is king, but that if he demands service to idols, he is a barking dog (a play on the word *nebah*, which sounds like the bark of a dog). The story of the three "servants of the Most High God," written, as I have noted, in the third century, is the earliest statement (although only implicit) of the doctrine of the separation of church and state: "Render to Caesar the things that are Caesar's, and to God the things that are God's" (Matt. 22:21).

The second tale of martyrdom, recounted in Daniel 6, is another story built on the theme of court rivalry. King Darius intends to appoint Daniel to be his vizier. Envious courtiers induce the king to forbid petitions to any god or man, excepting the king himself, for thirty days. Daniel naturally continues to invoke his God.

The royal edict that is the starting point of the story already perplexed the Greek translator of Daniel, who transformed the tale into an attack against ruler-worship; he has Darius forbid addressing requests to any god but himself. But in Babylonia, where the story takes place, the religious calendar forbade prayers (or particular kinds of prayers) on certain days regarded as unlucky. For instance, the king was warned not to pray to the gods Sin and Shamash (Moon and Sun) on five different days in the month of Nisan. To offer food, and thus the accompanying petition, to one's personal god in the month of Tebet was unlucky. Moreover, though Babylonian (and Jewish) months were lunar, Babylonian lists of lucky and unlucky days count thirty days for every month, which explains the thirty-day period of interdiction against requests that we find in Daniel. The Jewish tale-teller misunderstood Babylonian religious practice and, therefore, used the tale to contrast the absurdity of idolatry with the true faith of the Chosen People: a Jew could appeal to the God of his fathers at any time.

To help prove his point the Jewish author uses a popular theme of oriental folktales: A virtuous servant of the king is falsely accused, but in the end his innocence is proved. Accused of violating a royal edict, Daniel is cast into the lions' den, that is, he is subjected to an "ordeal." But the ordeal was generally used when there were no witnesses to an alleged crime. For instance, a woman suspected of adultery was forced to drink "the bitter water," which, should she be guilty, would cause her body to swell (Num. 5:11). In Daniel's case, however, his disobedience was witnessed directly by his accusers, which should have rendered the ordeal unnecessary. The three youths had flouted a royal order openly, which again should have obviated the need for any kind of test in their case. We can assume, therefore, that the court tale the Jewish author of this story was using probably involved a royal favorite falsely accused of a secret offense, who proved his innocence by undergoing an ordeal. Jewish authors and readers were not interested in the niceties of legal procedure. They wanted miracles—and so an angel descended to shut the lions' mouths and Daniel was found blameless before the king. In this way the stories about Daniel and the three youths became examples of ever-present divine help. Since then, men have recalled these stories in their synagogue prayers in order to invoke divine mercy yet again, while in Christian art the deliverance of Daniel and of the three youths became a symbol of victory over death.

But to the compiler of Daniel's tales and to his readers in the early Hellenistic age, the main and immediate value of these miracle stories was pragmatic, not symbolic. The compiler worked before the reign of Antiochus Epiphanes (176 B.C.E.), since there is nothing in the stories that refers to the Seleucid king and his persecution of the true faith. On the other hand, in the interpretation of Nebuchadnezzar's dream there is a clear allusion to the marriage between Antiochus II of Syria and the Egyptian princess Berenice in 251 B.C.E. (2:43), as well as to the war between Syria and Egypt in 245 B.C.E., demonstrating that the book was published between 245 and 175. Either the editor did not know or did not want to include several other tales about Daniel, such as the tale of Daniel's refusal to worship Bel of Babylon, which have been preserved in the Greek translation of his compilation.

At the time the editor was working, the diaspora from Egypt to Persia and from Greece to Arabia was exposed daily to the attraction of foreign deities immediately at hand, while the Lord of Jerusalem had his abode far away in his sanctuary on Zion, in the Promised Land. We can still read the story of a Jewish slave at Oropus, in Boeotia, who was a contemporary of the editor of Daniel's tales. The slave, in order to understand a dream of his, consulted Amphiaraus, the oracular god of Oropus. The oracle interpreted the dream as indicating that the slave would be set free by his Greek master. When this actually happened, the Jew, according to the instructions of Amphiaraus and the goddess Hygeia, recorded the whole episode on a stone in order to render homage to these Greek idols. Such testimony was invaluable in the fierce rivalry between polytheistic cults, each pretending that its deity alone was everywhere omnipotent. The Jewish minority, lost in the immense spaces of pagan empires and living for generations on foreign soil, wanted and needed to be reassured that the Lord of Jerusalem, although far distant, could offer His help anywhere. The Psalmist (148:11) called upon the kings of the earth and all the peoples of the earth to praise the name of the Lord. And in the four aretologies in Daniel, pagan kings do "tremble and fear before the God of Daniel" (Dan. 6:26). Belshazzar alone dared to affront the God of Jerusalem: "That very night Belshazzar, the king of the Chaldeans, was slain."

It is the art of the narrator, however, and not simply monotonous propaganda that attracted and still attracts readers to Daniel. The stories remind us of the Tales of the Arabian Nights. Daniel, the hero of the tales, is the man who against all odds, by virtue of his sheer intelligence and moral goodness like Joseph of old, succeeds at an oriental court. The king is the standard despot of oriental folklore; the conflict between the hero and his antagonists is purely personal. The contrast is not between Jewish light and pagan darkness, but between the caprices of the foolish caliph and the wits of the hero. And the compiler makes these oriental court stories even more fascinating by skillfully correlating, and at the same time varying, these materials. For example, in chapter 4 Daniel is summoned by Nebuchadnezzar, but in chapter 5 it is the queen mother who suggests calling him. Nor is the variation arbitrary: in chapter 5 Belshazzar, the new king, is ignorant of Daniel's reputation; in chapter 2 the first revelation to Nebuchadnezzar is narrated as if it were an entry in a chronicle—"In the second year of the reign of Nebuchadnezzar . . ."—but in chapter 4 the event is revealed in a royal proclamation.

In addition, the author of Daniel demonstrates a fine sense of artistic parsimony, avoiding the repetitions and digressions so common in folk-tales and making details serve the construction of the plot. We are told, for instance, that the three youths were thrown into the furnace fully clothed. This seemingly unnecessary detail later becomes the evidence attesting to the miracle: the garments do not show the least trace of fire or smoke.

Still, the primary appeal of Daniel's tales lay in the fact that in them propaganda and literary skill served a great cause. The author of Daniel convinced his readers because he himself was firmly convinced that his faith was the only true one.

PART II

THE
THIRD
CENTURY

TEN

Ptolemaic Palestine

Two events that happened to occur exactly a century apart allow us to speak of third-century Palestine as a single historical unit. In 301 B.C.E., after the defeat of Antigonus at the battle of Ipsus, Ptolemy I of Egypt reoccupied the southern part of the Syrian lands, this time, he thought, for good. But Ptolemaic rule ended a century later, in 200, when Antiochus III of Syria, by his victory at Panion, succeeded in recovering Palestine and Phoenicia for the Empire of Asia.

Five times in the course of this century, in 280–279, 276–272, 242–241, 219–217, and in 203, the kings of the South and the kings of the North (to use Daniel's language)—that is, the Ptolemies of Alexandria and the Seleucids of Antioch—went to war. The pretext for each conflict varied but in Syria, at least, the Ptolemies were defending Palestine, the bulwark of Egypt. Ancient strategists long before Napoleon had already seen that possession of this barrier was vital for the security of the pharaohs and their successors. For five thousand years before Bonaparte's Egyptian expedition of 1799, all the conquerors of Egypt had come by way of Palestine. Although the dominion of the North, as Daniel notes, was greater than the lordship of the South, the Seleucid armies, except in 218, could not pierce the Ptolemaic fortifications along the Litani River (the Greek "Leontos") and the ridge of Mount Hermon. On the other hand the triumphant expedition of Ptolemy III, who in 246 reached the Euphrates and stirred the imagination of his contemporaries, brought about no lasting territorial changes in southern Syria. A few cities in the frontal zone, such as Damascus, changed hands several times, but except for some temporary fluctuations the boundary traced in 301 remained virtually unchanged. The Nahr el Kebir, the "Great River" of the Arabs ("Eleutheros" to the Greeks) and the watershed between the Orontes and the Litani, a natural frontier, separated the Seleucid and the Ptolemaic dominions in Syria. The sea (once again, except in 218–217) remained under Ptolemaic control, while to the east strongholds and garrisons guarded Palestine from the Bedouin of the desert across the Jordan. Under the wings of the Ptolemaic eagle, the Holy Land enjoyed the blessings of peace throughout the century. Except perhaps for the experience of 218, three generations of the Chosen People knew only from the lips of their grandfathers or from reading their Bibles of the horrors of ancient wars. Israel again dwelled in safety, in a land of grain and wine.

Our information about Ptolemaic Palestine is scanty and haphazard: a few lines in Polybius, a hero tale in Josephus, isolated coins and inscriptions, and a few bits of archeological evidence. Greek papyri from Egypt, however, sometimes contain references to the province. Particularly important are the files of one Zenon, an agent of Apollonios, the treasurer general of Ptolemy II, who in 259 was sent on a mission to Palestine and whose archives provide some evidence about conditions in the country at that time.

Under Ptolemaic rule Jerusalem belonged to the province of Syria (also styled "Syria and Phoenicia"). A *strategos* headed the civil and military administration of the province and an "intendant of revenues" controlled the economy with the help of local agents, called *oikonomoi*. The province itself was divided into subgovernments *(hyparchiai)*, which in turn were divided into still smaller units, each of which was called a *nomos*. Thus the *nomos* of Lydda was a part of the Samaritan region (Samaritis). We do not know the titles of the heads of these districts, nor are the districts' exact boundaries known. Samaritis, governed from Samaria, joined Judea to the north; Idumea, whose chief town was probably Marissa, lay to the south and extended from the Dead Sea to the confines of Gaza and Ascalon. The administrative organization in Galilee remains unclear.

Within a "strategy" (or a Seleucid satrapy) there also existed areas that were directly governed by royal officers, as well as more or less self-governing communities, primarily cities of the Greek type. No Greek *polis* had existed in Syria before the Macedonian conquest, but since the Phoenician cities along the coast had enjoyed a limited autonomy under Persian rule, they maintained it under their new overlords and at first continued to be ruled by their native kings. Monarchy, however, was not compatible with the Greek idea of *polis*, and kings gradually disappeared from Phoenicia; the era "of the people of Tyre," for instance, began in 274 B.C.E. Nonetheless, the new republics remained in essence oriental polities: "judges" (the biblical *shofet* and the *suffetes* of Carthage) now replaced kings, but real power remained in the hands of the notables. It should be noted, too, that each of these cities dominated the surrounding countryside, the rule of Tyre, for example, running south toward Mount Carmel and east toward the Jordan.

The Ptolemies, however, did in effect free the seacoast of Palestine from the domination of Tyre and Sidon, which these Phoenician cities had exercised under Persian rule. From the Carmel to the Egyptian frontier, the coast was now divided among numerous cities of the Greek type. Before 261 B.C.E. Ptolemy II had renamed Acco "Ptolemais" and had established a mint there; in 218, Dora is mentioned as a Ptolemaic stronghold; and Gaza, which became yet another Ptolemaic fortress, was also awarded a Ptolemaic mint. And even though the inhospitable coast offered no safe anchorage south of Carmel, making Acco-Ptolemais the most important harbor of Palestine, in Zenon's correspondence Strato's Tower (Caesarea) and Joppa (Jaffa) are also mentioned as places of disembarkation and trading. Ascalon, which possessed only a small countryside, was busy on the sea, too. As early as the first part of the third century, traders from Ascalon were established at Athens. And although Gaza, the southern gateway to Palestine, "situated at the beginning of the desert," as a Greek writer says, lay upon a hill an hour's walk from the sea, among wells and gardens, yet it was the pivot of the caravan trade. It was here that the great land routes—to Egypt from Syria and from Arabia to the Mediterranean—crossed and together touched the sea.

There were Macedonian and Greek colonies in Palestine, too. As we have seen, Samaria, an impregnable fortress, had become a Macedonian colony under Alexander (under the Caesars it still honored Perdiccas, one of Alexander's generals, as its founder). However, the Ptolemies were also careful to establish other military colonies at strategic points along the caravan routes that connected Egypt with Syria and Mesopotamia. A Ptolemy planted a Greek colony at Beth-shan, a key point dominating the fords of Jordan on the historical highway from Damascus to Egypt. In 218 B.C.E. the Seleucid army marched from Tyre to Mount Tabor in Esdraelon, from there to Philotera—another Ptolemaic colony—at the southern tip of the Sea of Galilee, and then turned southward to Beth-shan and the Jordan. The Greeks, probably identifying the local Baal, Mekal, with their own god of wine, named their colony at Beth-shan "Nysa," in honor of the place where Dionysus was nursed by the nymphs. But because local antiquarians for some reason imagined that their city had been founded by Scythians, who (as Herodotus still knew) had overrun Palestine at the end of the seventh century, common usage was to call the city Scythopolis.

Crossing the Jordan near Scythopolis the Seleucid army, led by Antiochus III, continued to Pella, some eleven kilometers southeast of Scythopolis. Pella was another Ptolemaic stronghold, an almost impregnable fortress that was accessible only on its eastern slope and that dominated access to the river Jordan from the East. Like Beth-shan, it had already been mentioned in Egyptian records. The Greeks had renamed the city Pella, after the Macedonian capital, but under the Ptolemies it was called Berenice, after the wife of Ptolemy I. From Pella roads led to Gerasa and Philadelphia (now Amman), both of which became Greek settlements.

The route north from Scythopolis to Damascus and Arabia was also controlled by Greek colonies—the stronghold of Hippos, set above the gorge of Fik, east of the Sea of Galilee, and the settlement at Gadara. Abile and Dium, northeast of Gadara, along with several other military colonies, supplemented the defenses of the Transjordan region. A papyrus of 259 B.C.E. mentions such a Ptolemaic military colony, "Birta, in the Ammonitis."

This network of Ptolemaic strongholds across the Jordan was made both necessary and possible by the abandonment after the Assyrian and Babylonian invasions of all the territory beyond the lower Jordan—roughly, from the Sea of Galilee to the Dead Sea. Sedentary occupation of this fertile land and its rich pastures seems to have ceased after that time, leaving the territory to Arab nomads and their flocks until the coming of the Macedonians. Ptolemaic colonists could therefore be settled on the virtually empty tracts of land and the drift of nomads into Palestine be checked by armed husbandmen. The new Greek colonies also enriched the royal treasury. Polybius notes that the territories of Scythopolis and Philotera were easily capable of supplying food and other necessities to the entire army of Antiochus III.

A number of Ptolemaic colonies, such as Scythopolis and Philadelphia, were probably organized as Greek city-states with all their attendant democratic institutions. Because military service in a *polis* was the most important of civic duties, the city militia should have been sufficient to protect its territory from marauding nomads. But as shown by the document from Birta (in Transjordan) mentioned above, the Ptolemies also used the device of military land allotments in Palestine, as they did in Egypt. In Birta the "men of Tubias" and the "cavalrymen of Tubias" were established as holders of military land tenures *(cleruchs)*, which in all probability were cultivated by native tenants or slaves. The regiment included men of various nationalities. Tubias (Tobias) himself was a Jewish dynast, a descendant of Tobiah "the Ammonite," governor of the Ammonite land in the time of Nehemiah. The men under Tobias, like the Jewish military colonists in Persian Elephantine or the members of a military *hatru* in Persian Nippur, had to handle both sword and plow and to pay for their holdings with their blood. The Ptolemies also garrisoned a number of harbors, as we saw in the case of Gaza, and for the purpose of keeping order in their province placed military posts at places such as Beth-zur and in the Negev.

This military machine, particularly the founding of military colonies, was very expensive, even though the new settlements were apparently established on crown land. Most of this land had been inherited by the Ptolemies from the Persian kings, but sometimes they also resorted to confiscation. When the authorities in Jerusalem defaulted on the payment of their tribute, the Ptolemaic government threatened to seize Jewish territory and parcel it out to mercenaries.

The amount of land held by the crown in Palestine was extensive. Beside the balsam gardens, the Ptolemaic crown holdings probably included Transjordan, Galilee, and the valley of the upper Jordan. Ono (Lydda), Ekron, and perhaps Jamnia (Jabne) were also in the king's hand. The king, of course, could dispose of this land at will: he could exploit it directly, lease it, cede part of it for a colony, or transfer a tract in a revocable grant *(dorea)* to a favorite.

In the crown lands the village was the basic unit of organization. The revenues from the rents and taxes imposed on the village were generally farmed out to one person, the village contractor, who then subleased the land to native tenants. These native farmers, called *laoi* (commons), were headed by a village chief. Although, in addition to tilling their lots, they were required to donate a certain amount of labor to the government in other places, the village was their legal domicile. Moreover, because each taxpayer was compelled to state a place of origin *(patris)* in his tax declaration, control of the labor force was facilitated.

The *dorea* was also a form of lease, since holders of such grants were responsible for the taxes due on their land—although, of course, they regarded themselves as landlords. Ptolemy, son of Thrasea, a former Ptolemaic official and later the Seleucid governor, writes to Antiochus III in 200 B.C.E. of the "villages [in the vicinity of Scythopolis] that are mine." The same document goes on to show that a powerful landlord could protect, or try to protect, his villages from the billeting, the requisitions, and the violence of passing soldiers and officials—no mean feat in a preindustrial age. Of course, this protection also meant that the *laoi,* although remaining legally free, had in fact become villeins. A royal order of 260 B.C.E. speaks of *laoi* who had been bought, carried away, detained, or otherwise seized, and decrees their liberation.

As tenants, the natives paid their rent in kind, perhaps one-third of the yield of their sown crops and one-half of the yield of the fruits. They were also required to pay imposts on goods entering or leaving a fiscal district, in addition to various personal and capital taxes introduced by the Ptolemies. For instance, there was a sales tax on slaves and an impost on livestock called a "pasture duty." Accordingly a complicated system of tax returns was necessary. Around 264 B.C.E. a general census of slaves was made and in the actual year 264, every owner of flocks and herds in the "villages of Syria and Phoenicia" had to file a return concerning his "taxable" and "tax-exempt" animals. Simultaneously the head of each village (as well as a fiscal agent) had to declare the number of livestock owned by the inhabitants of a village, so that the government could verify the individual declarations. Probably, as in Ptolemaic Egypt, every kind of income and virtually every material object, including agricultural implements, were taxed. The returns were sworn to and false statements were severely punished. Those who failed to declare their slaves not only forfeited them, but also had to pay the enormous fine of one talent—that is, about ten times the going price—for each nondeclared slave.

Outside the crown lands and the Greek and Phoenician cities, the territory of the province of Syria and Phoenicia was left to the native towns and tribes, each of which lived according to its customary laws. Like all ancient overlords, the Ptolemies avoided bothering their subject communities unnecessarily or bothering themselves unnecessarily about the welfare of their subjects. Security and revenues were practically the only matters with which the king or his governor concerned himself.

Jerusalem belonged to this category of subject towns. Information about the relationship between the Ptolemaic administration and the Jewish *ethnos,* however, is scarce and accidental. We do not know, for instance, whether royal troops occupied the citadel of Jerusalem in peacetime or whether the Jews furnished recruits for the Ptolemaic army; we do not even know whether there was a royal governor in Ptolemaic Jerusalem. Some essential facts, however, are clear: the Jews of Judea constituted a more or less self-governing *ethnos,* the law of Moses was their law, and their Temple was sacrosanct. In other words the Ptolemies, like Alexander before them and the Seleucids after them, in this respect continued the policies established by Cyrus, Darius, and Artaxerxes.

Ptolemaic Judea was required to pay a lump sum of twenty talents, that is, over 500 kilograms of silver (equal in value to about 40 kilograms of gold) annually in tribute, if Josephus' figure is to be trusted. The Ptolemies, who needed ready cash, assigned the tribute as well as many other taxes to "contractors" who bid for them at auction in Alexandria, paying a lump sum in advance for the privilege. As a result local chiefs, among them the High Priest of Jerusalem in the later years of the third century, eagerly bid for the revenues of their own towns in order to preserve their power. The government, of course, lent a hand, including the use of its troops, to assist such publicans when necessary.

Once again there is much that we do not know. We don't know whether in addition to the tribute there was direct taxation of individuals by the royal government, or what the limits were of the fiscal autonomy of Ptolemaic Judea. Nor do we know anything about taxation by Jewish authorities, although we do know that the *Gerousia,* the governing body of the Jews first attested in a Seleucid document of 200 B.C.E., already existed under the Ptolemies.

To a superficial observer Palestine, and Judea in particular, may have appeared quite the same toward the end of the third century B.C.E. as they had one hundred years before. Yet the changes had been profound. To begin with, the Phoenician curtain that separated Judea from the Mediterranean had disappeared. Further, following the example of Alexander, the Ptolemies had opened their empire to the speculative energy of Greek businessmen. Apollonios, vizier of Ptolemy II, was also a great merchant: his caravans went from Egypt to Gaza, and from Gaza to Sidon or to the other side of the Jordan. The correspondence of Zenon, his agent, demonstrates that entrepreneurs had invaded Palestine as early as approximately 260 B.C.E. He writes, for instance, of two Greeks trafficking in the charms of slave girls at Ptolemais, at Joppa, at Pegae (northeast of Joppa), and in Transjordan, and of a Greek salesman who had visited Miletus and Halicarnassus in Asia Minor and had proceeded to Gaza, Ptolemais, and Philadelphia. He tells us that in 257 a Greek trader in Sidon met another Greek trader, just arrived, while a third watched at Joppa for an export opportunity, and a fourth, mentioned in the same letter, had brought slaves and merchandise to Tyre for transshipment. A tradesman brought mattresses from Egypt to Gaza and sold them at Philadelphia, and a caravan led by Zenon himself stopped in Jerusalem and Jericho on the way to Transjordan.

Further, Alexander and the Ptolemies had also introduced the general usage of coined money in the Orient, from the Nile to the Indus. Even camel drivers had drachmas now. Of course, landlords continued to receive payment in produce from their tenants, but Ptolemaic silver served to pay taxes as well as for such merchandise as imported reed mats, pickled meats, and Sicilian wine. Numerous Rhodian stamped jars of the Ptolemaic (and Seleucid) period attest the extensive diffusion of imported Greek wines and olive oil. One may ask why the Promised Land with its olive trees and vineyards needed foreign wine and oil (Apollonius was also the owner of a vineyard in Galilee), but the point is that the influx of expensive foods illustrates a raised standard of living in Ptolemaic Palestine.

At the same time, however, the Ptolemies cut their dominions off economically from the outside world by means of their monetary policy. In the Hellenistic world the weight of a silver drachma was generally about 4.3 grams (the Attic standard), but Ptolemaic silver was lighter (around 3.5 grams per drachma). One hundred Ptolemaic Egyptian drachmas were therefore worth only eighty Attic standard drachmas outside the empire. The result was that Ptolemaic silver coins circulated only within the Ptolemaic Empire and were the only silver coins used within it. Gold, of course, was an internationally accepted means of payment, but the Ptolemies ordered that imported gold coins be exchanged for gold of the realm, and reserved for themselves the exclusive right to carry out this operation. Furthermore, although copper coins elsewhere served as subsidiary money only, from about 270 B.C.E. the Ptolemies used copper coins of fluctuating value with respect to silver as a legal means of payment.

Nevertheless, despite the self-imposed isolation of their economy, the Ptolemies sought to obtain bullion by forcing exports and taxing imports, to the extent that even the movement of goods from Syria (and probably from other provinces also) to Egypt was subject to exorbitant custom duties. For instance, the Greeks in Egypt wanted olive oil, a commodity that for climatic reasons could not be produced in Egypt, but which was abundant in Syria. But the state had the monopoly on oil in Egypt and subjected Syrian oil to a duty of fifty percent *ad valorem*. Moreover, an oil importer needed a license, and the licensed oil had to be stored in the royal magazines. The government thus pocketed about 65 percent of the price paid by the customer in Egypt for oil. The cumulative effect of these measures caused Syria, and within it Palestine, to become economically dissociated from the Levant and attached instead to the Egyptian economy, a change that explains at least in part the importance of the Jewish diaspora in Alexandria.

The Ptolemaic government also interfered with the traditional economy of Syria. For example, in the ancient Orient parents in need often resorted to selling themselves or their children into conditional servitude. Defaulting debtors, too, were indentured to their creditors. Still, the new owner was usually a local man, and the bondsman ordinarily remained either in his own village or in its vicinity, so his personal misfortune, economically speaking, did not disturb the overall pattern of social life and behavior. The Greeks, however, bought slaves for export, which disrupted the local economy. Accordingly Ptolemy II forbade the enslavement of freeborn natives in Syria and ordered a census of those already so enslaved. The order was necessary to protect the constantly increasing numbers of native workmen who were becoming entangled in the new money and credit economy. But the benevolent king's decree destroyed an important source of labor on which the traditional economy of the country had depended. (It is significant that the treasury retained the privilege of selling into slavery those liable to governmental fiscal penalties.)

The worst colonial feature in the life of Ptolemaic Syria, however, was the preponderance of foreigners over natives. The administrative personnel were virtually all Greek. For instance, the five officials at Marissa, in Idumea, to whom Zenon wrote to complain about the escape of slaves he had bought there, were all Greek. Merchants, like Zenon himself, as well as trade agents—even the cooks of the Greek traders—were all Greeks, while the natives served as mule drivers and household servants and in other low-paying jobs. All these Greek officials and Greek businessmen who, like Zenon, returned to Egypt after a tour abroad, drained the wealth of Palestine, which local traders and officials would have put back into local circulation. The words of Edmund Burke about the East India Company and her agents are apt here: "Every rupee of profit made by an Englishman is lost forever to India." Nor is it necessary to adduce evidence of the corruption of this privileged foreign class. Josephus' sources speak candidly of the rampant bribery of Ptolemaic officials. In his praise of the Patriarch Joseph, the author of Jubilees writes that his hero was liked by everyone when he governed Egypt because his judgments were upright, he was no respecter of persons, and he took no bribes. In a land where Ptolemy himself expected and accepted douceurs from his subjects, the Joseph of Jubilees would have been considered miraculous. Yet for the natives caught in the mesh of a foreign, extremely complex, and unceasingly meddling administration, the bribe was a precious means of escaping the fiscal snare. An incorruptible official of the Ptolemies would never have been popular in a Ptolemaic province.

All the above notwithstanding, Macedonian domination also brought great benefits to Palestine. To begin with, the Greeks introduced new technologies. For example, although in the Orient (and apparently in classical Greece, too) the potter's wheel had always been turned by hand, the Hellenistic wheel was a foot-powered machine that left both hands free to manipulate and fashion the clay. Ben Sira (38:29) attentively describes this new synchronized operation: the potter sitting at his work turns the wheel with his foot while "fashioning the clay with his hand."

Ben Sira also tells us that the potter particularly "gives his heart" to perfecting the glazing, which required special attention to the firing. In another passage (38:28) the moralist describes a smith. He, too, "gives his heart" to perfecting his work, and his eyes, too, are constantly on the model of his vessel. These technical allusions become clearer in the light of archeological finds.

The Hellenistic age saw the extensive use of gold and silver plate by the rich; in 166 B.C.E. a courtier of Antiochus IV paraded a thousand slaves carrying articles of silver, none of which weighed less than approximately four kilograms. The middle class, unable to afford such expensive metals, demanded that they be imitated in clay and glass, with the result that replicas of this kind became common throughout the Mediterranean region. Ben Sira shows this fashion to have been in great vogue in Hellenistic Jerusalem: his smith hammers out metal plate and his potter molds the black-glazed tableware that imitates the brilliance of metal. Elsewhere (38:27) Ben Sira describes an engraver who endeavors to achieve his artistic effects by "variation" and who sets his heart on "equaling the painting." The Hebrew sage speaks here of the Hellenistic art of the cameo, in which, by exploiting the diverse layers of various stones, the artist was able to produce color effects that rivaled those of painting.

Another Hellenistic improvement concerned lighting. The traditional Palestinian lamp was a shallow open saucer containing oil, part of whose rim was depressed to form a spout that held the wick. These wheel-made lamps were cheap and remained in constant use by the poor of the land as late as the twentieth century. One kind of Greek lamp that began to be imported into Palestine in the second half of the fifth century was small, compact, and black-glazed, and utilized a muzzle to protect the wick. This lamp in turn was followed by a two-piece lamp that was molded rather than thrown on the potter's wheel. The top and bottom, both of soft clay, were fabricated in separate molds and then joined together—a method that allowed for the mass production of the lamps and for the use of a longer spout. These semi-closed lanterns gave light for approximately four hours without being refilled, which not only saved oil but also diminished the hazard of fire.

The mainstay of the Judean economy, and of ancient economies in general, however, was agriculture and not fine artisanal work. Yet we find Ben Sira speaking disdainfully of the man who handles the plow and drives the oxen. Did the Ptolemies endeavor in Palestine, as they did in Egypt, to improve the local breed of cattle or promote systematic fallowing? Were progressive methods used in the Galilean domain of Apollonios? We don't know. But with or without Ptolemaic help, some inventions came into use that saved both time and labor for the common man. For instance, in each household in Jerusalem, as everywhere at that time, women (including female slaves) were responsible for grinding the grain. In the early Hellenistic period in Judea, however, the primitive quern in which the grinding had been done with a hand-held stone seems already to have been replaced by the Greek rotary mill, which required the hand merely to set it in motion. It is also probable that the same period saw the introduction of machines for crushing olives and producing oil, of beam presses that pressed the grapes and produced the must, and of the vertical loom as well. The water-rising cogwheel with an endless rope (sakiyeh), which became popular in Ptolemaic Egypt, was also in use in Jerusalem in the middle of the third century B.C.E.; the author of Kohelet, describing the misery of the old, says, "The pitcher is broken, and the wheel is shattered on the pit" (Koh. 12:6). Still, it is curious that the author of Jubilees ascribes to Abraham the invention of a sowing device that was attached to the plow to protect the seed from birds, since this device seems to have been known to the ancient Babylonians. Unfortunately, as long as the tools found in the Persian and Hellenistic levels of Palestinian soil are not systematically studied, it is impossible to appreciate in any greater depth the history of technological progress in Ptolemaic Palestine.

The evaluation of the psychological impact of Ptolemaic domination is even more difficult. The essential and immeasurable factor was the secular character of Greek civilization, a civilization that had neither a priestly caste nor priestly scribes, and that was represented by an intelligentsia independent of both palace and temple. Thus, while one is able to read Homer without believing in Homer's gods, the Babylonian tablets relating the exploits of Gilgamesh or the scrolls of Moses are meaningless to an unbeliever. It was their secular point of view that prevented the Greeks from caring for oriental writings, yet it was precisely the secular quality of Greek civilization that made the impulses coming from it so powerful. Plato was the most religious of Greek philosophers, yet the Jewish philosopher Aristobulus could claim him as a follower of Moses, and later Philo interpreted Moses in the light of Platonic ideas.

Moreover, the values of Greek civilization were expressed in a language that, being Indo-European, was totally different from the Semitic languages spoken for millennia throughout the Levant, and a script that indicated vowels must have aroused wonder in Jerusalem. Certainly the Jews in Jerusalem had to learn this imperial language if they wanted to advance in the world governed by the Ptolemies, but again direct evidence relating to the impact of the Greek language in Jerusalem is lacking. It is true that four Greek names for musical instruments occur in Daniel (3:5, 7, 10, 15), but this chapter is in Aramaic and borrowings from the Greek language by the Arameans, or vice versa, are irrelevant to our question. As a matter of fact, our ignorance of the development of the Aramaic and Phoenician civilizations in the Persian and early Hellenistic periods makes the evaluation of the Greek impact on Palestine even more uncertain. For instance, banquets in Greek Jerusalem, as described by Ben Sira, appear to have been organized in the Greek manner: a master of ceremonies was appointed by the guests and songs, music, poetry, and philosophical discourses enlivened the proceedings. Ben Sira even advises his readers not to display their erudition at the wrong time when attending such a party! But was Jerusalem imitating Athens or just competing with Damascus or Sidon?

Other Greek customs must have appeared to residents of Jerusalem, as they would have to any oriental person, as foolish or even offensive. In the Orient new houses were built on the remnants of older ones; there was no digging of new foundations, and hardly any serious attempt to clear away the accumulated rubble. But when the Greeks built in Palestine, they began by removing what was left of the superstructures of previous buildings. In contrast to the typical oriental town, a maze of houses and narrow winding walks, the Jewish visitor to third-century Greek Marissa (the city that succeeded Lachish and was less than ten kilometers from the Jewish town of Keilah) would have seen an example of Greek city planning, albeit badly executed: an avenue, eight meters (twenty-seven feet) wide, forming an axis with lateral paved streets running perpendicular to it.

And what of Greek mores? Into a civilization in which nudity was extremely offensive, where even a harlot sitting by the roadside was veiled (Gen. 38:15), the Greeks brought naked athletes and images of naked goddesses, such as the terra cotta statue of Aphrodite found in a cave on Mount Carmel. Another example: when an oriental subject appeared before an oriental despot, even if he were in the king's favor, he became like Nehemiah, "very afraid." Oriental tales from ancient Egyptian stories to the Arabian Nights have made this attitude comprehensible to us; even an agent of the king was to be feared. In the Testaments of the Twelve Patriarchs, written around 200 B.C.E., it still seemed natural that a Palestinian trader, although innocent, should fall at the feet of a royal officer at the officer's first reproach. It even appeared natural to the same storyteller that the officer, without further ado, should scourge the trader. But this Jewish author, writing in Hellenistic Jerusalem, was retelling the adventures of the biblical Joseph in an older, pharaonic Egypt. The situation was very different in Ptolemaic Egypt. Here another Joseph, a man from Jerusalem, comes to Alexandria and happens to meet the king's chariot in the street; a courtier mentions his name to King Ptolemy, who greets the newcomer and seats him in his carriage beside his queen. Joseph tells a few jokes and is invited to the royal table. Later, more clever words of his addressed to the king win him a substantial tax-farming contract. Such "Greek levity" astonished and pained the Romans, wrapped as they were in their *gravitas,* but did the Greek sense of individual freedom attract or horrify the average Jerusalemite? However you look at it, Yavan must have been an odd guest in the tent of Shem (LXX Gen. 10:27).

ELEVEN

The Dispersion under the Ptolemies

FOR THE diaspora the consequences of the Macedonian conquest were threefold. To begin with, the new era divided the Jews politically: from 321 B.C.E. to 30 B.C.E. Asia and Egypt obeyed different masters. Second, the break was cultural: while the Near East from the Sinai to the Himalayas continued to think and speak in Aramaic, this language, which had been imposed by the Persian administration, disappeared in Ptolemaic and Roman Egypt. Here, a non-Egyptian had to speak Greek. And, finally, spatial and social mobility quickened as never before. For the Persians, a foreigner, even Nehemiah at Artaxerxes' court, always remained an alien. Now, however, one could not only become a Greek "in soul," like the Jew of whom Clearchus speaks, but one could even become a citizen of a Greek city. Nevertheless, citizen or not, a Jew who had learned the Greek language and Greek manners could feel at home in the Alexandria of Egypt as well as in the Alexandria of Sogdiana (Merv) in Central Asia. Compare Tobit, who was an alien not only legally but also psychologically in both Nineveh and Ecbatana. Oriental civilizations had no concept of naturalization and were averse to acculturation.

In no land were the changes wrought by Alexander's conquest more impressive than in Egypt. Alexander and the Ptolemies needed workers at hand for the immense task of modernizing the valley of the Nile, the richest agricultural country of the Mediterranean region. From the four corners of the world, from Italy, Gaul, and Cyrenaica, as well as from Greece and Asia Minor, immigrants streamed into the land of promise. "Of all the patrons, Ptolemy [II] is the best for a freeborn man," as a contemporary poet, himself from Syracuse, adroitly put it. Many immigrants naturally came from neighboring Palestine, some among them Jews. Alexander had already transferred Jews from Samaria to Egypt and the Palestinian campaigns of Ptolemy I brought more Jews to Egypt, this time as captives of the king and slaves of his soldiers. Political partisans of the ruler of Egypt, compelled by supporters of his rivals to flee Jerusalem in 320 and 312, found refuge in his realm. Then, of course, there were many who left voluntarily for this most desirable of countries. All these newcomers joined the Jewish settlers who had come still earlier, in the pharaonic period, or in the days of the Persian Empire. It is a pity that we know nothing of relations between later emigrants and their predecessors.

The primary sources of information about Ptolemaic Egypt are Ptolemaic (Greek) papyri, but of these we have only a few written before 270 B.C.E. and another few written between 216 and 180 B.C.E. Moreover, most of the papyri of the third century come from modern Fayyum, some sixty miles southwest of Cairo at the rand of the desert, and from other places along the Nile southward of Fayyum, as far as Elephantine at the southern end of the country. We have practically nothing from the Nile delta, which comprises half the cultivated land in Egypt, and thus nothing from Alexandria, the capital of the Ptolemaic Empire.

The scribes who drafted the legal records on these papyri (wills, contracts, petitions, and the like) regularly noted the personal status of all those involved: their given names, patronymics, origins, and, if required, their official positions. Native Egyptians gave their place of origin, naturally, as Egypt; citizens of the three Greek cities in Egypt, Alexandria, Naucratis, and Ptolemais, made known their citizenship in those cities; and immigrants gave the name of the foreign nations from which they had come (for example, Philon, son of Herakleides, a Cyrenean). In Egypt proper, outside the Greek cities, there was no procedure for naturalization; not only the immigrant himself but all his descendants were identified by his original place of emigration—forever. Since even the Ptolemies legally remained Macedonians, it is clear that when we find the qualification "Jew" or "Jewess," the term refers to nationality, not religion, which was irrelevant to the Ptolemaic administration. A Jew was a man from Judea. Whether a Jew coming from Persia would be recorded as a Jew or a Persian probably depended on individual circumstances and the decision of the recording scribe. The administration was only interested in fixing the prescribed three elements of personal identification, which, once recorded, could not be changed except by the government itself.

Unfortunately, the greatest number of papyri consist of tax lists, accounts, letters, and other private papers, which rarely give any direct indication of the nationality of the persons mentioned. To identify a Jew in these documents the researcher must depend primarily on given names, which are rarely revealing. For example, the earliest papyrus in which a man is officially qualified as a Jew, written in 259, records his name as

Alexander, son of Andronicus, a cavalryman. Only by chance do we learn that another cavalryman, Theodoros, son of Theodoros, was also known as Samuel. In a contract drawn in an Egyptian village in 201 B.C.E., all six witnesses were officially designated as Jews, but they and their fathers, with the sole exception of a Sabbattaios, bear Greek names ranging from Theodotus, which may be a rendering of the Hebrew Nathan, to Democrates, which is certainly not a translation from either Hebrew or Aramaic. When we attempt to use given names to identify Jews in Ptolemaic Egypt, therefore, we can record only those persons who either retained their Hebrew names or used the popular Greek equivalents for them. Jews named Diophantes or Herakles escape our search.

At any rate, to isolate those documents in which Jewish names can be identified is both illusory and senseless. In Ptolemaic Egypt, scribes did not deal with individuals as Jews or Lycians, but from the point of view of their social role in relation to the matter at hand: litigant, taxpayer, tenant, or the like. Consequently, owing to the nature of our sources, we can elicit from the "Jewish" documents only trivial and historically useless information: that a Jew received barley or that another had not delivered a mare. Such data can be used historically only as general documentation in, say, a study of the use of barley as food in Ptolemaic Egypt.

To understand the role of the Jews in Egypt in that period, we have first to know that all immigrants, of whatever origin, were assigned to the class of "Hellenes," in order to distinguish them from native Egyptians. "Hellenes" were aliens residing in Egypt. They were admitted to the country, protected, favored, and advanced because directly or indirectly they served the king. The record of the immigrant's personal status also indicated his military or civil position in the king's service, as we see in the designations "of the third cavalry regiment," and "in the service of Apollonius, the *dioiketes*." An alien not in royal service was officially styled a "sojourner," for example, "Jason, son of Kerkion, Calyndian, a sojourner *(parepidemos)*."

"Hellenes" lived in accordance with royal law, which like Egyptian common law was created by scribes, only in this case the scribes were Greek. (Native Egyptians had their own legal system.) Nor is there any trace of specifically national codes of law in our documentation. Some illustrations: In 227 a Jew brought an action of assault against a married Jewess before the Hellenic *dikasterion* (court). According to a general Greek rule a married woman was required to appear before a court with a male guardian. The Jewess complied with this Greek rule—bringing, incidentally, an Athenian—even though neither Jewish law nor Aramaic common law required such assistance. Likewise, in documents recording loans made by one Jew to another, the professional scribes, disregarding

the biblical prohibition, stipulated the usual interest rate of two percent
per month. In the same way, through the daily actions of anonymous
notaries, the Greek dowry was substituted for the so-called bride-price
in Jewish marriage contracts. The Septuagint, already reflecting this situation, renders the Hebrew term *mohar* as *pherne* (dowry).

Most of those we are able to identify as Jews in our documentation
are soldiers. As the dominion of the Ptolemies depended upon force, a
great many of the "Hellenes" in Egypt belonged to the royal army.
According to pseudo-Aristeas, a Jewish author writing in Alexandria
toward the end of the second century B.C.E., Ptolemy I had armed selected
Jewish captives from Judea and settled them in Egyptian forts in order
to intimidate the Egyptians. Such regiments would have been analogous
to the "Jewish force" in Persian Elephantine, but no documents referring
to these Ptolemaic strongholds have been recovered as yet.

We do, however, find Jewish soldiers settled in the Arsinoite district.
The Arsinoites, between the Nile and Lake Moeris (Qarun), was somewhat exceptional. In antiquity, as today, the basin of the Fayyum (Coptic
for "lake"), at the edge of the western desert, was famous for its fertility,
and the first Ptolemies further enlarged its productive area by draining
the marshes and instituting a system of irrigation. The reclaimed land
(now again covered by sand) was then assigned to the king's courtiers
and soldiers. The latter obtained allotments of from twenty-four to one
hundred *arourai* (that is, between approximately fifteen and sixty-eight
acres, or between something over six and a half hectares and twenty-
seven and a half hectares) depending on their rank, arms, and regiment.
The entire holding, or sometimes just a portion of it, was generally rented
out to a tenant farmer, usually an Egyptian.

When summoned, military settlers were obliged to report to their
regiments completely equipped. They were bound to the king not only
by an oath of fealty, rarely sacrosanct to mercenaries, but also by ties of
personal interest. Their sons, most of whom would inherit the lands and
military obligations of their fathers, had been raised and educated in
Egypt, and though legally registered as Athenians, Macedonians, and so
on, regarded Egypt as their fatherland and the pharaoh as their natural
leader.

In the Arsinoites, soldiers from different regiments and of various
nationalities (each regiment was multinational) lived side by side with
native Egyptians. In 201 B.C.E., in a village whose *gymnasion* was built
by a Cilician, six Jews witnessed a contract between a Paeonian from
the Balkan peninsula and four Egyptians. Because the first Ptolemies
forced recruiting in their non-Egyptian provinces, we find quite a high
number of Jews among the settlers in the Arsinoites in the third century

(about 6 percent); the proportion of Cyreneans was even higher (about 9 percent).

No Jewish officer, however, can be identified in Ptolemaic Egypt before 174 B.C.E., although Persian and other "barbarian" officers were not rare in the third century. Nor is any Jew, or any male with a Jewish name, to be found among those holding civil authority in the third century, either. Yet when even a simple soldier, a mercenary from the stony wastes around Jerusalem, or a highlander from the Peloponnesus, settled in Egypt, he became a landlord in the richest agricultural country of the known world, where the smallest military allotment was three times greater than the holdings of 94 percent of the Egyptian peasants in 1947 C.E.

On the other hand "Hellenes," and among them Jews, also worked in menial occupations: they were tenants, vine-dressers, and hired laborers. In a property declaration made by a Greek landowner in 240, six farm hands are named, not one whom was an Egyptian. A Jeab, who must have been a Jew, is followed in this list by a man bearing the Macedonian name of Krateros, by a Thracian named Sitalkes, and by Natanbaal, who was probably a Syrian. In another document, a granary guard called Samuel claimed that he did not receive enough food to nourish his children. We also find slaves (or perhaps just domestic servants) bearing Jewish names.

As a rule, however, "Hellenes" had higher and better paid positions than the average Egyptian, for they were better suited to carry out Ptolemaic plans for developing Egypt's natural resources than were the tradition-bound natives. For instance, the traditional Egyptian cereals were barley and spelt. The Ptolemies, however, favored the culture of wheat (which is considerably more nourishing than other edible grains) and introduced Syrian wheat into Egypt with a view toward improving the quality as well as increasing the size of the Egyptian wheat crop. Also, the demand for wine, the national drink of the Greeks, was constantly rising in Ptolemaic Egypt, but the natives, who were used to the local beer, could not furnish the specialized workers needed to work in the vineyards. In Judea, of course, the culture of the vine was traditional. No wonder that a certain Samoelis, together with a companion, could lease a large vineyard (ca. 40 acres) in 241 B.C.E.

Yet another example: The Egyptian peasant had always cultivated his land—and still did in the nineteenth century C.E.—with a wooden plow and a hoe, instruments sufficient for the thin black soil renewed year after year by the inundations of the Nile. But the Ptolemies introduced the use of iron in Egyptian husbandry, in order to exploit soil that was reclaimed from desert and swamp by Greek engineers. Because iron plow-

points, shovels, axes, and other implements had been in use in stony
Judea since the time of King David, Jewish laborers and other foreign
workers who knew how to handle such agricultural instruments were
most welcome in Ptolemaic Egypt.

Very few documents mention Jews living outside the Arsinoites. The
only Jewish trader and moneylender known to us in Ptolemaic Egypt
operated at the beginning of Ptolemaic rule, about 310 B.C.E., and still
recorded his transactions in Aramaic. Probably based in Elephantine, he
traded widely, from the eastern Delta to Syene, and the names of most
of his clients sound Jewish—indeed, two of his clients were Jewish priests.

As a matter of fact, the often acclaimed richness of papyrological
documentation is frequently disappointing to the historian. The documents we read deal chiefly with the ephemera of daily needs: accounts,
claims, receipts, complaints, and similar material. Even writers of private
letters are busy arranging petty business deals. The inner man discreetly
and prudently escapes our searching eye. There exist hundreds of papyri
from the archives of Zenon, but we never learn whether he was married.
In the Arsinoites, Persians were as numerous as Jews, but the only evidence we have of their religious life is the mention in a tax list of goats
belonging to Mithra, the popular Iranian deity.

We do have more luck with regard to Jews, however, since a number
of papyri and inscriptions in Greek speak of Jewish houses of worship
in third-century Egypt. A few of these buildings seem to have been rather
impressive, with gate entrances; the sexton of one village synagogue in
the Arsinoites bore the pompous Greek title of *neokores,* that is, "warden
of the temple." But the Jews in Ptolemaic Egypt had no temples or altars;
they called the place in which they worshipped *proseuche,* literally, "prayer."
The noun, condemned by purists, was used by the Jews metonymically
to designate a building and indicates the building's religious function.
Like their pagan neighbors, the Jews put their religion under the protection of the Ptolemies, although they avoided using the divine epithets of
the pharaohs in the dedicatory inscriptions of their sacred buildings.

Still, the life that went on inside a *proseuche* remains unknown. Who
were "the Jews in Crocodilopolis" who built themselves a house of worship? Were they a private association, or did they constitute the Jewish
community itself? A Hebrew papyrus, now ascribed to the second century
B.C.E., contains the Ten Commandments followed by the Confession of
Faith (Deut. 6:4), reaffirming the rabbinic tradition that in earlier times
the recitation of the Decalogue preceded that of the Shema. The papyrus
attesting this practice indicates that the synagogal service in Ptolemaic
Egypt was celebrated, at least in part, in Hebrew. But except for this
detail, the liturgy remains unknown. A few Aramaic *ostraca,* enumerating
identical contributions made by various persons, may record the payment

of congregational dues. Private devotion is attested in an anonymous account from an estate managed by Zenon that records the number of bricks delivered daily. On the third line there is no figure, but rather the word "Sabbath." Was this steadfast Jew who refused to work on the day of rest an exception, or does he exemplify the faith of Egyptian Jews in general in the middle of the third century B.C.E.?

Alexandria (as well as the other two Greek cities, Naucratis and Ptolemais), although under the rule of the Ptolemies, was situated legally and morally outside of Egypt proper. Many Jewish immigrants found new homes in the Ptolemaic capital, and although there are no early Ptolemaic papyri from Alexandria, Jewish names have been found in the earliest graveyards of the newly founded city. Some of these are still in Aramaic and some are already in Greek, as, for instance, that of Hedyne, wife or daughter of Mordechai. Two mint masters, Zabnai and Ammai, whose names are inscribed in Aramaic on the coins of a hoard buried in the delta around 318 B.C.E., were probably Alexandrian Jews.

In the big new city of Alexandria, whose population seemed as numerous as ants, the Jewish settlers naturally kept together at first, settling on the east side of the metropolis, close to the sea. From this "fourth" of five wards the Jewish population eventually spilled over into the other districts of the city. Yet here too we know next to nothing about the life of Alexandrian Jewry in the early Hellenistic age, for the simple reason that we do not know much about the city itself at this early date. We learn only some isolated facts: Dositheos, son of Drymilos, a Jew, was an influential man at the court of Ptolemy V, and in all probability the person identified as the priest of Alexander and of the deified Ptolemies in 222 B.C.E. In III Maccabees, written around 145 B.C.E., we read of Greeks in Alexandria who were the business partners of Jews. And we know that the Jews in Jerusalem were in contact with the Jews in Alexandria because Joseph, the tax-farmer and businessman, kept his money in Alexandria.

The question of Jewish "rights" in Alexandria has been treated anachronistically by modern scholars influenced by the history of Jewish emancipation in the nineteenth century. The question must be posed in Greek terms, however. Alexandria was a Greek *polis,* and the *polis* had invented the concept of naturalization, that is, the change of nationality by will and fiat. What was important was not what a person had been but what he or she could become. Certainly the Greek city demanded that a naturalized citizen worship the city gods, but this was the problem of the Jewish burgess and not that of his city.

It is probable that during the first forty or fifty years of Alexandria's existence, naturalization was easily procured. Later, however, in about the second quarter of the third century, the imperial city became virtually a closed corporation. This state of affairs was brought about by means of a legal innovation: in a *polis*, the citizens were divided into subunits *(demoi)*; no one could become a citizen who was not enrolled in a *demos*. In the course of time, however, as the influx of immigrants into Alexandria grew ever greater, the enrollment of new citizens in the *demoi* was stopped, a measure that at one stroke created a sharp distinction between the old citizens, hereditary members of the *demoi*, and the new immigrants, who were now styled "Alexandrians not enrolled in the *demoi*." Only the enrolled citizens possessed full civil rights, including the right to acquire real estate in the city. In addition, Alexandrians not enrolled in the *demoi* were even set under the jurisdiction of the "Court of the Foreigners." A royal decree issued in the first decades of the third century ruled that parties to lawsuits should, if they were citizens of Alexandria, indicate their *demos;* if they were soldiers, their origins, regiments, and land allotments; and if they were "others," their "origin and status." Included in the last group were the "Hellenic" residents of the city—Macedonians, Jews, Athenians, and others—who were not members of the military.

With regard to the Jews, this meant that the descendants of those Jews who had become citizens of Alexandria before the reform was instituted were full citizens, whereas those who arrived after the reform was instituted had but a slender chance of acquiring the position of burgess. As a result of this situation some of the new immigrants, both Jews and non-Jews, as well as their descendants, could be identified by the vague term "Alexandrians," while the majority continued to be identified simply by their original nationality, for example, "Jew" or "Macedonian."

As a result, these Jews, as well as the members of other nationalities who were legally merely resident aliens in the city where many of them had been born, formed national associations called *politeumata*, which coexisted with the various "citizen" bodies of the city, both types of association deriving their rights and duties from the king's will. Although there were several *politeumata* in Alexandria—for instance, that of the Boeotians—the numerical importance of the Jews in the city made their association particularly conspicuous. In the first century B.C.E., when the power of the Ptolemies had declined, the head of the Jewish corporation was said to behave "as though he were the magistrate of an independent community."

Accordingly, when the author of III Maccabees, toward the end of the second century B.C.E., imagines that Ptolemy IV has offered a fabulous reward to the Jews ready to embrace heathenism, he makes the king promise not only the "priceless citizenship" of Alexandria to the Jews of Egypt living outside the city, but also "equal citizenship" to the Jews already in Alexandria. Likewise, when Philo and Josephus later quote

Jewish claims, they do not write of Jewish "citizenship" in Alexandria (as modern scholars do), but of "equal rights" *(isopoliteia)* to those of full citizens for Alexandrian Jews who were not enrolled in the *demoi*.

According to both Philo and Josephus, Jewish privileges in Alexandria had been granted by Alexander and the first Ptolemies. Josephus, however, claims that conflict between the Jews and the "natives" of Alexandria was constant, while Philo says that these rights were not contested in the city before Caligula. This disagreement between the two Jewish authors is semantic. The Jews were clamoring for absolute equality (and the letter of the Emperor Claudius to the Alexandrians, written in 41 C.E., confirms that this pretension was opposed by the Alexandrians), but it does not mean that these Jewish privileges were contested before Caligula. A story, of which two versions have been preserved (in III Maccabees and in Josephus, respectively), tells of the persecution of the Jews by a King Ptolemy (Ptolemy IV, 222–205, in III Maccabees and Ptolemy IX, 146–117, in Josephus). But the tale was invented much later, in the first century B.C.E., and reflects the political situation in Egypt in the period of dynastic wars, after approximately 130 B.C.E., and therefore is irrelevant to the subject of this chapter.

With regard to the organization of the Jewish *politeuma* in Ptolemaic Alexandria, the earliest information we have about it comes from the Letter of Aristeas, composed toward the end of the second century, in which we are told that the Greek version of the Torah had been read to the entire Jewish community of Alexandria, gathered for this purpose on the island of Pharos. Afterward, the letter continues, "the priests, the venerable translators, those from the corporation [*politeuma*] and also the leaders of the multitude [*plethos*]" cursed anyone tampering with the translation.

It is curious that in this text the priests are listed first and form a separate class. In I Maccabees too "the priests and the whole multitude" praise the Lord after deliverance from the persecution. Yet the *kohanim* were essentially just sacrificers in the Temple of Jerusalem and had no prerogatives outside their sacrificial work. Further, we note that the Letter of Aristeas distinguishes between the *politeuma* and the *plethos,* that is, between full members of the Jewish political body and a "commoner" class. Likewise, Greek associations in Egypt and elsewhere had their "associated members." What is remarkable here, however, is that the Jewish *plethos* had its own leaders. Unfortunately we know neither the origins nor the history of this binary organization of the Jewish community in Ptolemaic Alexandria.

Jews also settled in other Greek cities ruled by the Ptolemies outside Egypt. Ptolemy I sent Jewish colonists into Cyrenaica "to strengthen his hold on Cyrene and other cities of Libya." Indeed, not only did the

Ptolemies foster the settlement of Jewish "corps" *(syntagmata)* as military colonists in Libya, but they probably followed the same plan elsewhere—in Cyprus, for instance, where the presence of Jews is attested as early as 140 B.C.E.

The kings needed Jewish and other "barbarian" mercenaries to check the independent spirit of the Greek cities, ever ready to defect. These foreign military bodies, living in the midst of these cities, formed a state within a state. At Berenice (Benghazi) the Jews constituted a *politeuma* that, as in Alexandria, paralleled the city organization. Under Augustus, in a decree honoring M. Titius, a Roman, "the organization of the Jews in Berenice" praises him for his kindness to the "citizens" of Berenice and "also to the Jews of our *politeuma*." In Cyrene, in 87 B.C.E., the Jews constituted a separate unit ("tribe") of the population, different from the burgesses but also from other resident aliens. No wonder that after the death of the last Ptolemaic king of Cyrene, in 96 B.C.E., the civic disturbances were complicated by strife between the Jews and the citizens. The existence of separate officially recognized Jewish organizations in the cities made the assimilation of Jews difficult, and the Greeks sometimes tried to get rid of the Jewish privileges. No one likes a privileged alien.

TWELVE

The Eastern Dispersion

B EYOND the Ptolemaic watchposts in Syria, the Jewish diaspora extended over the immense space of the Seleucid Empire. Before the Maccabean revolt Jewish colonists are attested in Asia Minor, in northern Syria, in the satrapies of Babylonia and Mesopotamia, and in Parthia and Persia. In Mesopotamia and Media the progeny of the Ten Tribes and of the Babylonian deportation were on their way to becoming the ancestors of the "myriads" of Jews (Josephus) who, around 70 C.E., in the last days of the Temple, peopled the Parthian Empire. Indeed, it was probably Mesopotamia, rather than Palestine, that furnished the emigrants to the new lands conquered by the Macedonians and to the new cities yet to be established by the Seleucids.

The Seleucids, no less than the Ptolemies in Egypt, had need of reliable people—of any nationality—to fill their regiments and to settle the colonies they were establishing as strongholds against the natives and as safeguards for their vital lines of communication. But although later generations in these places could pride themselves on the cities they had established and boast of their Macedonian ancestry, the emigrants, Macedonians or others, who about 300 B.C.E. left for Dura-Europos or for the fortress (recently discovered) on the Oxus (at the Soviet-Afghanistan frontier), were probably no more envied by their contemporaries than the passengers on the Mayflower in 1620.

According to Josephus, who in turn depends on his Jewish informants from the Eastern diaspora, Seleucus I of Syria established Jewish colonists in Antioch and in the other cities he founded in Seleucid Syria and Asia. (As Josephus sensibly remarks, when Antioch later became the Seleucid capital and a big city, Jews flocked there particularly.) Moreover, according to Josephus, Seleucus granted "privileges" to the Jewish colonists. This claim is credible. Seleucus had to urbanize a quadrangle of some 450 square kilometers on the inhospitable coast of northern Syria and build two artificial harbors there (Seleucia and Laodicea) as well as two new cities—the new capital of his empire, Antioch, and its military center, Apamea—in order to connect his lands on the Euphrates with the Mediterranean. At this early date (300 B.C.E.), since colonists must still have been at a premium, it is probable that many individual Jews were able to become citizens of these four new cities.

Josephus, however, speaks of "privileges" awarded to the Jews as such and engraved on bronze tablets in Antioch, and mentions their *politeia* in this city. This means that in Antioch, as in Alexandria, the Jewish community formed a separate political body that existed beside other corporations of the same kind. Thus we hear that after the murder of the High Priest Onias in 171 B.C.E. not only the Jews in Antioch but also many of the other "nations" in the capital complained about the crime. We also hear, according to a statement made in 70 C.E. by the Antiochene Jews to the Roman governor, that Seleucus I had ordered that money for oil was to be given to the Jews of the city since they were unwilling to use the "foreign" oil furnished by the gymnasiarchs. Oil, particularly in the Roman period, was frequently distributed to all citizens and sometimes even to noncitizens, but the term *gymnasiarchia* used by Josephus in this context and the role of the gymnasiarchs in his account suggest, rather, that at this early date (Seleucus I died in 281 B.C.E.), this grant was given only to Jews who exercised in the *gymnasia* naked, under the eyes and the patronage of Hermes and Herakles. In point of fact, physical training was the foundation of the Greek way of life; a Jew could only enter into the Greek community through the *palaestra*.

When he speaks of Jewish "privileges," Josephus, as he himself says, is describing the state of affairs only in the new cities. The situation was not the same in the old Greek cities of Asia, such as Sardes. In a *polis*, even in the Hellenistic age, as a Phoenician says in a sketch of Herodes, the alien lived at the pleasure of the city. Consequently the legal situation of Jewish communities may have varied from city to city, and even within the same city. For instance, a decree of the Roman period states that at Sardes the Jews "have continually received many great concessions from the people." But our information about the Jews in the old Greek cities begins only with Roman times.

New or old, Greek cities formed only isolated points on the map of the Seleucid Empire. Native populations continued to live according to their ancestral ways and the new kings of Asia continued to use the machinery of their Persian predecessors, including the transfer of populations to ensure law and order. Toward the end of the third century, for instance, the province of Lydia and Phrygia was troubled by a rebellion. In order to pacify the country, Antiochus III sent two thousand Jewish families from Babylonia and Mesopotamia to the fortresses and to the most endangered districts of the rebellious province. In his order, he promises the emigrants the use of their own laws, which meant of course that wherever they settled, they would constitute a separate group. In the same manner, some years later, between 197 and 193, the same king transferred the Carduchi (Kurds) from the far eastern part of his realm to the southwestern part of Asia Minor. Here, in Lycia, they settled as a separate "village of the Carduchi."

Antiochus granted each Jewish settler a site for his house, allotments for grain fields, and a vineyard, as well as various fiscal privileges and an allowance in kind until the first crop was harvested. He refers to the loyalty of the Jews, which, he says, is secured by "their piety to their God," and speaks of their services to his ancestors. In an age of mercenary armies, when oaths were violated daily, it was useful to him to put his trust in men who naively still believed that breaking an oath would draw heavenly punishment upon themselves. His faith was well placed. Like the Jews of Egypt, the Jews of the Seleucid Empire were proud of their military exploits in the service of their pagan overlord. II Maccabees (8:20) boldly ascribes to Jewish troops the glory of the most famous Seleucid victory, the defeat of the Gauls (who had invaded Asia Minor) by Antiochus I in 275 B.C.E.

We may infer from the Seleucid document just quoted that the Jewish communities in Mesopotamia also lived according to the Law of Moses. Nevertheless, the fact that the Law of Moses was universally valued from Cyrene to Ecbatana did not prevent a linguistic and cultural split between the two halves of ancient Jewry: the Jews in the Greek and graecised lands in Africa and Asia Minor, and the Jews in the Aramaic world, which reached from Jerusalem to Babylon and Ecbatana. Inscriptions in Syria were written in Greek, but the population outside the gates of Antioch continued to speak and think in Aramaic. Aramaic books written in the Hellenistic age have disappeared, except for some works of Jewish origin, but the characters in these Jewish books live, if not in the Holy Land, then in the Eastern dispersion: Baruch, Daniel, Tobit, Susanna, the Three Pages of Darius, the Three Youths, the Babylonians to whom pseudo-Jeremiah addresses his epistle. And we may add to this oriental series the Hebrew Book of Esther. Much later, when the visionary of the New Covenant of the Dead Sea Sect speaks of the holy war against Belial, he dismisses Egypt in one line, but dwells on the campaigns against the Assyrians and the other peoples of the East. Last but not least, Josephus wrote his history of the Jewish War in Aramaic for the benefit of the Eastern diaspora.

We have already spoken of the Book of Tobit and of the biblical tales about Daniel, but we may add some observations here on other stories of the Daniel cycle that have been preserved only in Greek, as well as on the just mentioned Epistle of Jeremiah, whose Semitic original has also been lost.

The story of Susanna has been preserved in the Greek Bible as an appendix to the Book of Daniel, but the Semitic idiom of the original can still be seen through the Greek. The story is well known: Two Elders attempt to seduce Susanna, the wife of a rich and honored Jew in Babylon. Scorned, they pretend to have witnessed a breach of her conjugal fidelity with a young man. Although condemned to die for adultery, she is saved by the cleverness of young Daniel.

This story combines two widespread motifs of folklore: the woman slandered by an unsuccessful suitor, and wisdom issuing from the mouths of babes. The doubling of the slanderous suitor, however, is unexpected, for the two Elders together declare their purpose to Susanna and, when she refuses, both bear false witness against her. The author of the Susanna story, needing two eyewitnesses for a conviction of adultery, borrowed this scabrous detail from another folktale that was used much later by the rabbis in the explication of a biblical passage: Jeremiah (29:23) speaks of two pseudoprophets "who have committed adultery," and the rabbis imagined that each commanded various women, in God's name, to yield to his companion. The seduction of a woman under the pretext of divine authorization occurred in reality (see, for instance, the story of Paulina in Josephus), and was also used as a theme in folklore. By means of this stratagem Nectanebus, the magician in the Alexander Romance, fathers the future conqueror of the world. The theme clearly lends itself to facetious elaboration. We may imagine that the motif of this kind of mutual pandering was invented for some "Arabian Nights" tale in the bazaars of the ancient Orient and from there found its way into the austere conversations of the ancient haggadists.

The story in the Septuagint is told with biblical terseness. Susanna's husband does not appear at all and her beauty is only alluded to: she is "of fine appearance." Nevertheless, we learn that seeing her just once, walking in the garden of her house at eventide, was sufficient to induce two venerable Elders to look no more "toward heaven." Nor, when Susanna refuses to yield, does she talk of virtue, duty, or the Law, but simply states her predicament: since guilty or guiltless she will be convicted, it is better to die without sin. Her prayer in court consists of one sentence and two sentences suffice to describe Daniel's intervention. The narrator only dwells upon Daniel's cross-examination of the witnesses, which is the main part of the story.

The divinatory power of a pure youth was well established in ancient religions, a fact which caused some ancient interpreters to postulate that Daniel was twelve years old at the time of Susanna's trial. But the kind of wisdom propounded by "babes" is always uttered unintentionally, as when by chance words such as *tolle, lege,* heard by Augustine, are so appropriate that the utterance is seen as prediction. Daniel, however, intervenes purposefully. Africanus, a Christian author writing around 230 C.E., observed that Daniel's gift of discernment in this story is unlike the idea of inspiration in the canonical Book of Daniel, and adds irreverently that the cleverness displayed by Daniel in his cross-examination (he asks each witness separately under which tree he had seen Susanna sinning, and each contradicts the other) resembles the gags in Greek comedies. But Origen compares Daniel's sagacity to that of Solomon in the story told in I Kings 3:16ff.

The narrator of Susanna's tale, however, is not telling it in order to demonstrate Daniel's wisdom, as is the author of I Kings with respect to Solomon; he is, rather, a preacher reciting a moral fable, and he concludes by praising the artless and God-fearing youth. Nevertheless, because the beginning of the sermon is lost, we are unable to learn the intentions of the moralist; nor do we know who he was, or where he preached, or why he speaks so glowingly of the "spirit of discernment and knowledge" in young men, an attitude that is somehow surprising in patriarchal Jewish society (as Bishop Asterius of the fifth century C.E. noted). That he contrasts the "Jewess" Susanna with the less steadfast "daughters of Israel" is also curious.

The homily can be dated within reasonable limits. First, the identification of the hero of the story with the prophet Daniel suggests the period when tales about Daniel's wizardy have already become popular, that is, after approximately 250 B.C.E. Second, as we have already shown, the use of the term "Sidonian" to designate a man of Canaan is Hellenistic. Third, execution by means of hurling a culprit into a ravine was unknown in Jewish jurisprudence, but was used by both the Persian kings and the Seleucids. Last but not least, the glorification of the wisdom of a youth at the expense of the Elders, who are represented, as Africanus also noted, as counterparts of the lascivious graybeards in Greek comedy, is yet another Hellenistic trait. Although the Jews might not have suppressed the Semitic original of the tale because of its censure of the Elders, as Origen supposed they did, still, in later Jewish variants of the story the seducers are no longer magistrates of the community.

The original Greek version of the Book of Daniel, as it is found in the Greek Bible, was composed around 150 B.C.E. and includes the Susanna story. This version of the story, however, was rejected by the Church in favor of the so-called Theodotion version and was subsequently forgotten. Rediscovered only in 1783, in a unique manuscript, it was also preserved in a papyrus codex that was published in 1968. Now that we have the original, it is interesting to note that the celebrated scene of Susanna at her bath, being spied upon by the lascivious Elders, is an interpolation of Theodotion's version. To quote Africanus again, in the version approved by the Church a homily has become a "romance."

Still, the original version, although less erotic, has the advantage of furnishing some information about the life of Babylonian Jewry in the early Hellenistic age. We learn that the Jewish community had jurisdiction over even capital cases, at least for offenses in the field of family law, and that the "whole assembly" judged the cases that came before it— under the direction of the Elders—according to the Law of Moses. As in the Torah, the concordant testimony of two witnesses was necessary as well as sufficient proof of guilt, and false witnesses were forced to suffer the same punishment they had attempted to have inflicted upon the accused. On the other hand, the Mishnaic rule that an execution must be delayed if someone offers to reargue the case makes Daniel's intervention understandable. This procedural similarity can hardly be coincidental; it proves, rather, that this rule, found in the treatise Sanhedrin, was already known in the Hellenistic age.

The question is how far the author was describing the institutions of his time and how much he was simply inventing. Africanus already claimed that it was unhistorical to ascribe to a Jewish community in exile the power to inflict the death penalty. To this objection Origen replied that under Roman rule the Jews in Palestine did enjoy that power. We ourselves prefer to suspend judgment pending further information.

As the Susanna homily shows, the figure of Daniel, prophet and wizard, was popular in the Eastern dispersion. In one of the many Daniel tales that were current, the prophet Habakkuk is introduced as a secondary character in a manner similar to that in which the famous Ahikar is introduced in the Tobit romance. A compiler gathering Habakkuk stories for a book (now lost) called the Prophecy of Habakkuk, Son of Jesus, of the Tribe Levi inserted this particular tale into his work. In his turn, the editor of the Greek Daniel picked up the novelette from the Habakkuk collection and added it to his own garland. As some Church Fathers (Africanus, Origen, Jerome) already noted, "a certain man, Daniel, son of Abal, a priest," in the Habakkuk collection cannot strictly speaking be the same as the Hebrew Daniel, who is of the tribe of Judah. But because each Daniel was presented as a friend of the Babylonian kings, the editor of the Greek Daniel, rightly or wrongly, identified one with the other.

In the Habakkuk story, Daniel (the priest) is asked by his king why does he not worship Bel (Marduk), the patron god of Babylon. Daniel claims that the provisions set before the god's bronze statue are consumed not by the idol Bel, but rather by the idol's priests. The stratagem by which Daniel proves this assertion is derived from folklore: ashes strewn on the floor of the temple show the footprints of priests who, each night, carry away the sacrificial offerings. The stratagem also proves, incidentally, that the anecdote is of Eastern origin, as Greek gods were not served daily. Nevertheless, the triumph of Daniel is deceptive; no one ever really believed that an idol consumed the offerings left for it. The sacrificial meal was openly and officially distributed among the priests in Babylon as well as in Jerusalem.

After this episode the Babylonian king points to a great dragon worshipped by the Babylonians, proclaims that it is a living god, and orders Daniel to worship it. Daniel's response is to offer to prove that the dragon is not immortal. Since this beast does eat and drink offerings, Daniel gives it a cake made of pitch, fat, and hair. After eating the cake the monster bursts asunder. Daniel's strange oblation, and in fact the entire tale of the slaying of the dragon, is of Iranian origin: monstrous serpent, invulnerable to weapons, succumbs to poison. Yet because the Jewish author omits any mention of poison, he renders his story unintelligible while revealing his dependence on Eastern folklore.

Daniel's actions naturally provoke the pagans. The populace gather against him and he is thrown into the lion's den. Six days later the prophet Habakkuk, carried by an angel "by the hair of his head," brings food from Judea (that is, kosher food) to the prisoner in the pit. The lions, of course, do not touch Daniel and the king proclaims the greatness of the Lord.

The story of Bel and the Dragon must be of Babylonian origin. There were sacred snakes everywhere, even in Greece, but no one, not even the Babylonians, ever pretended that sacred animals were immortal; the Egyptians even mummified them. Nor could the story have been invented in Syria-Phoenicia, where Bel was not worshipped before the first century C.E. But the Babylonians took the international motif of the invincible monster seriously: hundreds of reliefs of a horned serpent with the feet of a lion and the wings of an eagle protected the walls of Nebuchadnezzar's Bablyon. No wonder that Jeremiah (51:34) compared the all devouring king of Babylon to the Babylonian monster *(tannim)*, the attribute of the supreme deity, Bel (Marduk) of Babylon.

Daniel killed the invulnerable dragon by attacking him from inside, by feeding him indigestible ingredients. The destruction of a dragon who was revered as a god by a similar device also appears in old Persian folklore. The author of the Jewish version of the story may have followed some Persian fairy tale. Scoffing at idols was a Jewish tradition still approved of by later rabbis (San. 63b), but "Daniel" treated the subject in all seriousness. For him the story he had told confirmed the words of Isaiah (46:1): "Bel bows down."

The Palestinian Jews to whom Jerome told the tales of Bel and the Dragon (which he knew from his Greek Bible) observed that the hero, here as in the Susanna story, displays a keen wit rather than the prophetic spirit of the biblical Daniel. The Daniel who detects frauds is not the same as the Daniel who pierces the future: whereas Daniel the priest attacks paganism, Daniel the prophet defends his faith.

The story of Bel and the Dragon illustrates the wisdom of the commandment in the Greek Torah not to vilify "the gods" (LXX Exod. 22:28). On the other hand, the story also shows why a Babylonian Jew could be impelled to disregard this commandment, even if he knew of it. Greek gods were rarely fanatical and rarely sought proselytes, and Jews and Greeks had contempt for the beastlike gods of Egypt, but Bel and the other gods of the East were held in high regard by both Jews and Greeks. A Jew in the Eastern dispersion was not able to dismiss Bel with a shrug or a sneer. How could a Jew escape the pressure to bow before such an idol except by affirming that it had no breath of life? According to Jewish tales, Abraham himself abandoned the idols of his father only after discovering that they were unable to partake of food offered to them.

As a matter of fact, we have another tract of the same period whose purpose was to persuade the Babylonian Jews that they must revere their own God only, the sole true Deity, Who has "sovereignty over all flesh." This tract has been preserved in the Septuagint as "an exemplar of the letter which Jeremiah sent to those who were to be taken to Babylon as captives by the King of the Babylonians," that is, to those in the first deportation of 597 B.C.E. The author found the idea of such a message in Jeremiah 10:1–11. He wrote his pamphlet sometime between 300 and 100 B.C.E. First, "King of the Babylonians" is a graecism, since Nebuchadnezzar was, rather, "King of Babylon," as he is rightly called in Daniel, and further, a Greek fragment (v. 43–44) of the Epistle of Jeremiah, copied around 100 B.C.E., has been discovered at Qumran. Second, the author of the Letter to Aristobulus, which was fabricated in the middle of the first century B.C.E. and inserted into our text of II Maccabees (2:2–3), quotes the Epistle of Jeremiah. And last, fictitious propagandizing letters ascribed to famous men of the past seem to have been unknown in the ancient Orient, while such forgeries were common in the Hellenistic age.

As the Epistle does not refer to the worship of animals, it could not have been fabricated for circulation in Egypt, and since the author speaks of sacred prostitution (v. 43), he cannot have in mind Greek (or Egyptian) worship, either. Indeed, he himself tells us (v. 4) that just like the author of Bel and the Dragon, he too is speaking of the gods of Babylon. But while in Bel and the Dragon idolatry is held up to ridicule, pseudo-Jeremiah, like the true Jeremiah, is very much aware of the strong attraction exercised by the idols of Babylon. His homily is punctuated by the repetition of the refrain, borrowed from Jeremiah 10:5: Idols are nought, be not afraid of them.

At the distance of two millennia, the anxiety of the prophet and of his imitator may seem strange to us. But, as we have seen, polytheism had found many adherents among the Jews in Persian Babylonia, and the danger of heathen contagion was endemic. The religious situation of the average Jew in Seleucid Babylon was similar. First and foremost, he was deprived of the sacrificial cult that was the basis of religious life everywhere. Moreover, because the sacrificial worship of his Lord was permitted only in faraway Jerusalem, its practices were virtually unknown to him; otherwise the author of the story of Daniel and Bel would have realized that his sneer at the meals prepared for the god of Babylon would also strike at the ritual of the Temple of Jerusalem. In addition, the rare pilgrim who got to Jerusalem, like the author of Tobit, would have discovered for himself the penury of God's house there, so unlike "the first one," built by the mighty Solomon.

Instead, the Jew in Babylon, separated from Jerusalem for several generations by this time, saw each day the temples of the Babylonian gods, which, protected by the Macedonian kings, had regained their ancient splendor. He witnessed magnificent processions of idols made of gold and silver and adorned with purple byssus and precious stones. How could he help admiring the pomp of the clergy or fail to be impressed by their confidence in the power of their gods? The Babylonian priests proclaimed that the glance of Bel deposed potentates and that he gave the sceptre to the king who feared him. Belit, his spouse, humbled the rich, made the poor wealthy, released the captive, and grasped the hand of the fallen. Even a stout monotheist might have been tempted to think that there was something in these heathen rites; perhaps idols, in one way or another, were truly able to succor and avenge? (In point of fact, these same praises, almost word for word, were also addressed to the God of Jerusalem and later became a part of the daily prayer of the Jew.)

Although the actual service in the Babylonian temple was inaccessible to laymen, and in any case beyond the understanding of the Babylonian Jew because it was conducted in the Akkadian language, the servant of Belit who calls upon her (in a cuneiform text) to help him proclaim her power to the whole world must have carried on his propagandizing, oral or written, in Aramaic, the daily language of both native and Jew in Babylonia.

As if he were answering a missionary tract, the new Jeremiah point by point demonstrates once again the vanity of putting one's faith in idols. No, he says, they can neither establish kings nor depose them; nor can they bestow riches or exact the fulfillment of a vow. And because in Babylonian religious texts idols were described as though they could stand, sit, or otherwise move by themselves, the new Jeremiah asserts vigorously that if idols fall to the ground they *cannot* raise themselves again, or move, or in any way bring themselves upright. How, he insists, can anyone believe that they are gods? Only the righteous man who has no idols will escape the shame of the one who vainly expects help from a fetish.

THIRTEEN

The Greek Torah

LTHOUGH Hebrew and Aramaic literature continued to flourish in the early Hellenistic age, the Jews in the Greek dispersion slowly learned to think and write in Greek. The first fruit of their labor was a translation, the most important translation ever made: it opened the Bible to the world and the world to the Word of God. Without this translation London and Rome would still be heathen and the Scriptures would be no better known than the Egyptian Book of the Dead.

According to the tradition handed down among Alexandrian Jews, the Torah was rendered into Greek under the patronage of Ptolemy II Philadelphus (285–246 B.C.E.). Some seventy years after the death of Philadelphus, that is, between 175 and 170, Aristobulus, the first Jew known to have been a Greek philosopher, who belonged to the Aristotelian school, presented a work entitled "An Explanation of the Mosaic Scripture" to Ptolemy VI Philometor. Like Jewish Aristotelians in the Middle Ages, he was concerned with the relationship between Greek wisdom and Jewish faith. Addressing his king, Aristobulus tells him that the Greek version of the Law was made "under King Philadelphus, your ancestor, who displayed the greatest munificence [on this occasion]; while Demetrius of Phaleron directed the undertaking." The name of Demetrius, who was famous as a lawgiver and an adviser of Ptolemy I, may have been wrongly attached to the translation of the Jewish law, but Aristobulus' date for the translation is indirectly confirmed by the fact that another Demetrius, a Jewish historian who wrote in Greek under Ptolemy IV (221–205), already drew his quotations of Genesis and Exodus from it.

Some fifty years after Aristobulus, an Alexandrian Jew writing under the fictitious name of Aristeas, a Greek courtier of Ptolemy II Philadelphus, used the memorable undertaking of the king as the historical basis for a narrative of an imaginary voyage to Jerusalem—a narrative written to glorify the Chosen People. According to pseudo-Aristeas, Ptolemy II sent him, together with others, as envoys to the High Priest in Jerusalem in order to obtain qualified scholars to translate the Mosaic Law for the royal library. Assenting to the request, the High Priest dispatched to Alexandria seventy-two men worthy of the task—six from each tribe of Israel—together with a trustworthy copy of the Torah. The translators did their work in seventy-two days. The translation was then read to and approved by the entire body of Alexandrian Jewry and even by the king himself. In Philo's time the Jews of Alexandria celebrated each anniversary of the translation with a festival on the shore of the island of Pharos, where they believed the seventy-two translators had lived during the period of their labors. Christian authors and rabbis later embellished pseudo-Aristeas' account, but furnished no real new information.

The Jews always carefully distinguished between the Torah and the other Holy Books. In Jewish tradition, the Greek version of the Torah, made under royal auspices, was the authorized version; Philo even claimed divine guidance for it. But beginning in the second century C.E., Christian authors even began to ascribe later translations of the Prophets and the Hagiographa to the original company of interpreters. They designated this body by the round number seventy, a title that was subsequently transferred to the entire Greek Bible, which became known as the "Septuagint." In this chapter, however, when we speak of the Septuagint we mean the Greek version of the *Torah* only. This is the version that was published, apparently, in five volumes, or "rolls" (hence the name "Pentateuch," that is, five scrolls).

It is generally held that the Greek version of the Torah was produced by Alexandrian Jews who no longer knew enough Hebrew to understand the sacred Scripture when it was read aloud in the synagogue. But this hypothesis is anachronistic. The custom of reading the Law publicly within a cycle of lessons is not attested before the middle of the second century C.E. In the third century B.C.E., a passage of a verse pertaining to the day was perhaps read on Sabbaths and Festivals. The Mishna still offers a list of lessons appointed for these days; Leviticus 23:23–25 is appointed for the New Year service, for instance. It is even possible that there existed lectionaries of these selected passages in a Greek transliteration or translation as an aid to the reader unable to decipher the original Hebrew of the sacred scroll.

Under the conditions of ancient bookmaking, however, it would have been an extraordinary waste of money and manual labor to translate, copy, and recopy the five scrolls of the new Greek Torah in order to assist an inexperienced interpreter struggling with the oral translation of isolated passages. As a matter of fact, pseudo-Aristeas, writing more than a century after the translation of the Torah, gives no hint that any copies of the Septuagint were commissioned for the liturgical and educational needs of Egyptian Jewry. Indeed, he tells us that only two copies of the translation were made, one of which was deposited in the royal library and one of which was given to the chiefs of the Jewish community in Alexandria, in accordance with their request. In antiquity publication of a work was commonly effected by depositing the bulky manuscript in a place of safety; those who wished could then make their own copies of the book. Such private activity was quite different from the imagined mass production, for any reason, of the five "rolls" of the Greek Torah.

The error made by modern critics with respect to the traditional account of Alexandrian Jews is, so to speak, optical: they view the Alexandrian translation as if it were a unique undertaking. In fact, the task of the Seventy took its place in a long tradition of translation.

The Greeks never denied that the founders of their philosophy and science were disciples of the wise men of the Orient. But while oriental civilizations from the Euphrates to the Nile were scribal and thus bookish, Greek civilization was essentially a civilization of the spoken word *(logos)*. There were no Greek books before approximately 700 B.C.E., and more than three hundred years later Plato still regarded the invention of writing as harmful because it substituted dead letters for living dialogue. Thus, as we have seen, the Eastern wisdom that was transmitted to the early Greeks was transmitted not through books, but through personal contact with Eastern sages. (For this reason, so many Greek sages in the Greek tradition, from Pherecydes in the first half of the sixth century—the first philosopher, according to Josephus—to Plato, are said to have visited either Egypt or the other lands of the East.)

Moreover, the universal use of Aramaic in the Persian Empire facilitated the oral transmission of knowledge. Eudoxos, a disciple of Plato, did not need to read cuneiform in order to learn the Babylonian creation poem whose beginning he quoted, and Democritus (died ca. 470) probably knew the Aramaic story of Ahikar even though it had not been translated into Greek. Greek colonists in Egypt were intermediaries between Egyptian physicians and their Greek colleagues. As a matter of fact, the only oriental book whose translation may be placed in the period before Alexander is the Dialogues of Dogs, written by the above-mentioned Eudoxos. According to the opinion of some unnamed critics quoted in a late compilation, Eudoxos, who had lived in Egypt for eighteen months, translated the book from Egyptian. Indeed, if the work was a collection of animal fables, it could well be of Egyptian origin, since the Egyptians cultivated this genre.

The Torah, however, was neither fable, nor interesting narrative, nor philosophical discourse, but law, and the written translation of legal and official documents had been practiced in the Near East from time immemorial. The art of the dragoman, derived from the Babylonian term *turgeman,* was particularly useful in the Persian Empire, where Persian orders had first to be translated into Aramaic and then into a variety of other languages. As the Book of Esther tells us, royal commandments were sent to every province in its own script and to every people in its own language. For instance, the record of Darius' deeds was published in Persian, Elamite, and Aramaic, and read in Aramaic by Jewish colonists at Elephantine; the decision of a satrap dealing with worship in a temple in Xanthos (Lycia) was published on stone in Aramaic, Greek, and Lycian; and, as we have seen, on an order of Darius I a company of Egyptian scholars went all the way to Persia to produce an Egyptian law code and an Aramaic translation of it.

Outside the limits of the Persian Empire, the Buddhist king Asoka, a contemporary of the Seventy, published his edicts not only in Sanskrit but also in Aramaic and Greek. Further, we know that under the Ptolemies the Egyptian law code was read in Greek to the entire court and its officials. A recently published Greek papyrus offers a Greek translation of some Egyptian laws for which, by chance, we also have the demotic original, making it highly probable that the translation of the demotic law code of the Egyptians into Greek was, like the Septuagint, prepared by the Ptolemaic government.

At about the same time as the Seventy were engaged in their task, between roughly 280 and 260, a Babylonian priest was composing in Greek the story of his country from the Creation to Alexander the Great and "a high priest and scribe of the sacred shrines of Egypt" was compiling the story of the pharaohs from the divine dynasties who ruled in the beginning to the Macedonian conquest. The purpose of each author was to provide the Greek public with authentic information about his country in order to counteract the fabulous tales about the Orient then current in the Greek world. Like the Seventy, the Egyptian Manetho worked for Ptolemy II, while the Babylonian Berossus dedicated his compilation to Antiochus I of Syria, the contemporary and rival of Ptolemy II.

Berossus and Manetho, however, summarized countless original records in compiling their chronicles, whereas the Jews relied on a single document, the Torah. As for the history of the Jews after Moses, it was a matter neither of concern to the Greek reader nor of pride to the Chosen People; after the return from exile Jewish life had been reconstituted directly on the foundations laid down by Moses. Now there was a Greek version of this Torah that provided an authoritative image of the sacred history and of the faith of the Chosen People—a gift, as Ptolemy II is alleged by pseudo-Aristeas to have written to the High Priest in Jerusalem, to all the Jews throughout the world and their posterity.

We would like to believe, with Philo, that the Seventy gave us a faithful Greek rendering of the sacred text. In fact, although the translators undoubtedly aimed at fidelity, the Septuagint is often at variance with the Hebrew Bible. For instance, as Origen observes, the description of the Tabernacle (Exod. 35–40) in the Septuagint disagrees widely with the Hebrew description. Because of such differences, the Jews, after the destruction of the Second Temple, began to deny the authority of the Septuagint and in the second century c.e. produced rival translations of Scripture (such as the almost literal Greek translation of Aquila) for the needs of the diaspora. Thus, the Septuagint remained the Greek Bible only for the Church. Even within the Church, however, when Protestants after the Reformation began to appeal to the authority of the Hebrew original, the basic value of the Septuagint became a topic of confessional, and afterward scholarly, controversy. To account for the discrepancies between the Hebrew original and the Greek of the Septuagint, scholars offered various conjectures: the Septuagint was made from the Samaritan Bible, from a Hebrew text written in Greek characters, from an Aramaic Targum. A whimsical scholar even suggested that the Hebrew text depended on the Septuagint. More prudent critics spoke of the translators' faulty knowledge of Greek, or of Hebrew, or of both.

It is obvious, however, that none of the Hebrew manuscripts available around 260 B.C.E. could have offered a text identical to that found in our printed Bibles, since the latter essentially follows the edition made in Jerusalem three centuries after the publication of the Septuagint. Toward the end of the second century B.C.E. we find pseudo-Aristeas complaining that copies of the Torah were being penned carelessly and "not as ought to be." But even had the Greek translation been made—as he asserts it was—from the particularly splendid Hebrew scroll sent by the High Priest, the golden letters of that manuscript would not have guaranteed its trustworthiness. At the time of the Seventy, textual criticism was just beginning in Alexandria, to say nothing of Jerusalem, and any manuscript, so long as it was old, would have been regarded as authoritative. The Seventy, like, for example, the author of Jubilees, had before them an uncorrected text of the Torah.

It should come as no surprise consequently that the Septuagint often agrees with the Samaritan Pentateuch, the Book of Jubilees, the Qumran manuscripts, and similar variants of the Vulgate text, as against the Torah text later fixed by Jewish bookmen after, and in imitation of, Alexandrian editions of Homer. For instance, in the Song of Moses (Deut. 32:43) the Septuagint exhibits a conflated text: eight distichs, including a line adapted from Psalm 90:7, instead of the four found in the Torah. A Hebrew fragment from Qumran, which although not identical with the LXX text often agrees with its readings, is also conflated and repeats the same line from Psalm 90.

The Hebrew consonantal text was not frozen until sometime toward 100 C.E., but once it was accepted as authoritative, all scrolls deviating from the standard recension were suppressed by the rabbinic authorities. Divergent manuscripts of the Septuagint, however, continued to circulate freely. Around 90 C.E., Josephus, in his paraphrase of pseudo-Aristeas, suggests that his readers "amend" any text of the Septuagint manuscript that they possess if they find any addition or omission there. As Josephus does not advise the reader to compare the suspect reading with the original manuscript in Alexandria, his words can only mean that the reader should consult the standard Hebrew text. Thus historians attempting to understand the Greek Pentateuch as an Alexandrian interpretation of the Torah are hindered by two obstacles: they must decide first whether the Greek text that is being examined reproduces the original translation, and second whether the Greek reading follows or modifies the Hebrew manuscript used by the Seventy.

This dual problem is illustrated in the following two examples. In the Vatican codex, which is a mainstay of our printed Septuagint, Exodus 20:11 is inserted in Deuteronomy 5:14 in order to provide motivation for the commandment to keep the seventh day rest. The same interpolation appears in a first century B.C.E. Hebrew Deuteronomy from Qumran. Does the reading of the Vaticanus conform to the original text of the Septuagint or was the Septuagint text later modified by a scribe after a Hebrew scroll of the same text type as the Qumran Deuteronomy? On the other hand, the Septuagint asserts that God "completed His work" (the Creation) on the sixth day, while our printed Bible (Gen. 2:2) says that He finished His work on the seventh day. The rabbis had already recorded this variant among the changes "made for the King Ptolemy." Yet the reading saying that God completed His work on the sixth day also appears in the Samaritan Torah, that is, in a witness to the unrevised Hebrew text type of the pre-Hasmonean period. Thus we see that the Hebrew text of Genesis 2:2 had been tampered with in Palestine before the period around 300 B.C.E., and the modification from the seventh to the sixth day had entered into the Hebrew manuscript from which the Seventy worked. The verse had been doctored for the sake of the reader who might have misconstrued the original wording to mean that the Creator labored on the Sabbath day. As a matter of fact, the wording of Genesis 2:2 continued to embarrass Jewish commentators, including Rashi.

Because the work of the historical interpretation of the Greek Torah has hardly begun, we must limit ourselves to some observations on the methods of the Seventy with particular attention to their vocabulary.

To begin with, the Seventy rendered the entire—enormous—scroll of the Torah into Greek without amplification or condensation. This fact is fundamental, since translators of works of literature in the ancient world were generally free to adapt the original story to the needs of new readers. When a hellenized Egyptian translates a tale of the miracles of his god Imhotep into Greek (at Imhotep's command), he tells us that he straightened and simplified "the divine book" (of Imhotep) and "filled in defects and struck out superfluities," and that he did so "in accordance with divine favor." His task, he says, is to make every Greek tongue praise Imhotep.

The Torah, however, is no missionary tract, but God's ordinance: "Whatever God says is not words, but deeds," Philo says of the Decalogue. Accordingly the Seventy, following the practice of the dragomans when translating legal records, endeavored to render the original exactly. Of course, like every translator, they had trouble expressing foreign idioms—the Hebrew cognate accusative, for example—in the Greek language, and found themselves at times compelled to change constructions and to omit or add words. But generally speaking the greatest fault of their version is, paradoxically, its very servility to the original. Lacking dictionaries, grammars, and commentaries, and adhering as they did to the practices of the dragomans, the Seventy rendered the original literally, clause for clause, even to the point of following the word order of the original. In this way they made the Greek Pentateuch into an un-Greek book. Nevertheless, where they felt surefooted they were true to the Alexandrian taste for variation and rendered the same Hebrew term differently in different places. The Hebrew word *keber* (grave), for instance, is *taphos* in Genesis 23:4 and *mnemeion* two verses later. Of course they also blundered, sometimes through ignorance and sometimes by virtue of simple human frailty. For instance, as Jerome noted, by taking the adverb *ulam* in Genesis 28:19 as part of the proper name that followed it, the Greek translator created the nonexistent city of Ullammaus.

Historians, however, are not interested in variations or accidental errors. What matters to them are the changes made by the Seventy intentionally, for the Greek Pentateuch is the earliest extant interpretation of the Torah and often incorporates even earlier exegetic traditions. An adequate treatment of this topic would require a special and voluminous work, but I would like to give some examples here of the kind of purposeful interpretation (or reinterpretation) introduced by the Seventy.

Jerome supplies us with one example when he notes that, to his surprise, the Hebrew word *mth*, which is correctly rendered as "bed" in the Greek version of Genesis 48:2, is translated as "staff" in Genesis 47:31.

Actually, the consonantal group *mth* has both these meanings in Hebrew, but the Seventy were embarrassed when dealing with the second passage by the idea that Jacob would bow down "upon the bed's head," and chose to assess the value of the Hebrew word differently. Let us add that no commentator has as yet been able to explain adequately the meaning of this word in this verse.

Again, in Genesis 39:1, Potiphar is called the *saris* of the pharaoh. Taking the term literally, as Jerome later did in his own translation, the Seventy, writing at the court of Ptolemy II, could not have understood how a eunuch could have been "Commander of the Guard." But because the Hebrew word for "guard" can also be derived from the root *tbk*, meaning "slaughter," they were able to transform the eunuch Potiphar into the head of Pharaoh's cooks.

Some mistranslations were tendentious. For instance, listed among the unclean animals (Lev. 11:6 and Deut. 14:7) is the hare, the Greek for which was *lagos*. However, because *lagos* also happened to be the name of the grandfather of Ptolemy II, the Seventy substituted the synonym *dasypous* ("hairy-foot") for *lagos;* the rabbis recorded this change as among those made for Ptolemy. Again, the word *mlk* ("king"), which is common to Aramaic, Hebrew, and Phoenician, was rendered exactly by the dragomans and by the Seventy as *basileus*. Nevertheless, in Deuteronomy 17:14–15, when the Hebrews are warned never to choose a foreigner for their king, the Seventy, loyal subjects of the Ptolemies, chose instead to render *mlk* as *archon* ("ruler"), an innocuous word often used for the chief of a local community or tribe. (For the same reason *archon* appears in the Greek text of Deuteronomy 28:36 and in the predictions of Genesis 49:20 and Deuteronomy 33:5.)

The same consonantal group, *mlk*, was also troublesome in Leviticus 18:21 and 20:2–5, where the Torah forbids the cult of *mlk*, that is, of the heathen deity worshipped as "king." We do not need to discuss here the real meaning of these biblical passages; we only need to note that the Seventy again prudently rendered the word *mlk* as *archon*. Thus, the injunction in Leviticus 18:21 becomes, in Greek: "You shall not give your seed to serve an *archon*," a meaningless and therefore innocuous injunction.

Because Alexandrian society valued polite manners, Alexandrian scholars omitted several lines in Homer that might have shocked the well-bred gentleman's sense of decorum. In the same vein, the Seventy revised the divine promise that covenanted Israel will "devour" all the peoples God delivers to it (Deut. 7:16), so that it read, in Greek: "Thou shalt devour the booty." Similarly, an admonition to circumcise the foreskin of the heart becomes, in Greek, an injunction to prune the obstinacy of the heart (Deut. 10:16).

For the same reason the translators exercised a fine sense of discrimination in their treatment of the anthropomorphisms in the Hebrew Torah. It is true that in the Greek version, as in the Hebrew, the Lord "smells" the sacrificial odor of Noah's offering and "descends" to Sodom in order to learn about its sins; but that is because in the context of the epic tales of Genesis, this kind of figurative expression would not offend the ear of the Greek reader. Yet, although the Seventy were reluctant to call on a "Man of War" or a "Rock," even in poetical passages (Exod. 15:3; Deut. 32:4), and although when the Torah reports that Israel complained "in the ears" of the Lord (Num. 11:1), the Seventy write in Greek, "in the presence of the Lord," still, when God speaks of Israel's complaint to Moses and Aaron, the exact Hebrew reading—"what [they] have said in my ears" (Num. 14:28)—is retained. It is clear, therefore, that in speaking to men the Deity is permitted to use anthropomorphic figures of speech. Similarly, Moses may converse with God, but the elect of Israel may see only "the place where the God of Israel had stood" (Exod. 24:10). Translating the Torah exactly, the Seventy write that Moses saw God "face to face" (Exod. 33:11), but when the Torah adds that God spoke to Moses "as a man speaks to another," they ennoble this everyday expression by reassessing the value of the word *rea,* which can also mean "friend." The trite Hebrew idiom becomes in Greek, "as someone talking to his friend." Since the word *philos* occurs only twice in the Greek Pentateuch (the second time in Deuteronomy 13:6), the change in meaning is clearly intentional. From the fourth century B.C.E., Greek philosophers had insisted that good and wise men are the friends of the gods and enjoy their particular favor.

For the Seventy, Mosaic law was the fundament of human life. As Philo remarked, when Moses tells us that Terah left Chaldea for Haran, his intention is not to register a historical accident, but rather to teach us a lesson of great value for our lives. Accordingly there exists a category of changes by means of which the translators aim at bringing the biblical text up to date. For instance, Exodus 25:25 directs that the table of shewbread in the Tabernacle be gilded. But because in the Temple of Jerusalem the table of shewbread was constructed of pure gold (I Kings 7:48), in the Greek version the passage was changed to reflect that fact. And because in the Second Temple salt was used with all offerings, the Seventy add salt even to the composition of the shewbread (Lev. 24:7). They also updated some geographical names: "Caphtor," for instance, is wrongly identified with Cappadocia in Deuteronomy 2:23. They speak of "On, that is, Heliopolis" (Exod. 1:11) and even of "Potiphar, priest in Heliopolis" (Gen. 41:45). Curiously, they even changed the Egyptian name of the Patriarch Joseph (Gen. 41:45): in the Hebrew text the Egyptian name means "God has said, he lives," while in the Septuagint the

Egyptian name means "the sustainer of life." Working in Alexandria, the Seventy probably regarded themselves as experts in Egyptian matters, although they also transformed the tribal Elders of the Hebrew Torah into the "Senate" (Greek, *Gerousia*), the term that in their time was used for the governing body of Jerusalem and Judea.

The translation of the legal sections of the Torah, which again, following the practices of the dragomans, had necessarily to be precise, was often difficult. Still, the translators could sometimes rely upon the traditional oral exegesis of Jewish priests and judges. For instance, the Lawgiver in Leviticus 23:11 directs that the offering of the first barley sheaf of the new crop should be made "on the morrow of the Sabbath" of the Feast of Unleavened Bread. This can be understood to mean the Sunday in the middle of the festival week, as the Samaritans and the Sadducees believed. The sectarians of the Dead Sea, however, in agreement with the Book of Jubilees, interpreted the passage, rather erratically, as referring to the first Sunday after the feast. The Pharisees, taking a third position, maintained that here "the Sabbath" meant the first day of the feast and, accordingly, that the sheaf-waving should be performed on the sixteenth day of Nisan. It is commonly held, not without reason, that the Sadducees generally followed the ancient and priestly tradition, but in the present matter the fact that the Septuagint translates the verse as "on the morrow of the first day" demonstrates that here we have a rare case in which we find the Pharisees, rather than the Sadducees, following an earlier, obviously priestly interpretation of a biblical injunction.

Another example illustrating the influence of traditional exegesis on the Seventy is found in their translation of Exodus 21:10, in which it is ruled that the husband of a bondmaid, if he takes a second wife, may not diminish the food, clothing, or *nth* of the first wife. The meaning of the term *nth* is unknown. Cuneiform documents and such biblical passages as Hosea 2:7 and Ecclesiastes 9:7–9 seem to indicate that the threefold obligation of support included food, clothing, and oil; but whatever the original meaning of the clause, later interpreters could only guess at it. Jerome translates the enigmatic term as *pretium pudiciatiae*, although the prevailing view among rabbis was that the word *nth* referred to the conjugal rights of the first wife. The Seventy translated the enigmatic term as *homilia*, a word which had the same euphemistic meaning in Greek as "intercourse" does in English (to understand this ancient interpretation of biblical law we need only recall the story of Leah and Rachel, spouses of Jacob [Gen. 30]), and by adopting this interpretation demonstrate that this exegesis was prevalent in Jerusalem of the third century B.C.E. and that it was transmitted to the rabbis teaching in Palestine some five centuries later.

The Septuagint rendering of Exodus 21:22–25 is particularly interesting. The law deals with a miscarriage caused by unintentionally injuring a pregnant woman during a fight between men and dictates that the person who causes the miscarriage must pay compensation to the husband for the loss of the fetus. But, the law continues, if *swn* ensues, the law of talion is applicable. The meaning of the term *swn* is unknown and was already unknown to the rabbis; they decided, however, that the word meant "death," and referred to the death of the pregnant woman (for which the culprit would incur the penalty of death). This interpretation agrees with Mesopotamian law and is generally accepted by modern commentators. The Seventy, however, omitted the unintelligible term *swn* and understood the continuation of the law as also dealing with the fetus; that is, according to them, the second part of the law states that in the event that the fetus was already fully formed (and consequently viable) the culprit would incur the death penalty. Thus, this interpretation regards the embryo as part of the mother's body until it is fully formed. The distinction is Aristotelian. Yet around 200 C.E., R. Isaac, who was hardly influenced by Aristotle, and who surely did not consult the Septuagint, also taught that the culprit is to be punished by death only if he kills a viable child. Did R. Isaac arrive at this conclusion independently, or did he and the Seventy follow a very ancient halakah?

Having illustrated some of the problems that bore upon the translation of the Hebrew original by the Seventy, we will now consider the other aspect of the translation, its language. Grammar aside, the discussion of which belongs rather to comparative philology, we shall deal here with lexical material, and that only insofar as it can throw light on the attitude of the Seventy toward the Torah. As the vocabulary of the Greek Pentateuch has never been studied with regard to the Greek usage of the Hellenistic period, we can offer only a few examples.

To begin with, the Seventy often employed the traditional terminology used by the dragomans. For instance, because circumcision was also practiced by the Egyptians, the dragomans already had a term for the operation, *peritome*, which, with its derivatives, was also used by the Seventy to cover various Hebrew words pertaining to the rite. The Hebrew word *nephesh* (also found in Phoenician and Aramaic) was rendered in Greek by the dragomans as *psyche*, and the Seventy clung to this translation even when the Hebrew word meant "corpse" and not "soul." *Bomos* and *hagios*, Greek equivalents of West Semitic terms meaning "altar" and "holiness," are other examples of terms fixed by the dragomans long before the translation of the Torah and adopted by the Seventy. Following the practice of the dragomans, they even clung to the standard dragoman rendering of the word *krisis* for the Hebrew *mishpat*, regardless of the context.

Second, striving for literalness of translation, particularly in legal passages, they often gave a Hebraic character (as ancient Christian readers already noted) to the Greek version. For instance, in Hebrew the distributive idea "anyone" is expressed by the iteration of the word *ish* ("man"). After the Hebrew manner, the Seventy double the Greek word for "man," *anthropos*, and write: "*Anthropos, anthropos,* who shall become unclean . . . " (Num. 9:10).

And third, because the Greeks employed their own political terms, *polis, demos, ecclesia, phyle,* and others when describing the organization of foreign societies, the Seventy could not avoid some of this terminology if they wanted to be understood by their readers. The result is that in the Septuagint, Kiriath-arba (Hebron) becomes a *polis* in the age of Abraham and the word *polites* (citizen) is used by Ephron the Hittite (Gen. 23:11) for the Hebrew "sons of my people." Yet, other terms current in the Greek political language of the time—for example, *eunoia* (loyalty), *presbeutes* (ambassador), *symmachia* (military help or alliance)—are never used by the Alexandrian translators. Why?

The truth is that the use of Greek political terms by the Seventy frequently lacks precision. While it is easy to understand that they regularly rendered the two biblical terms for "the community of Israel assembled," *kahal* and *edah,* by the vague word *synagoge,* which can be applied to any gathering, of crops as well as of men, it is not easy to understand why the term *kahal* in Deuteronomy is sometimes rendered in Greek as *synagoge* (Deut. 5:22 [19]) and sometimes as *ecclesia* (Deut. 9:10), that is, "popular assembly."

Still, when they have to deal with terms of practical importance for their readers, they can be careful. The common Hellenistic term for "resident alien" was *paroikos,* and it is used by the Seventy in two different situations: when the original speaks of a Hebrew who is residing *(toshab)* or sojourning temporarily *(ger)* abroad; and when the Lawgiver specifies the religious duties and rights of a stranger residing among the Chosen People. But when the Torah speaks of the "stranger" *(ger)* in Israel, and when the community of Israel is described as a "temporary sojourner" in a foreign land ("You shall not wrong a stranger . . . for you were strangers in the land of Egypt" [Exod. 23:9]), the Seventy used the term *proselytos* ("incomer"), which has not been found in non-Jewish Greek yet.

The usage of the Greek Pentateuch reflects the legal situation of the Jews outside Judea and of the non-Jews in Judea at the time of the translation. Since no foreign cult was tolerated in the Holy Land, only an alien in Jerusalem who agreed to worship the Lord could be a *paroikos* there in the full sense of the word. But the Jew residing in a foreign country was welcome to worship his deity there. Thus the Seventy refused to blur the differences between Greek and Hebrew institutions. For the same reason, except for "Judah" *(Jehudah)* and "Mouses" *(Mosheh* [Moses]), they abstained from using the current Greek transcriptions of Jewish names, preferring to transliterate (and vocalize) as indeclinable nouns names such as Abram, Sara, Esau, Nachor, and so on. Such barbaric nomenclature provoked the scorn of the Greeks, but for the Seventy, the patriarch remained "Isaak" and not "Isaakis," as the name was Hellenized by Greek scribes.

The religious vocabulary is also peculiar. In the first place, the Seventy took pains to avoid using the technical terms of heathenism. It would be easy to compile a long list of words commonly used in Greek religious language that could have been, but that were not, employed by the translators. The singularity of the Greek Pentateuch in this respect appears clearly when comparing its language with that used by the Greeks for Jewish institutions. For the Greeks, the Temple on Zion was, as was a temple of their own, a *hieron;* the adjective used to define the "holy" things in Jerusalem was *hieros;* and the head of the Jewish colony was the *archiereus.* In a Greek document of 200 B.C.E. the Jewish sacrifical system is elegantly called *kallierein.* Greek sovereigns speak of the Jewish *patrioi* (ancestral laws) and of animals in Jerusalem that are either *apagoreuomenoi* (forbidden) or *thusima* (fit) for sacrifice. Describing the Temple on Zion, Greek authors speak of its *bomos* (altar), *sekos* (enclosure), and *adyton* (inaccessible room). But rather than use these common Greek equivalents whenever possible, the Seventy use them only with reference to heathen worship.

Again, Hellenistic Greeks used the common vocables *eusebeia* and *hosiotes* to describe their religious feelings: Greek overlords spoke of their *eusebeia* (piety) toward the Lord. In the Greek Torah, however, the root *sebomai* appears only twice (Exod. 18:21 and Gen. 20:11), both times as a rendering of the Hebrew "fear of God," when this expression is used of or by Gentiles. Everywhere else the Seventy translate this formula literally. The term *hosion* (devout) often appears in Jewish inscriptions of the Roman age, but it occurs only once in this sense in the Greek Pentateuch, for *hasid* (Deut. 33:8).

One would think that the word *monos* would occur frequently in material about a "monotheist" revelation, but with one exception the Seventy do not use the word to refer to the Lord, because the epithet is common in Greek prayers that stress the superiority of the deity being invoked over other gods. For the same reason the word *protos,* which occurs so often in Greek hymnology, is never applied to the Lord in the Greek Torah. He is, rather, *heis,* "One." He is *unus,* not *solus.*

When speaking of pagan deities the Seventy naturally used pagan terminology. The Greek word *alsos,* for instance, means "sacred precinct," and in the Septuagint the term is used only of the pagan *asherah.* Nevertheless, when speaking of the images of pagan deities, the translators never use the common Greek term *agalma* or *eikon;* they use *eidolon* (our "idol"), that is, properly speaking, "phantom"—surely the right name for idols who were nought.

It was impossible to avoid pagan terminology altogether, however, and the Seventy relaxed their vigilance when dealing with poetry. In Moses' song, for instance, we do find the word *monos* applied to the Lord (Deut. 32:12). Moreover, as we saw in the case of common Greek terms for foreign political institutions, it would have been impossible to eliminate some of the Greek religious terms for Jewish rites or dignitaries that had been employed by the Greeks long before the Seventy (as the relevant passages in Hecateus and Theophrastus prove) without making the Septuagint unintelligible to its readers and hearers. Thus, *kohen* was still *hiereus* in the Septuagint, and the Greek word *thusia* was used for both Jewish and pagan sacrifice. In addition, some technical terms of heathenism, such as *aparachai* ("firstlings") or *holocautoma* ("burnt offering"), were probably used by the Seventy because there were no convenient Greek synonyms.

Yet even when using pagan terms for Jewish institutions, the Seventy tried to indicate the difference between the true faith and pagan error. The Hebrew Scriptures candidly use the same word, *mizbeah,* for both the Jewish and the pagan altar, while the corresponding Greek term *bomos* appears in the Greek Torah with reference to heathen worship only. The altar of God is *thusiasterion,* a rare term in Greek cults. *Prophetes* was still the most dignified Greek name for one who reveals the divine will, but the word *mantis* and its cognates in the Septuagint refer only to heathen soothsaying. The Seventy stretched and even changed the meaning of some terms of Greek religious language in order to translate certain Hebrew terms of worship. In Greek, "votive offering" is *anathema,* but the Seventy translated the Hebrew *korban* as *doron* (gift), while using the term *anathema* for *herem,* that is, the Latin *devotio* (vow). In Greek, the word *eulogia* means "praise," and does not belong to cultic language, but in the Septuagint the word renders the Hebrew religious term *berakha* (blessing).

Two religious terms in the Greek Pentateuch demand special attention. The first is *Torah,* which became *nomos* (law) in the Septuagint, although this use of the singular did not follow official Greek terminology. When speaking of Mosaic legislation the pagan authorities used the plural *nomoi,* since for them the Torah was similar to any Greek constitution. By using the Greek singular to render the Hebrew singular, the Seventy, however, made it clear that for them the Torah was not just another code, but the revealed, fundamental order within which man, all other creatures, and all the elements of the cosmos as well ought to live. This was also the basic meaning of the Greek singular, *nomos; nomos* is "king of all," as the Greek poet Pindar says. And Josephus, noting that Homer does not use the term, adds that the *nomos* of Moses embraces the whole conduct of life. Although *Torah* and *nomos,* to be sure, are not identical in all their shades of meaning, no Greek word exists that can express the Hebrew idea more exactly. Four centuries after the Seventy, Aquila himself, whose goal was to translate the Torah literally, could not find a closer equivalent.

Another concept central to Jewish faith is that of *berit. Berit* bound the Chosen People to the God of the Patriarchs. Reading into the term connotations deriving from modern translations of it as "covenant" or "alliance," which in turn derive from Jerome's use of the Latin *foedus,* modern commentators are at a loss to understand the Septuagint translation of *berit* as *diatheke. Berit,* however, does not mean "agreement." The Hebrew word refers to the particular relationship that obtained between a lord and his client, whereby the former grants his protection to the latter unilaterally. *Diatheke,* on the other hand, originally signified "promise" or "pledge," and then in legal usage, the unilateral disposition of property, hence "testament." By translating the Greek term into Latin as *testamentum* we arrive at that strange term, the "Old Testament." Later translators, Symmachus and Aquila, who rendered the Torah into Greek, translated *berit* by *synthekai,* that is, "agreement." This rendering, however, also effaced the peculiar connotation of the Hebrew term.

In the eyes of the pagan administration the Jews formed a "nation," an *ethnos,* just like the Idumeans, for example. In the Septuagint, however, *ethnos,* with some exceptions, refers only to pagan peoples, while the *laos,* a poetic word, is in principle reserved for the Chosen People. "You are My treasured host [*laos*]," says the Lord to Moses in the Greek Bible.

The Seventy judged, perhaps better than we, the inherent impossibility of translating the full meaning of a sacred text. An Egyptian predicted that when the Greeks would try to translate Egyptian religious writings into their own tongue, they would disturb the sense of the text and cause much obscurity. The grandson of Ben Sira also pointed out that things originally spoken in Hebrew did not have the same force when rendered into Greek. Four centuries later, a rabbi, referring to the oral translation of Scriptural texts in the synagogue service, stressed the difficulties of this task: "He who translates a verse literally is a falsifier, and whoever makes additions to it is a blasphemer."

In a Greek version of an Egyptian myth, not only did the translator avoid Egyptian anthropomorphisms (such as the idea that a god has a sense of smell), substitute Greek anthropomorphic deities (Hermes, for instance) for the divine animals of the original, and omit sentences that had a particular Egyptian flavor, but, in addition, he introduced the

Sphinx, well known to the Greeks, into his adaptation. The Alexandrian translators, by comparison, although beset by innumerable linguistic difficulties, made the knowledge of God's word available to the Greek-speaking world without repudiating the peculiarity of the Hebrew Scripture. They did not intend to hellenize monotheism, nor did they; they made it known to the Greeks in all its uniqueness. When, many days later, the Hellenes lost faith in themselves and their gods, and even in the critics of their gods—when the Greek universe collapsed—only those who believed in the Bible remained unperturbed. They had known the end beforehand: "Except the Lord build the house, they labor in vain who build it" (Ps. 127:1).

FOURTEEN

The End of the Kingdom of the South

W RITING some eighty years afterward, Polybius considered the almost simultaneous accessions of Antiochus III of Syria (summer, 223 B.C.E.), Ptolemy IV Philopater of Egypt (winter, 221), and Philip V of Macedon (fall, 221), as signifying the beginning of a new historical period. He was right. The uncompromising rivalries of these young monarchs upset the traditional balance of the Hellenistic powers and opened the way for Roman legions from the west and nationalist uprisings in the east.

The prognostic of the new era was the appearance of Seleucid soldiers in Ptolemaic Palestine, the first enemy to be seen there in three generations. Antiochus III, beset by the rebellion of his satraps in Iran and Asia Minor, began the war in 221 as a demonstration of his military might and as a warning to the Egyptian court, which was supporting Achaeus, his rebellious cousin at Sardis. We do not, however, need to deal here with the military operations of this four-year war (221–217), since it touched Judea only indirectly. It is true that in the winter of 218–217 Antiochus was able to take up his winter quarters at Acco-Ptolemais (north of Haifa) and thus was probably the overlord of Judea at this date, but we have no actual information on the subject. Two generations later, Daniel (11:10), using the words of Isaiah (28:15) to describe the campaign of Antiochus III, wrote that he "shall come on, and overflow, and pass beyond."

The next summer, however, on 23 June 217 B.C.E., Antiochus lost the decisive battle of the war at Raphia, south of Gaza, at the Egyptian frontier, and Palestine again came under Ptolemaic domination. Yet the war really ended in a stalemate. To quote Daniel again: "The King of the South succeeded in striking down myriads of his foes, but still he had not prevailed" (11:10). The peace, indeed, brought no important territorial changes. Ptolemy IV gave up Seleucia, the port of Antiochia conquered by his father in 245 but lost to Antiochus in 219, and abandoned the cause of Achaeus.

Ptolemy remained in Syria and Phoenicia for four months in order to complete the subjugation of this province, many of whose cities had sided with Antiochus. Naturally, to show himself again as the legitimate ruler and as the mediator between mankind and heaven, he visited the shrines of the reconquered province and sacrificed to the gods of its people. Did he also go up to Jerusalem? A later historical romance, III Maccabees, tells of his thank offering at the altar of Zion and of his sacrilegious attempt to enter the Holy of Holies, an attempt thwarted, of course, by divine intervention. We are unable to say whether the tale has any historical substance. On 12 October 217, Ptolemy IV returned to Egypt.

His triumph and the honors decreed for him by the Egyptian clergy were dearly bought, for in order to finance the war the government had been forced to resort to a policy of monetary inflation. Moreover, a political crisis accompanied these financial difficulties. For his war with Antiochus, Ptolemy had formed an Egyptian phalanx, which meant that natives had been admitted to the arm of the military that was regarded as the deciding factor in the battles of the Hellenistic age. According to Polybius, these native soldiers, proud of their success at Raphia, were afterward no longer disposed to obey. Revolt broke out. At first it seems the Egyptian peasant-soldier carried on his own war against his oppressors, Egyptian as well as Greek; even some native temples were despoiled. But from about 206, the whole of southern Egypt, including Thebes, was in a state of secession, and for some twenty years the Thebiad was ruled by native pharaohs.

Philopator's death in the summer of 204 left the kingdom to a child, Ptolemy V Epiphanes. His rivals, Antiochus III of Syria and Philip V of Macedon, now entered into a secret compact to divide between themselves the Egyptian possessions in southern Syria and around the Aegean Sea. Having seized the Ptolemaic cities in the southwest of Asia Minor in 203, Antiochus launched his next attack against Ptolemaic Palestine. In 202, he besieged Gaza, taking it the following summer. In the winter of 201–200 B.C.E. the Egyptians, in a counteroffensive led by Scopas, their general, recovered the whole of Palestine—only to fall back to the coast (toward Sidon) after Scopas was defeated at Panion, at the source of the Jordan, in the summer of 200. In the spring or summer of 199 Scopas capitulated, and the next year found Antiochus employed in reducing the cities of the province that had remained loyal to Ptolemy V. In the meantime, the Roman war with Macedonia (200–196) provided Antiochus with a welcome opportunity to regain the coast of Asia Minor toward the Hellespont, a portion of the heritage of his ancestors now controlled by the king of Macedonia. Finally the Alexandrian court concluded a peace with Antiochus. Egypt gave up all its possessions in Syria and Palestine, and in Asia Minor and Thrace as well. In the fall of 196, Ptolemy V was betrothed to Cleopatra, a daughter of Antiochus III.

The unpredictable and recurring changes of fortune in the wars of 221–217 and 203–197 meant that every city in Syria and Phoenicia spent these years in expectation of being besieged either by Antiochus or by Ptolemy. Daniel's "King of the North" came "with a big army and a big train" (Dan. 11:13), and whether he won or lost, the cities were crushed between his successes and his defeats.

Although Jerusalem probably escaped the horrors of the war of 221–217, it was occupied by Antiochus in 202 or 201. Scopas reconquered the city in the winter of 201–200 and stationed a strong garrison in the citadel of Zion (the future Antonia), northwest of the Temple. The result was that when Antiochus returned later in 200 he was forced to institute a long siege. Still, "the King of the North" cast up "a mound and took by storm the fortified city" (Dan. 11:15). At the end of it, the Jerusalem of 200 lay in ruins; even the porticos of the Sanctuary were gravely damaged.

To the inhabitants who had not fled the city during these chaotic events, and to those who should return before the end of the year, Antiochus granted a three-year exemption from taxes. He also granted the permanent remission of one third of the tribute. The inhabitants who had been sold into slavery were declared free and their property restored. Measures for the rebuilding of the Temple were set in motion. It is probable that Ben Sira's praise of the High Priest Simon refers to this work of restoration.

Jerusalem, caught between "Assyria" and Egypt, was again, as in the days of Isaiah and Jeremiah, torn asunder by opposing factions, one favoring Antiochus, the other inclining to Ptolemy. As happened often in Hellenistic cities, an external war had become the cause of internal dissension. According to Daniel (11:14) the majority stood against "the King of the South," with only the "evil" among the people disagreeing— that is, the Holy City sided with Antiochus. In 201–200 the Ptolemaic general, Scopas, had been compelled to "subdue the nation of the Jews" and to "take Jerusalem" by force. Now, on Antiochus' return in 200, the Jews helped him retake the city.

Considering that the Ptolemies had ruled the country for a century, we would expect that the ruling class in Jerusalem would be loyal to the Egyptian crown. The population of Syria and Phoenicia is said to have favored the Ptolemies; we have seen that Antiochus III was compelled to spend more than a year after his victory over Scopas in subduing its cities. How then can we explain Jerusalem's defection from the Egyptian cause? A guess is, perhaps, possible.

Under the Ptolemies, the right to farm the taxes for each city was auctioned each year in Alexandria and was usually bought either by the leaders of the city or by its leading citizens. In this way the local aristocracy perpetuated its domination. The resulting absence of any real competition, however, diminished the royal revenues. Toward the end of the reign of Ptolemy III (246–221) a certain Joseph, a member of the family of the Tobiads, accused the native bidders (probably correctly) of collusion and promised to pay a much greater amount into the royal treasury than it had thus far received. His offer was accepted and he was awarded the contract to farm the taxes of all of Ptolemaic Syria. Because its fiscal system was the heart of the Ptolemaic administration, Joseph in a single stroke deposed the local aristocracy and achieved for himself, in deed if not in law, a status unrivaled in the entire province. He was empowered to use royal troops if he met with resistance, and even executed some of the principal citizens of Ascalon and Scythopolis.

Joseph remained the general contractor for the taxes of Ptolemaic Syria for twenty-two years—until practically the end of the Ptolemaic domination of Syria. His tenure coincided with years of growing inflation. Before approximately 220 B.C.E., copper had circulated in the Ptolemaic Empire alongside silver, the international currency, and was exchanged for silver at the rate of sixty to one. But the war of 221–217 and the subsequent native rebellions had led, or compelled, the government to pay its expenses in copper, thereby increasing the issue of copper abnormally. The price of silver coins expressed in copper coins of the same weight doubled and quadrupled, and around 210 B.C.E silver pieces disappeared from daily circulation. In addition the government debased silver coins, to the extent that toward the end of the third century an authentic old silver piece was worth four new ones.

Because Ptolemaic taxes were paid partly in kind, partly in silver, partly in copper, and partly in copper with agio, it is easy to see the possibilities that such inflation opened up for tax contractors and collectors. Joseph, as his biographer (quoted by Josephus) proudly acknowledges, stripped Syria to the bone, reaped enormous profits, and raised "the Jewish people" from "poverty and weakness" to a "splendid situation." In other words, Joseph used his new wealth to establish and secure his power in Jerusalem. From the biblical Joseph to Joseph the Tobiad, the best way to riches and power in an absolute monarchy was through the royal court.

In Jerusalem, Joseph's position was a special one. He was an outsider whose power base was on the other side of the Jordan. Tobias, one of his ancestors, had been the Persian governor of the Ammonite territory and a rival of Nehemiah, and since that time, at the very least, the Tobiads had succeeded in establishing their predominance there. Nevertheless, when he became the general contractor for the entire province of Syria and Phoenicia, Joseph displaced none other than the High Priest, who had traditionally been the one to farm the royal taxes in Judea. As a result his position in Jerusalem became so strong that when, about 210 B.C.E., his son Hyrcanus bribed the Ptolemaic court in order to supplant his father, a civil war exploded between the faction of Hyrcanus and that of his brothers. Hyrcanus lost and was forced to withdraw across the Jordan to his Ammonite lands. But the continued predominance of the Tobiads in Jerusalem alienated the old oligarchy of the city, led by the pontifical family of the Oniads, from the Ptolemaic cause. In Jerusalem, as in Egypt, the financial needs of the Ptolemies were the cause of dissatisfaction and secession. Shortly after the Seleucid conquest, Ben Sira wrote that dominion passed from one nation to another because of injustice, arrogance, and money.

After he took the city in 200 B.C.E., Antiochus III, aided by the traditional aristocracy of Jerusalem and the clergy of the Holy City, punished his adversaries, "the adherents of Scopas," and demonstrated his gratitude to his supporters by relieving the secular aristocracy and the priestly caste of personal taxes. Most important, he restored the High Priest to his position as head of the nation and once again delegated to him the responsibility for the collection of the tribute. Real power was returned to the traditional ruling families of Jerusalem. Under Seleucus IV (187–185 B.C.E.), Hyrcanus the Tobiad continued to be a rich and important figure, but he no longer directed the politics of Jerusalem.

Here we touch on an important point in the evolution of Hellenistic Jerusalem. In ancient times, victory and defeat appeared to be a result of devine dispensation. The fall of Jerusalem and its restoration by Cyrus still had the ring of providential interpositioning; as late as 332 B.C.E the High Priest had hesitated to break his oath of allegiance to his Persian overlord. In the conflict between Antiochus III and Ptolemy V, however, Jerusalem found itself for the first time in a situation that had become common in other Hellenistic cities. The populations of the cities of Ptolemaic Syria had oscillated between the Seleucid and the Ptolemaic magnetic poles throughout the third century. Now this situation had taken hold in Jerusalem, too; the Jews were divided into two parties, each subservient to one of the two warring superpowers, both of which were equally indifferent to the biblical promises to the Chosen People. The Greeks had secularized politics in the Holy City; the struggle was no longer between the Holy City and heathen power, but between partisans of two rival heathen powers. Whoever won punished his enemies—the pro-Ptolemaic "optimates" had to flee to Egypt in 200—but protected Jerusalem and the Temple for the sake of his own party among the Jews. Agrippa II, who in 70 C.E. besieged Jerusalem, and Johanan ben Zakkai, who made peace with Titus, both followed a precedent established in 200 B.C.E. Thus, Providence was now on the side of success. Daniel, although writing at the time of the persecution of Antiochus IV, regards the Ptolemaic party in Jerusalem as "evildoers" *(benei parizei)* who vainly tried to resist the preordained course of events (Dan. 11:14: *hazon*).

Consequently, for the first time since the days of Jeremiah the men of Jerusalem interested themselves in world politics. Writing toward the end of Persian rule, the editor of Ezra-Nehemiah confused the succession of Persian kings, and in Daniel's tales, Darius the Mede succeeds Belshazaar of Babylon and is followed by Cyrus the Persian; but the author of the vision in Daniel 11 gives us a precise outline of the Seleucid-Ptolemaic struggle in which every apocalyptic allusion corresponds strictly to historical facts. It is remarkable that a thorough knowledge of contemporary secular history could have been expected from readers in Seleucid Jerusalem.

FIFTEEN

The Kingdom of the North

A NTIOCHUS III renamed the conquered Ptolemaic province of Syria and Phoenicia "Coele-Syria and Phoenicia," frequently abbreviated to "Coele-Syria." Also, the province was no longer called a "strategy," but a "satrapy." A governor-general, called a *strategos,* was the administrative head of the province as well as in command of the troops. The management of fiscal affairs was entrusted to an "intendant of revenues." The *strategos* was a personage of considerable importance in the Seleucid hierarchy (there were only about thirty satrapies in this immense empire, which extended from the Hellespont to the Indian Ocean) and thus ancient historians have preserved the names of six governor-generals of Coele-Syria and Phoenicia for the period from 200 B.C.E. to the death of Antiochus IV Epiphanes in 164. The first of these was Ptolemy, son of Thraseas, a general formerly in the service of Ptolemy IV who had gone over to Antiochus III.

The subdivisions of the satrapy were called "portions" *(merides).* The governor of the portion of Samaria, which probably included Judea and Galilee as well, had the title of "chief of the portion" *(meridarches).* These districts were further divided into units called *toparchiai,* or, following the Egyptian usage, *nomoi.* The coexistence of administrative and financial organizations, the former headed by the *strategos* and the latter by the intendant of revenues, created a double line of command. For instance, a letter of Antiochus IV dealing with a Samaritan petition went not only to the appropriate *meridarches* but also to a royal financial agent. The complexity of this bureaucratic machinery appears clearly in the treatment of the requests of the governor-general Ptolemy just mentioned: the decisions of Antiochus III regarding these requests were always transmitted to several local officials who had to cooperate in executing the royal mandate—to two *dioiketai* (financial agents), for instance, on one occasion, and to four agents of the government on two other occasions.

Still, despite its complexity this administrative and fiscal framework managed to regulate a large variety of political units—the Macedonian military colony of Samaria; the graecised settlements like Philadelphia (Amman); the semiautonomous, originally Phoenician cities on the coast, like Acco-Ptolemais; the territories under direct royal administration, like Galilee (but even in Galilee some of the crown lands had a unique status, having been conceded as *dorea,* that is, as a temporary gift to royal favorites like the governor-general Ptolemy); and last but not least, national or tribal bodies, among them "the nation *(ethnos)* of the Jews."

In the ancient world, because each city and each people was considered a particular and peculiar unit, a conqueror had to determine the future of each such unit newly added to his dominions. In general, he confirmed the preexisting position of a city. If the inhabitants of the city had supported the winner in an international and imperial contest, it received its franchises back and sometimes even obtained new privileges. Of course, if the city had resisted long and stubbornly, it was often punished or even sacked. In the absence of explosives, the siege of walled places was a protracted and costly undertaking, and a city's attitude of docility was of great military value. When, in 200, Jerusalem went over to Antiochus III, the conqueror, following the example of his Macedonian predecessors, confirmed and perhaps even extended the privileges of the city.

The text of the charter that Antiochus III granted to the "Nation of the Jews" has been preserved by Flavius Josephus. Considered together with other contemporary evidence, it allows us to delineate the status of Judea under Seleucid domination.

The Seleucid government classified the self-administered units within their realm as *polis, dynasteia,* and *ethnos.* The Jews did not constitute a rajaship *(dynasteia),* subject to a prince, nor a city in the Greek sense *(polis),* a unit governed by magistrates elected by the people, but rather a tribal nation, an *ethnos* in possession of its own territory (in 200 B.C.E. this more or less corresponded to the extent of the Persian province of Judea.) Accordingly, a Jew *(Ioudaios)* was not just a person of the Jewish faith, but a person of Judaic parentage, whose place of origin *(idia, origo)* was legally Judea and not, say, Ascalon or Antioch. This definition also meant that such an individual was obliged to worship the God of Jerusalem, just as an Aetolian in Greece was obliged to revere the Aetolian gods. Therefore, in his charter Antiochus proclaims that "all members of this *ethnos* shall be governed in accordance with their ancestral laws." The reference to ancestral laws was a customary formula in granting privileges to a city or a people, but to the Jews of the time it could only have meant the laws of the Torah. Thus, as in the Puritan Commonwealth of Massachusetts under the charter of Charles I, no extraneous cult was tolerated in Judea. Following the tradition established by Artaxerxes I in 457, Antiochus III endowed the Law of Moses with the status, in Judea, of royal law. As usual in ancient times, the royal charter was declaratory, stating what the old law was and had always been.

To be granted the privilege of living according to its own law implies that the group in question administered its own affairs. And indeed the crown appears to have had neither a permanent agent nor royal troops in Jerusalem. The Jews seem to have settled their own problems, fulfilled their duties to the crown, and above all paid their taxes without any external pressure. Ben Sira tells us that it was the High Priest Simon who fortified the city of Jerusalem against siege, and it is probable that the Jews also manned other defensive works in their territory—the citadel of Beth-zur, for instance, or the tower of Jericho. But when the security of the empire was endangered, or when taxes fell in arrears, the old citadel that overlooked the Temple was garrisoned by royal troops and the commanding officer also charged with fiscal and administrative work. A military presence, it was assumed, would arouse the conscience of the taxpayer.

The preamble to Antiochus' charter shows that the "nation of the Jews" was represented by its "Senate" (*Gerousia* in Greek, probably *zekenim* in Hebrew) and that this body had already been in existence in Ptolemaic Jerusalem. The Seventy sometimes render the Hebrew term "Elders of Israel" as "*Gerousia* of Israel," and the later Hellenistic sources of Josephus represent Moses and Joshua as acting with the advice of the *Gerousia*. The term appears for the last time in a letter ascribed to Judas Maccabeus, but this letter was fabricated around the middle of the first century B.C.E., when the word was no longer in use in Roman Jerusalem. The composition of this body, in either Ptolemaic or Seleucid Jerusalem, is not known; nor do we know how and by whom its members were appointed. We do know, however, that Antiochus exempted the *Gerousia* from some (perhaps all) personal taxes.

The Popular Assembly, gathering in the Temple, continued to function alongside the Senate. In the allusions of Ben Sira, its role appears as important as it is elusive. It would seem that the people acted as judges in cases in which the charge was adultery and in cases in which the legitimacy of children was contested. The utterance of a wise man was sought in the assembly. To be praised there was the goal of the sage, who advised his disciples not to offend the multitude. Under the Ptolemies, Joseph, the son of Tobias, an enterprising demagogue, called the people together in an assembly and manipulated them into sending him to the king as the representative of the Jews. Debates, seem to have been conducted only by the nobles, however, and the multitude restricted to approving or disapproving by clamor. The practice of taking and counting votes, the foundation of Greek constitutional government, seems never to have been introduced in Judea. Flavius Josephus describes the Jewish polity before the Maccabean era as "aristocratic-oligarchic." The only administrative officer of the "nation of the Jews" at that time known to us is the *agoranomos,* the overseer of the market, who by virtue of his position controlled the entire commercial life of Jerusalem, particularly the supply of food. Still, the manner in which he was appointed is unknown.

The most important lacuna in our knowledge of the Jewish polity under the Ptolemies and the Seleucids, however, is our ignorance of the political role of the High Priest. No royal letter is addressed to him until the usurpation of the pontificate by Jonathan in 145–144; the Hellenistic kings, rather, write to the "Nation of the Jews," or address their instructions to some high functionary. Thus, the charter of Jerusalem is in the form of a letter of the king to the governor-general Ptolemy. Yet, in order for Joseph to convene the Popular Assembly to discuss a political question, that is, his being sent to Ptolemy as the representative of the Jews, the permission of the Pontiff was required. And we know, according to Ben Sira, that the High Priest was in charge of the fortifications of Jerusalem. Still, he is not mentioned in the charter of Jerusalem. He is not even mentioned in the mandate of Artaxerxes to Ezra (Ezra 7), although this text deals with the priesthood, sacrifices, and other religious matters. Outside Jerusalem, in the towns and villages of Judea, the local Elders represented the people. We may assume that the organization alluded to in the Book of Judith, a book of the Maccabean period, already existed under the Seleucids. According to Judith, three *archontes* (probably *sarim* in Hebrew) preside over the town of Bethulia and convoke the Elders. The local popular assembly, in which youths and women also took part, ratifies the proposals of these authorities by acclamation.

As a matter of fact, in normal times, as we have noted, a king's interest in his provinces was purely fiscal. The "Nation of the Jews" as a political unit paid a yearly tribute to the crown. In addition to this, Antiochus' charter specifically mentions a "head tax" (a tax on persons, not their property), a "crown tax" (which had originally been a voluntary and occasional gift to the ruler, but which had become a yearly tax), and a salt tax (which may have been another personal impost, or perhaps an obligation upon individuals to purchase a certain amount of salt at a fixed price from the state). Because the charter deals only with those imposts, from which the privileged classes were exempt, no mention of property taxes is to be found in it. Nevertheless, because such levies are mentioned in later Seleucid documents dealing with the "Nation of the Jews" and could hardly have been totally absent in an agricultural economy, we may assume that some kind of tithe was already paid by land-owners under the first Seleucids. Finally, the charter mentions tolls on commodities entering Jewish territory. Supplementary tolls also seem to have been levied at the gates of Jerusalem, although we don't know how these tolls were collected or their amounts. Nor do we know from what sources the expenses of the Jewish government were met.

But neither the Senate of the Jews, nor the molehills of Jerusalem, nor even the little nation itself, was of any importance to the outsider—diaspora Jew or heathen overlord. The Temple took precedence chron-ologically, legally, and psychologically over all these. The worshippers of the God of Heaven had been permitted by Cyrus to return from their captivity for the purpose of rebuilding the Temple on Zion. What was Jerusalem, what were the Jews without the Sanctuary? Speaking of An-tiochus III, Polybius writes that the king subjugated "those Jews who dwelt around the sanctuary called Ierosolyma," and a Jewish author roughly contemporaneous with Polybius introduces his people as "the godly men who dwell around the great Temple of Solomon." Pseudo-Aristeas, an Alexandrian Jew writing at the time of the Maccabean ex-pansion, nevertheless uses only a few lines to describe Judea and Jeru-salem and concentrates on describing the Temple. Antiochus' charter names "in first place" the royal grants to the Temple, bestowed upon it "by reason of piety." In Jerusalem, as elsewhere, the brutal force of the conqueror was checked by the superstitious awe of an alien and unknown deity.

The importance of the Temple in the Holy City is further reflected in the list of fiscal exemptions granted by Antiochus. Such exemptions had already been granted to the entire clergy (priests and Levites) of the Temple—and only to it—by King Artaxerxes in 445 (Ezra 7:24). An-tiochus' grants are more selective. In the first place, he includes a small group of laymen, the Senate of the Jews. Second, although his exemptions still cover the entire priesthood, only two Levitical groups are specifically mentioned: the Temple singers, whose presence was required during the sacrificial service, and the "scribes of the sanctuary" (II Chron. 34:13: *soferim*), that is, the managerial staff of the Temple. Nothing better illustrates the ascendance of bureaucracy in the Hellenistic age than this partiality toward a group that is not even mentioned in Artaxerxes' document. Thirdly, Artaxerxes' exemption covered all taxes, including tolls, whereas Antiochus' exemption, as we have seen, covered only the head tax, the crown tax, and the salt tax.

It is obvious that the formulation of this as well as other benefits granted by the Seleucid king must have been drafted with the participation of Jewish experts. We notice, for instance, that the king does not promise to furnish the fuel for public offerings. The reason for this omission was that the wood offering was a traditional obligation of rich Jewish families in Jerusalem (Neh. 10:35, 13:31). Indeed, we learn by chance (II Macc. 4:11) that Antiochus' charter was secured "through" a certain John, whose son Eupolemus forty years later, in 161, arranged the alliance between Rome and the "nation of the Jews," led by Judah the Maccabean.

As they did in Greek cities, the Macedonian sovereigns sharply distinguished between Jerusalem's secular and sacred financial systems. Unlike pagan sanctuaries, the Temple was not liable to taxation, for the House of the Lord had neither extensive landholdings nor other independent revenues. The Hebrew legislator, while showering emoluments on the clergy, had neglected to provide funds for maintenance of the Temple and the Temple service. In point of fact, Solomon's Temple was originally the royal chapel adjoining the palace of the king, and became the sole legitimate sanctuary of the Chosen People only at the time of Josiah's reformation of 622 B.C.E. Accordingly it was the kings who reigned in Jerusalem who maintained the Temple, and after them their Persian and Macedonian successors were obliged to bear the Temple costs. Darius I built the Sanctuary at his own expense. Antiochus III, however, although he authorized the restoration of the Temple after it had been damaged during the siege of Jerusalem in 200 B.C.E., did not pay the costs of the restoration; he only exempted the necessary building materials from taxes and duties. It was the business of the Jews to provide the wood, stone, and labor; Ben Sira praises the High Priest Simon for completing the repairs of the Temple. It was only in the Maccabean period, between 125 and 88 B.C.E., that the Temple became the beneficiary of a head tax levied on every male of the Jewish confession aged twenty years and over and collected in Judea as well as in the Diaspora.

The Seleucid court fixed the amount of the Temple subvention once and for all. Wheat and salt alone were provided in kind: salt seems to have been a royal monopoly and the wheat, too, could have come from the royal domains in Palestine. For public sacrifices approximately 150 *ephahs* of flour were needed yearly and almost the same quantity was needed for the shewbread, making a total of about 165 attic *medimnoi* (approximately 190 bushels or 6700 liters). The king promised 1360 *medimnoi* of wheat, indicating that in order to produce the required quantity of the "finest flour," the sacred millers of Jerusalem needed an eightfold amount of wheat. As for the salt that was added to every offering, the Temple needed 375 *medimnoi* (approximately 430 bushels or 15,000 liters) yearly.

Further, Antiochus promised to give 20,000 silver drachmas yearly for sacrificial animals, wine, oil, and frankincense. The public offerings required 113 bullocks, almost 1200 head of sheep, 342 *hins* (about 1900 liters or 550 gallons) of wine, and the same quantity of oil yearly. We do not know the price of these commodities in Seleucid Jerusalem, but according to the general price levels at the end of the third century, it appears that the allowance of 20,000 drachmas was quite generous. Taking into account the approximate value of wheat and salt, the royal grant amounted to about 30,000 drachmas or, in the value of metal, about 7500 gold dollars.

Another privilege, conceded perhaps by Seleucus IV Philopator (187–176), was the promise to pay the subvention from the king's own revenues, making the grant independent of the unsteady and fluctuating income from the taxes collected in Judea. The term *syntaxis,* used by Antiochus to describe his grant, shows that it was meant as a permanent contribution and not as an exceptional gift. Thus, under Seleucus IV, and surely under Antiochus IV, the crown continued to defray all the expenses of the sacrificial cult out of its own revenues. In exchange for providing this money, however, the king assumed control of Temple finances and appointed an "overseer of the Temple" who was entrusted with this task. The royal subvention was credited to the special "account of sacrifices."

About 180 B.C.E. this financial arrangement occasioned a conflict between the Temple and the Treasury. The question was whether a surplus that had accumulated in the sacrificial account belonged to the Temple or should be refunded to the king. This legal controversy led to the intervention of Heliodorus, vizier of Seleucus IV, who tried to withdraw the surplus. The Jews naturally saw his attempt as a sacrilegious seizure of Temple funds. In his miraculous chastisement—described in II Maccabees and painted by Raphael and Delacroix—the Christian clergy in 388 and again in 1791 saw a warning to the would-be spoliators of church property.

The intervention of Heliodorus and his miraculous discomfiture was an ephemeral episode. Seleucus IV continued to respect the letter and the spirit of the charter granted by his father and the Holy City, to quote II Maccabees, continued to be "inhabited in unbroken peace." But under Antiochus IV, who became king in 176 B.C.E., Jewish reformers led by the new High Priest, Jason, brother and successor of the pious Onias, convinced the young king to set aside the charter and to introduce new customs contrary to the Torah. The reformers wanted to assimilate: since we separated from the neighboring gentiles, they said, many evils have come upon us. It was this violation of the charter that led first to the religious persecution, then to the Maccabean revolt, and finally to the loss of Judea and Palestine by the house of Seleucus.

PART III

PERMANENCE
AND
INNOVATION

The reign of Seleucus IV Philopator, during which the Temple triumphed over the wiles of Heliodorus—the age of the High Priest Simon and of Ben Sira—was the last peaceful period in the history of Hellenistic Jerusalem. The accession of Antiochus IV Epiphanes in 176 B.C.E. marked the beginning of fundamental changes in Jerusalem. Thus, the historian may stop at this moment to survey the life, manners, and ideology of the Jews at the beginning of the second century, on the threshold of the Maccabean age. It is important to note the innovations of the early Hellenistic age, but it is even more important to note the persistence of the old, for the structure of social life, at least before the Industrial Revolution and the beginning of modern times, changed slowly, indeed almost imperceptibly. Certainly the new is loud, "but a man of understanding remains silent" (Prov. 11:12).

SIXTEEN

The Temple

THE Temple of the Lord dominated Jerusalem physically and spiritually. Towering over all other buildings of the city, it was the sole edifice that struck the eye: the tightly packed houses and narrow streets below the "Temple hill" (I Macc. 13:52) appearing, as pseudo-Aristeas says, like the seats and passages of a tiered theater seen from above.

Built on the ruins of Solomon's Temple, destroyed by Nebuchadnezzar in 586 B.C.E., the sanctuary of Zerubabel covered a small rectangular area approximately 500 feet by 160 feet (150 by 44 meters). A stone wall separated the sacred precinct from the city. A double gateway gave access to an open court surrounded by offices, storerooms, kitchens, chambers for sacrificial meals, and priestly cells, all built into the surrounding wall. A second wall separated this outer court from an inner one in which stood the altar of burnt offerings. Approached by a ramp, the altar, made of unhewn white stones, was approximately fourteen and a half feet (4.4 meters) high and twenty-nine feet (8.8 meters) square. This inner court, it seems, was flushed with water from an underground supply system; the High Priest Simon is praised by Ben Sira for having constructed a reservoir "as big as the sea." (Ancient sources also mention a spring within the Temple precinct, but none has been found to date.) Both courts were bare of growth, to the surprise of foreign visitors; a woodland scene was the usual background of pagan sanctuaries.

Hard by the altar stood the House of the Lord. Although its dimensions are unknown, we do know that its axis was east-west, that its facade was adorned with gold ornaments, and that a curtain covered the entrance. Like Solomon's, this tabernacle was probably divided into three parts: the Vestibule *(Ulam)*, the Holy Place *(Hekal)*, and the Holy of Holies *(Debir)*. Crowns, vases of gold, and other precious offerings were probably deposited in the Vestibule. The table of incense, the table of shewbread, the seven-branched candlestick that burned day and night, and other sacred vessels of gold were placed around the *Hekal.* The Holy of Holies, however, was empty and dark: the Ark of the Covenant, lost when the Temple of Solomon was burned by Nebuchadnezzar, had never been returned to Jerusalem. In the course of time the Sanctuary naturally underwent a few architectural changes—in the beginning of the second century, for instance, the High Priest Simon built a "high retaining wall for the Temple rampart"—but the line of the wall as built at the time of Darius I remained the same until the persecution of Epiphanes.

The Temple was the abode of the Living God. It radiated its holiness over Jerusalem. In the name of the city, "Ierousalem," or "Ierousaleme," Greeks and graecised Jews discovered the Greek root *hieros,* that is, "holy." Eupolemus, around 160 B.C.E., has already asserted that "Hierousalem" had received her name from the Sanctuary, the *hieron.* A Seleucid document shows that the rabbinic classification of the ten degrees of holiness, which begins with Palestine, the land holier than all other lands, and culminates in the most holy place, the Holy of Holies, was essentially known in the days of the High Priest Simon the Just, that is, around 200 B.C.E.

Consequently, it is not surprising that the Jews endeavored to prevent the desecration of the Holy Land by pagan worship. As late as 37 C.E., a Roman army on the march to Petra avoided Judea at the urgent entreaty of the Jews, lest the Roman standards, the divinities of the legions, pollute the land of Israel. Nevertheless, since aliens were not forbidden, even in theory, to live in the land of Israel, they must have been accorded the right to worship their gods there, in the same way that Jews in Alexandria or in Athens had the right to serve the Lord of Jerusalem in those cities. The contradiction is only apparent: Jewish zealots attacked only the public worship of idols, the public display of their might, so to speak. As for Jewish worship in pagan cities, it was a general rule in pagan societies that although aliens needed express permission to erect a temple or altar for the public worship of their deities, private and domestic cults were unhampered. Consequently, the Jewish "prayer houses" in the diaspora and the services there, without sacrifices or divine images, could not offend the pagans.

Jerusalem, however, needed more protection than even the land of Judea because the presence of the Temple made her exceptionally vulnerable to impurity. Neither the Torah nor parallel pagan codes required unconditional ritual cleanliness, that is, ritual cleanliness for its own sake. A Jew might remain in a state of impurity indefinitely, so long as he or she abstained from contact with holy things or hallowed persons. But although ceremonial cleansing was necessary to avoid any defilement of the Tabernacle, a defiled person even after a ritual bath remained unclean until the night and during this period could spread contamination through any contact with people and things. Thus, so that the priests and the pilgrims might not be contaminated, everyone in Jerusalem was obliged to follow the rules of Levitical purity. In the Roman period the clothes of a Pharisee, who certainly may be supposed to have been a ritualist, were considered capable of contaminating a priest preparing to partake of an offering.

To protect the Levitical purity of Jerusalem, Antiochus III issued a proclamation that was posted at the gates of the city and probably at the entrance of the Sanctuary as well. Of the four principal sources of impurity specified by the Torah, three were beyond his control: the leper fell under ordinary police jurisdiction, and pollution through contact with the dead and sexual pollution, including that engendered through childbirth, were not amenable to legislation. It was impossible to prevent birth and death from occuring in Jerusalem, as had been done on Delos, the holy island of Apollo. Thus Antiochus' proclamation was necessarily limited to measures designed to prevent the defilement of the Holy City by an animal carcass. He forbade the breeding in the city of animals unfit for Jewish consumption, as well as the introduction into the city of the flesh of such animals. Only animals permitted for sacrifice were allowed to be slaughtered within Jerusalem. Furthermore, no Jew was permitted to penetrate the altar court of the Temple except after a ceremonial ablution, and no alien was permitted to enter the altar court at all. This last exclusion is not attested in the Torah. It was probably derived from some biblical passage (Exod. 30:20, for example) by some Temple lawyers after Alexander's conquest, when the number of foreigners in Jerusalem had increased. As a matter of fact, the exclusion is problematical, since the Torah obliges the sojourning alien (ger) to offer sacrifices to the God of Jerusalem (Lev. 17:8), but Antiochus probably had tourists in mind.

In Greece, anyone who was ritually clean could, as a rule, enter a temple, even a slave or a stranger. But in the Orient, only the clergy was thought fit to approach the idols; the laity, both native and alien alike, were restricted to the forecourt of the sanctuary. The particularity of Jerusalem was that here only the children of Israel could be ceremonially clean. Because the Law was addressed to Israel alone, the cultic purity of a heathen was of no concern to the Jews. The difference between the Jewish and the pagan view here is striking. For the pagan, sacred enactments only classify and limit the effect of an impurity that is both external and *ex natura,* like childbirth. For the Jew, impurity is solely *ex lege.* As Johanan ben Zakkai said: "Death does not make unclean, nor water make clean. It is a decree of the Sovereign King of Kings." It was for this reason that Paul of Tarsus insisted that guilt is a matter only of law.

Still, all those relegated to the outer court—foreigners, women, and Jews in a state of impurity—were able to follow the ceremonies enacted by the priests from where they stood. The liturgy was performed twice daily, at dawn and at dusk, and consisted of three acts. First, in the Tabernacle before dawn, unseen by the multitude, the priests dressed the oil lamps on the golden candlestick in the Holy Place *(Hekal)* and burned the incense on the golden altar that stood in the same room. Outside in the altar court the Levites sang psalms, among them the last strophe of Psalm 44(43): "Awake, why sleepest Thou, O Lord . . . Arise for our help and redeem us for Thy mercy's sake." Then, on the stone altar in the court, the priests offered the standing holocaust *(tamid)* of a yearling, accompanied by gifts of vegetables and libations of wine. The congregation of male, ritually clean Israelites assembled in the court around the altar served only as mute witnesses of the ceremony, while the priests examined the victim, carried the wood, oil, and spices, and threw pieces of the flesh on the altar. After the libations, at a signal given by priestly trumpets, the Levites again chanted psalms—this time 105:1–16 and 96—while the assembly prostrated itself before the altar. In addition, each day the Levites sang the psalm designated for that particular day: Psalm 92(91) was sung on the Sabbath, followed by Psalms 24(23), 48(47), 82(81), 94(93) and 81(80), in that order, ending with Psalm 93(92) on Friday. The people responded with benedictions. When the service was ended, the priests, descending from the altar, pronounced the priestly blessing (Num. 6:23–26), and the congregation prostrated itself again upon hearing the Name of God thrice pronounced in this passage. In the evening an offering of incense and the lighting of the lamps in the Tabernacle followed the holocaust.

In this description of the daily liturgy as it was performed about 200 B.C.E. we have mainly followed the account of Ben Sira, an eyewitness. What may be surprising to the modern reader is the absence of prayer in any part of the service. The priests at the altar did not pray; in fact, their silence during the complex sacrificial operation impressed pseudo-Aristeas, another eyewitness. The congregation did not pray either; nor were the Levitical songs supplications, but rather hymns of praise to the Lord. The offering of the sacrifice was a sacral action, and like every such action, was self-sufficient. In the covenanted system of daily oblations a prayer would have been superfluous; the priests only supplicated the Deity to accept the gifts of the Chosen People. So long as the Temple stood, the altar atoned for Israel.

Yet already in Ben Sira's time public prayer had been integrated into the sacrificial service. While the fire was consuming the sacrifice on the altar and before the priestly blessing, the people supplicated the Lord with prayer. This collective prayer was a civic prayer, which, like similar

Greek supplications, asked God to grant health, welfare, and a prosperous agricultural year to His people, and to be compassionate toward Jerusalem, His city, and Zion, His abode. The appeal "Hear our voice" concluded the prayer. While the statutory sacrifice was a purely priestly business, "the remnant that has escaped" offered their hearts, just as the pilgrims who came to Zion prayed for the Holy City: "*Shalom* be within thy ramparts" (Ps. 12:6).

We do not know exactly when and how the civic prayer came to be included in the Temple liturgy, but it was the intense apprehension of their unworthiness that led the Jews in postexilic Jerusalem to supplement the daily sacrifice with a special prayer for the protection of the Chosen People. This collective prayer became the nucleus of what today is called the *Amidah* (because it is recited standing), the sole daily prayer for well-being in the synagogal service.

Our sources offer only a few more bits of information about statutory worship in the pre-Maccabean Temple, but it goes without saying that the other ceremonies prescribed in the Torah and later attested for the Herodian Temple were also performed in the period around 200 B.C.E. The Septuagint rendering of Leviticus 23:11 and 15 shows that at this time the sheaf of the first ripe harvest was waved before the Lord on the 16th of Nisan and that the Feast of Weeks was celebrated fifty days later. Further, the Septuagint rendering of Exodus 12:6 suggests that the paschal lamb was sacrificed toward evening and not in the afternoon, as was the practice in the Herodian Temple. But was the Passover lamb eaten by the worshippers in the Sanctuary, as the Torah apparently prescribes and the author of Jubilees demands, or in homes throughout the city of Jerusalem, as was the practice in the first century C.E.? The use of the palm branches *(lulab)* during the Feast of Tabernacles and the procession around the altar are mentioned in the Book of Jubilees. And last, since Hanukkah was originally a new "Feast of Booths" (II Macc. 1:9), the singing of Hallel, which includes Psalms 113–118, on Hanukkah, makes it virtually certain that the same Psalms were already being recited on Sukkot long before the creation of the Maccabean feast.

For the Jews in Palestine, the three festivals connected with the agricultural year—Passover, Pentecost, and Sukkot—were the primary religious events of the year. The proper celebration of these festivals required the direct involvement of laity; on these occasions, the pilgrims ascended to Zion, carrying with them their offerings and tithes and bringing trade and life to the Holy City. It is possible that the messages from Jerusalem to the dispersion calling for the celebration of these holy days outside the Holy Land had been sent out even in the pre-Maccabean period, but the custom is not attested before 145 B.C.E.

Such appeals were necessary because the seasons of Judea did not coincide with the seasons and thus with the agricultural solemnities, of Egypt or of other parts of the diaspora. This climatic difference also explains the difference in attitude toward the Day of Atonement in Palestine and in the dispersion. Outside the legal commandments in the Torah, this fast day is not referred to in the Bible and is hardly mentioned at all in early Hellenistic sources. The reason for this lack of comment was that the celebration of this holiday was part and parcel of the institutional Temple worship, that is, it was a priestly matter. The participation of the people in the ceremonies of the day was, so to speak, negative: they observed a fast and refrained from working. Accordingly, the story of Ezra (Neh. 8–9), which evolves outside the Temple and its sacrificial apparatus, passes over the tenth day of Tishri. And when the author of Jubilees, in a very Greek manner, wants to give a historical explanation for this day of fasting, he says that the day of affliction commemorates Jacob's sorrow upon hearing of the disappearance of Joseph. As this explanation shows, the Palestinian author did not attach much importance to the biblical day of expiation. It was, rather, in the diaspora that *Yom ha-Kippurim* became the most solemn day of the religious calendar.

Deprived of the sacrificial cult that daily redeemed their brethren in Jerusalem, the dispersion clung all the more to the "Fast," as they called the Day of Atonement, for obtaining the yearly expiation of their daily transgressions. The Septuagint, forcing the meaning of the Hebrew text (Lev. 23:28), already states that this day, by itself, "expiates you." In the Greek translation of Isaiah 1:13, made in the first half of the second century B.C.E., the Day of Atonement is called "the Great Day." On this day, when even a humble layman felt the presence of the Almighty, some Jews at Delos in the second century B.C.E. appealed to the Deity to avenge the blood of two murdered children. In this way the "Sabbath of Sabbaths," as the Septuagint literally renders the Hebrew formula (Lev. 16:31), became for the Chosen People outside the Holy Land the foremost day of awe.

Let us now return to Jerusalem and the Temple. Beside the statutory sacrifices, there were "many myriads," as pseudo-Aristeas says, of sacrifices offered by individual worshippers, and occasionally even one by the entire Jewish polity. For instance, when the Seleucid vizier Heliodorus came to despoil the Temple treasury, a service designed to avert the danger was held, and after Heliodorus' failure, a service of thanksgiving. Finally, the High Priest celebrated an office of expiation for the repentant Heliodorus. Moreover, because voluntary public and private sacrifices were necessarily accompanied by prayers stating the occasion and meaning of the offering, in this context the Temple could be called a "House of Prayer for all peoples" (Isa. 56:7).

The burnt offering on behalf of the pagan overlord, apparently made daily, was from the point of view of Jewish sacral law a voluntary (or votive) sacrifice. For the royal government, however, this holocaust and the prayer for the sovereign that accompanied it expressed the recognition of the pagan king as the legitimate ruler of the Chosen People.

Traders selling animals fit for sacrifice and ritually clean vessels for sacred meals, moneychangers, butchers, cooks, and other auxiliary personnel roamed the outer courts of the Temple and gave them the aspect of an oriental bazaar. No one took exception to this traffic, for every renowned sanctuary, whether in Greece or in the Orient, was also a center of trade. Every temple was both slaughterhouse and eating place, a condition inseparable from the sacrificial system. (It was miraculous, as the rabbis later contended, that no woman ever miscarried because of the smell of the roasted animals and that the sacrificial flesh never stank.) Yet except for a few Greek philosophers no one was disgusted by this atmosphere of butchery, neither Socrates nor Jesus. It was the Roman Emperor Titus who in 70 C.E., by destroying the Temple of Jerusalem, put an end to the bloody sacrifices of the Jews and the Christians and thus eventually to paganism itself. He was certainly the greatest religious reformer in history.

SEVENTEEN

Priests and Levites

T
HE TEMPLE was God's dwelling place. Here He was ministered to by His priests—all male descendants in the line of Aaron, Moses' brother, and thus direct descendants of Levi, Jacob's son. Aaronites alone were qualified to officiate at the altar and in the Tabernacle. Their status was hereditary and immutable. Although a physical defect made an Aaronite unfit for ministering, it did not deprive him of the right to eat "the bread of his God"—the hallowed food of sacrifices and offerings. Because rabbinic jurisprudence recognized that even a schismatic priest continued to belong to the hereditary order of Aaron's sons, the utmost care was taken to keep the lineage pure. A priest could marry only a virgin or a widow. When Ezekiel further restricted the choice among widows to the widow of a priest, he was emphasizing the intention of the restriction. As Jacob advises Levi in the Testaments of the Twelve Patriarchs, a priest's wife has to be a Jewess without blemish or pollution.

Despite the hereditary nature of the priesthood, an act of investiture was required to qualify an Aaronite to approach the Lord and serve in His house "as the Angels of the Presence and the Holy Ones officiated in heaven," to quote Levi's testament. The Torah does not state and the sources of the early Hellenistic period do not indicate at what age a priest was consecrated, however.

The priests (and Levites) were divided into "courses," which attended to the liturgic service of the Temple and which changed each Saturday. Each course was formed from members of a separate clan that supposedly descended from a common ancestor; the Maccabees, for example, were accounted as belonging to the children of Joarib. As for the number of clans, it is given as twenty-two in the list in Nehemiah 12 and twenty-four in I Chronicles 24 and in later accounts. Each clan in turn was divided into several families ("fathers' houses"), the number of families in each clan, according to rabbinic tradition, varying between five and nine.

The priest was indispensable to the Jewish polity. He alone could perform the ceremonies of public worship upon which the existence and welfare of the society depended. He alone mediated between the individual worshipper and Heaven. For example, although the sacrificial victim might be slaughtered by the individual bringing the offering, only the priest was qualified to sprinkle the blood of the victim on the altar. The priest also heard confessions of guilt and trespass and made atonement according to the sin. But while in the oriental cults, in Babylonia for instance, the clergy was organized into numerous groups of specialists, the officiating priests of Jerusalem formed a single body. Further, even if the ministers of the Sanctuary were "holy" to God, God also demanded holiness of the entire Chosen People: "You shall be holy, for I, the Lord your God, am holy" (Lev. 19:2). Thus the distinction between the clergy and the laity in Israel was not the same as in Babylonia; the priest of the Lord had no particular standing aside from his liturgical functions in the Temple and wore his consecrated garments only during his ministrations.

The primary reason for the ascendancy of the priesthood in the Hellenistic period was the tendency of Macedonian rulers to distrust the secular aristocracy of the conquered peoples. The result was that the native clergy, who could be neither eliminated nor displaced, became the leading privileged group among the native populations and their natural spokesmen. In the eyes of the Ptolemies, the Egyptian priestly synods represented the Egyptian people; in Persian and then Seleucid Babylonia, too, the temples were the centers of privileged native groups. Among the laity in Jerusalem, only the members of the Senate were exempted from personal taxes by Antiochus III, while the same privilege was granted to the entire priestly caste. Although they curtailed the political and economic privileges of oriental sanctuaries, the new rulers bestowed riches and honors on the native clergy. This union between native altar and alien throne can be illustrated by the history of the High Priests of Jerusalem.

In the Torah, the High Priest is only "chief among his brethren" (Lev. 21:10), and his privileges, even according to later jurisprudence, are minimal, such as the right of choosing his portion of a sacrifice; we don't even know whether he possessed any disciplinary power over the rest of the clergy. As late as 408 B.C.E., as the Jews of Elephantine saw it, the "*kahana rabba* and his associates, the priests who are in Jerusalem" formed the collective leadership of the Sanctuary. The temples of late

Babylonia were similarly headed by a "big brother" and by the other priests who were his "fellows." Accordingly, in the Persian period, the chief priest of the Temple of Jerusalem was only the "governor" *(nagid)* of the House of the Lord (II Chron. 31:13).

The new lofty station of the High Priest is first marked when he, alone, is awarded the right to be anointed with the sacred oil (an act that confers a state of holiness upon the one anointed). According to Exodus 30:30, all the sons of Aaron were to be consecrated with the sacred oil, but by 520 B.C.E. the High Priest was the only anointed one among the clergy, just as the king was the only anointed one in the secular realm (Zech. 4:14). The result was that the requirements assuring the holiness of the High Priest necessarily became more stringent. While the Law permitted him to marry any "undefiled virgin" (Lev. 21:13), the Septuagint limited his choice to his own kin. The Septuagint (Lev. 4:3) also uses the Greek title *archiereus* for the words "anointed priest" in the original Hebrew. This term was used by the Greeks for the head priests of the Egyptian and Phoenician sanctuaries as early as the fifth century B.C.E. (it corresponds to *kahana rabba* in Aramaic terminology); around 300 B.C.E., Hecataeus is already using it for the spiritual leader of the Chosen People. Hecataeus also makes him the mediator between the Lord and Israel, but he was mistaken on this point. Interested in the comparative study of religions and thinking in abstract sociological terms, Hecataeus bestowed the prerogatives of an oriental *archiereus* on the High Priest of Jerusalem. In fact, some fifty years after Hecataeus, the Septuagint still does not indicate that any particular sanctity attaches to the *kohen hagadol,* as the chief priest of the Temple is sometimes called in the Torah (Num. 35:25, for instance). Indeed, this title is still used for him by Ben Sira.

Nevertheless, although it appears that the "Great Priest" of Jerusalem was not held in awe as a living symbol before Ben Sira's generation, Ben Sira needed eleven poetical figures to describe the effects of the High Priest's appearance at sacred ceremonies and compared him with the shining sun. The author of the Testament of Levi, in his turn, imagined that the angels themselves had put the vestments of the Pontiff on Levi and had consecrated him. Each part of this garment acquired a symbolic value—the outer robe, for instance, symbolizing truth. And although the Torah confers on any priest the authority to interpret the Law (Deut. 33:10), and although even for Malachi (2:7), that is, in the Persian period, any priest could be a messenger of the Lord, Ben Sira reserved this role for the High Priest alone (45:17).

The supremacy of the house of Zadok in Jerusalem is a matter of history, not of law. It is a historical fact that the pontificate remained in the same family for eight centuries: the pedigree of the Oniads in Seleucid Jerusalem began with Zadok, High Priest under David, and the first High Priest of the Second Temple was Jeshua, a grandson of Seraiah, the last Pontiff of the First Temple. When the legitimacy of Zion was challenged by the schismatics at Shechem, the unbroken succession of the Zadokite High Priests in Jerusalem was offered as the main proof of the sanctity of God's House in Jerusalem. Foreign overlords came and went, but in the Holy City a Zadokite continued to protect and lead the Chosen People. As Ben Sira says, although God gave kingship to David for two generations only, He established the seed of Aaron forever. No wonder that in the eyes of Ben Sira and his contemporaries pontifical dignity ranked above royal title: "As the heaven is higher than the earth, so the priesthood of God rises above earthly kingship; except if, because of sin, it is cast off by God and lorded over by earthly kingship."

Two generations later, the princely Maccabean High Priests and the Roman rulers placed the Pontiff at the head of both Judea and the dispersion. Philo believed that the High Priest had monarchically ruled the Jews at the time of Ptolemy II, around 260 B.C.E., and Josephus, concurring, asserted that the Jews had been ruled by the High Priests until the rise of the Hasmonean dynasty. In II Maccabees, the history of the Holy City itself is presented as conditioned by the conduct and character of the successive Pontiffs.

This view of the pontificate, docilely accepted by modern scholars, is anachronistic. The High Priest of Jerusalem was neither the head of the state, as were the spiritual dynasts in Syria and Asia Minor, nor even the master of the Sanctuary. Nor was the Jewish polity a "church-state." In the Seleucid charter, the "nation of the Jews" is represented by the Senate— the High Priest is not even mentioned. As late as 124 B.C.E., when the Maccabean High Priest John Hyrcanus was in power, festival messages were still being sent out in the name of "the brethren in Jerusalem and Judea," with no reference at all to the reigning Pontiff.

In the controversy about the legitimacy of Zion submitted to the decision of Ptolemy VI, the parties involved were only "the inhabitants of Jerusalem and Judea" and the Samaritans; in the Book of Judith, written in the second half of the second century B.C.E., authorization to use sanctified victuals for secular purposes is requested only from the Senate of Jerusalem.

As we have noted, foreign overlords tended to favor the native clergy for reasons of policy. They favored the native High Priests particularly for the simple reason that the heads of the clergy were appointed by the king. On his side, a Levitical High Priest had every reason to side with an overlord who kept David's seed out of the way and thus left the

Zadokites without rivals in Jerusalem. Moreover, as we have also noted, the High Priests, at least under the Ptolemies, were responsible for collecting the royal taxes in Judea. It is significant that Joseph the Tobiad denounced the tax operations of the High Priest Onias II in order to damage his alliance with the Ptolemies. Let us add that the tax farming of the Oniads must have made them the richest house in Jerusalem, and that wealth, royal favor, hereditary prestige, and the sacredness of the office combined to win for the High Priests the natural leadership of the Chosen People.

Nevertheless, the memory of the Zadokite pontificates soon faded in Maccabean and Roman Jerusalem. Josephus is already ignorant of the exact history of the Zadokite dynasty in the postbiblical period. He draws on two versions of a list of those who followed the High Priest Joshua, who served under Darius I. Josephus begins his list with a Jaddua who was a contemporary of Alexander the Great, but who is identified by Josephus with the Jaddua in the list of Nehemiah 12:10, who held office around 400 B.C.E. On the other hand, at the end of Josephus' list the apostate High Priest Menelaos, who was not even a Zadokite, appears as a brother of Onias, the last legitimate High Priest. As the falsification benefited the Hasmoneans, who had supplanted the legitimate line in 153 B.C.E., it is probable that Josephus here followed a Hasmonean list. A true list, reconstructed with the aid of the sources Josephus himself used, but avoiding his mistakes, should read as follows:

1. Jaddua (II?), ca. 330 B.C.E.

2. Onias I, ca. 300 B.C.E.

3. Simon I

4. Onias II, ca. 225 B.C.E.

5. Simon II, ca. 217 B.C.E.

6. Onias III

7. Jason

According to Josephus, Eleazar and Manasses held office during the minority of Onias II. We are unable to check this statement, although it is probable that pseudo-Aristeas found the name of Eleazar as a High Priest under Ptolemy II in some Hasmonean source. We do not know anything about Simon I, either. The approximate date of Onias I is furnished by a letter written to him by King Areus I of Sparta. The letter is really a Hasmonean forgery, but the Hasmonean chancellery could probably correctly identify the High Priest who was a contemporary of Areus I. Onias II figures in the story of the tax-farmer Joseph; Simon II is glorified by Ben Sira; and Onias III, Jason, and Menelaos are well known from II Maccabees.

A dethroned dynasty is of interest only to antiquarians. Ben Sira asked God to grant the pontificate to the seed of Simon II forever, but Ben Sira's grandson, writing in Egypt at the time of the Maccabean priest-king John Hyrcanus, omitted the request in his Greek translation of Ecclesiasticus. Still, even at this date a Zadokite was officiating at the temple in Leontopolis in Egypt. But Leontopolis was not Zion.

Nevertheless, Simon II was enshrined in Pharisaic tradition and afterward in rabbinic tradition as well. The Pharisees first appear in history toward the end of the second century B.C.E., but it is not until about a century later that, in the fashion in which the Greeks noted the succession of masters within a philosophical school, the Pharisees constructed a genealogy of the masters of *their* school in the form of a chain of tradition that linked them to the biblical age. They made it clear that the deposit of faith given to Moses on Sinai had been handed down ultimately to Hillel and Shammai—not to the Sadducees, or to the Essenes, or to the sectarians of the Dead Sea.

According to the Pharisees, the first link between the biblical prophets and themselves was the mysterious body called *Anshe Kenesset ha-Gedolah*, "The Men of the Great Assembly." The formula seems to refer to some general convocation, as when Simon the Maccabee was honored "on Elul 18th . . . in a great gathering of priests and people." The "Great Assembly" may perhaps have been a council called by a Ptolemaic king, a gathering somewhat similar to assemblies of the Egyptian clergy. The next link is Simon the Just, who apparently is the High Priest Simon II, and who is described as one of the "survivors" of the "Men of the Great Assembly." His role in the Pharisaic list requires comment. Why under the Hasmonean High Priests should the Pharisees appeal to the authority of a Zadokite High Priest and make him their spiritual ancestor? Neither the saying attributed to him by the Pharisees nor the anecdotes about his piety—for instance, his opposition to the Nazarite vow—helps us to understand his position in the Pharisaic chain of tradition.

Yet, a guess is possible. Simon II was the last Zadokite High Priest whose authority was indisputable. Onias III was involved in the power struggle under Antiochus the Persecutor; Jason, his brother, apostatized; and Onias IV was a schismatic who founded a temple in Egypt. By claiming Simon II as their predecessor the Pharisees were guaranteeing the reliability of their tradition. Accordingly, they and, as it seems, they alone, gave to Simon II, and to him alone (besides the biblical saints), the agnomen *ha-Zaddick,* "the Righteous." We remember that the Sect of the New Covenant likewise called its founding Master "Moreh ha-Zaddik."

The minor clergy, however, was not favored in Hellenistic Jerusalem. The Levites, like the Aaronides, were divided into twenty-four "courses" that officiated in rotation. But they were merely assistants "at the side of the sons of Aaron": they slaughtered and flayed the animals to be sacrificed, kept watch at the Temple gates, and performed other similar services. Artaxerxes exempted the priests and the Levites, as well as other Temple servants (including the *netinim,* who performed menial duties), from personal taxes. Two and a half centuries later, Antiochus III rescinded these tax privileges with regard to the Levites and the other minor ranks of the clergy. This action was consonant with the fiscal policies of the Ptolemies and the Seleucids, who sought to lessen tax advantages of both the sanctuaries and the lower clergies. Yet Antiochus makes an exception for the "sacred musicians" and the "scribes of the Temple." The musicians, who are not even mentioned in the Torah as a separate class, originally formed a group inferior to that of the Levites proper. By the time of the Second Temple, however, they had become an honored organization: the Chronicler already counts them among the Levites, and by Antiochus' time they had risen to take the first rank among the Levites. In the true spirit of the Hellenistic age, function now determined social prestige, and by 200 B.C.E. the Temple musicians held the same privileged tax status as that of the Aaronides.

The advancement of the Temple scribes illustrates the same point. This group took no part in the Temple rites (as the musicians did), had no religious privileges, and is mentioned neither in the Bible nor in Artaxerxes' edict. The Chronicler, however, does mention certain Levites who were set over the stores and the treasures of the House of God. These also performed other clerical duties: a Levitical secretary, for instance, compiled the roll of priestly "courses," and a "Comptroller of the High Priest" is also mentioned in Chronicles (he also appears as the treasurer of the Temple in 54 B.C.E.). Clearly the accounting of royal subventions and of the deposits in the Temple required experienced officials. By 200 B.C.E. the secretariat, climbing the social ladder, had attained the third rank in the Temple hierarchy and the same tax exemption as the priests and the sacred musicians. The bureaucratic tendency of the Hellenistic age is exemplified in this promotion.

Yet neither the "scribes of the Temple," nor the Temple singers, nor the Levites in general, constituted a sacred order. Marital restrictions did not apply to the lower clergy and there is no reference to the consecration of Levites. Thus, while in the Persian age Ezra, Nehemiah, the Chronicler, and even Tobit, deal with the Levites, the minor clergy is forgotten by the authors of the Hellenistic age. Even Levi, the common ancestor of the Levites and the sons of Aaron, speaks of his priestly descendants in his testament, but does not mention the Levites. This social degradation of the Levites is in some way connected with their loss of the second tithe (Num. 18:21).

EIGHTEEN

Economic Life

THE Temple dominated not only the panorama of the Holy City but its economy as well. In pre-Maccabean Jerusalem a great part of the city population was still engaged in agriculture. Fields, vineyards, and gardens were the regular sources of livelihood for the Jerusalemites and the raising of cattle, sheep, and poultry also flourished, even within the city walls. When Seleucid soldiers raided Jerusalem in 168 B.C.E., they led captives and cattle away. Spinning for the family was probably still confined to the home and the sound of turning millstones still came from the doorways of individual houses—even though the kneaded dough might be sent to the ovens of the bakers' street.

But beside those who pursued agriculture or home industry, there were also artisans living in the city, those Ben Sira speaks of as people of small means who "rely upon their hands." The carver, the smith, the potter, and the perfumer are specifically mentioned by him and goldsmiths are mentioned in Nehemiah. Other trades, of course, must have existed in Ben Sira's Jerusalem, since it is probable that villagers from outlying areas obtained tools and implements in the city's workshops. The Temple, however, was the greatest single consumer of the products of the artisans' labor. For example, skilled craftsmen were needed for new building projects, such as those undertaken by the High Priest Simon II, or to make the necessary Temple repairs, such as those financed by Antiochus III. Interestingly, the abundance of hides taken from animal sacrifices turned the Temple itself into the most important purveyor of the basic commodity of the leather trade.

Larger industrial endeavors could not flourish in Jerusalem because, except for the excellent building stone and the plentiful leather, raw materials were lacking in Judea; the land possessed no ore, probably no wood, and no superior potter's clay. The industrial centers mentioned in the Bible or later in rabbinic sources were all situated outside the tiny territory of Judea.

Ptolemaic and Seleucid Jerusalem was not a commercial center, either. The international caravan trade that enriched Gaza and Petra bypassed the mountains of Judah. This does not mean, of course, that no foreign traders were to be seen in Judea and Jerusalem. On the way from Strato's Tower (Caesarea), on the northern coast of Palestine, the caravan of Zenon passed through Jerusalem and Jericho, and Ben Sira speaks of Jewish merchants several times and distinguishes them from retail dealers. He also speaks of Jews who sail the sea, while the Epistle of Enoch and the Testament of Naphtali mention Jewish ships on the Mediterranean (which probably sailed from the Greek city of Jamnia [Jabne]). Indeed, the author of the Testaments of the Twelve Patriarchs attributes to Zebulon the invention of the first fishing boat.

Nor was the Holy City a financial center. The gold and silver deposited in Temple vaults were not available for commercial purposes. When Joseph the Tobiad needed a large amount of money to bid on the taxes in Alexandria, he had to turn to his friends in Samaria. In fact, in the early Hellenistic age Jerusalem was still an insignificant, poor town. Although Joseph was able to buy all the equipment for his voyage to the Alexandrian court, including expensive clothing and luxurious drinking vessels (the latter probably imported) in Jerusalem, he still appeared poor and plain to the wealthy Phoenicians who met him on the road. Only after the Hasmonean expansion did Jerusalem, now the capital of the whole of Palestine, become a city "skilled in many crafts," to quote pseudo-Aristeas. Still, the incorporation of Judea into the economic structure of the Ptolemaic Empire did accelerate the exchange of goods and the expansion of trade; it even created a psychology of acquisition, as attested by Kohelet and exemplified by the Tobiads.

The attitude of the Bible toward business activity is determined by the morality of an agricultural society: lending is either usury or an act of charity, and going surety for someone else is foolhardy, as it was in archaic Greece; the garment and the bed of anyone who stands as security will surely be taken from him by the usurer. For Ben Sira, on the other hand, although he is a traditional moralist who distrusts businessmen, a loan is simply a commercial transaction. Nonetheless, he is careful to remind his hearers that many are dishonest and, reckoning a loan as a windfall, have banqueted and built houses on borrowed money. He even warns his hearers not to lend to anyone more powerful than themselves, and completing the thought in the next verse (8:16) he says: "Do not go to law with a judge."

In giving this kind of financial advice Ben Sira is probably thinking of the conditions under which the Ptolemaic system of taxation operated, for elsewhere he also speaks of contractors for public works who fall prey to lawsuits. Under the Ptolemies a person who contracted to farm a tax, or who made any other financial contract with the government, usually acted with partners and had to be secured by bond. Even small investors committed their money to such ventures with the royal government. The problem was that not only were the partners liable if the contractor failed to meet the terms of his contract, but that the creditor could exact the debt from the bondsmen as well. In this way a publican with the right connections was able to crush his small partners and bondsmen while evading his own responsibility.

The countryside was almost exclusively agricultural; after the Seleucid amnesty of 164 B.C.E. the Jews, as II Maccabees states, "devoted themselves to agriculture." Yet we know virtually nothing about the peasant economy of Judea under the Ptolemies and Seleucids. Foreign observers were interested only in the mysterious Temple on Zion, while the intellectuals of Jerusalem, as Ben Sira put it, had no care for people who talked to bullocks and whose thoughts were for fodder and furrows (38:25–26).

Like agricultural societies everywhere (except for those that, like Egypt, relied on irrigation), the Jews depended for their very life on rain. Since rain came only during the winter, storage of rainwater was essential; thus, Kohelet built cisterns. Sowing was done in the fall, hard wheat (siligo), barley, and millet being the principal cereal crops. Agricultural techniques were elementary; fallowing the land every second year, the rotation of crops, and systematic manuring are not attested before the Roman period. We have noted that a water machine (sakiyeh) that came to be widely used in the Hellenistic East seems to be referred to in Ecclesiastes 12:6. It is curious that in Jubilees, Abraham is praised as the inventor of a device that attaches to the plow and scatters seed, since this implement was already known in ancient Babylonia. It is probable that, in order to have so impressed the author of Jubilees, the device must have been introduced in Judea only in the third century B.C.E. We may also note that for this author Abraham's invention is important only because it prevents the birds from devouring the seed (which occurred when the seed was scattered by hand); he ignores any savings in time and labor. In a primitive agricultural society man produces bread by the sweat of his brow.

Another important branch of agriculture was the breeding of cattle and sheep. The needs of the Temple alone should have made animal husbandry profitable in Judea, but evidence about the pastoral economy in early Hellenistic Judea is lacking. We learn only incidentally that when Mattathias and his followers fled to the wilderness in the wake of the persecution of Antiochus IV, they took with them their sons, their wives, and their cattle. We also learn that the Patriarch Judah, according to the Testaments of the Twelve Patriarchs, had a "chief shepherd"—obviously because of the size of his herds. Judah is also a great hunter who not only chases game such as hind and wild oxen and tames a wild horse, but also slays bears, lions, and panthers. He does it partly to protect his flocks and crops—he snatches a kid out of the jaws of a lion and slays a wild ox feeding in his fields—but he also hunts for food: he catches a hind and prepares a meal for Jacob. The enthusiastic description of the joys of the chase in the Testaments tells us that hunting was both a favorite pastime of a citizen of Jerusalem around 200 B.C.E. and an important economic resource. A Seleucid text of 200 B.C.E. indicates that wild asses, panthers, foxes, and hares were to be found in Judea and that panther hides were exported from Ptolemaic Palestine. A contemporary fresco at Marissa pictures a chase of panthers and wild asses.

The cultivation of fruit trees, olive groves, and vines was also a valuable source of income for the agriculturist. But this was an endeavor for which peace was essential. When the enemy came, cattle could be driven to safety; if crops were destroyed, the land could be resown; but fruit trees and vines burned or cut down were lost for a long time. Indeed, the olive tree, which flourishes in the stony soil of Judea, needs some fifteen years of care before it begins to bear its fruit, making the olive branch the most fitting emblem of peace. From the time of Ptolemy I to the time of Antiochus III, that is, for several generations, the olive groves, fig trees, and vineyards of Judea were untouched by war.

Furthermore, in addition to preserving the peace in Judea, the Ptolemies, by incorporating Judea into their economic system, opened a new and ever-expanding market for Judean olives and their oil, for, as we have noted, Egypt did not have extensive olive groves. Alexandria and the Greeks in Egypt had to import the oil they needed. As we have also noted, however, the system of monopolies and the high custom duties imposed by the Ptolemies made the retail price of oil in Egypt three times higher (and sometimes more) than the price in Greece. Thus the export of oil from Palestine was very profitable, particularly as the Ptolemies apparently favored importing oil from their own province of Syria, which included Judea, over importing foreign oil. Moreover, the price ratio between grain, on the one hand, and wine and olive oil on the other, would have made a small vineyard or olive orchard as profitable as a grain field four or five times as large. The Ptolemaic peace, which allowed olive trees and grapevines (which Egypt also lacked then, and still lacks) to take the place of annual crops of cereals, made the thin soil of Judea more precious than ever.

In describing how he acquired more wealth than all the men who had come before him in Jerusalem, Kohelet tells about how he built houses and planted vineyards, gardens, and orchards, and about the water supply in his forest, which was sprouting with trees, and about his great herds and flocks, and about buying and breeding slaves. The era of Ptolemaic security made it possible to say with Ben Sira that whoever tills his land will heap up his harvest, that the green shoots of grain delight the eye, that young cattle and planting make one rich—and that a man who has no home was likely to be a roving bandit!

Philo observed that wealth necessarily follows peace and orderly government, and we see in Judea that the imperial peace also encouraged the growth of the human crop. In addition to the fact that Jews abhorred infanticide and gloried in the number of their children (Hecataeus, about 300 B.C.E., noted that for this reason the Jewish nation was "rich in men"), wars and their accompanying epidemics had ceased and prosperity was reducing undernourishment and improving resistance to disease. It was also the Jews' good fortune that even when the Judean fields withered from lack of rain the produce of Egypt was at hand to feed them.

The statistics of population in preindustrial Europe indicate that in agrarian societies the birth rate was a function of the price of bread and that the annual excess of births over deaths was three times greater after a good than after a bad harvest. Also of demographic importance was the custom of very early marriages, which produced a higher birth rate; the story of Dinah (Gen. 35), as told in Jubilees, shows that in early Hellenistic Jerusalem it was possible for a girl of thirteen to marry without her father's consent, a practice later accepted by the rabbis. On the other hand, it was the Jewish custom to suckle a child for three years, which tended to delay the next birth. Yet despite this limitation, and despite the very high rate of infant mortality and the high death rate of women in childbirth, we may confidently surmise that the century of Ptolemaic peace may well have doubled or even tripled the population of Judea.

Emigration offered an outlet for excess population. When in the last decades of the third century inflation and native rebellions made Egypt less inviting, the vast Seleucid Empire was still wide open to enterprising men. Young men from Greece who were in pecuniary embarrassment or who wished to get rich quickly sailed to serve the kings of Asia or the Ptolemies of Egypt as mercenaries. A "warrior in want through poverty" was a sad abnormality in the eyes of Ben Sira (26:28), and Jewish mercenaries were highly appreciated by kings, who knew, as Menander said, that lands where livelihood comes hard make men courageous. Ben Sira tells us of the well-to-do who, having lost their land, went abroad, and Issachar in his Testament speaks with horror of those who, impelled by evil desires, abandon husbandry in the Holy Land and are dispersed among the nations and serve them.

On the other hand, mercenaries who did make something of themselves, as well other emigrants who made money in the diaspora, often returned to the Holy Land to spend the rest of their lives there. By 200 B.C.E. the diaspora had begun to make Jerusalem its world center. The stream of pilgrims that brought "myriads" of Jews to Judea in the time of the Caesars had only begun to flow in the days of Ben Sira. But if Jason and Menelaos, around 175 B.C.E., outbid one another in soliciting the pontificate, there must have been profits to be made in Zion even earlier.

The priestly caste constituted the hereditary aristocracy of Hellenistic Jerusalem. Antiochus III, and probably before him the Ptolemies, granted tax exemptions to all the priests. Yet their economic status did not correspond to their social position. The Torah (Deut. 18:2, Num. 18:20) explicitly refrains from allotting to the clergy a portion of the Holy Land, leaving them in a position very different from the revenues of sacred estates. The priesthood in Jerusalem was, rather, to be provided for out of the dues of the individual worshippers. Thus the priests in Jerusalem, like the priests of all ancient religions, were assigned a share of all sacrificed animals (except those of the holocausts and of some sin offerings); they received, for instance, the breast and the right foreleg of each peace offering. Likewise, the flesh of the firstborn unblemished male animal, a mandatory sacrifice, fell to the priest, as did the cereal oblation, only a small portion of which had to be burned on the altar. There were also some fees paid in silver, for instance the ransom of the firstborn son.

Yet the number of Zadokite priests grew so great that in Hellenistic Jerusalem they were divided, as we have noted, into twenty-four courses, which meant that each course served in the Temple for only two turns of one week each. Thus an individual priest could count on only some fifteen dinners containing meat a year. For the rest of the year the main source of priestly revenues were agricultural levies: a part of every loaf of kneaded dough *(hallah)* and a tithe of every agricultural produce of the soil, as well of every increase in flock and herd.

In this archaic system of dues, tailored originally to the conditions of life in a small agricultural community with local altars and local priests, neither property as such nor income other than that derived from farming and animal husbandry was taxed. The clergy was therefore dependent upon the contributions of that particularly sluggish and unwilling taxpayer, the agriculturist. Issachar surely brought his first fruits to the Lord punctually, but had such practice been common, the author of the Testaments of the Twelve Patriarchs would not have added that Jacob rejoiced in the rectitude of his son. Nor would Ben Sira and the author of Jubilees have needed to insist that the tithe should be given cheerfully and that first fruits be delivered in full measure. In fact, the clergymen themselves were compelled to go from one threshing floor to another in order to collect their tithes. Although we learn from the Book of Judith that at Bethulia the first fruits of grain and the tithes of wine and oil were stored to be sent to Jerusalem, this innovation, like the rule that every priest was qualified to share in the priestly meals, favored the priests of the Holy City over priests living in the country such as the Maccabean family in Modiin. Only priests living in Jerusalem could sustain themselves in affluent circumstances; only priests permanently attached to the Temple administration, say, for the preparation of incense or as treasury officials, could become rich. The economic division of the clergy was not without importance for the history of Jerusalem: the fat prebendaries of the Temple favored Greek ideas in the time of Antiochus Epiphanes, while the Maccabees were country priests.

Nevertheless, when Ben Sira speaks of the powerful men in Jerusalem, he is not thinking of the clergy: the "lords" (mostly *sarim* and *nadibim* in Hebrew, *megistanes* and *dynastes* in Greek; both sets of terms used synonymously) are laymen. A wise man should learn to serve them (8:8) and show deference to them (4:7, 13:9, 20:27, 23:14, 32:9), but one should also be prudent in dealing with them (8:1), for they can sway justice (20:28, 7:6). Wise rulers *(sarim)* make the city habitable (10:3). When the moralist speaks of a skillful physician (38:3), he stresses that the art of the healer wins him the admiration of the *nadibim*. When Ben Sira addresses his instructions to the "grandees" *(megistanes)* of the people and the leaders of the Popular Assembly (33:18), we cannot doubt that he means the members of the Senate and their families who ruled Seleucid and, in all probability, even Ptolemaic Jerusalem.

For Ben Sira, the middle class is the class of craftsmen, who undoubtedly had their workshops and retail shops in one or another of the bazaars of the Holy City. Ben Sira speaks with respect of these artisans. Although they are not to be found on the judge's bench, they do take part in the Popular Assembly, and although completely absorbed in their work, it is they who maintain the fabric of the world (38:33). Paraphrasing Proverbs 21:17, Ben Sira (19:1) warns that a worker who is a drunkard will not become rich, a commonsense adage that, however, implies that a sober worker *will* be rich. As for the intellectual class, all we learn is that physicians, of course, have their fees; we learn nothing about the economic situation of Ben Sira himself and his peers.

We have no specific information, either, about the economic status of farmers, the backbone of a rural economy. Nevertheless, even without the Testaments of the Twelve Patriarchs we would have known that in the early Hellenistic age the peasant, like Issachar, whom Scripture (Gen. 49:14) already calls a servant burdened with taskwork, continued to bend his back and toil in the field. No wonder that in the new economy, which opened easier ways to success, many peasants abandoned husbandry. It is this situation that Ben Sira has in mind when he warns against abandoning toil and agriculture (7:15).

With regard to the poor, the Torah tells us that the poor shall never cease out of the land (Deut. 15:11), and solicitude for them is demanded in the Law. No wonder that Ben Sira, a pious moralist, after speaking of the dues owed to the priests adds an appeal for generosity to the poor (7:32) and often reminds his hearers to help the poor "for the commandment's sake" 29:9. He is naturally horrified by a man who cheats a worker of his wages (32:22) and, in agreement with Testaments of the Twelve Patriarchs (T. Ash. 2:5), indignantly condemns one who offers sacrifices from the possessions of the poor (34:20).

Appeals to aid the poor were not new in Jerusalem; from Amos on, the prophets in Israel preached against greed and inveighed against maltreating the weak and the needy. What was new in Ben Sira's time, however, was a polarization of society that sharply opposed the wealthy oppressors to the needy poor. Ben Sira speaks of the poor as often as of the rich and it is significant that his grandson and translator, as a rule, renders the Hebrew terms Ben Sira uses for "poor" by the Greek word *ptochos,* which means "destitute."

Yet the term "rich" (*ashir* in Hebrew), as Ben Sira uses it, is relative. When he advises his listeners against associating with rich men, and on this occasion refers to the proverbial collision of the iron kettle and the clay pot, he is not speaking of destitute people. This "poor" *(dal)* man is poor only in comparison to the possessor of great wealth and has funds that may be needed by a "rich[er]" man (13:4). Ben Sira is really saying here, as he says elsewhere (27:9), that birds of a feather should flock together.

This salutary advice is followed, however, by an angry denunciation of the rich as such: just as the sinner has nothing in common with the righteous, so there can be no peace between the rich and the poor. A long tirade, in which he uses several Hebrew synonyms to describe the poor, ends with his rewriting Proverbs 29:29, in which the righteous are opposed to the wicked; using the key word of the biblical passage, "abomination," he contrasts humbleness with arrogance, the poor man with the rich (13:20).

The traditional moralist in this case agrees with the frenzied author of the Epistle of Enoch, another writer of the early Hellenistic age. For pseudo-Enoch, too, a chasm separates the rich from the poor; he even condemns slavery as no part of the natural order, but only the result of oppression. He delivers a firey sermon against men of wealth who acquire gold and silver unrighteously, but who, by pretending to be righteous and "by words of error," lead many astray. The rhetoric of Ben Sira and pseudo-Enoch is biblical, but the cool-headed Kohelet also speaks of the tears of the oppressed and of the power of the oppressors.

Nevertheless, neither Kohelet, nor Enoch, nor Ben Sira talks about any specific unrighteous actions; while denouncing traders, Ben Sira merely says that sin "will thrust itself in" between buying and selling (27:2). They do not speak, like the prophets of old, of land grabbing, of hoarding grain, of false weights and measures, or of usury. In Ptolemaic Palestine the *agoranomos* supervised the market of Jerusalem, and a maximum rate of interest was probably established by the Ptolemies in Palestine as it had been in Egypt (where it was fixed at twenty-four percent). As for land grabbing, the high plateau around Jerusalem, rugged and stony as it was and broken into ridges and slopes, was unfit for latifundia. (Of course, the rich men of Jerusalem could and did possess estates outside stony Judea; the Tobiads, as we know, owned large tracts of land on the other side of the Jordan.) Nevertheless, it is true that in the days of Nehemiah the people on this same stony ridge were forced to mortgage and lose houses, fields, and vineyards and to sell their sons and daughters into bondage because of their poverty or in payment of taxes. Under the Ptolemies, as we have seen, it was forbidden by law to buy or to receive free men in pledge. But the Jerusalem of Ben Sira would not have been the first place where such laws were disregarded.

A period of inflation followed by a period of deflation had aggravated the economic situation in Judea. In the last decades of the third century B.C.E. the inflation instituted by the Ptolemies had accelerated. This burden was borne by wage earners and salaried officials, including soldiers, because the adjustment of wages to rising prices was, as usual, slow. On the other hand, the inflation also weighed heavily on landowners. Because credit terms were short (generally one year or less) and the assessments on land were mostly fixed in kind, the Ptolemaic inflation, by disturbing the delicate system of credit, worsened the situation of the debtor in an economy where cash was always scarce. Thus, in 203 B.C.E., a defaulting debtor who was obliged to pay a penalty had to disburse five times more than he would have paid ten years earlier. Of course, in 203 the payment was made in debased silver or in constantly depreciating copper coins. Higher taxes also hit the landowners particularly hard, because they could not hide their property, whereas businessmen could easily conceal their profits. Furthermore, because transactions in silver continued to be legal and because one could demand payment in "old Ptolemaic silver drachmas," businessmen were not touched directly by the inflation.

When Palestine became Seleucid however, in 200 B.C.E., a sudden deflation ensued. Seleucid currency was based on silver, and the Ptolemaic silver drachma of 3.6 grams' weight was worth only five-sixths of the Seleucid (Attic) drachma of 4.3 grams. The economy of the land was still, of course, mainly based on payments in kind, but every valorization of crops now involved a monetary transaction. In the language of the times, the metaphor of the ledger took its place beside the traditional images of testing and weighing.

Still, the wealthy men of Jerusalem could not be blamed for monetary fluctuations imposed by foreign overlords. In fact, wholesale condemnation of the rich denies the axiom of the sapiential writers that God is the maker of both the rich and the poor and that it is diligence that makes one rich (Proverbs 10:4, 10:22, 22:2)—an opinion also shared by Ben Sira (11:14 and 29). In Israel's past, he tells his readers, "men of wealth" were honored in their generations (44:6). Ben Sira's final position is that wealth is good as long as it is not tainted by sin (13:24). (Pseudo-Enoch also attacks those who acquire wealth in unrighteousness.) In a long passage (31:1–11) he makes clear to us what he condemns as folly and sin: *auri sacra fames,* to speak with Vergil—the unending and accursed hunger for gold, that limitless avarice Plato regarded as Levantine, but which actually the Greeks had brought with them to the conquered East.

In the oriental society of the Hebrew prophets or, for example, the Egyptian sages, rank and wealth had been static and had imposed upon those who possessed them the moral obligation of comforting the weak and the needy and assisting the widow and the orphan. Even in the individualistic society of the *polis,* if mutual self-help was unavailing or unavailable, condescending charity was. In Hellenistic Jerusalem, however, rich and poor were no longer permanently fixed in their places in a social complex governed by reciprocal rights and duties. Hereditary rank and wealth had been replaced by new plutocrats who cared for nothing but money. It was money that now conferred power and nobility; in the new society of avarice and social mobility, wealth and power appeared merely as the transitory attributes of individuals. The difference between rich and poor was now only quantitative, for which reason it was even more burdensome and irritating. In Athens in 316 B.C.E., a character in Menander's *Dyskolos* calls a rich landowner "generous" because he talks on equal terms with a landowner of only moderate means. Some fifty years later, Callimachus, the court poet of Ptolemy II, praises Sosibios, an influential courtier, for being friendly with men of lower rank, a rare attitude seen only in a wealthy man whose soul was superior to his social position.

In Jerusalem, Ben Sira advises his hearers that just as they should show deference to a powerful man, so should they incline their ears to a poor man (4:7–8). Ben Sira, who is more optimistic than Kohelet (9:16), is sure that the poor man *(dal)* who is full of wisdom will be honored (1:23, 10:30, 11:1), and he says the same about the clever slave (10:25). The haughty poor man, however, is named among the three kinds of men who arouse his anger (25:2).

Nevertheless, in this rocky land of Judea, where riding on horseback was a mark of wealth but stubble was used as fodder, in a society where clans and clanship had disappeared, a neighbor who got rich quickly was a mote in the public eye. When poor men had to huddle together to keep warm in the winter night—"How can one get warm alone?" (Koh. 5:11)—great wealth was both provocative and overwhelming: "Do not curse the king in thy thought nor the rich even in your bedchamber, for a bird of the air may carry your voice" (Koh. 12:20). The contemporaries of Kohelet and Ben Sira were not the first to worship the Golden Calf, but now they danced around him in the new, Hellenistic manner of an acquisitive society. (On this topic, however, we refer the reader to our *Four Strange Books of the Bible*.)

Slaves stood on the lowest rung of the social ladder; consequently our information about them in early Hellenistic Judea is very poor. We may believe, however, that the institution of temporary bondage for debt, still attested in the time of Nehemiah—Nehemiah protested against the selling of Jews to their Jewish "brethren"—became extinct afterwards. Such civil bondage is never mentioned either in Hellenistic sources or in those of the Roman period, except in theoretical discussions of the relevant biblical laws by the rabbis. It seems that imperial peace, by improving the economic situation in Judea, made the very idea of debt servitude obsolete.

In Hellenistic Judea the demand for slaves, the articulate instruments of production in the ancient world, could now be satisfied by the supply of foreign slaves who, as the absolute property of their masters, were not protected, as were Jewish bondsmen, by scriptural law, jurisprudence, and public opinion. There were consequently no sons or daughters of Israel among the slaves of a Jewish master, yet, because slaves mostly accepted the faith of their masters, there were numerous slaves who were Jews by religion. Such slaves were probably household servants; female slaves, of course, were often also concubines of their masters. Ben Sira (41:22) advises his students that if they want to live in peace, they should not covet another man's wife and should keep away from the bed of a slave girl. The role of slaves in husbandry and crafts remains obscure, although men such as the husband of Judith (who had numerous slaves), or Kohelet, undoubtedly used their slaves for tilling the soil and tending the gardens, as well as in other productive occupations.

Like Aristotle, Ben Sira believed that food, work, and punishment were all a slave needed. Chains, collars, and whips subdued the stiff-necked slave; instruments of torture awaited the evil one. Even the sweet Sarah in the Book of Tobit scourged her maid in anger. As Ben Sira says, the hands of a slave should never be idle, or from too much idleness he will seek his freedom. Still, he frowns upon any excessively inhuman treatment, even if only out of self-interest—such treatment would cause the slave to run away. Accordingly, he advises the slave owner not to abuse a good worker. When he observes that free men will be at the service of a clever slave and that a man of understanding will not grumble about it, we remember the clever slaves of Greek comedy. We also remember that a slave was the trusted agent of the Tobiads in Alexandria and that a female slave of Judith's was in charge of her inherited wealth. Our sources offer no information on the private lives of slaves, except for the incidental passage in the Testaments that tells us that when selling Joseph, his brothers put a "slavish" garment on him (probably the *exomis* of the Greek slave, a tunic that was either sleeveless or had only one sleeve).

The attitudes we have noted are common to all slaveholding societies. A famous and instructive, although always mistranslated, saying of Antigonus of Socho, a younger contemporary of Ben Sira, shows, however, that around 200 B.C.E. the new economic forces and the intensified greed of the period began to destroy the traditional relationship between master and slave and to make the exploitation of slaves not only profitable but acceptable to the public. Antigonus speaks of the kind of men who serve God as "slaves who minister to their masters in expectation of receiving their regular food rations." This simile indicates that food, one of the three things, according to Aristotle and Ben Sira, that it is necessary to supply in order to assure obedient slaves, was distributed in Jerusalem, as in Greece and Rome in the same period, in a measured, probably monthly, allotment *(demensum)*. This is significant. In a patriarchal economy the slave ate with his master; for this reason the slave of a priest was qualified, according to the law, to partake of sacred offerings, something forbidden to the free Israelite layman. The system of food allowances that Antigonus refers to, however—a system that came to be customary even in small households—raised a barrier between master and slave and made the exploitation of the latter all the easier. Meat and wine were now served to the master only, while the standard ration for slaves was barley. To these slaves who worked for the sake of their rations, the sage contrasted those who attended their masters *without* expectation of rations—and he exhorted his disciples to fulfill the Law in the manner of the latter.

To understand Antigonus' simile we have to realize that the slave is a "permanent hireling," as the Stoic philosopher Chrysippus defined him, and that his maintenance, as Aristotle had already pointed out, represents his wages. Just as the entrepreneur seeks to reduce the salary of his free workers in hard times, in every slaveholding society, ancient and modern, masters in a time of scarcity tried to diminish the food allowance of their slaves, even at times to withhold it altogether. In the Hellenistic age the Stoics debated whether a gentleman was morally bound to feed his slaves when food prices were high. Several centuries later the rabbis, in a similar manner, discussed whether a master could say to a slave, "Work for me, although I will not support you." Under such a system, the slave would have either to earn his living by working for himself in his free time, or he would have to depend on charity.

In a Jewish household that observed the Sabbath, a slave who was fed for seven days but who worked for only six, by virtue of this fact alone could have been more costly than free help hired by the day. Moreover, slaves who did not work hard were not worth the bread they ate. Indeed, until the coming of a consumer society, the same rule was also valid for the free workman; as the Apostle Paul put it, "If any would not work, neither should he eat." Nevertheless, as Aristotle also pointed out, to make a slave work without feeding him would be oppressive and exhaust him. Such exploitation, of course, violated the moral basis of slavery, since security was the slave's sole compensation. The Stoic Epictetus, himself a former slave, pictures a manumitted slave who, having to earn his living, is nostalgic for the time when his master kept him clothed, shod, fed, and tended in sickness.

Yet slaves continued to hope for freedom, and Ben Sira advises the slave owner not to deprive a good servant of his. Some fifty years later, Judith allows her faithful maid to go free. It is curious that the voluntary emancipation of slaves is never attested in the Bible; however, Jews in Egypt who lived according to Aramaic common law did manumit slaves.

In a predominantly rural society the hireling is landless, and although legally free lives on a slave level without enjoying the slave's security. Ben Sira talks of them both in the same couplet (7:20), advising a master not to ill-treat either the slave who works faithfully or the hired servant who puts his heart and soul into his work. In another passage a lazy slave and a sluggish hireling are again considered side by side (37:11).

NINETEEN

Scribes and Sages

ETWEEN and beside the nobles and the common people there had always existed groups of technological experts whose power was based on knowledge. For Homer, the healer was more worthy than other men, and from time immemorial the knowledge of ritual techniques had made the priest and the sorcerer influential. In Hellenistic Jerusalem, also, the physician's skill, as Ben Sira says, lifted up his head. Honored by the grandees, the physician was rewarded by the king as well. "Royal" doctors and governmental medicine are well attested in Ptolemaic Egypt, and it seems that the Macedonians introduced the same organization into Palestine. Although it sometimes happened that the more medicines the physician used the worse the patient became, nevertheless Ben Sira expressly advises his audience to resort to a doctor's help—since his knowledge is of God (38:14).

The priest was the professional man of the Torah. "Listen to Levi, because he will know God's law," Levi (quoting Hosea) says to his posterity in the Testaments of the Twelve Patriarchs; "The light of knowledge shalt thou light up in Jacob." For Ben Sira, this meant that it was the prerogative of the Aaronides to teach the divine ordinances to Jacob (45:17) (a privilege, unfortunately, that the priests could and did abuse; the author of the Testaments reproaches them for teaching commandments contrary to the ordinances of God). This does not mean, of course, that the priests taught the Scripture to laymen, only that laymen were to go to the priests for opinions and decisions in legal and ritual cases.

As soon as the conditions of life became more complicated, however, to find right even "between blood and blood and between stroke and stroke" the technical knowledge of a jurist was required. Indeed, the time had come when expert opinion was necessary even with regard to purely ritual controversies. When the Torah says "You shall not eat any flesh that is torn of beasts in the field" (Exod. 22:30), a question immediately arises about the flesh of an animal killed by beasts or birds of prey in town. The priest, however, was essentially occupied with the ritual of the sacrifice; whether he was permanently attached to the Temple or was only serving his turn with other priests, his exacting duties occupied him in the altar court from before daybreak until sunset.

The requirements of the new age made it impossible to deal desultorily with legal matters in Hellenistic Jerusalem. The principle of priestly authority did not impress the royal official who came to verify the account of the sacrifices; nor did it suffice to settle the legal problems created by private deposits in the Temple treasury. Further, professional jurists were needed to advise the Macedonian rulers about Jewish law. The ordinances of Antiochus III relating to Jerusalem show the work of technicians versed in both Jewish law and Greek usage. For instance, the distinction between animals bred in the city and animals brought into it is one that appears also in Greek legal texts.

But the legist was also in demand outside the Sanctuary. The vastly increased use of written documents, the requirements of the Greek bureaucracy, and above all the bilingual character of the Macedonian administration multiplied the need for them. Both the Greek masters and their native subjects were flooded with returns, declarations, petitions, tenders, and questionnaires. Figs and pressed grapes could not be delivered by the tenants of a farm without a written agreement and the intervention of the tax contractor. Even the peasant had to put a request to the administration in the proper form of a Greek *enteuxis* (petition). Down to the shepherd in the wilderness of Judah, everyone was entangled in the red tape of the Greek fiscal system and needed the help of a professional scribe. According to Enoch's third parable, it was Satan himself who instructed mankind to confirm its good faith with pen and ink: "And thereby many sinned from eternity to eternity and until this day."

The professional scribe, the *sofer,* was in the first place a penman, like Baruch, who inscribed Jeremiah's words upon a roll at the prophet's dictation. But a *sofer* was also a notary who drew up contracts, bills of divorce, and other deeds; we have seen him at work in Persian Elephantine. Like the demotic scribes in Ptolemaic Egypt, an official draftsman of documents in Hellenistic Jerusalem probably needed a license. But whether licensed or not, a scribe needed knowledge of legal formulas and experience in their utilization and interpretation.

There was no conflict between sacerdotal and scribal jurisprudence. According to the Chronicler, priests, Levites, and laymen served in the court of Jerusalem under the kings of Judah (II Chron. 19:8). Many scribes surely belonged to the priestly class, but whether clerics or laymen, their profession was that of "scribe," and as such, they were distinct both from the priest who sacrificed in the Temple and from the Temple singers. We may compare them to the Roman *juris periti* of the same period, who were the legal advisers of the pontifices, and to other priestly interpreters of Roman law. In Rome, as in Jerusalem, the jurisconsult in due course supplanted the priest as the interpreter of the law because although he could manage his business without sacerdotal rank, the clergyman could not deal with legal matters without legal skills. No wonder that as early as 200 B.C.E. "the scribes of the Temple" formed a privileged group in the Temple hierarchy.

We can actually observe the rise of this group of technicians. The Chronicler calls Ezra "a ready scribe in the Law of Moses," and in II Maccabees, Eleazar, who suffered martyrdom under Antiochus Epiphanes, is called "one of the first among the scribes." By the time of IV Maccabees, however, written around 30 C.E., Eleazar, according to the phraseology of the Roman period, is styled *nomikos,* that is, legist. In 162 B.C.E., when Demetrius I sent his general Bacchides and the High Priest Alcimus to restore peace in Judea, an "assembly of scribes came together" to deal with the royal commissioners; but in the Herodian Temple it was the *grammateus* (that is, the *sofer*) and not the priest who sat in Moses' seat. Later, the rabbis sometimes even quote the *dibre soferim,* the legal decisions of the ancient scribes, for instance, in the discussion concerning marriage laws.

Modern scholars misrepresent the *soferim* by confusing these notaries, accountants, and legists with the rabbis. It would be a rather amusing metonymy if the rabbis, who discouraged their students from writing down their opinions, had styled themselves "writers." The error goes back, it seems, to Luther, who translated *grammateis* in the Gospels by *Schriftgelehrte.* But the Greek word does not have this meaning: *grammatikoi,* not *grammateis,* was the Greek term for scholars who studied books. The whole category of "biblical scholars," as Luther's term was rendered in English, is a phantom.

In fact, the rabbis of the Talmud never called themselves *soferim,* reserving that name for penmen, drafters of documents, and teachers of elementary reading and writing. The ancient use of the term *sofer* with reference to the interpretation of the Torah disconcerted the rabbis. Accordingly, neither Philo, nor Josephus, nor the competent Church Fathers called the rabbis *grammateis.* The rabbis, rather, took over the traditional title of "Wise Men" in Israel, for while the Torah belonged to the priest, and oracles came from a seer, "wisdom was from the sages." But for the talmudic rabbis the idea of wisdom acquired a new meaning, one that was unknown in ancient Israel, and the first man who was accorded the new title was Ben Sira.

The root *hkm* means natural sagacity. Ants, locusts, and spiders have it (Prov. 30:24); a rich man regarded himself as "wise" (Prov. 28:11). Through his wisdom King Panamu succeeded in winning favor with his Assyrian overlord. In short, *hokmah* means right conduct toward God and man. Teachers of wisdom in the Orient, like the gnomic poets in Greece, taught prudence to the simple. The advice, of course, carried more weight if it was the result of experience and wide knowledge—at which point "wisdom" became a liberal art.

On the other hand, because knowledge is power, arts and skills were as a rule transmitted orally from father to son (or to an apprentice) and as far as possible kept secret. Aristotle, a physician by profession, traced his genealogy back to Machaon, son of Asclepius, the god of healing. The Hippocratic oath obliges a physician to give instruction to none but his own son, the son of his teacher, and the sworn members of the medical order. The cuneiform manuals of astronomy consist of computational formulas that could not have been used by the uninitiated without further oral instruction. In Jerusalem, arts and crafts were likewise transmitted within a family or a particular group. Specialists were organized into guilds; the priesthood was hereditary. Accordingly, when the word *talmid* appears in the Bible (I Chron. 25:8), it refers to the children of the Levites who, "under the hand of their fathers," were instructed in singing for the House of the Lord.

The art of reading and writing, however, could not be transmitted orally, nor could it be kept a secret skill. Although recipes for ceramic glaze, for instance, were written cryptically, educational texts were written to instruct everyone. The scribe had to be able to write for everyone and to read anything written. His art was needed for the conduct of public affairs and private affairs, for temples, for accounts, and for correspondence. For this reason, schools in our sense of the term existed for the scribal profession from the beginning. Furthermore, because writing and books were the proper subjects of instruction in these schools, it is understandable, for instance, that the Egyptian literature that has been preserved for us has come mainly from school texts. Moreover, because scribal instruction involved reading and interpreting texts, the scribes came to be the repositories of whatever knowledge had been collected in books. The priests of Babylon and Jerusalem kept their technical knowledge to themselves, but when Daniel and his comrades learned the "writing and language" of the Chaldeans (cuneiform) at the Babylonian court, Daniel, with God's help, became a master of Babylonian divination. The distinction between a liberal education, general and literary, and a technical education begins in this antagonism between desire for secrecy on the part of the professionals and the public nature of anything written.

"Wisdom" was not a technical subject: it dealt not with nature and its riches, but with the nature of man. Solomon, who exceeded all the kings of the earth in riches and wisdom, speaks of the cedar that is in Lebanon and of the hyssop that springs out of the wall, not in order to instruct anyone literally in the use of these ingredients for ceremonial purification, but merely in an allegorical sense in his proverbs devoted to teaching the rules of behavior.

Still, in order to secure happiness and success, the recommended rules of behavior had to be widely known and accepted. "Wisdom crieth aloud in the street," and people from all over came to hear the wisdom of Solomon. Though directives concerning right conduct were originally private fatherly admonitions, they became perhaps the first books used in the general curriculum of the scribal schools and published for the general reader. The Instructions of the Egyptian vizier Ptah-hotep were compiled in the middle of the third millennium, and the earliest extant manuscript of the book was copied in the beginning of the second millennium B.C.E.

It is probable that reading and writing were widespread in Hellenistic Judea; the skills were most likely transmitted from fathers to sons. The author of the Testaments of the Twelve Patriarchs takes it for granted that all his heroes were able to read and write. Canaan would not have been seduced by the perverse doctrine of the Watchers had he not been taught to read by his father, Arphaxad. Esau, however, in contrast to Jacob, did not learn to write because he was a hunter and a "man of the fields," which suggests that in pre-Maccabean Judea only city children received an elementary education.

Since the mother tongue of the Jews in Hellenistic Jerusalem was Aramaic, the study of the sacred tongue was not identical with learning to read and write. We are told in Jubilees 12:27 that Abraham learned Hebrew "during six rainy months," that is, in the winter season; his teacher (in this case, an angel) explained the difficult passages to the Patriarch. In Egypt, in the same period, when demotic was becoming the daily language of the country, children in the priestly schools learned the hieroglyphs according to the same method.

In Hellenistic Jerusalem, as elsewhere in the classical Orient at that time, the study of wisdom, that is, the study of doing right and acting justly, was part of a person's general education, the popular notion being that wisdom would bring success in life. Varying a saying in Proverbs 17:2, both Kohelet and Ben Sira speak of the value of the wise slave and of the fact that a poor man, too, can have insight. Kohelet says of himself that through his wisdom, meaning "shrewdness," he acquired wealth, and Ben Sira recognizes that from scribe to potter, every man is wise in his art.

Yet in speaking of *hokmah* Ben Sira distinguishes between the practical ability to succeed in one's calling, like the ability of a wise woman to build her house (Prov. 14:1), and sapience, that is, intellectual effort. Search and inquire, he says, and sapience will be made known to you (6:27); because most men do not do so, it is not manifest to them (6:22). Before Ben Sira, Kohelet had already spoken of *hokmah* in the same vein. He had already discovered, like all scholars after him, that research, which he calls *hokmah*, is a sore task. The thought that *hokmah* could be a great vexation must have confused minds used to hearing that with the help of *hokmah* one could easily climb the social ladder. On the other hand, the word "fool," like *aphron* in contemporary Greek philosophy, meant a man who lacked the right education, rather than a simpleton or a vicious man, as in ancient Hebrew.

In other words, *homkah* had acquired something of the meaning of the Greek *sophia*, as the term was used by the pre-Socratic philosophers, or of *paideia* in Hellenistic Greek. *Hokmah* now meant culture, and Ben Sira was its prophet and teacher. This reevaluation of the meaning and essence of *hokmah* changed the social status of its servants. The *hokmah* that was sagacity was transmitted by leading men of practical experience, from the vizier Ptah-hotep and King Solomon to the vizier Ahikar and "the Convoker, the son of David, king in Jerusalem." But Ben Sira's sage, like a Greek philosopher, is an intellectual.

The sage he describes must, in the first place, have leisure for learning. That is why Ben Sira, like the Greek philosophers, excluded those who toiled from the class of people for whom it was possible to acquire sapience. This exclusion was not meant to cast aspersion on those who worked with their hands; Ben Sira says that without artisans no city could sustain itself. But for him, as it was for Plato, and as it is in every genuine civilization, education did not come to an end when a diploma had been obtained; true education continued throughout one's life. Under the technological and social conditions of the ancient world, however, it was impossible for the average worker to take part in this kind of continuing study. As Ben Sira says, the thought of a technician is on his handiwork alone, and in saying so he divided the idea of an education in sapience, the "liberal arts," from an education in technical matters: "From your youth choose up education and unto gray hairs you will find sapience" (6:18).

Ben Sira draws a parallel between the discourse of sages and the conversation of elders; the sage, he says, educates his people. The editor of Kohelet states that the author was *hakam* and "taught people understanding." We are reminded of the personified Wisdom who, in Proverbs, appeals to the crowds in the streets, at the gates, and in the concourse. In some Psalms, the forty-ninth, for instance, Wisdom addresses the crowd in poetical form: "Give ear, O my people, to my instruction." In a few of his chapters Ben Sira preserves this sermonizing style. As for Kohelet, he must have been famous as a street preacher, for the title that replaced his name for his followers and for posterity was the "Convoker," which means *concionator,* he who summons crowds to listen to him. When they come, he delivers his message: "I, Kohelet, have been king over Israel in Jerusalem." Classicists will easily recognize the similarity to the missionary sermons of Hellenistic philosophers. Like Kohelet, his Greek contemporaries Bion and Teles preached in the marketplace, calling to men to abandon their folly and acquire sapience; like Kohelet, they used epigrams, sarcasm, and paradox (which explains how the anonymous Convoker could introduce himself as a king of Israel); like Kohelet, they wanted to "restamp" the conventional currency in opinions. Diogenes entered the theater through the exit, saying that this was the right way to move forward in everything.

Of course, in Jerusalem as well as in Athens there were quieter mentors. Ben Sira offers no paradoxes. We may imagine him having discussions with friends and followers, sometimes in the open, at other times at home. A younger contemporary of his, Jose ben Joezer, gave this advice: "Let your house be a meeting place of sages; sit in the dust of their feet and thirstily drink their words." Like the Greek philosophers, the sages in Hellenistic Jerusalem talked and talked, giving and receiving knowledge. They spoke at the city gates, in the shade of a tree, or assembled under a roof when the weather was inclement. One can understand neither the Greek philosophical dialogues, nor the discussions of the rabbis recorded in the Talmud, nor Kohelet, nor Ben Sira if one does not hear in the background the constant murmur of the spirited and spiritual conversation of the sages—all carried on without the blessing and curse of printed books. It was an earlier contemporary of Ben Sira, Callimachus, who said that a long book is a long evil.

Although the sage established no school in the pedagogical meaning of the word, he did have followers, young and not so young; one thinks of Socrates and his group. If you have found a sage, advises Ben Sira, "cleave" to him: "Let your feet wear out his threshold." To this true disciple the sage transmits not technical skill, but the secret of happy and successful life.

As a philosopher, the sage knows that water, bread, a garment, and a roof over one's head should be sufficient for happiness. Nevertheless, in listing the necessities of life, besides water, fire, iron, and salt, Ben Sira adds wheat, flour, milk, honey, wine, oil, and clothing. His godly man wears golden jewelry and bracelets on his right arm and appreciates meats and dainties. As in all ancient ethical admonitions, from those of the ancient Egyptians to those of the Stoics—who discussed whether a sage should grab the best piece of meat at the table—the dos and don'ts of everyday life play an important part in Ben Sira's advice. For instance, a sage should not peep into the houses of other people; he should be polite to everyone, answering the greeting even of a poor man; he should visit the sick and bewail the dead (but for no more than a day or two). He should avoid gossip. He should know how to preside at banquets, how to speak and how to listen. When invited as a guest, he should not greedily put his hand into the common dish. If, however, he should happen to overeat, he should leave the table, like a gentleman, and go elsewhere to vomit.

As for the intellectual duties of the sage, Ben Sira says that he will interpret the hidden meanings of maxims and be conversant in dark parables (craftsmen, of course, are "not found among the speakers of parables"); the wise Kohelet, for instance, was busy with *meshalim* (12:9). This bewildering terminology is derived from the wise men of olden times, from the age of Ahikar, who spoke in proverbs, and from the age of Solomon, who spoke of trees, beasts, and fishes. In the sapiential psalms, "riddle" (*hidah,* plural *hidot*) denotes a piquant and thought-provoking speech. The *hidot* of Psalm 49 expound the paradox, probably of Egyptian origin, that the poor but just man will receive his reward after death. In Psalm 78, the preacher speaks of all three—*Torah, mashal,* and *hidah*—in a sketch of the history of the Chosen People from the "Deuteronomic" point of view (which was probably new and paradoxical in his time). Therefore, for Ben Sira, he who would become a sage should listen to the discourse of famous men and interpret their "parables." He should also travel to foreign lands to try "both good and evil things" among men, as Ben Sira himself did.

Moreover, because sapience is both with the Lord and from the Lord, its blessing cannot be acquired, according to Ben Sira, without prayer, contrition, and grace. The search for God requires supplication for forgiveness of one's sins, after which, if God desires it, the student will be filled with the spirit of understanding: From him will pour the words of God's sapience and he will praise the Lord; God will set right his counsel and understanding and he will understand God's secrets; God will make perceptible his education, and he will glory in the Law of God. The name of such a sage will live forever among all the nations of the world (Ben Sira 39:6–8).

Through the mouth of the sage, sapience reveals the secrets of God's works to the assembly. We may think here of the young Daniel, to whom the angel gives "a spirit of understanding" and so enables him to save Susanna by his cross-examination of the false witnesses. It is worth noticing the presence of the mystical in the life and meditation of the sage. For him, Scripture is not merely a text to be rationally interpreted, but an oracle, full of hidden meaning. The same idea, we saw, underlay the explication of all sacred words in the classical Orient: the sacred word has to be decoded, just as the significance of an omen has to be deciphered by a diviner. Thus, as we have noted, in the decree of the Egyptian priests of 196 B.C.E. recorded on the Rosetta Stone some religious symbols are said to mean that the reigning pharaoh (Ptolemy V) "illuminates" Egypt.

The author of Daniel 9, a younger contemporary of Ben Sira, after much prayer and contrition, is vouchsafed a revelation that divulged the true meaning of Jeremiah's word about the Seventy Weeks of the Exile— a word whose meaning, as the rabbis later said, had provoked many vain speculations—and a man of the same age identified the Servant of the Lord in Isaiah with the martyrs of Epiphanes' persecution. The exegetes of the prophetic writings in the Sect of the New Covenant also followed this method of deciphering ancient oracles. Indeed, the readiness with which Philo and the rabbis made use of the allegorical method in the interpretation of Scripture was inspired by the practices of the wise men of an earlier age.

That the foundation of wisdom is in God was, of course, no discovery of Ben Sira's; Naphtali, in his testament, advises his sons to "become sages in God." The tendency to claim a religious basis for a moral teaching prevailed in the later Orient. Toward the end of the fourth century, the Egyptian priest Petosiris considered that "great fear of the Deity" was identical with happiness and the "way of life [wisdom]" with the "way of God." In an Aramaic inscription found in Cappadocia it is said that "the wise man (hkym) stands before Bel and [the other] gods." And in the Book of Proverbs, Ben Sira read: "Fear of the Lord is the beginning of knowledge." Nor was it new to state, as Ben Sira does, that although sapience was imparted to all nations, Israel became its permanent abode and the Torah its permanent expression.

Every people believes itself to be in possession of perfect wisdom and therefore it is the one property of their neighbors that they do not covet. In the inscription from Cappadocia, the Mazdaic religion is called "very wise." Even Artaxerxes' letter to Ezra called the Torah the "wisdom of thy God," and in Deuteronomy it is said, almost naively, that if Israel observes the divine statutes, which are good and righteous, other people will say that the children of Jacob are "wise and understanding."

Ben Sira's contribution, however, was the discovery that sapience, that is, culture and education, was identical with the wisdom of his God: "All sapience is the fear of God and in all sapience is the fulfillment of the Torah" (15:1). His enthusiastic praise of sapience ends with a reference to a passage in the Torah: "All that is the Book of the Covenant of the Most High God, the Torah which Moses commanded, the inheritance of the congregation of Jacob" (24:23). Ben Sira's insistence on the identification of the whole of wisdom with the Mosaic Law shows that this view was new and disputed. It would hardly be acceptable to Kohelet or to the High Priest. It meant that the Torah of the priest and of the scribe was to be the foundation and the fulfillment of secular, liberal education.

It is often, but gratuitously, supposed that Scripture commanded the Hebrews to study the Law. In fact, however, the Israelite is enjoined to learn by heart and teach his children only two formulas: the Shema and a list of curses and blessings. He is also exhorted to remember three great events of his sacred history: the Exodus, the revelation on Mt. Horeb, and the settlement in Canaan. In the same way, a Babylonian father was admonished to tell his son of the deeds of Marduk. To read the whole Law was imposed on the king alone; for the common people the Lawgiver prescribed only the public reading of the Torah every seventh year, on the Feast of Tabernacles. When Ezra had the Law read and translated by his Levitical assistants, his activity was juristic and not pedagogic. It was, rather, in some Greek cities and in Rome that the national law was memorized at the elementary school level.

Of course the whole nation was expected to observe the Law, but children, instructed by their families, learned by doing (for instance, by observing the Sabbath). The pious Susanna was no biblical scholar, but she was taught by her parents how to live according to the Law of Moses. In the early Hellenistic period only a visionary could imagine children studying the Law—and then only in the messianic age (Jub. 23:26); around 200 B.C.E. it was taken for granted in Jerusalem that the Torah was taught only to the sons of priests. In the Testaments of the Twelve Patriarchs, Levi, and he alone among the sons of Jacob, instructs his sons to teach their children to read (unceasingly) the Law of God. Levi himself learned the laws of the priesthood from his grandfather. It is hardly an accident that centuries later Jewish children still began their reading of Scripture with Leviticus, the priestly book.

Toward the end of the second century B.C.E., the grandson of Ben Sira clearly distinguished between the "students of Scripture" and "the outsiders." It was for the latter that his grandfather had written his book, to instruct them in how to live according to the Law. In the first decades of the first century C.E. we learn of a school, annexed to a synagogue, established in Jerusalem for the study of the Torah and its commandments; to still later rabbis, it seemed natural to believe that when Jacob reached his thirteenth year he began to study the Torah in the *beth hamidrash* of Shem. (Let us note here that the term *beth midrash*, as used in a poem added later to the work of Ben Sira [51:23], is a figure of speech in imitation of the "House of Wisdom" in Proverbs 9:1 and not a reference to a rabbinic school.)

Ben Sira, however, proclaimed that the Torah as a whole—that which guided both priests and scribes in their professional work—must be the central subject of Jewish culture and education. In order to be wise, one had to ponder not only the intricacies of ritual impurity but also the statute concerning parapets on roofs. That his idea of wisdom apparently included the prophetic books as well, those obscure oracles about forgotten events, did not make the suggestion more attractive. Everyone knew, and pseudo-Aristeas still repeats, that a godly life could be better achieved by listening and by conversation than by study. Now wisdom was to be like a heavy stone that could be lifted only by an athlete. Passive acceptance of Scriptural precepts and the memorization of traditional words and formulas was to cede place to inquiry and discussion in the Greek manner.

In Ben Sira's time, instruction in the liberal arts was given by professional teachers in Jerusalem. The tax gatherer Joseph, "wishing to learn which of his sons was inclined to virtue," sent them one after another "to those who were famed in education." Unfortunately, all except one of the boys were lazy, and so these came back as "foolish and ignorant" as before. Were their teachers wise men of the old style, or were they Greek professors? We don't know, but the story itself reflects Greek discussions about the importance of the innate qualities that are necessary in order for any education to proceed, and, above all, it demonstrates that the Greek idea and ideal of *paideia,* of the notion that education forms a man, had already entered Jerusalem by the end of the third century B.C.E.

The Greek idea of *paideia* was based on a book, that of Homer, whose poems were memorized; Homer "has educated Greece," Plato says. In school, Greek boys, and the Jewish boys who studied with them, began their education with Homer. Indeed, Greek philology developed out of the task of preparing Homer's text for the schools; the interpretation of Homer was the foundation of the liberal arts. What could a Jew oppose to this bible of the Hellenes? Ben Sira had an answer: Moses. Not the masses, of whom Ben Sira does not think on this occasion, but the intelligentsia of Jerusalem would be obliged to learn the Torah.

This idea, which may or may not have originated with Ben Sira, prevailed; we can still make out some of the milestones on the new road to wisdom. About 150 B.C.E. the first use of the word *grammatikos* ("a scholar who studies books") appears in Jewish sources. This means that at that date there were already *soferim* busy correcting the biblical text. For Ben Sira's grandson, one generation later, the Torah and the Hebrew books related to it offered a reason to be proud of the national "education and culture" of the Jews. At the same time, however, he distinguished, as we have noted, between those who studied Scripture and those who were "outsiders," already establishing the later rabbinic habit of ranking men according to their capacity for studying the Law. (On the other hand, the rabbis never excluded anyone from the study of Torah.)

The first teacher in whose name the rabbis transmitted their legal interpretations was a priest, Jose ben Joezer, who died around 160 B.C.E. But toward the end of the second century the author of the Letter of Aristeas, inventing the list of those versed in Scripture who translated the Torah into Greek, found it natural to distribute the names equally among the twelve tribes, so that out of seventy-two scholars versed in Scripture, he named only six who were sons of Levi: the Torah no longer belonged only to the priest and his scribal adjuncts.

Scripture now became a book from which, as a sectarian text states, everything could be learned exactly. The verb *darash*, with reference to the Torah, originally meant "to seek to fulfill the Torah." The same expression now meant "to study Scripture." In the Sect of the New Covenant, "study in the Torah" *(darash ba-Torah)* went on without interruption, day and night. Somewhat later, instruction in the Torah became a part of the general curriculum of the schools; in 4 B.C.E. two "expounders of the Law" were popular in Jerusalem "on account of [their] education of the youth."

Nevertheless, with the extension of Ben Sira's idea the new education became something different from what he originally intended. For Ben Sira, the sage was an independent seeker of sapience. But the authority of the "master" *(rabbi)* was based, as in the Greek philosophical schools, on the right of magisterial succession, in which the rabbi and his disciple were links in a chain that led back to the revelation at Sinai.

Following the path marked by Ben Sira and the sages who were his contemporaries (and perhaps by others even before them), Jewish civilization, through education, became "Torah-centric." The theory, initiated to oppose the force of the Greek spirit, triumphed with the Maccabees; yet its fundamental idea, that of an education based on a unique book, was itself Greek. Even the new religious fervor that identified wisdom with revealed truth was only a Jewish wave—and a belated one— in the large movement that pushed the whole of Hellenistic civilization toward an uncharted spiritual sea. The philosophy of Plato, who had something of the hierophant in him, but who had remained a prophet without honor in his own city and in his own time, began to prevail over the positivism that had ruled in Ben Sira's time and in the Hellenistic environment in general. Young men, who in Socrates' time had aimed at obtaining practical wisdom and who had flocked to the study of facts and phenomena in the Academy and in the Lyceum, began toward the middle of the third century to turn away from research and to seek "virtue" in the philosophical schools.

Long before Ben Sira, the Stoic Cleanthes proclaimed that man's highest reward lay in worshipping the universal law. If Ben Sira's sage prays to God in order to obtain sapience, the Stoic sage does the same: the gift of grace is required before either can attain right knowledge. According to Clement of Alexandria (Strom. 4.6 = *SVF* III, 221) the Stoics taught that when, by training and self-discipline man has become possessed of true wisdom, then, suddenly, at some particular moment, his soul "will convert to sapience." Torah-centric Judaism became possible only when the Hellene, too, identified *philosophia* with *theosebeia*. Josephus believed that both Moses and Plato required of the citizen, above all, that, he must study the law exactly, but Josephus could not have known that the idea was originally Greek. The study of the law by laymen was a Hellenistic innovation in Jerusalem.

Babylonia and Egypt, and, it seems, the populations of Syria and Iran as well, apparently stood aloof from this Hellenistic development and their native civilizations shrank instead into priestly dependence. On the Nile, as well as on the Euphrates, a double barrier separated the layman from native learning. Babylonian priests continued to copy their sacred texts in the original Akkadian, written in cuneiform, and Egyptian priests continued to do the same in the old (although somewhat barbarized) Egyptian language and its hieroglyphs at a time when everyone around them—and they themselves in the street—spoke Greek or Aramaic or, in Egypt, demotic. The result was that, so far as I know, no new work was written in either cuneiform or hieroglyphs, or in their languages, during the Hellenistic age.

This does not mean that the priestly intelligentsia in Egypt or Babylonia set their face against all innovations; these priests were also in contact with Greeks and with Greek wisdom. Greek grammatical science seems to have penetrated into the Egyptian priestly school of the Ptolemaic period and Egyptian wisdom as well as Egyptian novels were written in demotic and exhibit traces of Greek ideas. There was also an exchange of data and ideas between Babylonian and Greek astronomers. But for the most part the grip of tradition immobilized native learning in Babylonia and Egypt. Writing during the apogee of Greek science, the Babylonian priest Berossus could say that all the acquisitions of civilization were the gift of Oannes—half-fish, half-man—at the dawn of history, and that since then nothing had been invented. When a Babylonian or an Egyptian priest of the Hellenistic age wanted to say something new and to say it to the world at large, he usually said it in Greek.

More to the point, however, is that while Scripture became the basis of education in Jerusalem, even for laymen, in other parts of the Orient only priests continued to study their ancestral texts. The extinction of this sacerdotal class or a decline in its learning thus meant the end of a civilization. Because they spoke Aramaic, the Magi in the Persian diaspora were unable to read their own holy books. In Uruk (Erech), out of some twenty priestly clans that had existed under Persian rule, only seven survived into the second century B.C.E., and by about 150 B.C.E. perhaps only a dozen persons in that city were still capable of writing cuneiform; the last extant cuneiform tablet is dated around 75 C.E. And while the learned priests studiously copied and ingeniously manipulated hiero-glyphs already in use in the time of Cheops, the common people on the Nile forgot all about the builders of the Pyramids. In the popular imag-ination the pharaohs became mighty magicians of old.

The Book of Moses, however, could become the fountainhead of Jew-ish education because the Torah was different from the sacred books of the East. The words of Zoroaster were preserved as a part of the apparatus of worship, but the simple believer played no role in the Avestan religion. The libraries of the Egyptian temples displayed the scrolls, the knowledge of which enabled the priest to dispose of an evil spirit or drive away a crocodile, but the worshipper was permitted to look at these scrolls only from afar. In Israel, however, all the people were called to holiness: "You shall be holy unto Me, for I the Lord am Holy." Thus, paradoxically, religion in Jerusalem, like philosophy in Athens, was basically non-priestly. When attacking the philosophers, the Church Father Tertullian cried: "What has Athens to do with Jerusalem?" He overlooked one essential point: the nature of both Greek wisdom and Hebrew faith was universal. That made possible, first, the Hellenization of Jerusalem and, in the course of time, the worship of the God of Abraham, Isaac, and Jacob in Athens.

But all this was still "on the knees of the gods" at the time that Ben Sira sponsored Torah-centric education. His aim was to prepare future leaders of the nation who would be wise in speech. In antiquity, the art of persuasion was a necessary prerequisite for political activity. Ben Sira, however, counts on sapience and not on Greek rhetoric to develop the skill of his students: The skill (Hebrew, "wisdom of hands") of a crafts-man is manifest in his work and the wisdom of a leader of the people is manifest in his speech (9:17); sapience raises its follower above his neigh-bors and makes him eloquent when he speaks in the Assembly (19:5); "They inquire at the mouth of the wise man in the Assembly and they ponder his words in their hearts" (27:17). But although the sage will be sought out in the Public Assembly (38:33) and will sit in the judge's seat because he ponders and explains judgments (38:33), his eloquence and his sapience are derived from his fear of the Lord and his mastery of the Torah (15:1; 39:1).

Like Plato, Ben Sira is convinced that one cannot know what is just without being righteous. Yet power in Jerusalem belonged to the aris-tocracy and not to the sages or their disciples. Ben Sira himself can only apostrophize men of authority: "Hear me, grandees, and harken with your ears, leaders of the Assembly" (33:18). To exercise influence, however, the disciple of the sages often had to enter into the service of those who held the power: sapience "lifts up" the head of the humble and places him "among the great" (11:1), Ben Sira says, and also that the sage advances himself with his words and that the prudent man will "please the great" (20:27). Still, the great, with much talk and many smiles, tested their intellectual friends and advisers. Ben Sira vividly describes the miseries attending the life of a philosphical client in a lord's house. Like Dean Swift, he advises the sage to let the noble lord repeat the invitation to him before he accepts it.

On the other hand, a lord needed the intellectual, who could present a case equally well before the Popular Assembly in Jerusalem or the royal court. The coexistence of Jewish and Greek systems of administration and law produced a need for advisors, stewards, and secretaries outside the scribal guild. Native wit and clerical apprenticeship were no longer sufficient in an age that was both technical and encyclopedic. As the cook in a Hellenistic comedy says, knowledge of astronomy was now required in order to prepare a good meal. We may suppose that Joseph the Tobiad, who as an enterprising young man upbraided the High Priest himself in the Popular Assembly in Jerusalem; that John, who secured privileges from the Seleucids; and that Eupolemus, his son, who negotiated the alliance between Judah Maccabee and Rome, had sages as advisors, if they were not themselves students of the sages. Yet only a century before Ben Sira, the Jewish nation appeared to Greek visitors as the classic example of obedience to the authority of the High Priest, appointed by God.

The Stoic Chrysippus named royal service among three ways a philosopher could earn a living, and Kohelet, his contemporary, speaks of the Jewish courtiers of a (Ptolemaic) king (8:2). And although Ben Sira (7:4) advises his pupils not to seek a seat of honor at a pagan court, Daniel, counselor of Nebuchadnezzar and vizier of Darius, who in all matters of wisdom and understanding was "ten times" wiser than the pagan sages of the realm, continued to excite the imagination. The myth of Jewish intellectual superiority began to take shape in Jewish thought. We read how the future tax-farmer Joseph seduces Ptolemy by his cleverness, his wit (stale to our taste), and his behavior (which appears boorish to us). But toward the end of the second century, pseudo-Aristeas presents a new portrait of the ideal intellectual of Jerusalem. He not only knows the Torah and lives according to its precepts, but also knows how to draw applause from the Greek philosophers at the royal table by virtue of his knowledge of the best way of life and the best manner of government. The biblical paragon of the Jewish servant of a pagan king, the

Patriarch Joseph, became the model for youth. As Levi says in the Testaments of the Twelve Patriarchs: "Whoever teaches noble things and does them shall be enthroned with kings, like Joseph."

The Jews of the Syrian and the Egyptian diasporas also needed the kind of sages who were formed in Jerusalem. As a contemporary of Ben Sira says, a man who learns letters and knows the Torah will gain friends everywhere; his earthly possessions may perish, his land and city may be destroyed, but his wisdom will gain him fame even in a strange country. The author of the Testaments of the Twelve Patriarchs puts his praise of learning into the mouth of Levi, the ancestor of the priests, whose hereditary authority had been devalued. Levi now admonishes his progeny to "get wisdom in the fear of God with diligence." The Age of Education had opened in Jerusalem.

TWENTY

The Midrash

THE Torah is more than the Law of Moses; it is the memorial attesting the deeds performed by the Lord for His Chosen People. Long before the Scriptures became a subject of study in Jerusalem, their stories were told and retold countless times in the public places of Israel and Judah. Those who heard Hosea at Samaria understood his allusion to Jacob seizing his brother by the heel (Hos. 12:3). The Prophet of the Return comforted those in captivity: "Look unto Abraham your father and unto Sarah that bore you (Isa. 51:2). Before the rabbis formulated the rule that all Jews are obliged to regard themselves as if they personally were delivered from Egyptian bondage, thirty generations of them had, every Passover, lived through the Exodus again.

The traditional lore of God's people was transmitted from parents to children, not as tales of a dead past but as a living and life-giving force in the present. In order to remain vital, however, the past must be capable of being revitalized by every generation; every generation must be able to express its own fears and hopes in retelling the stories of the forefathers. No civilization can survive without pouring the new wine of the spirit into the old bottles of the letter. The rabbis called this work of actualization "Haggadah," a term that intimates that Scripture itself is "telling" its new meaning.

The first step in the logical, though not necessarily the chronological, development of scriptural exegesis is the attempt to explain the plain meaning of the text. The Septuagint bears evidence of this kind of philological work. For instance, the technical term *azkarah* in the sacrificial ritual was understood to derive from the verb *zakhar*, "to remember," because it was considered to be a memorial for the one who offered it, and consequently was rendered in Greek by *to mnemosynon*. According to Scripture, the mysterious objects *urim* and *tumim* served for inquiring as to God's will; as the Septuagint translation of these words—*delosis* and *aletheia*—shows, they were understood to mean "command" and "truth." The Hebrew Bible explicitly states the meaning of the name given to Noah: "And he [Lamech] called him Noah, that is to say, he shall comfort us *(yenahamenu)* . . . in our toil." Some readers, however, found fault with this explanation, which contains no reference to the Deluge, and suggested other derivations. The Greek translators of Genesis derived the name from the root *nuah,* "rest," and attributed to it the meaning "he will give us rest." A story of Noah, originally written in Hebrew and Aramaic and partly incorporated in the Book of Enoch, followed the same philological lead, but interpreted the name of the patriarch as meaning "remnant." In Jubilees, the similarity of the words *shebuot* and *(hag) shabuot* leads to the inference that the first (Noachic) covenant was concluded at the time of the Feast of Weeks.

There were also discordant statements in Scripture that had to be dealt with, as well as other kinds of exegetic difficulties. For example, Moses' sister, Miriam, and his brother, Aaron, spoke against him because of his "Cushite" wife. But Moses' wife was Zipporah, daughter of a Midianite from the peninsula of Sinai, and not from Cush-Ethiopia. Yet the historian Demetrius identified the Cushite wife with the Midianite wife on the basis of the biblical statement that Abraham sent the sons of Keturah, among them Midian, the ancestor of Zipporah, to be "colonists" (as Demetrius interpreted the text) in the East. Another problem arises because of Abraham's marriage to Keturah after the death of Sarah. Why did he not call back Hagar, driven out by Sarah? The answer, found in the Book of Jubilees, is that Hagar had predeceased Sarah.

In this manner numerous problems of biblical interpretation, particularly problems of the identification of persons and places and of chronology, were posed and solved by succeeding generations of readers and interpreters of Scripture. Their work was surely used by the Seventy, who were men of learning, as pseudo-Aristeas says. When, for instance, the Seventy translate the expression *"Abram ha ibri"* as "Abram the Crosser," or speak of Adam's "trance" and Enoch's "translation," they are probably repeating the results of earlier exegesis.

Sometimes the difficulties were more complex and required the use of hermeneutics. Adam was warned that he would die on the day he ate of the tree of life, yet after his transgression he lived to the age of 930. But that only showed, according to the author of Jubilees, that, as the Psalmist says, a thousand years are but as one day for God. Here, the early Hellenistic author of Jubilees used a principle of interpretation, later formulated as a norm by R. Ishmael, to the effect that when two scriptural passages appear to be contradictory, a third passage may be used to remove the difficulty.

The exegetical rule that one biblical passage may be elucidated by means of another naturally led to combinations that to us sometimes appear arbitrary. In Jubilees, divine law and sacred history are often correlated on the basis of inference. The Law directs that a male child be brought to the Temple forty days, and a female child eighty days, after birth. Accordingly, the author of Jubilees postulated that Adam entered Paradise when he was forty days old and Eve eighty days after her creation, apparently equating the Temple and the Garden of Eden. According to the Law, the shoe of a brother who refuses to enter into a levirate marriage must be removed by his brother's widow *(halizah)*. In order to make sense of this strange ceremony, Zebulon, in his Testament, reasoned as follows: Amos speaks of those who sell the righteous *(zaddik)* for silver and the needy man *(ebyon)* for a pair of shoes. This was understood to be a reference to the sale of Joseph *(ha-zaddik)* and consequently to imply that the money received from the sale of Joseph was spent on shoes by his brothers. Therefore, because the ceremony of *halizah,* according to the Law, degraded the brother who refused to fulfill his brotherly duty, it was fitting to regard it as a remembrance of Joseph's betrayal by his brothers.

A further logical step was historical Haggadah, the embellishment and amplification of biblical narrative with the help of other traditions or even just with guesswork on the part of the interpreter. For instance, the Greek translator of Joshua tells us that the stone knives used to circumcise the people at Gilgal were buried with Joshua and remain in his grave "until today." The discovery in 1870 of Stone Age artifacts at Timnath-Serah, the burial place of Moses' successor in the hill country of Ephraim, gives us a clue as to the origin of this tale. In the third century C.E., R. Joshua ben Levi quoted a Roman tradition to the effect that Esau had been killed by Judah. Because the Romans were regarded as Esau's descendants, the source of R. Joshua's information was considered particularly authoritative. In fact the tale was already known to the author of the Book of Jubilees, writing about 200 B.C.E. Here Judah advises Jacob to slay Esau; he cannot do it himself because Esau resembles Jacob. As usual, the compiler brushes aside the divergent version at the same time that he refers to it.

The remarkable fact, however, is that Jewish exegetes seem never to have known a historical tradition independent of the Bible. While the Jews of the Hellenistic age could still obtain some information concerning the last Babylonian king, Nabonidus, who is not mentioned in Scripture, they apparently preserved no written or oral memory, for example, about the fall of Jerusalem, except the brief and dry report in the Bible. When R. Simeon ben Azzai, around 300 C.E., quoting a "haggadic tradition," says that Nebuchadnezzar was a stepson of Hiram of Tyre, he reproduces the fanciful idea of some earlier rabbi who wished to connect the destroyer of the Temple with its builder.

Yet Nebuchadnezzar's conquests were not forgotten in Hellenistic Babylon, and legends continued to cluster around the names of Semiramis and Nitocris, two ancient queens of the same city. Herodotus could collect anecdotes about Amasis of Egypt, counterparts of which have also been preserved in demotic. Did no one in Jerusalem ever gossip about Solomon and his wives, or about Athalia, who, after seizing the throne, lost her life in a revolution? Anathot was repopulated after the Exile; it is difficult to believe that no tale about the prophet Jeremiah was recounted at his birthplace.

But the learned men of Jerusalem, who are our informants, looked down on the tales told at the gates or in the places of drawing water. In the Levant civilization was essentially bookish and the memory of the past was entrusted to writers; matters that escaped their notice seemed both irrelevant and untrustworthy. The proud claim of oriental writers, recorded by Josephus, was that their histories of the past were not dissonant. Thus only the stories fitting into the framework of the biblical tradition could find a place in our learned sources.

The case of Jeremiah may illustrate this point. For the Chronicler, the reason for God's destruction of the Temple of Jerusalem was the evil conduct of Jeremiah's generation, who polluted the House of the Lord and scoffed at the prophet. Variations on this historico-theological theme are presented again and again. Ben Sira says that because Jeremiah was treated evilly, God made the streets of Jerusalem desolate. A generation later, Eupolemus writes that the Jews mistreated Jeremiah because they wanted to worship Baal. In the Bible, King Jehoiakim flings Jeremiah's oracles into the fire. Eupolemus repeats a haggadic story to the effect that the king tried to burn the prophet himself, but adds that Nebuchadnezzar, hearing of Jeremiah's prophecies, avenged him. On the other hand, to account for the absence of the Ark of the Covenant and of the incense altar in the Second Temple, another story suggests that Jeremiah had been charged with hiding these sacred vessels after the fall of Jerusalem. His bones, as we shall see, sanctified the soil of Alexandria for Jewish immigrants. In other words, the clergy and the literati were not interested in an authentic or even anecdotal biography of the prophet for its own sake; they were interested only in using Jeremiah's name and reputation for their own purposes.

Accordingly the Haggadah, in embellishing the past of the Chosen People, became a compendium of the inventions of exegetes. Inferences developed on the basis of the sacred text itself seem to have been rare and rather elementary. From the punishment of the serpent in the Garden of Eden ("upon thy belly shalt thou go") they inferred that before the Fall the snake had walked on four feet. They explained that Moses, though brought up as an Egyptian prince, had learned about his origins from his true mother, who, according to the Bible, nursed him. The Bible says that Tubal-Cain, living seven generations after Cain, was a smith who made weapons. Accordingly—to believe the exegete-author of the Book of Jubilees—Cain killed Abel with a stone and not with a sword and, in agreement with the principle of *lex talionis,* he in turn was killed by the stones of his house, which fell upon him.

For the most part, however, the imaginations of the exegetes were stimulated by the quantity of fanciful lore with which generations of readers had already embroidered the biblical text, such as that the forbidden fruit was similar to the clusters of a vine, or that Abraham had burned the idols belonging to his father Terah. No writing of any kind is mentioned in Genesis, so the historian Eupolemus concluded that Moses had learned the art from the Egyptians and had transmitted it to the Hebrews. But the haggadists of the early Hellenistic age also speak freely of books written by the antediluvian patriarchs. Repeated by the rabbis, the fable of antediluvian writers reached Augustine, who rightly observed, "I do not know how it can be proved."

By way of such additions, even pagan mythology insinuated itself into the traditional interpretation of the Bible. Paradoxical as it may appear, the main reason for this intrusion was the intense dread of mythology in God-fearing Israel. The prophets would not dignify Baal by mentioning his myths, and later the rabbis on the same principle ignored the sacred lore of their neighbors. Yet the mythopoeic faculty of the Hebrew craved expression, and since it could find no outlet beyond the limits of the Bible it embroidered the Bible itself. The rabbis, who in principle were eager to explain that biblical anthropomorphisms were merely figures of speech, themselves spoke of the Lord adorning Eve as a bride and of His complaining to the Messiah about Cyrus' behavior. In nonrabbinic sources Enoch, the heavenly scribe, is the counterpart of the Egyptian Thoth and the Babylonian Nabu. Thus, even when frowned upon by the rabbis, the myths attached to biblical names in the minds of the people continued to be repeated and were transmitted from generation to generation; a Ugaritic myth, recorded in cuneiform tablets in the fourteenth century B.C.E., reappears twenty-seven centuries later in a medieval compilation of haggadic lore.

Some mythical tales used in the early Hellenistic Haggadah throw light on the thought-world of the Jews in the third century B.C.E. The Bible says that "the sons of God saw the daughters of men that they were fair, and they took them as wives, whomsoever they chose" (Gen. 6:2); and, it continues, the sons resulting from this union of celestial beings and mortal women became mighty men of renown (like the children of the gods in Oriental or Greek mythology). This mythological fragment embedded in the Torah naturally attracted the fancy of readers. It appears that in the early Hellenistic age two forms of midrash on the passage were popular. One version describes the sons of God as "Watchers" (that is, sentinels) of the celestial palace. Led by Azazel, the demon to whom the scapegoat was sent on the Day of Atonement, the "Watchers" descended to earth at God's command, in order to teach men crafts and to instruct them to do right. But, falling in love with the daughters of men, the "Watchers" forgot their mission and, as a result, lost their celestial rank. This interpretation of the biblical passage makes use of two foreign motifs. The first is the civilization myth: celestial heroes, like Oannes of the Babylonians or Triptolemus of the Athenians, descend to earth in order to teach men art and crafts. The second motif is folkloric: celestial beings lose the privilege of immortality by joining themselves to mortals, for immortal angels may not marry.

The fact that in the Bible the story of the Deluge immediately follows the story of the sons of God also suggested a second, more pessimistic, interpretation of the Fall of the Angels. Their sin was concupiscence. Lusting for the fair daughters of men, two hundred angels, led by Shemihazah, decided to rebel and, against God's will, descended to earth. Their gigantic offspring began to devour mankind until God put a stop to it and punished both fathers and sons. Josephus noted the similarity of this tale to the Greek myth of the Titans, and, indeed, both stories are variants of the widely diffused folkloric theme of demonic rebellion against celestial power, an idea already referred to in the Psalms and in the Book of Isaiah.

Thus it is impossible to estimate the age of these interpretations of the Fall of the Angels. The versions became conflated and were again and again embellished and amplified, and although the rabbis never directly referred to the Fallen Angels, their somber rebellion continued to capture the fancy of Jews through the ages and in modern times to fire the imagination of writers and poets from Milton to Anatole France. It is interesting to note, on the other hand, that the idea that the Fallen Angels were teachers of mankind seems to have found no later adherents. Men preferred to ascribe to less notorious inventors the creation of the arts that enhance life.

In the early Hellenistic age, however, another mythological fragment embedded in the Torah, the story of the Tower of Babel—today practically forgotten—was even more popular than that of the Fallen Angels. Ben Sira (16:7) could refer incidentally to the "giants of old who revolted in their strength" against God and know that his audience would understand him immediately. A Samaritan author of the same age, writing in Greek, as well as the Jewish Sibyl, tell us that the giants, who had escaped the Deluge, were the builders of the Tower of Babel: they aimed at "climbing up to the starry heaven." As the Alexandrian polemicists already noted, we have here the Greek theme of the Aloadae, who piled the three loftiest mountains of Greece on top of each other in order to reach heaven.

Although nothing in the biblical account suggests that the builders of the Tower of Babel, mortal children of mortal men, aspired to overthrow divine rule, this Hellenistic midrash became the foundation of the rabbinic exegesis of the scriptural passage. According to the rabbis, the tower was built by Nimrod, king of Babylon, in order that he and his people might brave the waters of a new deluge. Then, deeming themselves secure from divine wrath, they planned to take vengeance on God for the flood. Even a Hellenistic detail, that the tower was overthrown by a mighty wind, reappears in the mouths of the rabbis.

The theme of these tales is *theomachia,* rebellion against God. This Luciferian complex appears strange and foreign in a religion in which every sin was considered to be a rebellion against the Lord, and in a thought-world in which, as Manetho says of a pious pharaoh of old, a ruler preferred to give up his country to the invader rather than "fight against the deity." But in Greek myth and Greek consciousness, men and titans freely contested the sovereignty of the Olympians, who were jealous of the success of mortals. It was a current mode of flattery in the third and second century B.C.E. to say of a prince that he ascended Olympus or that he threatened the domination of Zeus. In a similar vein the Jewish Sibyl addresses Rome: "Stouthearted Rome, after the Macedonian spear, thou too flash forth to Olympus. But God wills that of thee no more shall be heard." A difference is, however, apparent: the Jewish poet, though using a Greek motif, is here expressing the more traditional mono-theist abhorrence of *theomachia.* Is it fanciful to think that the popularity of the concept among the Jewish intellectuals of the early Hellenistic age is in some way connected with their new knowledge of Greek mythology, necessarily acquired in learning Greek? In any case, men whose fancy embellished the biblical hints of rebellion against God were unconsciously turning their eyes from Job and looking to Prometheus.

A second distinctive group of *haggadot* popular in the early Hellenistic age is politically inspired. The Torah narrates that the people of God received gold, silver, and raiment from the Egyptians when departing from Egypt. In the third century B.C.E., this booty embarrassed the Jews of Alexandria. But an exegete found a decent reason for the spoliation of the Egyptians: it was, he said, the recovery of wages due for the work the Hebrews had been forced to render during their Egyptian bondage. This rejoinder appears both in the Greek tragedy of Ezechiel, *The Exodus,* written in Alexandria, as well as in the Book of Jubilees, written in Hebrew by a Palestinian.

The same attention to the feelings of the Jews in Egypt manifests itself in the Septuagint rendering of the biblical formula "A wandering Aramean was my father," which is a part of the confession spoken by a pilgrim offering his first fruits in the Temple. This formula seemed to the Jews of Egypt to affirm a kinship between the Jews and the Syrians, the hereditary enemies of Egypt. According to the Seventy, however, the biblical expression means, rather, "My father abandoned Syria and descended into Egypt." It is remarkable that the Passover Haggadah, as it is still read today, is also anti-Syrian. In the service for the Passover meal, the same biblical expression, by means of a different vocalization, reads, "An Aramean sought to destroy my father." This allusion to Laban and his plans against Jacob is not fortuitous. The opening of the midrash in the Passover Haggadah was apparently formulated with the intention of softening the markedly anti-Egyptian features of the biblical history of the Exodus. In other words, the Passover Haggadah of today offers an interpretation of a biblical passage that agrees with the Septuagint, but deviates from all other forms of the text. No one would have prevented the Jews from rehearsing the traditional story of their deliverance from Egyptian bondage. The poet Ezechiel, although writing in Greek in Alexandria, shows no compunction in mentioning the plagues inflicted on the Egyptians. But the High Priests in Jerusalem probably thought that the paramount importance of the pilgrim feast of Passover made it advisable, under the rule of the Ptolemies of Egypt, to soften the holiday's basic anti-Egyptian position.

The political relationships between peoples are often projected onto a mythological screen. Esau, the ancestor of the Edomites, the Bible tells us is the twin brother of Jacob, and in biblical tradition a kinship, once fixed, remains unaltered; Edom's inveterate enmity against Jerusalem did not cause the redactors of the Bible to change the Deuteronomic statement that an Edomite was a brother of the Israelites. Greek myth, on the other hand, was unstable. In Greece, the role of a mythological figure could shift from villain to hero and back again, depending upon the state of the relationship between the figure's country and Athens. The early Hellenistic reinterpretation of "A wandering Aramean was my father" is an example of this Greek thought-form applied to a biblical passage.

Fictional kinship is also used for a political purpose in another early Hellenistic tale. We learn from II Maccabees that in 170 B.C.E. both the Jews and the Spartans believed that they were related by blood. Nothing was more common in the Hellenistic age than the invention of a tie of kinship between a famous Greek city and some barbarian tribe, for whom such a relationship was a ticket of admission to the Hellenic club. Although scholars vainly tried to find a rationale for the choice of the Spartans as kinsmen of Abraham's race, there seems to have been none; neither in Greek mythology nor in the political history of the third century B.C.E. was there any reason to connect Jerusalem and Sparta. But it is not necessary to suppose that the idea of this kinship evolved in either Jerusalem or Sparta. The Samnites were promoted to kinship with Sparta not for the sake of the Lacedaemonians, but for the sake of Tarentum, a Spartan colony and a neighbor of the Samnites. We may guess that, in similar fashion, the Spartan relationship to the Jews was thought out at Cyrene, another Spartan colony, in order to improve the status of Jewish settlers there. It is a pity that we do not know what would be the most historically important feature of this genealogical fiction: Was some ancestor of the Chosen People identified with a Greek hero, or did the Spartans as a whole become associated with the descendants of Abraham? The Maccabees chose the latter interpretation, but their choice may have been a deliberate innovation. Generally, it was an ancestor of the barbarian group who became attached in some way to Greek mythology.

In fact, the men and women of pre-Maccabean Jerusalem were not interested in what was happening beyond the sea, on the Spartan shore; they were too busy quarreling with their immediate neighbors. In the small extent of the Promised Land mutual dislike between tiny entities that had no room within which to move was natural and endemic. Tacitus, speaking of an Arabic force that took part in the siege of Jerusalem in 70 C.E., says that these troops were "hostile to the Jews with the usual hate between neighbors." The mutual aversion of Phoenician and Syrian cities to one another was proverbial among the Greeks, who, one would think, would also score well in this game of bickering. In the third century B.C.E. the Jews reproached the Samaritans, who were "flourishing at this time," with laying waste their land and carrying off slaves.

The situation was similar in the west and south of Jerusalem. Ben Sira announces that he abhors Philistia and Edom. In the story of the Three Pages, the Jewish hero, having won a prize for his discovery that truth prevails, proceeds to tell the lie that the Edomites had burned the Temple "when Judea was made desolate by the Chaldeans." For this reason, he maintains, the Edomites should pay for the rebuilding of the Temple and also for the costs of the Temple service; in addition, they ought to relinquish the villages of the Jews that they had occupied. In the east, the Jordan did not restrain enmity, either: the Chronicler disliked the Ammonites.

Authentic Hebrew tradition asserted that the Holy Land had been promised by God to Abraham (just as the land of Seir was given to the sons of Esau) and that God had dispossessed the Ammonites because they had blocked the passage of Israel to the Promised Land. Jephthah told this to the king of the Ammonites, adding: "Will you not possess what Chemosh, your god, gives you to possess?" (Judg. 11:24).

But as early as the compilation of Deuteronomy, the redactor took pains to state that the Hebrews had not seized the land that belonged to the children of Esau, nor the territories of Moab, nor the land of the children of Ammon. The territorial losses suffered under the Assyrians, and later the fall of Jerusalem, made the traditional interpretation of the conquest untenable. Having known defeat, Jews could no longer appeal to the God-given right of victory, as Jephthah had done in the days of the Judges. In the territorial contests with the Samaritans, who pretended to be the true Canaanites, and with the Phoenicians, that is, the Canaanites on the seacoast, and with the Idumeans and the Arabs, the people of Persian and Macedonian Jerusalem must often have heard that even according to their own tradition they were intruders in Palestine.

In the third century B.C.E., however, the author of Jubilees offered a secular, and purely legal, justification for Jewish possession of the Holy Land: Noah, dividing the earth among his sons, bound his descendants by a solemn oath not to seize other people's possessions. Canaan alone broke the pledge and wrongfully occupied Palestine, which had been alloted to Arphaxad, the ancestor of the Hebrews. Under Joshua, therefore, the Chosen People had simply resumed possession of their ancestral portion. The destruction of Canaan's seed was a realization of the curse that had sanctioned the oath sworn by Noah's sons. It was good to know that if others had settled in the Promised Land before the Hebrews, they had done so in violation of a solemn compact.

The author of Jubilees does not mention any biblical arguments; he emphasizes, rather, the respect due to a contract. The idea that unlawful occupation cannot create proprietary right was a pillar of Greek law and was accepted by the rabbis. It may even have been known in the international law of the pre-Greek Levant. The notion of immutable boundaries is biblical: Israel was warned not to take so much as a foot of the land of Esau. The Achaemenids, too, regarded Asia as their legitimate domain and resented Greek claims to it. On the other hand, Greek historians never impugned the Jewish right to Palestine and curiously believed that the Hebrews had entered an empty land.

Patriotic tendencies also explain some stories about Hebron, a city which had fallen into the hands of the Edomites after the fall of Jerusalem. The Seventy, mistranslating the original Hebrew (Num. 32:12), describe Caleb as one "who had separated himself," which attests to the early origin of the exuberant rabbinic midrash about the spies sent by Moses into the Promised Land. The Bible tells us that Caleb, who with Joshua retained his faith in God's promises, received Hebron as his portion. The author of Jubilees, on the other hand, connects the building of Hebron with Abraham; claims that all the patriarchs except Joseph are buried there; and, finally, tells of the conquest of the city by the children of Israel in the generation preceding the Exodus. Thus Jewish historical rights to Hebron were abundantly documented.

Another popular tale again opposed the sons of Jacob to hostile Edom. Helped by Moab, Ammon, the Philistines, and other inimical neighbors of Israel, Esau's sons break the oath of reconciliation between Jacob and Esau (unknown in the Bible) and start a war to recover Isaac's heritage. But the cause of right prevails, and the sons of Edom are compelled to pay tribute to the sons of Jacob forever. Note that in this story the men of Hebron side with Jacob.

A related story told of the triumphant wars of Jacob and his sons against other cities and princes of Canaan. An obscure passage in Jacob's blessing gave a biblical pretext for this glorification of ancestral prowess. There was, however, the ticklish case of Shechem. The city was now the seat of the schismatic Samaritans and thus called the "City of Imbeciles" in the Testament of Levi and it must have been very tempting to dwell on the conquest of Shechem by the Patriarchs. Unfortunately, however, according to Genesis, Simon and Levi had captured Shechem through treachery and had been condemned by Jacob for ruining his reputation. The result was that the author of Jubilees, like Joseph later, felt it better simply to omit the unsavory episode in his paraphrase of Genesis. In Levi's testament, however, we are told that the men of Shechem intended to ravish Sarah, that they had vexed Abraham when he was their guest, and that they generally persecuted all visitors and carried away their wives. The author retorts thus to the Samaritan claim that their deity was the protector of guests and that Abraham had been received as a friend at Shechem.

Another martial haggadah popular in the early Hellenistic age, which described the wars of old between Egypt and Canaan as seen from an asiatic point of view, was interestingly enough not of Jewish origin. A fictional echo of the struggles between the pharaohs and the rulers of Asia, it may reflect the tumult of the wars of Thutmosis and Rameses. The version of it used by the Jews was composed in the Persian age, when kings of Assyria appeared as the heads of the first world empire and as rivals of the pharaohs. Manetho, who places the Assyrians in the period of the conquest of Egypt by the Hyksos, reproduces the same anachronistic confusion. Asia, represented by Assyria, is opposed to Egypt in his history, as it is in the Jewish story, in the same way in which Herodotus speaks of the eternal struggle between Asia and Europe. The Jews judaized the tale by attaching it to the story of Joseph, who was, as the Bible tells us, "the first minister" of the pharaoh.

The heuristic value of this tale is great; it directly links the historical and patriotic Haggadah with the patriotic novel (oral or written) of the Hellenistic Levant. A Greek observer, writing shortly after 300 B.C.E., spoke of the glorification of Nebuchadnezzar by the "Assyrians," who ranked him above Herakles, and we have noted how the "mighty deeds of Semiramis" were celebrated "among the Assyrians," that is, in the Aramaic tongue, also spoken in Jerusalem.

Jewish storytellers may have begun to compose their romances of chivalry under the Persian kings, when Jewish mercenaries kept watch on the borders of the Nile in the service of the Achaemenids, heirs of the Assyrian might. For although the rabbis, pacifists by necessity, were not interested in the mighty deeds of Jacob's sons—for them, the Patriarchs spent their days studying Scripture—martial stories continued to be told behind their backs. When later, in the age of Roland and Digenis, tales of chivalry again became poular in the East and the West, the Jews again felt the need for public recognition of the martial spirit of their ancestors. Hence the popularity of *Yosippon,* of the *Sefer Milhamot Benei Jacob,* and of other such tales among the medieval Jews. And hence the inclusion of the story of Jacob's war, in a new elaboration, in the vast compilation *Sefer ha-Yashar,* written in the twelfth century.

Modern scholars, as is their wont, happily discover in these old martial stories precise allusions to the Maccabean conquests. The parochial character of these fictional campaigns excludes such late dating. Greeks are mentioned in them merely as mercenaries in Edom's service and Egypt is merely the background for Palestinian conflicts. A Persian or a Ptolemaic date is therefore more likely. Squeezed between Shechem and Adora, Persian and Ptolemaic Jerusalem enhanced its self-esteem by repeating and embellishing stories of ancestral triumphs. In these tales the listener could admire a skilled swordsman outfencing the heathens, a warrior hurling a stone of sixty pounds against a horseman, and mighty men climbing up a wall of iron that protected the besieged city. Let us not forget that Jewish mercenaries were sought after by both Persian and Macedonian kings and that Jerusalem often had occasion to quarrel with her neighbors. In accordance with the date proposed, Hellenistic motifs are rare in these tales; but they can be found, as for example in Esau's contention in one tale that no oath of friendship is valid forever in political relations, or in the sentimental note that we hear so often in the productions of Hellenistic Jews, which is also sounded by the author of this tale. The Bible simply says that Esau planned to revenge himself on Jacob after the death of Isaac, their father, but the Hellenistic storyteller has Esau strike just when Jacob is mourning for Leah.

In fact, even the martial heroes of the early Hellenistic Haggadah were neither ambitious nor even particularly adventurous; Jerusalem was now a quiet provincial town where Abraham's war against four kings from afar aroused no interest. It may seem curious at first that in an age when Jews were emigrating to far away shores storytellers in Jerusalem were not more venturesome, but David, too, was now remembered only as the lad who slew Goliath and who was the sweet singer of Israel. Although his (or Solomon's) dominion, which extended from Kadesh in Galilee to Kadesh in Sinai, was forgotten, Hezekiah's engineering works in Jerusalem were still talked of. The Jew who left Jerusalem was not looking for a new kind of opportunity; he merely wanted to continue his ancestral manner of life in a larger country. The storyteller only wanted to impress upon the Jewish settlers in Persian Elephantine and in Ptolemaic Arsinöe and upon their fellows in Palestine the lesson of obedience to God, His Law, and His prophets. Success was equated with goodness and godliness, and one hated the troublemaking schismatics in the north and the marauding Arabs in the south. But although the glory of Rameses troubled the sleep of Egyptian priests, Jerusalem and those who had emigrated from Jerusalem were satisfied to be ruled by a benevolent, though pagan, overlord. As Augustine put it: "Of what importance is it under which government man, this mortal being, lives, as long as they who command do not compel him to act impiously or injustly?"

Later Jews, writing in Greek, imagined the mighty deeds of their ancestral heroes on a larger scale: Abraham taught the Phoenicians; Moses, as an Egyptian prince, conquered Ethiopia; and Solomon, like Antiochus III, had the title of "The Great King" (the rulers of Phoenicia and Egypt, his "paternal friends," were merely kings). But even in these exuberant stories the horizon was still limited by the Euphrates and the Nile. By contrast, Taharka (Tirhakah in the Bible), a pharaoh who did not prosper in real life, became the fictional conqueror of remote lands in tales concocted by the Egyptian priests. It was only under the Caesars, who ruled the whole world, that the rabbis imagined Solomon and Ahab in the guise of world emperors.

The overwhelming number of *haggadot,* however, carried no political or theological implications. Many *haggadot* merely answered questions raised by attentive readers of Scripture. For instance, "there is a difficulty" as to why Benjamin received a five-fold portion of food from Joseph. The exegete answers that this was done to equalize the shares of the sons of Rachel and the sons of Leah. "It is queried" where the Hebrews of the Exodus got their weapons. This problem, posed and answered in a Greek book, puzzled the readers of the Septuagint (the Masoretic reading does not mention weapons). Both of these passages are from an Alexandrian source and the questions and answers are formulated in the manner used in the interpretation of Homer. But there must also have been exegetes of the Bible in Jerusalem, even though Ben Sira offers no *haggadot* in his book. He and his fellow sages probably regarded Haggadah with the same attitude with which the Greek philosopher of his time regarded the *mythoi* told by and for the populace. Philosphers excepted, however, everyone liked to listen to *mythoi*—or haggadic exposition—because these tales provoked discussion. In a civilization in which so much was oral, interesting conversation was always welcome. This was the reason for the popularity of parables (Jesus spoke in them), anecdotes, and puzzles. The philosopher Clearchus asserted that it was this kind of material that was right for table talk, and not prattle about food and sex.

In the third century B.C.E., haggadic narratives already existed that roughly followed the outline of the Bible, in a manner similar to that of the later Genesis Apocryphon discovered among the Dead Sea Scrolls. The author of Jubilees made use of this guileless literary genre in order to palm off on the reader his presumptuous revelations. Such haggadic books, together with wandering storytellers, kept the haggadic tradition alive and transmitted it to the rabbis, who rightly stressed its usefulness for popular education. They gave haggadic talks on various social occasions and suited the style and the content of their exposition to the aptitude of their audience.

This method of transmission explains the ideological coherence of haggadic exegesis in space and time. Opposed to crude anthropomorphisms, the philosopher Aristobulus of Alexandria ventured to opine that the Deity had never descended on Mount Sinai. Rewriting the Sinaitic revelation, the Palestinian author of Jubilees was unable to dispense with the meeting between Moses and the Glory of God, but elsewhere he carefully eliminated both the story of Abraham's entertaining the angels and the story of Jacob's striving with God near the river Jabbok.

The schismatics of Shechem also interpreted Israel's past in the spirit of the orthodoxy of Jerusalem. Except for a reference to Mount Gerizim, the haggadic history of Abraham, written in Greek by a Samaritan and erroneously transmitted under the name of Eupolemus, could have passed as having actually been composed by this orthodox writer. For instance, Eupolemus as well as pseudo-Eupolemus presents the Patriarchs as the inventors of the arts. The author of Jubilees, writing in Hebrew, concurs. Pseudo-Eupolemus tells us that the pharaoh who had taken Sarah into his home was unable to approach her, and that Egyptian seers explained to the pharaoh that because he kept Sarah captive his people were afflicted with plagues. The Genesis Apocryphon and the rabbis embroider the same motifs. Historical taste was the same in Jerusalem, Shechem, and Alexandria.

The characteristic feature of early Hellenistic Haggadah was its additive tendency. It was not only deduced from, or sustained by, the biblical text, but it complemented Scripture. Enoch, for instance, became the inventor of writing and, if we may believe the poet Ezechiel, Moses received a report in the wilderness about the appearance of the immortal bird, the phoenix, seen at the sources of Elim. The Torah does not name the pharaoh's daughter who saved Moses, but the rabbis discovered her name in a passage in Chronicles: Bithiah, the daughter of the pharaoh and the wife of Mered (I Chron. 4:17) was identified with Moses' foster mother. In the Hellenistic period, however, the Jews had called her either Termouthis or Merris, both names borrowed from Egyptian lore. In the same way, a Greek version of Isis' deeds added the Greek myth about Demeter holding a baby over the fire in order to make him immortal to the sequence of the ancient Egyptian myth. But we must leave it to learned talmudists to produce a historical study of Jewish exegesis of the Torah and its relationship to Oriental, Greek, and Christian hermeneutics.

TWENTY-ONE

The New Jurisprudence

AFTER the end of the Kingdom of Judah in 587 B.C.E., Mosaic Law could only be reinterpreted; it could not be supplementeed or amended. The Lawgiver was now the heathen suzerain of the Chosen People: Artaxerxes I, who promulgated Ezra's Torah, was the last Lawgiver of Israel.

The development of the "Traditions" or of the "Oral Law," as a later expression put it, was an unavoidable consequence of this lack of legislative power. The Torah was, in itself, final: "Thou shalt not add thereto, nor diminish from it." As the Book of Jubilees and the regulations of the New Covenant show, some groups did not abstain from new codifications, but the validity of these new laws rested on free agreement. Modifications of the statutory law, because they were not sustained by the authority of the (now pagan) state, necessarily took the form of precedents established by men learned in law and then followed by the courts and the royal officers. In this way Hillel could circumvent the biblical law regarding loans and Yohannan ben Zakkai could do away with the biblical ordeal of jealousy.

The earliest extant document of legislation by reinterpretation is the proclamation of Antiochus III regarding the Levitical purity of Jerusalem. As we have seen, Jewish jurists who prepared the proclamation extended to laymen wishing to enter the altar court the same requirements with regard to ablutions as those for the ministering priests. Probably basing their opinion on Leviticus 17:9, they forbade pagan sacrifice in Judea; without any scriptural support they excluded pagans from the altar court in the Temple; and they made it virtually impossible for a visitor to Jerusalem to partake of unclean meat. All these interpretations were sanctioned by Antiochus III as the "ancestral laws" of the Jews. Here we must note that although the sanctity of ancestral observance seemed the best and most natural source of law for the Greeks, for rabbinical jurisprudence the law emanated from God. Was the reference to "ancestral laws" in Antiochus' proclamation a concession to the Greek view, or did the jurisconsults of the Temple, differing from the rabbis, accept the legislative validity of customary rules? Similarly, although the fine prescribed in the royal proclamation was a common sanction in Greece, it is unknown in Jewish law, in which damages are collected in favor of the injured party but an offender is not mulcted. On the other hand, monies collected as penalties were assigned by Antiochus III to the priests, a practice that agrees with the biblical rule that restitution made for a trespass committed against the Lord belongs to the priest.

The applicability of the Jewish legal system, however, could be affected by royal statutes, which overrode native (as well as city) laws. The ensuing conflict in Macedonian Jerusalem can be illustrated by two examples. The Torah prohibits taking interest from an Israelite but expressly allows it without limitation on money lent to gentiles, while Ptolemaic law allowed interest but set up a maximum rate. Again, Scripture enjoins the Hebrews to use honest weights and measures but fixes no penalty for transgression. According to rabbinic principles of interpretation, this implies that a fraudulent seller must make restitution to the wronged buyer. In the law of the Greeks, on the other hand, possession and use of false weights and measures was a public crime harshly punished by the magistrates. Under the Seleucids, and surely under the Ptolemies, there was a Jewish market commissioner *(agoranomos)* in Jerusalem who fined or flogged the trader caught with false weights and measures in his possession.

A Ptolemaic ordinance mentioned earlier is of particular value for the study of the interrelation between royal law and Mosaic law. The ordinance issued in 262–261 B.C.E. for "Syria and Phoenicia" forbids the purchase of free natives of the lowest classes *(laoi* in Greek) or the acceptance of their persons as a pledge; persons aleady enslaved were to be declared free (and probably were freed). Kidnapping a free man and selling him as a slave had always been a crime; it seems that the new Ptolemaic ordinance was directed against businessmen who tried to transform some of the modes of oriental bondage that did *not* deprive the bondsman of his legal rights into chattel slavery (on which point Ptolemy II was in complete agreement with Moses and the Jewish jurists).

In Syria, Ptolemy II was dealing with the abuse of two particular forms of enslavement. There was, first, the sale of either oneself or one's family into slavery. This practice, which was common in the ancient Near East, had been limited by the Hebrew legislator. According to the Torah, a daughter could be sold by her father only as the concubine of the buyer or of his son. This eliminated the possibility of her being resold as a bride, of her being used as a slave-concubine for prostitution, or even of her being used simply for work. On the other hand, the sale of oneself (and, by analogy, the sale of one's son or wife) had been transformed into indentured service by means of the rule that every "Hebrew slave" must be released in the seventh year of bondage. Because, according to another norm, such persons could not be resold, their bondage was a kind of contractual general service of limited tenure, like the Greek *paramone*. As the biblical text says, and as the Septuagint version stresses, the impoverished "brother" was to be "like a hired hand," and was not to serve as a "household slave." The later rabbinic discussion of the status of the Hebrew slave, which appears meaningless (or "humanitarian") to a modern reader, is, on the contrary, full of meaning when viewed against the background of the *paramone*.

The second form of enslavement was debt servitude, which since Solon (594 B.C.E.) had virtually disappeared in the Greek world, except in the case of debt to the state, but had continued to be practiced in the Near East, where men often mortgaged themselves or their families. Nehemiah himself made loans secured by the person of the borrower. Mosaic law, however, prescribes the release of every pawned pledge in the seventh year.

It is interesting to note that the Greek version of the Torah formulates this norm differently from the Hebrew original. It reads: "Release every private debt that thy neighbor owes thee." By implicitly excluding public debts from the benefit of cancellation the Septuagint is in agreement with Greek law, as well as with the ordinance of Ptolemy II, which in a similar manner reserves for the government alone the right to sell fiscal debtors into slavery.

Nevertheless, the essential point to understand about the Septuagint rendering of the Hebrew text is that the biblical problem of debt slavery has become the Hellenistic problem of money debts. The insolvent debtor was now not enslaved, but rather put into detention, in order to compel him to pay. Ptolemy's ordinance, in this instance, was directed against usurers who on their own authority seized native debtors and sold them as slaves. A relatively fluid money economy had made borrowing easier.

At Elephantine, in 401 B.C.E., a loan in kind *(emmer)* was taken by a man who, twelve days later, bought a house. To secure his debt, he attached his whole property—but not himself or his family. Ben Sira shows that in his own time, around 200 B.C.E., credit transactions in Jerusalem were common and the payment of a debt was guaranteed by the property and not the person of the borrower or his surety. As Ben Sira says, many men of wealth lost their homes through standing surety, which implies that a guarantor, and consequently the principal debtor too, pledged his entire property as security against repayment of a debt.

This idea of a general lien in favor of the creditor had already been used by Jews at Elephantine toward the end of the fifth century B.C.E. When Simeon ben Shetah, a century after Ben Sira, gave to a wife a general lien on her husband's property as security for her *ketubah,* he applied to her case a general rule that already governed commercial transactions. The essentials of the talmudic law of obligation, in which a man's property stands as surety for him, had been formulated by the jurists of Jerusalm before 200 B.C.E.

The Macedonian overlords, like the Achaemenids before them, generally left private law to local authorities and private agreements, as long as its autonomous development did not hurt the fiscus. We have seen how the case law of notaries modified the status of Jewish women in the marriage contracts of Persian Egypt. With regard to Palestine, we have a somewhat anachronistic, yet valuable, rabbinic tradition on the history of payments in connection with marriage. In the beginning, the rabbis report, the groom paid money to his future father-in-law for the maintenance of the bride in case the marriage was dissolved. This practice agrees with that reflected in the biblical story in which Laban's daughters complain that their father sold them to Jacob and devoured their "silver" (that is, their bride-price). In the next phase, the bride-price was left in the hands of the husband to hold in trust for his wife. This, as noted, is a stage similar to that reported in the fifth-century Elephantine papyri: the bride "brings in" her marriage-price, which is returned to her at divorce. In the third stage the bride, to secure the divorce indemnity, transformed the nuptial price into silver objects, a common method of storing wealth in the ancient world. Confirming evidence is still lacking for this last phase, but the rabbinic report presupposes a wide use of coined money. This brings us to the Macedonian period in Palestine, when toward the beginning of the first century B.C.E. Simeon ben Shetah, as we have just seen, substituted for the payment of the bride-price in cash a pledge made by the groom and secured by a general lien on his property. It is also significant that this historical reconstruction of the rabbis deals exclusively with the evolution of the groom's settlement upon the bride. As late as the fifth century B.C.E., as evidenced by the Elephantine marriage contracts, dowry in the proper sense of the term was not given among the Jews.

For the average Greek, however, it was the dowry that distinguished a legitimate alliance from concubinage. It is significant with respect to the hellenization of the Jews that the rabbis accepted this idea and, no less than the Greeks, insisted on the principle that there could be no dowry outside legitimate marriage—this despite the fact that the Jewish law of marriage, as we have just seen, was centered on the *mohar* (the bride-price) and despite the significant lack of a fixed term for "dowry" in Hebrew (Aramaic) legal language. Indeed, the rabbis often resorted to the Greek term *pherne*.

The Seventy, however, by rendering the biblical term *mohar* as *pherne*, demonstrate that in the first half of the third century B.C.E. the use of dowry was already well known among the Jews. Toward the end of the same century, in the Testaments of the Twelve Patriarchs, a store of gold goes with Judah's wife and a hundred talents of gold are given to Joseph with his Egyptian bride. Ben Sira considered a dowry to be a kind of bait; he warns against being enticed by the beauty or by the goods of a girl, and he speaks of the disgrace of a husband who depends on his wife's support for his livelihood.

Thus, if the Elephantine documents are admitted as evidence for Palestine, the Jews in Jerusalem passed from a regime in which the estate of the wife was held apart to the dotal system in which at least a great part of the wife's property was managed by the husband and was used for the maintenance of the household. This evolution was made possible—indeed almost necessary—by the money economy brought about by Macedonian rule in Palestine. Earlier an endowment of a bride would have meant the transfer of furniture, equipment, and cattle to the bridegroom (a father would have had no right, according to custom, to alienate land from his sons by settling it on a daughter). In a developed economy, however, with the new mobility of coined money, raising a crop for market easily secured the necessary cash for the dowry; while at the same time, in an agnatic society from which the clans, as we have seen, had virtually disappeared, a young bridegroom needed capital in order to start a new household.

Nevertheless, economic conditions alone cannot explain the new role of the dowry in Jewish marriage, because it is clear that different financial arrangements governing the monies and properties of the married parties can coexist under similar conditions of social development. Economics does not necessarily dictate that one and only one arrangement is appropriate. In Hellenistic Jerusalem, the desire to imitate Greek ways must have provided the stimulus for the introduction of the institution of the dowry into the Jewish system of marriage payments, so that the contribution that the wife made to the husband for the expenses of the household was in addition to the settlement made upon the bride by the groom. As we have mentioned, the rabbis used the Greek term *pherne* (as well as the catchall expression *ketubah*) to describe the dotal arrangement. In fact, in a papyrus of 218 B.C.E., a certain Helladote, probably a Greek woman, sues her Jewish husband Jonathan in a matter of dowry *(pherne)*.

The dowry was probably first introduced into Jewish marriage contracts by the scribes of the diaspora. On the other hand, the scribes, in the interest of the wife, evaded the principle of the agnatic devolution of property established in Mosaic law. The notion that a last will becomes valid only after the death of its author is foreign to the Jewish legal system. For this reason the scribes utilized the form of the *donatio inter vivos* and made it into a quasitestamental disposition. It is significant that in rabbinic language this instrument is called, improperly, *diatheke*, that is, a testate succession. Thus, while the Torah grants no succession rights to the widow, the Jews in Elephantine stipulated at the time of the marriage that either spouse could inherit from the other if there were no children. Two centuries later, Judith's husband left her his whole estate unconditionally, and before she died she disposed of her goods in her own right. The Book of Judith is Maccabean, but even in pre-Maccabean times Ben Sira had spoken of women who inherited their husbands' (or fathers') property.

Thus, about 200 B.C.E., the right of a widow to inherit was recognized by the Jews from Egypt to Persia; about 180 B.C.E., a great part of the deposits entrusted to the Temple for safekeeping belonged to widows and orphans. One is reminded of complaints made in Sparta during the middle of the third century B.C.E. that too much property was owned by women. In Sparta, this evolution was made possible by a new law validating such testaments. But in Jerusalem, nobody abrogated or amended the Law of Moses, which of course made it possible for the rabbis in later years to return to a far stricter interpretation of the property rights of women. In the Persian and Hellenistic periods, however, the scribes, by using the device of the private agreement marginal to the law, succeeded in evading its rules. By explicitly articulating the rights pertaining to a wife in the marriage contract itself, which were not expressed and were therefore unprotected in biblical law, the scribes raise the status of married women in Jerusalem. Rabbinic tradition rightly regarded the *ketubah*, the "writ" par excellence that today still forms the legal basis of a Jewish marriage, as an innovation of the scribes.

Most important, the family was now monogamous. Ben Sira's book is explicit on this point. While polygamy, permitted in the Bible, was certainly not outlawed and continued to be practiced by the Jews under the Caesars even after its general interdiction by Diocletian, the desultory appetite of the male was generally checked by stipulations agreed on in the *ketubah* and sanctioned by monetary penalties. A clause in the oriental *ketubah* of today still repeats the promise of the bridegroom, which appeared at Elephantine in the fifth century B.C.E., not to take a second wife. The occidental form of the *ketubah* expresses the same idea by obliging the bridegroom to provide the bride with food, clothing, and other necessites, and to perform his conjugal duties, a formulation already found in the Septuagint.

In Ben Sira, adultery leads to the same punishment for both the man and the woman: the unfaithful husband "will be judged in the squares of the city," where the court met, and the woman who leaves her husband "will be brought out into the assembly." As in Persian Elephantine, the marriage contract in early hellenistic Jerusalem established the equality of the spouses with regard to divorce.

Literature reflects the new status of the fair sex. Potiphar's wife now offers not only herself but also all her property to the incorruptible Joseph, and Rebecca advises her son about his marriage even before Isaac does so. She blesses Jacob, who not only gives sustenance to his father, but also sends gifts to his mother four times a year. In a somewhat later text, Sarah is praised for her understanding as well as her beauty. In the Book of Jubilees, Ham and Shem, like Hellenistic kings, name cities after their respective wives. Later, Judith is the first woman among the Hebrews who prays for the nation and is elected to save Israel. It is not by chance that erotic motifs began to adorn popular stories.

Equal to her husband in private law by virtue of the marriage contract, a woman now also had the advantage of both dowry and an independent estate. Some women were even able to maintain their husbands. But such financial advantages over men, in addition to the social advancement of women, were bound to be resented by the old-fashioned moralists. The misogynist virulence of Kohelet and Ben Sira is unparalleled in earlier Hebrew literature. Ben Sira forcefully attacks the idea of emancipation; his ideal is still the woman who cannot do as she pleases and who abstains not only from impudence and wine, but also from jealousy. His ideal, actually, is a silent wife. Speaking of the wedded wife, he sometimes alludes to the warning in Proverbs against foreign women. It is even more significant that Ben Sira is the first writer who sees the origin of sin and the source of death in Eve's fall.

The spirit of emancipation seems to have created new problems for the fathers of marriageable girls, too. Ben Sira tells us that a willful daughter should be watched, "lest discovering license, she abuses it." The father not only had to worry about whether his daughter would find a husband, or whether once she did she would be barren, or whether she would misbehave after marriage, but now he also had the added fear that his daughter might be seduced and become pregnant while still in his home. It would seem, thus, that marriage no longer coincided with puberty. Moreover, it seems that, in agreement with later rabbinic jurisprudence, a daughter more than twelve years old was already regarded as no longer subject to *patria potestas,* at least with regard to her betrothal.

It is a remarkable fact that rabbinic jurisprudence, at least from the end of the second century C.E., tended to return the wife to the protection of her husband. The developed rabbinic system excludes the possibility of a divorce initiated by the wife, and by establishing the concept of community property in marriage makes it virtually impossible for a wife to own anything independently. In this system the wife does not inherit from the husband. He, on the other hand, inherits not only the dowry she brought with her into the marriage but all her property as well. It is particularly remarkable that the rabbis in this way opposed the tendency of Roman (and Roman-Egyptian) law to emancipate the wife.

In Ptolemaic Egypt, as long as the direct interests of the government were not involved, all crimes except homicide and highway robbery were regarded not as public wrongs, but as private offenses punishable by damages. Prosecution was introduced by the injured party, even in homicide cases. Since there was no royal administrator in Hellenistic Jerusalem, it is hard to believe that first the Ptolemies and then the Seleucids removed penal jurisdiction of this kind from the Jewish authorities in the city. On the other hand, the Jewish authorities could hardly prevent a party from appealing to royal jurisdiction. With these contradictions in mind, we may ask whether the substitution of money compensation for the biblical rule of talion in assault and battery cases was not stimulated by the fact that in Greek law the penalty in these matters was financial.

It is interesting to note, however, that the principle of "an eye for an eye" was somewhat foreign even to the mentality of the ancient Hebrews. Except in a few rules of criminal law borrowed from the earlier oriental codes, the rule of talion is not held to in the Bible: if a man afflicts the widow and the orphan, he is to die by the sword. Yet in the Hellenistic books of the Jews the idea of talion is obsessive: "By what things a man transgresses, by the same also is he punished"; in the Book of Esther, Haman is hanged on the gallows he prepared for Mordecai. In Greek thought the principle of exact retribution was always present, its validity never disputed; even when the courts no longer applied it, the gods continued to do so. The Jews of the Greek age, it would seem, and after that the rabbis, took this dual attitude over from the Greeks. Although they, too, generally substituted monetary compensation for the physical penalties prescribed in biblical criminal law, they also supported the firm belief that divine justice strictly repays evil in kind.

We must limit ourselves to these rather unsatisfactory and random observations, since a history of Jewish law can be written only by a competent talmudist who is also versed in the general history of the legal systems of the ancient world. It is a pity that specialists in talmudic studies, who eagerly look for any trace of earlier Halakhah in late sources, like Philo, have never tried to evaluate the evidence offered by the Septuagint, Philo's source, or that offered by other books of the Hellenistic age. As a matter of fact, the cursory observations of Z. Frankel, written more than a century ago, remain the best work on the Jewish law of the Greek version of the Torah. Lacking a palingenesis of Jewish law, the historian can only note some legal facts and tendencies of general import which, by external evidence, may be assigned to the pre-Maccabean period.

TWENTY-TWO

New Literature

A PECULIARITY of the Jewish literature of the Hellenistic age is the abundance of pseudonymous works. On the eve of the Great Rebellion against Rome in 66 C.E., for instance, the sectarians of the New Covenant in their settlement at the Dead Sea had in their library the *Psalms of Joshua,* as well as a speech made by Moses on Mount Nebo, scrolls signed by such worthies as Enoch and Noah, and many other similar works. This pseudepigraphic aspect of postbiblical literature attracted attention at an early date. From Irenaeus (ca. 180 C.E.) on the Church Fathers speak about it; Jerome warns an avid reader that all apocryphal books are not necessarily written by those to whom they are ascribed. The argument of spuriousness was, in fact, of no little weight in the ecclesiastical controversy over the value of the apocrypha.

Modern critics for the most part hold that postbiblical authors concealed their identity under one or another of the great names of old in order to impress their readers, while other critics have recourse to various psychological hypotheses. In fact, however, the problem of pseudepigraphy belongs to the history of literary genres. In the ancient pre-Hellenistic Orient, literary production was generally anonymous. All narratives (history as well as belles lettres and myth) followed this stylistic rule because they all purported to be factual records of actual happenings. An official historiographer "put into writing, according to the facts," the victories won by Thutmose III of Egypt, but in the royal annals, carved upon the walls of Egyptian temples, his account appears as an anonymous and objective report of the Pharaoh's deeds. The name of the narrator would have introduced a subjective element into the narrative and impaired its absoluteness. This attitude explains the paradox that Egyptian and Babylonian scribes signed the copies they made of literary works while the authors themselves remained nameless. The signature of the copyist and the anonymity of the author both served as assurances of the veracity of the text.

On the other hand, everything that was written in order to regulate the conduct of the reader required the name of the authority delivering the precepts. It is obvious that the laws of Hammurabi had to bear his name in order to be considered valid. Consequently, sapiential books, which had the form, content, and name of "Instructions," could not be published without the name of the author, who naturally was a man of authority: King Solomon, the vizier Ptah-hotep, or even Saggil-kinam-ubbib, an incantation priest and the author of a Babylonian dialogue between a sufferer and his friend. When an Egyptian scribe speaks of the eternity of literary fame that survives the pyramids, this predecessor of Horace names only celebrated sages as examples of writers who are revered forever.

Accordingly there is no clear evidence for the existence of pseudonymous works in the ancient Near East, where literary fabrication took the form of anonymous records. For instance, an Egyptian apocalypse, composed probably approximately 2000 B.C.E., is presented to the reader as a report of predictions made to the Pharaoh Snofru, who had reigned around 2700. A seer predicts to Snofru events that occurred four centuries later. It is a moot question whether this presentation is more or less convincing (and disingenuous) than the cloak of a famous pseudonym.

Writing in Hebrew or Aramaic, Jewish authors of the Hellenistic age continued to conform to the literary conventions of their ancestors. Following the example of King Solomon, of Agur the son of Jakeh, and of other wise men of old, Ben Sira put his name to his book of sage advice, but Esther, Judith, I Maccabees, and later the *Seder Olam Rabbah* and *Megillat Antiochus,* following the example of the historical books of the Bible, were published anonymously. Similarly, collections of traditional materials, like the sectarian commentary on Habakkuk found at Qumran, bear no author's name. Indeed, the so-called pseudepigrapha are to a great extent technically anonymous writings. For instance, the Book of Jubilees is in form an objective report concerning the commandments given to Moses on Sinai; the reporter is not named—just as he is not mentioned in the biblical description of the Sinaitic theophany itself. In fact, only visions, epistles, and similar autobiographical works are actually pseudonymous: the Words of Enoch, the Words of Moses, the Epistle of Enoch, the Revelations of Abraham. The difference in form between the stories about Daniel and the books containing his visions illustrates the point. Generally speaking, anonymous works were written *ad narrandum* and the pseudepigraphs *ad probandum.*

In the Hellenistic age, archaism was a part of the general reaction of the ancient civilizations of the Near East to their new barbarian masters.

When the Egyptian priests who wrote under the Ptolemies endeavored to imitate their classical language, already obsolete for some twelve hundred years, and when the Hasmoneans started to use an ancient Hebrew alphabet on their coins, writers, too, turned back to the times of the Flood. The books about or ascribed to men of ancient renown compensated the native intelligentsia for the inferiority of its present status; even the Greeks ascribed profundity and wisdom to the spiritual ancestors of these modern writers in Jerusalem and Memphis. Jewish books about Moses or the sons of Jacob written in the Hellenistic age paralleled Egyptian stories, written at the same time, about Setne, a son of Rameses II, the pharaoh of the Exodus, and about Imhotep, a deified sage who lived some fifteen hundred years before the Exodus. The fashion having been set, who could hope that his own plebeian name or the story he was telling would attract the reader's attention? The name of an antediluvian patriarch not only objectified the advice given by the author; it clearly secured a larger audience.

Authors had yet another motive for producing pseudepigraphs. Hellenistic civilization in spite of all its innovations remained a traditional civilization in which novelty was suspect. The author and his readers, therefore, felt the need to seek counsel from the worthies who had already been accepted as teachers of previous generations. Frivolous Greeks might contrast the recollections of Menelaus, as recorded in an interview with an Egyptian priest, with the story of Homer, but a Jew could find no name to set against or beside those of Moses and other biblical heroes. To put it in modern terms, the Jewish literature of the Hellenistic age belongs, in great part, to the genre of historical fiction.

Yet pure fiction, "the fact invented, but which could have happened," as Cicero defines the genre, was thought to be unworthy of serious attention; in order to be considered worthy a story had to be a part and parcel of history. As Aristotle observed, names of historical persons in a work of fiction enhance its credibility; we doubt, he says, whether something that is not known to have happened could have happened at all.

Moreover, in an age in which books were meant to be read aloud, it was important to set a story in a framework already familiar to the audience. Just as the name of Oedipus evoked the whole myth in the mind of an Athenian spectator, so the mention of Jacob helped the Jewish listener to relate to a new tale. But while Athenian dramatists chose their themes from a small number of popular myths known to the average theatergoer, and Hellenistic authors borrowed from the stores of half-forgotten myths as well as from local lore, for the Jew, as we have already observed, the Bible was the sole source of information about the national past. Thus Jewish literature of the Greek age was in great part parabiblical, a kind of midrash on Scripture. For this reason, too, the Jewish author felt no need to authenticate his tale. In the scribal literature of later Egypt, a historical romance is presented as being derived from the inscription engraved by the hero, King Petubastis, at the temple of Heliopolis; but the author of Tobit, like the author of Ruth, does not feel it necessary to indicate the source of his family story. The Jewish listener, accustomed to the way biblical stories were told, did not ask how the narrator of the new stories he was hearing knew of the happenings he was reciting.

In the Greek terminology of the Hellenistic age, the parabiblical book would have been styled a *mythos*. According to Stoic theory a *mythos* was a fictional embellishment of actual facts. Cities and lawgivers invented this genre in order to educate the common people, for man is fond of knowledge and listening to tales is the beginning of knowledge. To put it in our terms, the ideological concepts of a society are made visible in its myths. This is particularly true with regard to the parabiblical books: their heroes are the founders of Israel and, for the most part, the direct ancestors of the readers of these books. Moreover, since these tales discretely strengthened the attachment of the Jew to his faith, we may compare them to the miracle plays of the Middle Ages.

The so-called Testaments of the Twelve Patriarchs, written in Hebrew toward the end of the third century B.C.E., but except for some Hebrew and Aramaic fragments preserved only in Greek, may illustrate the genre of parabiblical books. The Testaments, in fact, are "Copies of the Words" spoken on his deathbed by each of Jacob's sons to his own progeny. Each address, given in the first person, is preceded by and concludes with historical notes on the occasion of the discourse and by a final remark about the death and burial of the Patriarch. These last constitute the framework of the address and are written in the third person.

The combination of third-person reportage with first-person narrative, necessitated by the difficulty of relating a long speech in indirect discourse, is biblical. Actually, the idea of the entire work is biblical: the blessings Jacob gives his sons in Genesis 49 are alluded to and imitated by the author of the Testaments. In the Testaments, however, Jacob's sons also give moral instruction to their sons, an idea not found in Genesis. Yet here, too, the author has followed a biblical model: the injunctions of Moses and Joshua to the people of Israel and David's advice to Solomon, his son. Tobit's address to his family also links the Testaments chronologically with its biblical models. The genre survived in later centuries as the "ethical wills" of Jewish sages and worthies.

Still, in the biblical models, and also in Tobit and in wisdom literature generally, the advice given is impersonal and the wisdom anonymous and objective; there are no self-revelations in Ben Sira, and Kohelet, although speaking of and from his personal experience of good and evil,

offers no self-portrayal. But the twelve patriarchs in the Testaments mor-
alize on the basis of their own life histories. Each farewell address contains
an account of those incidents in the life of the speaker which are apt to
teach a moral lesson. Everyone knows that anger is a deadly sin, but Dan
tells us how the spirit of anger almost caused him to murder his brother
Joseph. It is easy to thunder against fornication, but when Reuben reveals
to his sons the hideous secret of his life, his defilement of his father's
concubine Bilhah, we are better prepared to heed his advice to resist the
bewitching beauty of women.

The Bible, by representing our great ancestors as weak and corruptible
and by leaving all the glory to God alone, made such a treatment of the
founding fathers of Israel possible. But although everyone knew that a
contrite heart was a sacrifice to God, the technique used in the Testaments
to elicit such contrition was new. Confession was added to instruction.
Publicly repentant sinners now become the teachers of those still unre-
pentant. This literary device can of course be traced back to the actual
practice of confession, but in the Testaments penitential self-scrutiny is
used as a means of dramatization. The author of the Testaments is a
forgotten forerunner of Ephraim the Syrian, Jerome, and Augustine, all
of whom made the confession of sins into a literary genre. But the spurious
humility of the Christian imitators and their self-glorification through
self-abasement is absent in the Testaments. If Simon and Reuben, when
sick unto death, acknowledge their transgressions, Benjamin and Joseph
with the same outspokenness tell of their virtuous actions. *Longe iter est
per praeceptum, breve et efficax per exemplum.*

As the Byzantine copyists of the Testaments noted, each patriarch
concentrates on a particular topic. Reuben warns against unchaste thoughts,
Simon against envy, and Judah against greed and fornication. Dan attacks
anger and lying; Issachar offers a pattern of innocent simplicity; and
Zebulun preaches compassion. Naphtali praises natural goodness and
Asher uprightness, whereas Joseph shows the value of self-control, and
Benjamin recommends purity of mind. Only Levi's address, which con-
cerns the priesthood, preaches no moral lesson, but then Levi's sons are
priests and his admonitions deal with sacerdotal duties. Still, like his
brothers, Levi is a prototype. His self-disclosure, like self-disclosure in
Greek literature generally, is the description of a manner of life. For the
Greeks, a man's actions not only reveal his character, they create it.

The exemplification of virtues and vices that we find in the Testaments
is also Greek. Penitents of the pre-Greek Orient speak impersonally, as
they do even now in the liturgy of the synagogue. What matters are their
sins, not their subjective feelings or personal accidents. The psychological
self-portrayal of the patriarchs in the Testaments, however, is a product
of the Hellenistic study and schematization of human character. Theo-

phrastus' Characters and the Peripatetic biographies, in which an individual is presented as an example of a *bios,* or particular way of living, are the necessary background of the Testaments. Popular philosophy appropriated the results of this kind of psychological classification and disquisition for didactic purposes: famous men of the past were cited as paragons of certain qualities or faults. If Zebulun is a model of compassion in the Testaments, Aristides was a model of justice for the Greeks, and Cato a model of severity for the Romans. A good part of the imaginary epistolography fabricated in the Hellenistic age, such as the letters of Diogenes, simply serves for the psychological portrayal of types of men. Yet, as much as the Greeks liked gossip and filled volumes with personal anecdotes, there is no literary confession in Greek paganism. A Greek would never have accepted Augustine's statement that "tears of confession" are a sacrifice to God.

The modernization of biblical stories was not only possible but unavoidable in our period. Because pure fiction did not exist at this date, in order to express new ideas an author had to remodel an existing factual narrative. For this reason the historical narratives of the masters of Alexandrian poetry were permeated with erotic themes. To depict contemporary Alexandrian lovers, Apollonius casts them as Medea and Jason, and in Dictys' retelling of the Trojan War, Achilles falls in love with Polyxena at first sight. Similarly, if the thoughts of a Hebrew writer who was a contemporary of Apollonius or Dictys turned to the beauty of women who adorn their heads and embellish their faces to allure the children of men, he could only express his longings in biblical symbols.

"The sons of God" who, according to the Bible, "came in to the daughters of men," was a tantalizing story, yet the pre-Hellenistic (or early Hellenistic) variations on this biblical theme stressed, rather, its grisly aspects: the mutual curse by which the Fallen Angels bound themselves; the man-devouring giants begotten by them; the dire punishment of the celestial transgressors by God. The attitude of the hellenized writers of Jerusalem was different; they were interested in psychology. The Bible records Reuben's sin in a short, matter-of-fact sentence and mentions it again only in order to explain Reuben's loss of primogeniture. The Hellenistic author, on the other hand, tries to determine the psychological background of the episode: had Reuben not seen Bilhah bathing, he would not have succumbed to the seduction. (This Bathsheba motif seemed to please Jewish authors; it also appears in the Susanna story.) Further, we are told that Bilhah, sunk in a drunken slumber, remained unaware of the outrage. According to another writer, however, she was ashamed and therefore not only let Reuben flee but failed to report the matter to Jacob until he wanted to approach her.

Joseph's temptation provided another occasion to dwell on erotic psychology. An author whose account of this tale came to be included in our text of the Testaments of the Twelve Patriarchs described at length the wiles of Potiphar's wife—how she embraced the hero under the pretext of maternal feelings, how she sent him a love potion, and how she bared her body before him, "for she was very beautiful and splendidly adorned." In this author's description of the duel between manly self-restraint and female desire, he makes use chiefly of motifs from the Greek Phaedra stories. But he uses these Greek elements in the same manner as he uses the biblical incidents he introduces, that is, as materials for a new psychological picture of men and women and their doings in his generation. For instance, the idea of suicide for love's sake derives from Greek erotic literature. Jews saw things differently; thus in the Book of Tobit, Sarah thinks of ending her life not because of love but because of her sense of honor. The author of the Testaments, however, uses the motif of suicide in order to develop psychological insight into a woman's character: when Joseph dissuades the Egyptian woman from her plan to kill herself, she takes that as evidence of his love for her.

Particularly interesting is the new understanding of the Tamar episode. Tamar, who one way or another must become a mother by the kin of her deceased husband, is a true heroine to the original narrator of her tale; but because the tribal idea of honor was not only incomprehensible but shocking to a man of the Hellenistic age, Josephus omitted the incident and Philo allegorized it. In Jubilees the episode is retold in biblical terms, although the author attaches the prohibition of incest to it and stresses Judah's penitence. Later, some opposed the synagogal reading of this portion of the Torah. The contrition of the Patriarch is also stressed in the Testaments, but here the author wants above all to understand Judah's beavior: how was he, a *paterfamilias,* not ashamed to take a harlot before the eyes of all, at the city gate? (We remember the lascivious graybeard in the Greek comedy.) How could he not have recognized his daughter-in-law in her disguise? The author simply supposes that the Patriarch was drunk. But when he tries to understand how Judah could have believed Tamar's proofs of his visit to her, since Tamar could have obtained the pledges he left with the (supposed) harlot from her, it is clear the author is thinking of the tokens of recognition in Greek comedy.

Moreover, thinking of Hellenistic courtesans, the author of the Testaments (as well as the translators of the Septuagint before him and the rabbis after him) could not understand Tamar's attire as described in Genesis. But having heard the Herodotean tale (or a similar one) of a bride's sacrifice of her chastity, the author attributed the same custom to the "Amorites," and had Tamar sit at the gate in her bridal array. One final innovation: Judah's fall from grace was seen to be a direct result of his boasting about his self-control. The love described by these

Jewish authors is, as in most Alexandrian literature, only carnal. Of course, they deal only with illicit relationships; marriage was distinct from love in a society in which maidens were kept within doors until married off by their fathers.

While Genesis narrates, the author of the Testaments moralizes. Another erotic story that seemed unbecoming to national heroes told how Simon and Levi treacherously massacred the city of Shechem to avenge their defiled sister. Because the ravisher, in agreement with Mosaic law, had offered to marry Dinah, and because such a marriage would have repaired the outrage according to the standards of Hellenistic society, the murderous actions of the sons of Jacob seemed totally unjustifiable. The author of the Testaments resolves the situation by transforming the vendetta into a police action: the men of Shechem customarily attacked foreign women and it is for this that they were punished by Simon and Levi.

Another new, and at first sight surprising, feature of the literature of the period is the chastity of the Jewish hero. A bachelor at the age of sixty-three, Jacob tells his mother that he is still innocent. Issachar, too, knew no woman before his marriage. In the Bible, Joseph refuses the advances of Potiphar's wife because of his loyalty to his master; in Jubilees and in the Testaments, although struggling with a "burning flame," he rejects adultery and conquers his desire by means of fasting, tears, and prayer.

It would be erroneous to look for any ascetic tendency in the emphasis on this behavior; it is simply a means of idealizing the hero, a tendency paralleled in Greek romance. Cyrus, Alexander, and Scipio Africanus were praised for their self-control with regard to captive beauties. In a Hellenistic historical novel, Ninus, king and conqueror, nevertheless abstains from any commerce with woman, although it is true that his motive is not self-control but the desire to be worthy of and faithful to Semiramis, his love. After this work, perseverance in chastity until wedlock becomes an important feature of virtually all Greek romances, even of the salacious Daphnis and Chloe. Greek popular philosophy preached the same ideal of purity for both men and women. Philo asserts that among the Jews both parties entered marriage in a state of virginity. Indeed, Judith, though childless, remains a widow, in agreement with the Hellenistic ideal. It is sufficient to remember Tamar and Ruth in order to appreciate this ideological change, which mirrored a new status for women in Hellenistic society.

Of course, reality fell short of the ideal: Ninus remarks that although he is already seventeen years old and still pure, few boys were pure even at the age of fifteen. Joseph, the famous tax-farmer of Ptolemaic Jerusalem, was ready to risk his life in order to satisfy the desire aroused in him by the sight of a dancing-girl. The youth in love with a courtesan was a stock figure of Hellenistic comedy, and in the Testaments Judah speaks to Tamar with a biblical plainness that would have shocked even the lecherous old men trying to win the favors of courtesans in the New Comedy.

The author of the Testaments also pays attention to the other passions, such as envy, anger, and hate, whose symptoms and consequences are analyzed in the best manner of Greek science. The sale of Joseph is described four times by four different eyewitnesses, each of whom stresses a particular point of view. But whereas Simon, Zebulun, and Gad each discusses his own guilt, the innocent Benjamin reports the impressions of Joseph himself. It is especially fine that the victim of his brothers does not mention these impressions in his last words.

The author also ponders the tender emotions: Jacob was not angry with Reuben for defiling his concubine, but comforted his son and prayed with him that the Lord might forgive his sin. This sidelight on the character of a Hellenistic father would have pleased Menander himself. And hand in hand with the new sensibility, Hellenistic emotionalism also colors the picture. In the Bible, as in oriental literatures generally, and even still in Tobit, tears are ceremonial: one cries on separating, meeting, or in sorrow. In the Testaments, however, not only does Joseph cry when asking his brothers to let him off, but Zebulun also begins to wail, unable to bear Joseph's lamentations. Jacob weeps when he remembers Joseph, and Naphtali cries with him. And again in the best Alexandrian manner, these emotions are interwoven with action: when Joseph sees that Zebulun is sympathetic he tries to hide behind his compassionate brother.

In a similar vein, the author of Jubilees delights in adding sentimental traits to the austere and monumental brevity of Genesis. Although Scripture expends exactly two words on the description of Abraham's death—"Abraham expired"—in the Book of Jubilees the death of the patriarch is elaborated in the Alexandrian manner. Jacob sleeps in Abraham's bed, on the bosom of his grandfather, and does not realize that the latter has already left this world. Awakening, Jacob feels Abraham's cold body. He calls him: "Father, father . . ." He runs to tell the news to Rebecca, who brings the news to Isaac. All three return to Abraham's chamber, Jacob holding a lamp in his hand. Their voices arouse Ishmael, and now the whole family weeps over Abraham. This is a magnificent genre scene, written as if by Callimachus.

Alexandrian too is the glorification of the virtue of rustic simplicity in the Testaments of Issachar. The corresponding Hebrew terms *tam* and *peti* have no glamorous connotations. *Tam* is the sacrificial victim without ritual defect; a man who is *tam* is *vir integer*. But guilelessness alone did not satisfy the Hebrews. *Vir simplex* had also to be *vir justus*, who, like

David, kept the divine statutes: "And God justified a man according to his innocence *(tam)* and righteousness." In the Testament of Issachar singleness of mind appears as the cardinal and all-embracing virtue against which the spirits of deceit have no power, but this singleness of mind is directed to preserving the innocent rustic life. The Issachar of the Testaments is the prototype of a rustic who cares for nothing but husbandry and bravely fulfills his duties.

This equation of moral goodness with a simple rustic mind—because "every word of Belial is twofold and has no simplicity"—leads to a glorification of the husbandman that is Greek. The *Phaenomena* of Aratus, the most popular book of the Hellenistic age, tells of olden times when, under the rule of Justice herself, people lived simply, without war or dispute, navigation or trade; "oxen and the plough" satisfied all needs. The happy farmer of Virgil and the merry shepherds of Theocritus are figures from the same stock. In Jewish life and letters, the line is prolonged by the Therapeutae of Philo, who, abhorring city life and trade, devoted themselves to husbandry and related crafts. The Covenanters of the Dead Sea, too, spoke of "the simple *(peti)* of Judah, who observed the Torah." This glorification of plainness is neither biblical nor rabbinic. As much as the rabbis insisted on truth and sincerity, they believed with Hillel that no boor fears sin and no uncultured man *(am ha-arez)* can be a *zaddik*. For them, Issachar, "a servant under taskwork," as he is called in Jacob's blessing (Gen. 49:14), was the prototype of the scholar whose "taskwork" is the Torah, and his brother Zebulun, dwelling on the shore of the sea, was a navigator and trader. Following the same line as the rabbis, the author of the Testaments ascribes the invention of the first sailing boat to Zebulun. Still, according to him the patriarch uses his sailing ship for nothing more than fishing, for besides the farmer, the fisherman is another favorite type of the simple, contented figure in Hellenistic literature.

The Testaments of the Twelve Patriarchs is a primitive historical novel, a story of characters and happenings that indirectly inculcated in the reader proper notions concerning pious men and right behavior—just as the moral novels of the eighteenth century did. But the popularity of the Testaments among ancient readers, attested by the many and varied recensions and translations of the work, proves that it was primarily a good story that entertained its readers.

Many parabiblical books, however, were sectarian tracts in which Enoch or Noah or other great figures of the primeval past attack the adversaries of the author in veiled language and promote his own ideas about the final judgment and other matters impenetrable to common men. A pseudo-Enoch, for instance solves the problem of demonology: evil spirits are the offspring of the Fallen Angels and mortal women.

(Gen. 6). Inheriting the immortality of their fathers these half-breeds are, however, degraded by their half-human origin and for this reason take vengeance on men. This kind of revelation made the Enochic books very successful among zany zealots, the New Covenanters of the Dead Sea among them.

One parabiblical book of this class published in the early Hellenistic age and still deserving of consideration is the Book of Jubilees, composed between approximately 250 and 175 B.C.E. Written in Hebrew, the book is a report of sacred history from the Creation to the Revelation on Sinai, as dictated to Moses by the Angel of Presence. In effect, the author of Jubilees takes it upon himself to improve upon Moses' narrative. The rewriting of the annals of the kings of Israel and Judah by the Chronicler, or the Aramaic Genesis Apocryphon (first century B.C.E.), found at Qumran, offer literary parallels. The author of Jubilees follows his ancient source closely, but adds new materials and, like every historian, corrects his main source when its data do not agree with his own presuppositions. From our standpoint, Jubilees and the Genesis Apocryphon embellish their source by the use of legendary materials. But the author of Jubilees could honestly believe in the authenticity of the supplementary traditions he used: they are sometimes also known, for example, to the author of the Testaments (the traditions about the name of Lamech's wife and the duration of Abraham's wanderings appear in both). Thus the parabiblical authors were able to enrich the parsimonious statements of Genesis with the help of abundant lore, written and oral, that had enriched the sacred history for generations.

The author's own conjectures are artless. The Bible says that Esau threatened Jacob "in his heart," but that it became known to Rebecca. Taking every word of the biblical account literally, the author of Jubilees supposed that Rebecca learned of Esau's intentions in a dream. It is the kind of elementary solution of real or alleged difficulties in the sacred text that we find, for instance, in the work of the historian Demetrius.

In contradistinction to the historian, however, the author of Jubilees is interested in morality rather than causality; he has no scruples about correcting the biblical account, but his alterations are mostly expurgatory. The Genesis Apocryphon dwells on all the details of the difficulties Abraham faced on account of Sarah's beauty; the author of Jubilees touches on the topic as briefly as possible and omits mentioning that the Patriarch passed his wife off as his sister. The Chronicler had already taken offense at stories that showed God tempting His servants. Now, in Jubilees, we are told that it was Satan who suggested to God that he try Abraham, and that it was the same Evildoer who slew the firstborn in Egypt and hardened the heart of the pharaoh. The magic performed by Moses before the pharaoh is also omitted in the new story of the Exodus; nor does

Jacob wrestle with the angel. And since a heroic Jacob could not have been afraid of Esau, we find him saying in Jubilees: "If he wishes to kill me, I will kill him." The rabbis later blamed Jacob for having left his old father, but the author of Jubilees already knows the reproof and parries it by stating that Isaac himself sent his son away. Of course, the author sometimes forgets or is unable to change the biblical account. Not only does Moses still flee to Midian in fear of his life in Jubilees, but the Angel of Presence is tactless enough to mention this detail while supposedly dictating the book to Moses himself.

The author, like his Greek contemporaries, rewrote the ancient tale to suit the Alexandrian taste we have already met in the Testaments. His heroes are sentimental and he himself is pedantic and bookish: Noah was drunk when found naked by Ham because it was a festival day; Noah had a library, which he left to Shem; Jacob educated Joseph from the books of Abraham; and Abraham quoted the books of Enoch and Noah.

Some of the author's additions are motivated by his political or theological biases. His angel again and again dictates peculiar rules of behavior unknown to Moses—an interdiction forbidding marital cohabitation on the Sabbath, for instance. Isaac curses the Philistines. And the division of the earth among Noah's sons is not only given in detail, but is also rewritten in order to prove that the conquest of Canaan by Israel was rightful. But the author is mostly a compiler. War stories, for example, are borrowed from various sources (some of them can be found in the Testaments) and added for their own sake. In an age of Jewish mercenaries, martial prowess excited the interest of readers in Jerusalem.

As for his halakic statements, which so often appear sectarian from the point of view of rabbinic Judaism, these were still accepted in his time by many, or at least some, influential groups in Jersualem. For instance, the rule prohibiting cohabitation on the Sabbath referred to above is followed even today by the Samaritans, Karaites, and Falashas; it is derived from the literal interpretation of Exodus 34:21. The rabbinic rule enjoining marital cohabitation on the Sabbath is obviously a counterattack against a popular opinion. Even the quaint calendar of the Jubilees is taken from Enochic literature.

The religious calendar of the Jews was lunisolar and for this reason in disarray; it was not easy to coordinate the monthly revolutions of the moon and the course of the sun. A Jewish author who wrote under the pseudonym of Enoch in the Persian period tried to synchronize the movements of both luminaries. But although he knew that the twelve lunations amount to 354 days, he believed that the sun completed its course in 364 days, an error resulting from uncertainty about the actual duration of the solar year (as late as 190 B.C.E. the Roman poet Ennius spoke of the 366 days of the solar year). Still, this pseudo-Enoch derived his astronomical wisdom from Babylonian sources; he never mentions God in his scientific treatise, nor the idea of the week, an original and essential part of the Jewish calendar. The author of Jubilees, however, realizes that a year of 364 days amounts to 52 weeks exactly. Accordingly, he disregards the moon, which he says disturbs the seasons, and promotes his pseudosolar year, which has the advantage of fixing the arrival of every feast on the same weekday forever—the first of Nisan, for instance, would always fall on Sunday.

The religious calendar is the most visible sign of confessional allegiance. For almost two centuries the Anglican Church refused to accept the Gregorian calendar, preferring, as Voltaire said, to disagree with the sun than to agree with the Pope. The Torah-centric but schismatic Karaites were abhorred by the rabbis, who nonetheless tolerated the followers of Abi Isa, who acknowledged Jesus and Muhammad as true Prophets. Asked about this incongruity, a rabbinic authority explained to Qirqisani, a Karaite scholar of the tenth century, that the sect of Abi Isa continued to follow rabbinic time-reckoning, while the Karaites celebrated Jewish holidays on days other than the ones on which Rabbanites celebrated them.

Thus the esoteric group that follow the time-reckoning of Jubilees separated itself by virtue of its calendar from catholic Jewry. Catholic Jewry, on the other hand—according to our author—sinned by celebrating its feasts on days that he considered to be profane; a sin that, again according to him, was equivalent to eating all kinds of blood with all kinds of meat. About a century after him, the sectarians on the shore of the Dead Sea accepted the calendar of Jubilees, thus proclaiming their break with the "faithless" Jews of the Temple.

The author of Jubilees, however, grants only a few pages to the calendar. His main interest is chronology: using his fixed year of 364 days, he establishes a rigid chronological framework for biblical history, from the creation to the Exodus. His time unit is septenary, "a week of years," an obvious imitation of the Greek system of dating by quadrennial Olympiads. Seven "weeks of years," then, constitute a jubilee period. We learn, for instance, that Cain built the first city in the first year of the first week of the fifth jubilee, that is, *anno mundi* 197. Although the author invents many dates of this kind, he also uses biblical evidence. For instance, we know from Scripture that Jacob served seven years for Rachel; because, according to his reckoning, Jacob went to visit Laban in the first year of the second week of the forty-fourth jubilee, he must have asked for the hand of Laban's daughter in the first year of the third week of the same jubilee. Likewise, our author has Abraham separate himself from his idolatrous father in the year of his reckoning that corresponds to the year 1890 after Creation. He arrives at this date because according to his chronology Abraham reached his fourteenth year, that is, the age of discernment, in 1890.

Demetrius, Jose ben Halafta, the author of the *Seder Olam Rabbah,* and later chronologists such as Petavius and Archbishop Usher in the seventeenth century, similarly tried to deduce dates that are not indicated in Genesis from biblical evidence. Jose ben Halafta, for instance, argued from the Bible that the confusion of languages (Gen. 11:1–9) must have happened in the days of Peleg (here he follows the rabbinic tradition based on etymology; *peleg* meaning "division" in Hebrew), whom he placed 340 years after the Flood; while Petavius calculated that the Flood began on the twenty-third of November in the year 239 B.C.E. All these chronologists naturally dated biblical events according to their own systems of time-reckoning: Jose ben Halafta states that the world was created 3828 years before the destruction of the Temple by the Romans—a date that is totally unrelated to our own dating system and therefore meaningless to us.

Although the last date given in Jubilees corresponds to 2450 *anno mundi,* the author nowhere indicates what period of time intervened between the theophany on Sinai and later history. The reader cannot even measure this distance for himself, because the dates calculated by the author widely disagree with the Masoretic text. For instance, he places the Exodus in the year 2450 after the Creation, whereas the computation based on the Hebrew Bible gives the year 2666. Let us add that because the figures in the Septuagint and in the Samaritan Bible differ not only from each other but also from Jubilees and from the Hebrew Bible, there were consequently at least four divergent systems of biblical chronology.

We must ask, therefore, what the meaning was of this rigid chronological scheme that was unintelligible even to the ordinary reader of Jubilees. Moreover, this leads to still another question: What was the real aim of the author? Although he embellishes it, he does not offer a radical alteration of biblical history. Even as a belletrist he is rather timid. He doesn't offer a sensuous description of the beauty of Sarah, nor does he offer a conversation between Lamech and his wife about the legitimacy of Noah, her son, as does the author of the Genesis Apocryphon, written in the first century B.C.E. It was hardly necessary to move heaven in order to state that no one should give his younger daughter in marriage before the elder, or to tell us that for every newborn male of Israel cast into the Nile on the order of the pharaoh, a thousand of his soldiers sank in the Red Sea. Nor does the halakhah in Jubilees offer any surprises, except for the monotonous insistence on capital punishment for almost every ritual transgression. The question, for instance, about the right time for slaughtering the paschal lamb (which later occupied both the Sadducees and the Pharisees) scarcely deserved to be discussed on the top of Mount Sinai. Even if the author wanted to assert divine approval of the ritual used by his congregation (the Oral Law of the rabbis was also given on Mount Sinai), the disproportion between the apparatus used by the author and the results of its use lends a touch of the comic to his work.

It was its chronological schema and its (esoteric) meaning for the author and his followers that saved the book from oblivion. Its basic assumption is that history had been preordained—its chronology inscribed on heavenly tablets (1:29)—and would end when God would descend from the heavens to dwell with His people through eternity (1:16). As its title, *The History of the Division of the Days . . . into their Jubilees and Weeks throughout All the Years of the World,* indicates, the book purported to mirror the contents of those heavenly tablets, which bore the same name, and thus to reveal the divisions of the years from the time of the Creation until the coming of the Lord. Nevertheless, the angel who dictated the book to Moses and announced the future corruption and coming punishment of the Chosen People—which, he says, will last until God will heal His servants (23:9–32)—does not reveal the dates of those future woes and blessings: the history recited by the angel stops at the Exodus.

But for the author of Jubilees and his followers the past prepares for and indicates the future. Through a particular combination of numbers—which was a well-guarded secret—the group (or its founder) was certain that it could calculate the interval that separated the revelation on Sinai from its own time, a number intentionally not even hinted at in the body of the text. Without the secret oral teaching about the date of the Mosaic revelation and the arcana of years and numbers, the Book of Jubilees, and with it the knowledge of the future, remained inaccessible to the casual reader. On the basis of their calculations about the sacred history, however—newly arranged chronologically according to the "new" Sinaitic revelation recorded in Jubilees and interpreted in the light of the secret code—the initiated believed that they could pierce the secret of the future. While their contemporaries blindly followed the lunisolar calendar, this group knew itself to be in possession of the true rhythm of the eon.

By ending his historical narrative and his reckoning of time with the period of the Exodus, the author made certain that his numerical code would be well kept. The Covenanters at the shores of the Dead Sea had already lost the key to the code. They read *The History of the Division of the Days* in an attempt to learn the exact extent of the epoch of Israel's blindness (wickedness), but were unable to understand it rightly and were left willy-nilly to peer into the future by the vulgar means of reinterpreting Scriptural passages, a game in which everyone was, or could pretend to be, a master. The teaching of the Book of Jubilees was truly esoteric and at the same time complete. Like the Enochic dream vision, it paralleled the future and the past. But the imaginative contribution of the author of Jubilees was to make the entire sacred past of Israel mirror the entire course of its future.

It is vain to search for allusions to contemporary events in the Book of Jubilees; intelligible hints would have opened the code to everyone. Still, in rewriting the Table of Nations the author uses Greek geographical names, such as the "Celtic" mountains and the river "Tina" (the name also appears in the Aramaic Genesis Apocryphon)—that is, the river Tanais (Don) in Japhet's portion. This political geography is of Greek origin, since for the Greeks the Tanais was the boundary between Europe and Asia. And because all the nations between the Tiber and the Euphrates regarded nakedness with the same horror as the Jews, when he speaks (3:31) of the gentiles uncovering themselves, the only gentiles he can mean are the Greeks and the graecised orientals who exercised stripped in the *palaestra*.

His use of the Greek system of dating proves that the book could not have been written before the middle of the third century B.C.E. The *terminus ante quem* is suggested by the passage in which, on the occasion of Abraham's circumcision, the angel announces to Moses that the children of Israel will cease to circumcise their sons. Circumcision was universal among the neighbors of Israel, (the Arabs, the Syrians, and the Phoenicians), but, as Herodotus noted, many of them began to abandon the ancestral practice in the Greek age. It is therefore quite possible that many Jews, particularly those outside Judea, followed the trend. The prediction of the angel cannot, however, refer to these individuals: it is a general one and its purpose is to illustrate the future wickedness of the Chosen People as a whole (23:9). In fact, when the Jews of Judea were ordered to abandon circumcision under Epiphanes, a great number of them preferred to obey God and not the king. It would have been strange, therefore, for an author writing in Maccabean times not to have alluded to these steadfast people. Thus, the Book of Jubilees was written before 170 B.C.E. The still unpublished manuscripts of the book found at Qumran are said to have been written toward the end of the second century B.C.E.

Two sapiential books composed in the early Hellenistic period have come down to us: Kohelet and the Ecclesiasticus of Ben Sira. Kohelet, a singular creation, has been examined in *Four Strange Books of the Bible,* and we won't discuss this extraordinary work again here. Ben Sira's work, on the other hand, is written in the traditional manner of wisdom books of the ancient Near East. Even its original title imitated that of the biblical Proverbs; it was "Masloth," as Jerome transcribes it.

Ben Sira has been discussed in detail above. We will therefore limit ourselves here to some observations on the textual history of the work. The oldest Hebrew manuscripts of Ecclesiasticus are a fragment (6:21–31) found at Qumran and a scroll containing a substantial portion of the book (39:27–44:17) copied in the first half of the first century B.C.E., about a century after the publication of the work. Medieval manuscripts from the Geniza in Cairo cover about two-thirds of the book. The complete work is extant in a Greek translation made by the grandson of the author in the last decades of the second century B.C.E. and in versions made from the Hebrew and the Greek texts in the first centuries C.E. All extant Greek manuscripts of Ecclesiasticus are derived from a codex written in Egypt, probably in the third century C.E., in which a quaternion was misplaced. Yet the Old Latin version, made from the Greek in Roman Africa in the first half of the third century, exhibits the (right) order of pages of the original.

The text of a popular book was often enriched by the addition of extraneous but similar material. For instance, in Roman Africa the authorship of Ecclesiasticus was ascribed to King Solomon; consequently, in the Old Latin version, Solomon's prayer in I Kings, chapter 8, was appended to the book. In a psalm scroll written in the first half of the first century C.E. and found at Qumran, several pseudo-Davidic compositions follow the traditional text, among them a hymn to personified Wisdom whose verses, like those in the praise of a good wife in Proverbs (31:10–31), are arranged alphabetically, and in which personified Wisdom is described in erotic language. Likewise, an appendix was attached to the Greek version of Ben Sira and to the Syriac translation from the Hebrew, which consists of two parts. First, there is a prayer giving thanks for deliverance, the authorship and date of which are unknown. The second piece, however, is a translation of the hymn to Wisdom found at Qumran, although the Greek translator mutes the sensuous expressions of the original. Further, in the Cairo Hebrew an interpolated canticle separated the prayer and the hymn. This piece is modeled on Psalm 136 and contains many expressions from synagogal prayers, particularly from a later recension of the "Eighteen Benedictions." The mention of the "Sons of Zadok, chosen for the priesthood" may come from the terminology of the Qumran sect or from some similar group. The divine title, "King of the Kings of Kings," presupposes the existence of the secular title "King of Kings," which was employed by Persian kings, rejected by Hellenistic monarchs, and reinstated by Parthian kings from the first century B.C.E. onward.

Let us add that the manuscript tradition sharply separated the book of Ben Sira from its later appendix. After the original colophon (50:27), the Greek version gives the title of the appendix: "The prayer of Joseph, the son of Sira." On the other hand, in the Syriac and in the Cairo

Hebrew, two further colophons are placed after the appendix. It is curious that in these bibliographical notes the author is called Simeon ben Joshua.

Thus far we have dealt with books written in Hebrew and Aramaic. The books written in Greek by Jewish authors of the early Hellenistic age have not been preserved in full; what we learn about them comes only from patristic quotations made for apologetic purposes. In fact, what the Church Fathers quote are parabiblical books in Greek. Yet the simple fact of having been written in Greek put these particular parabiblical books in a class distinct from the others. Greek style demanded the name of the author, so a Jewish book written in Greek could not be ascribed to a biblical hero; it had to be either openly the work of a modern author or else fathered on a Greek worthy of the past—in which case, of course, the author attempted to imitate a Greek classic and not Moses. Thus the author, no less than his Greek-thinking readers, needed to adapt himself to the Hebrew mentality. Ben Sira was a modern in pre-Maccabean Jerusalem but his book, translated into Greek, does not sound like a Greek book. The verses of Philo, Theodotus, or Ezechiel, however, although their spirit is that of pure Hebrew orthodoxy, can be read as Greek books.

Further, the Jewish writers in Hebrew or Aramaic addressed themselves to their brethren, at least to their brethren in spirit. Should a non-Jew of Aramaic tongue have begun to read a scroll of Enoch in Aramaic, he would not have been out of his mental world; but the work of those who wrote in Greek on biblical topics was extramural. Although these authors may have had the Jewish reader in mind, their works were also accessible to every Hellene. If the subject was strange to the Hellene, it was also strange to the Jewish reader of Greek tongue and education. No rabbi surpassed Philo in the veneration of Scripture, but biblical figures appear only as phantoms or symbols in Philo's pages. Thus Jewish works in Greek on Jewish topics have a tinge of apologetics; consciously or not, the author had to vindicate the strange ancestral tale for the sake of his own peace of mind.

Other oriental intellectuals writing in Greek about their national history and religion found themselves in the same situation. Of the Egyptian author Apion, who offered a rationalist explanation of the Egyptian worship of beetles, Pliny the Elder says that he sought "to free from blame the rites of his own people." Cast down, but representing hieratic and now immovable civilizations, Egyptian, Babylonian, Phoenician, and Jewish intellectuals looked back to the primeval age. Contemporaries of Euclid and Archimedes, they spoke of Abraham and Oannes. Berossus, in his Greek history of Babylon, coolly stated that the prediluvian manfish Oannes had taught arts and crafts to mankind, "and since that time nothing more had been invented."

Speaking as orientals, but in Greek, these intellectuals from the East all display the same apologetical accent, and are univocal in the face of the Greek conqueror. Josephus and Philo of Byblus, Manetho and Berossus, all reproach the Greeks for their ignorance of oriental history and wisdom. Josephus explicitly opposes the true glory of the Orient to the pretentious self-praise of the Hellenes; yet he writes his book on the antiquity of the Jews in answer to a pamphlet of the Egyptian Apion mentioned above. The peoples of the Greek East naturally envied one another and vied one with the other to win the ear of their Hellenistic masters. Though primarily seeking to persuade themselves, these apologists, speaking in Greek, had nonetheless necessarily to adopt the Greek mode of reasoning. Accordingly, in order to secure the historical claims of their respective peoples, these oriental intellectuals had first and above all to deal with the Hellenocentric dogma of Greek historiography. As Josephus states, every nation tries to trace its own origin to the remotest antiquity so as not to appear to be the imitator of other peoples.

Beginning with the first Greek historian, Hecataeus of Miletus (ca. 500 B.C.E.), Greek scholars, by rationalizing their myths, established a scientific prehistory that no other people of the ancient world could match or invent. Greek method having evolved from Greek material, Greek scientific prehistory was Hellenocentric, and the beginnings of "barbarian" peoples were integrated into the Greek system. In this way Aeneas, son of the Homeric Priam, became the ancestor of the Romans, and Ninus, the Assyrian, was reckoned by Herodotus as the third in descent from Herakles. Even the Persian king issued from the Greek hero Perseus.

Unfortunately for their claims, the Greeks were unable to antedate the beginnings of their history. A Greek savant, contemporary with the Seventy translators of the Torah, placed Cecrops, the first Athenian king, in 1582 B.C.E. But the Egyptian priests, trusting their holy books, assured Greek inquirers that civilization had originated in Egypt more than ten thousand years before Alexander the Great, that their pharaohs had reigned for five thousand years before Cleopatra, that Herakles had been an Egyptian general, and that Athens had been founded by the Egyptians. All great Greek thinkers, it was claimed, were disciples of the Egyptians, and brought from Egypt everything for which they gained admiration among the Hellenes. In short, the Greeks had simply appropriated to themselves the glory of Egypt, as well as that of the colonies founded by the Egyptians.

This inversion of Hellenocentric claims was impressive. The Greeks knew, and the orientals who read Plato or Herodotus knew that the Greeks knew, this essential fact: the Greeks were striplings and upstarts, lately civilized disciples of the East. Many of the barbarians, says a Greek author, hold that they are the aborigines of their countries, that they were the first men to discover the things that are of use in life, and that the events in their history were the earliest to be recorded. The author of *Epinomis* could assert that the Greeks had improved what they had borrowed, but this was feeble comfort, for the Greeks were persuaded that wisdom is at the beginning, and that the descendants must be like the ancestors.

In the contest for the glory of having the oldest recorded history, the Jews were handicapped by the Torah, which presents them as a junior branch of mankind and as the invaders of their Promised Land. Still, it was possible to adjust biblical chronology to the demands of the Greek age. From the lives of the Patriarchs, as recorded in Genesis, the elapsed time between the Creation and the Exodus can be ascertained. As computed in the earliest Jewish work of chronology extant in its entirety, the *Seder Olam Rabbah* (probably written about 150 C.E.), the Flood occurred 1656 years after the creation of Adam; Abraham was born 292 years after the Flood; and Moses led the Chosen People out of Egypt 500 years after the birth of Abraham, that is, 2448 years after the Creation. As the Exodus connected sacred and profane history, these figures were inadequate not only in the face of the fabulous antiquity of Egypt but even with regard to Greek calculations. Dicaearchus, a pupil of Aristotle, dated the first pharaoh, whom he called Sesostris, to 3719 B.C.E. according to our reckoning. The great Greek chronologist Eratosthenes, a younger contemporary of the Seventy translators of the Torah, put the Greek flood around 2400 B.C.E., probably in order to adjust Greek chronology to the high figures of oriental reckonings.

By manipulating the figures referring to the Patriarchs, the Seventy succeeded in putting the Flood 2242 years after the Creation and the birth of Abraham 1072 years after the Flood. These figures offered a large chronological range for the pre-Abrahamic period, notably a millennium for the interval between the Flood and Abraham. Thus, some eighty years after the compilation of the *Seder Olam Rabbah,* the Christian chronologist Africanus, using the figures in his Greek Bible, could calculate that Moses led the Hebrews from their Egyptian bondage in 1785 B.C.E. according to our reckoning; that is, in the time of the Ogygian flood in Greece, some 190 years before Cecrops, the first king of Athens. The anteriority of the Chosen People had thus been proven mathematically. More than 1400 years after Africanus, the Jesuits in China, confronted with the (fictitious) long chronology of Chinese annalists, used the figures of the Septuagint and not the dates of the Latin Bible, translated from the Hebrew, in their discussions with Chinese intellectuals.

Proud of the antiquity of their peoples, oriental authors, such as Berossus, Manetho, Menander, and Dius, began to present their respective national histories in Greek, using Greek forms of historical thinking but following their own national sources and so avoiding the Greek bias. Demetrius, the earliest known Jewish writer in Greek, undertook during the reign of Ptolemy IV (221–204) the similar task of eliciting a pragmatic narrative from the Bible. The preserved fragments deal with the events narrated in Genesis and Exodus, although since he refers in a chronological note to the fall of Samaria and the captivity of Jerusalem his history continued at least until the end of the kingdom of Judah (586 B.C.E.). But because the only Christian authors who quote him, Clement of Alexandria and Eusebius of Caesarea, knew his work solely through excerpts in the compilation of Alexander Polyhistor, a Greek polygraph who wrote *On the Jews,* it is rather difficult to appreciate the man and his book.

It seems that Demetrius, like Berossus and Manetho, gave a matter-of-fact abridgment of his materials, placed skillfully in an accurate chronological framework. These oriental historians wanted to replace the romances of Herodotus, Ctesias, Megasthenes, and other Greek authorities of the Orient with a dry but authentic recapitulation of native records. Isaac's binding by his father for the sacrifice, one of the most moving episodes of Genesis (chap. 22) and one of the central themes of Jewish theology, was recorded by Demetrius in the same dry manner as the birthdates of Jacob's sons. Jacob's wrestling with the angel (Genesis 32) was retold as follows: When Jacob was on his way to Canaan, God's angel wrestled with him and "touched the hollow of his thigh, so that the latter grew stiff, and he limped."

History in Genesis is recorded in effect as a succession of generations, a *genealogia,* to use the Greek term. With the help of genealogies Greek authors arranged men and events in a chronological sequence. For instance, Hellanicus was able to calculate that Theseus was fifty years old when he carried off Helen, who was only seventeen. Demetrius organized the biblical material in the same way. His readers learned that Jacob had fled to Harran at the age of 77 and married Leah and Rachel at the age of 84.

Sometimes Demetrius complemented his source with his own ideas. He says, for instance—basing his statement on Genesis 46:34—that Joseph in Egypt did not send for his family because he feared Egyptian hostility toward shepherds. Sometimes he propounds historical problems using the well-known introductory formula of Greek scholarly discussion: "A question arises . . ." Some problems ventilated by Demetrius reappear in talmudic controversies. The question of where the Children of Israel obtained their weapons during the Exodus is based on the Septuagint text. The reference shows that Greek-speaking Jews discussed the Greek version of the Torah.

Having reconstructed the primordial events as a jejune but punctilious chronicle, Demetrius, again like Greek chronologists, related the remote past to his own time by calculating the number of years that had elapsed from the fall of Samaria and from the captivity of Jerusalem to the accession of his own sovereign, Ptolemy IV.

The purely historical approach to the Torah, the attention to chronology, the rationalization of exegetical difficulties, the resolution of the epic of the Bible into ordinary history—all this follows the pattern set out by Greek historians like Hellanicus, who continued to be popular in the third century for his retelling of Greek prehistory. This does not mean, of course, that no Babylonian before Berossus or no Jew before the Greek age used his sources rationally. The Chronicler already explains Solomon's building a house for his Egyptian wife outside the City of David (I Kings 9:24) by the fact that the Ark was kept in the City (II Chron. 8:11). The sign of Greek thinking is, rather, the systematic use of the rational method.

The establishment of a rational system of biblical reckoning was the essential achievement of Demetrius. The author of *Seder Olam Rabbah* and Africanus, as well as Eusebius and the scholars of medieval and modern times, followed in his steps. But Demetrius' influence on Greek historiography was nil. The same was true of the historical works of Manetho and Berossus. Berossus became famous as an astrologer and Manetho's theological dissertations became an important source for Greek writers on Egyptian religion, but nobody read or believed their historical works; no Greek historian or chronologist ever took note of Berossus. Greek scholars, despite Berossus' indignation, continued to repeat that Babylon had been founded by the Assyrian queen Semiramis. (As a matter of fact the same Greek compiler, Alexander Polyhistor, some time after 80 B.C.E. saved from oblivion both Berossus and the earlier Jewish writers in Greek, among them the historian Demetrius, by publishing excerpts from their works. Josephus and Christian writers came to know Berossus only through Alexander Polyhistor and his abbreviators.)

The average Greek continued to regard the Greek sagas as historical. An ambassador of the city of Teos, at the end of the third century, quoted mythical tales in order to prove the ancient friendship between his city and the Cretans, although since Ephorus (ca. 340 B.C.E.) Greek scholarship had given up the pretension of being able to discover the historical facts underlying the myths. The realm of legend was considered to begin somewhere around 1200 B.C.E. Still, at a time when Eratosthenes was refusing to discover history in the Homeric tale of Odysseus' wanderings, Berossus was asserting that in his land kings had reigned for more than thirty thousand years before Alexander the Great, and Demetrius was computing the dates of events before the Flood.

But the oriental historical tradition was hallowed by sacred memories:

the primeval history of the Hebrews was enshrined in the Torah ark and Egyptian priests transmitted to their successors the holy books of Egyptian history. Both Manetho and Berossus were priests; the latter appeared as a spokesman of the god Bel. The Greeks, however, lacked both priestly caste and sacred history; even the tales about the gods were just "tales" *(mythoi)*. Indeed, the first Greek historical work, that of Hecataeus of Miletus, began as follows: "I write what in my opinion is true. For the stories told by the Greeks, as it seems to me, are ludicrous." Josephus, however—again in agreement with other Eastern intellectuals—asserted that the proof of historical veracity was universal agreement, and contrasted the singleness of the Hebrew tradition with the diversity of Greek opinions: Greek historians disagreed among themselves and censured each other in their works. The incapacity of oriental historians, even when writing in Greek, to reject ancestral traditions and accept the Greek point of view made their works unpalatable to the Greeks. The Greeks knew that by writing in Greek, the oriental historians "wanted to glorify" their own peoples and not the sons of Yavan who now reigned in the East. Unable to refute oriental claims, the Greeks ignored them.

On the other hand, although united in opposition to Greek claims, oriental intellectuals did not miss an opportunity to enhance the prestige of their own peoples at the expense of their neighbors. According to the Egyptian priests, not only was Athens an Egyptian colony, but Babylon as well was founded by the Egyptian Belus. Through many different channels, claims and tales promoted by malevolent neighbors entered the current of Greek thought and caused or had the potential to cause much damage to the reputation of the slandered people. For instance, a Greek writer by the name of Mnaseas from the Lycian city of Patra quoted, among other curiosities, a strange Idumean story, to wit: In an ancient war, an Idumean promised to deliver the Apollo of the Idumean city of Adora to the Jews. The sly Idumean, however, posing as the Apollo, succeeds in this way in penetrating the Temple of Jerusalem, from which he snatches the cult image, the golden head of an ass, and returns home.

This tale is based on the idea that the loss of its idol dooms a city; the Assyrians for this reason deprived Babylon of the statue of Marduk. The theme of carrying off the idol of the enemy by stealth is well known: Ulysses, we know, carried off the palladium of the Trojans. To these themes the Idumean storyteller, on his own, added the well-known folklore motif of a man who, posing as a god, plays a trick on someone.

The point of the story, however, was that the palladium of Jerusalem was an ass, or a man-ass. It often happens that one's neighbors are scoffed at as dolts. In this case the Jews were derided not only as credulous, but as worshipping the symbol of stupidity itself. Later the anecdote was used and twisted by the apologists of Antiochus IV Epiphanes, from which point in time the notion that the Jews (whose blind faith often surprised the enlightened gentiles) adore the ass became a feature of anti-Jewish, and later, of anti-Christian, polemics.

The tale of Mnaseas is quoted by Josephus in his work against Apion and other Jew-baiters, among whom Josephus also places Manetho, the Egyptian priest who, around 270 B.C.E., published in Greek an Egyptian history based on native records and legends. It does not seem that Manetho found any mention of the Jews in Egyptian annals but, speaking of the conquest of Egypt by the Hyksos in the seventeenth century B.C.E., he reports that when these Asiatics were driven out of Egypt they returned to Syria, where they founded the city of Jerusalem in the land "now called Judea." This geographical reference attracted the attention of Josephus. Believing wrongly that the term "Hyksos" meant "captives" and "shepherds" in Egyptian, he identified this people with the Hebrews because, as he says, "our ancestors" lived a pastoral life, an illogical inference of the kind that was and is favored by biblical scholars (even in our century, some well-intentioned Egyptologists have tried to discover in Manetho's report a reference to Israel in Egypt).

Egyptian popular literature offered many pseudohistorical tales about the invasions of Asiatics and their eventual expulsion. Quite early on, the Greeks adapted these Egyptian stories to suit their own purposes. Euhemerus, a contemporary of Manetho, tells us in a utopian novel that Ammon, an Egyptian god whom he regards as a mortal who became divine, drove an alien group from the (imaginary) island of Panchaia for religious reasons. Fifty years before Manetho, Hecataeus of Abdera, also basing his claim on the accounts of Egyptian priests, related that the Egyptians had expelled a group of aliens dwelling in their midst because, by differing from Egyptian practice with regard to ritual and sacrifices, they had offended the gods of Egypt. Among these aliens Hecataeus names Cadmus and Danaus (two Greek heroes who, according to Greek mythological tradition, were fugitives from Egypt) and the Jews. Manetho also mentions Danaus, whom he identifies with a rebellious Egyptian prince, but he does not mention either Cadmus or Moses in this context. Elsewhere, however, he tells a tale not found in the public records, as he states expressly, about a pharaoh who put all lepers and impure men into the stone quarries. The prisoners escaped and occupied the city of Avaris (Tanis), the ancient Hyksos capital in the Delta. Allying themselves with the Jerusalemites, they devastated Egypt, but after thirteen years were driven out and fled to Syria. Their leader was Osarseph, a priest of Heliopolis, who ordained new anti-Egyptian laws for his followers.

It is obvious that the story about this Osarseph who made an alliance with the impure shepherds in Jerusalem and founded a community where the sacred animals of Egypt were consumed has been fabricated in order to blacken the reputation of the clergy of Heliopolis. We may surmise that it was authored by the priests of some rival sanctuary, say, that of Ptah in Memphis, during some civil strife in the land of the Nile. Anyway, the tale has nothing to do with Jews. Manetho, however, adds cautiously: "It is said that when Osarseph, named after Osiris, the god of Heliopolis, joined the lepers, he changed his name and was called Moses." We do not know who was the author of this addition to the original tale; it may have been invented in the Persian period. But in the first century C.E., when the communal strife between the Jews and the Greeks in Alexandria became acute, Manetho was enrolled in the company of anti-Jewish witnesses and consequently came under the fire of Jewish apologists.

Modern scholars, following the apologists, have either made Manetho out to be an enemy of the Jews or have attributed the Osarseph-Moses tale to an interpolator. In fact, Manetho does not accept responsibility for the identification of the leader of the lepers with Moses. His account is no more anti-Jewish than Aristotle's statement that the city of Locri in lower Italy was founded by slaves is anti-Locrian, although Timaeus of Locri abused Aristotle, and Josephus attacked Manetho, on account of these claims. The point, however, is that because his words were both misunderstood and misused Manetho came to be an authority on Jewish primeval history.

Let us return now to Jewish authors writing in Greek. Although the Greeks, as we have seen, refused in principle to admit the anteriority of the East, they were ready to believe that one or another of their masters, be it Homer or Plato, had been a disciple of oriental wisdom. For the Greeks, civilization was continually developing—an attitude that explains the apparently strange poem in which Orpheus, the first musician and prophet of the Greeks, sings the praises of Abraham and Moses. This "Sacred Discourse," quoted by the Jewish philosopher Aristobulus, cannot have been written later than the first quarter of the second century B.C.E. The poem became very popular and the Church Fathers eventually preserved several variants of it.

In order to understand the origin and meaning of this Jewish work, we have to remember that the oracles of the legendary pre-Homeric bard and prophet were favorite objects of falsification among the Greeks from the middle of the sixth century B.C.E. onward. The Pythagoreans, and later the Stoics, seem to have been particularly busy at this task. One Orphic poem of Pythagorean or Stoic inspiration glorified Zeus, the ruler of the universe, who is self-begotten and from whom all things spring. Invisible, he reigns over all, sitting upon a golden throne in a brazen heaven. Although a Jewish litterateur who came across this pagan quasi-monotheist text was impelled to recast it, the original of the Orphic poem continued to be read, and some of its variants, as we have noted, were later inserted in the above-mentioned Christian quotations of the hymn. Such crossbreeding of different variants of the same poem is not at all exceptional in manuscript tradition, resulting in many hybrid texts.

In the Jewish version, the Jewish adapter used the Greek hexameter easily and fittingly and employed words gleaned from classical Greek epics and ancient oracles. The study of poets and their vocabulary in the schools put versification of this kind within reach of any educated reader. What is remarkable in the Jewish adaptation, however, is the biblical coloring that is added. A metapor from Isaiah 66:1, already noted by Clement of Alexandria, embellishes the Homeric description of Zeus; Moses is "rush-born" (*hylogenes;* see LXX Exod. 2:3), and received "the two-fold Law" (LXX Exod. 34:4). On the other hand, Abraham, the founder of astronomy, is described in the language of Orphic poetry as *monogenes,* a being who is the only one of his kind. It is interesting to note here that several centuries after Aristobulus the rabbis interpreted Isaiah 51:2 and Ezekiel 33:24 as meaning that Abraham was unique.

The original Orphic text was also reinterpreted. In the original, it was said in the language of Hesiod that it was Zeus who sent evil to mankind. Greek philosophers, however, refused to attribute the authorship of evil to the absolute Good; following their teaching, the Jewish adapter states that although evil, like strife and hate, goes with man, God "from his goodness does not lay evil upon mortals." Nevertheless, whereas the original text asserted that no mortal could see the cosmic Zeus, the Jewish interpolator, less spiritual than the Greek pantheist, made an exception of Abraham.

In the Torah, revelation is continuous: the Lord speaks to Moses throughout the journey in the wilderness and in the plain of Moab. But in the Greek age, the giving of the Torah was conceived of as a single event, occurring at Sinai. The scenario of the second revelation in the Book of Jubilees already presupposes this shortened perspective, and the Jewish Orphic bard likewise speaks of a single theophany on Sinai. In this way, the giving of the Law was adjusted to the ideal, and the Jewish author could call upon the gentiles to flee men's laws because God had established His own Law for all.

The Jewish Orpheus was not unique. Aristobulus also quotes a series of isolated verses from Homer, Hesiod, and the mythical singer Linus that proclaim the holiness of the Seventh Day. He probably used some pamphlet glorifying the Sabbath; and here again the hexameters are tampered with or fabricated outright. Homer calling the Sabbath "a holy day" and Orpheus singing the praises of Abraham and Moses to his amanuensis Musaeus—these appear to us historically impossible. Yet an ancient hellenized Jew would have seen matters differently. In the days of Homer and Hesiod, artistic motifs and ideas, like merchandise, often crossed the Aegean Sea. Homer speaks of the Sidonians, so why should he not speak of the Sabbath? From the lack of references to the Jews in the extant Greek texts before Alexander we, being positivists, conclude that Orpheus or the Greek contemporaries of Amos had no knowledge of the Chosen People. But a hellenized Jew, in accordance with Greek canons of historical criticism, regarded an Orphic poem of monotheist coloring that did not refer to the Chosen People as obviously corrupt.

Eusebius may help us understand the position of the Jewish interpolator. The Church Father argues as follows: by their own admission the Greeks received their philosophy from the Orient; thus they must have obtained their knowledge of the One Supreme Being from the Jews, the sole monotheistic people. This conclusion is much better founded than Voltaire's suggestion that the Orphic hymn is evidence for the existence of a secret monotheistic doctrine among the Greeks. From the Torah, Jews knew positively that Abraham and Moses, who had lived long before Orpheus, were the originators of monotheism and that the Seventh Day had been sanctified at the Creation. Therefore it was impossible for any Greek poet of old to have expressed a monotheistic thought independent of the Mosaic revelation. Let us observe that modern scholars use the same kind of argumentation as Eusebius when they speak of, say, the dependence of the Mosaic cosmogony on Babylonian creation stories.

Thus, if the Orphic poem glorifying the Supreme Being lacked a reference to the Source of Truth, the only possible explanation was that the transmitted text must have been mutilated and that the true "original" should be restored. Greek critics also altered manuscripts in conformity with this way of thinking. Crates, a contemporary of Aristobulus, inserted a line in the Iliad (after verse 14:246) to the effect that the earth is round, because from his point of view it was impossible for the sage not to have known the real shape of the globe. A century after Aratus had written a poetical description of the starry heaven, an editor—also a contemporary of Aristobulus—corrected the text, as he himself stated, in order to bring it into agreement with new astronomical theories.

This kind of "setting right" appeared to be justified by the nature of the manuscript tradition of the time. The text of an author, copied by many hands, soon became fluid and untrustworthy; manuscripts diverged, verses were added or deleted—as papyri have shown for Homer—and there was always room for disagreement on the question of the original wording. It was, rather, the oral tradition, the living memory of some famous passage or episode, that preserved a text from meddlers. Aristobulus, quoting the famous hymn to Zeus which opened Aratus' poem, expressly notes that he substituted "God" for "Zeus," because he thought that this was more fitting for the piece. In other ancient editions the same hymn was tampered with in other ways or even just omitted.

Taking these facts into consideration, we may understand the adaptation of an Orphic hymn by a Jewish critic, and understand as well Aristobulus' use of a poem that had been "set right."

To our knowledge Aristobulus is the first Jew who, like Philo two centuries later, was completely at home in the Greek spiritual world. To quote Eusebius, "He partook of Aristotelian philosophy in addition to the native one." According to a later Jewish source, he belonged to the high-priestly family of Jerusalem and was *didaskolos*, a royal "tutor" (or "reader") at the Alexandrian court. Between 176 and 170 B.C.E., he published *An Explanation of the Mosaic Scripture*, dedicated to Ptolemy VI Philometor and purporting to answer his questions about the Torah. This Greek literary form is fictitious; the boy who in these years sat on the Egyptian throne could hardly have been interested in the mysteries of revelation. But King Gelon of Syracuse, to whom Archimedes dedicated a mathematical work in which he apostrophizes the king—"You are aware . . ."—was also hardly interested in the problem of calculating the number of grains of sand in a certain sphere.

While scanty fragments of Aristobulus' work, preserved by Clement and Eusebius to serve as props for Christian doctrine, do not allow us to appreciate it as a whole, some lines of his thought are discernible. Aristobulus speaks of "our sect," using the term *hairesis*, which to the Greek ear meant a philosophical school. As a matter of fact, not only were the philosophical systems of Aristobulus' time also religious creeds, but there was no better term in the Greek language than "philosophy" to describe a body of beliefs concerning the Deity, man, and the universe. Accordingly Aristobulus parallels and identifies the Peripatetic image of wisdom as a beacon that leads men with Solomon's commendation of wisdom. But he deludes himself. The Greek and the Jew both spoke of wisdom and both approved of similar rules of right conduct, but for the Greek philospher behavior was right because it agreed with nature or was rational, while for Aristobulus right conduct was ordained from above: "The whole structure of our Law is arranged on account of piety and justice and self-control and other goods which are real." Aristobulus' terminology is Greek: moral virtue alone has real value, such external things as wealth or success being by themselves neither good nor bad. Yet we note that although he speaks of moderation *(sophrosyne)*, a notion essential to Greek moral philosophy, he does not speak of the knowledge of good and evil, the primary condition of all right behavior according to the common Greek view. And while for Greek philosophers piety was a subdivision of the general virtue of fairness *(dikaiosyne)*, the virtue that should govern man's conduct towards men and gods, Aristobulus gives the first place to *eusebeia*, by which term the Septuagint rendered the biblical formula "fear of the Lord," the cardinal virtue that alone leads to the knowledge of good and evil and the desire to fulfill the divine law. Aristobulus belonged to the school of Aristotle, but he would not have subscribed to Aristotle's dictum that the gods, having no measure in common with men, cannot be virtuous according to the human meaning of this term.

On the other hand, identifying the Torah with the rational wisdom of the philosophers, Aristobulus states that those who cling to the letter of Scripture are devoid of intelligence and unable to understand Moses, who announced profound thoughts in terms applicable to external things: the Sabbath is in reality the first birth of intellectual light, in which all things are beheld; hence it is identical with wisdom. The Seventh Day is holy because it refers to the proportion of seven, whereby we have knowledge of all things human as well as divine.

Addressing his royal pupil directly, Aristobulus insists that anthropomorphic descriptions of God's activity should not be taken literally. Thus God, who is always everywhere, could not descend on Mount Sinai; rather, He miraculously created a fire that blazed without consuming in order to manifest His might to all. A Jew reading about the "arms" and "feet" of the Deity in the Torah knew by tradition that such expressions were figurative and that the Lord does not use His "hands" like a man. But the Olympians were created in the image of man and were worshipped in the form of their idols, their manlike images, and in their human form they helped morals. In 229 B.C.E., for example, Athena, apearing in the flesh, fought the Aetolians back at Pellana. The danger was that a Greek, and even a Jew of Greek education, hearing that the Lord brought Israel out of Egypt "by His hand," would instinctively see the Lord as similar to the Olympians. Let us remember that the pious authors of Heliodorus' story and of II Maccabees speak of angels who, in human form and wearing the armor and weapons of men, punished God's enemies and even served as bodyguards of Judah Maccabee. But the Lord was not an animated idol, and Aristobulus warns the reader not to take the biblical narrative for a "mythological fable."

His intention, however, is not apologetical only. He asks the reader to blame him alone, and not the Lawgiver, if his interpretation should miss the veritable meaning of the sacred text, for he wants to grasp at the meaning "below the surface" *(hyponoia)*, to use a Greek term. In the same way, Babylonian cosmogony and the ancient legends of Egypt were allegorized, the first by Berossus and the second by the Egyptian priests; even the obscene Attis tale received a Stoic interpretation. This kind of search for the hidden meaning of a venerable text had been practiced in Greece from the end of the sixth century B.C.E. At first the aim was to reinterpret those mythological tales in Homer which did not seem to befit the gods, but in the Hellenistic age the method served above all to turn an old and somewhat outdated text into an eternal classic. Allegory, to use the term in a broad sense, opened endless sources of reinterpretation: every sentence, even every word of the Torah—or of Homer, or of another enshrined book—could now acquire new meaings that responded to new needs. Haggadah is but another method of dealing with the unavoidable necessity of pouring new wine into old bottles in order to preserve it—just as this proverbial expression substitutes "bottles" for the "wineskins" of Jesus' saying.

Clement of Alexandria says elegantly that God gave philosophy to the Greeks as their peculiar covenant. We would like to know, then, how the philosopher Aristobulus succeeded in uniting the Hebrew and the Greek covenants. But the Church Fathers who quote his "thick volumes" were more interested in such topics as his proof, to quote Eusebius, that "the Peripatetic philosophy depended upon the Law of Moses and other prophets." Even on this subject we mainly learn that in order to explain the dependence of Greek philosophers on Moses' teaching, Aristobulus postulates that a partial translation of the Torah into Greek must have been made long before the Septuagint. Neither he nor, as far as we know, any other Jewish intellectual dared to imagine that Pythagoras or Plato had visited Jerusalem, even though the Greeks themselves spoke of the voyages of Greek sages to the East in quest of wisdom.

It is often asserted that, using forged Greek credentials, the Jews tried to convince the Greeks of the eminence of Israel. But as we have had occasion to note a number of times, the Greeks never hesitated to acknowledge their debt to the Orient. The Peripatetic Aristoxenus supposed that Pythagoras had learned from Zoroaster. Another Peripatetic, Hermippus, said that Pythagoras was a plagiarist of Thracian and Jewish opinions. In like manner we have seen that Aristobulus, another Peripatetic scholar, agreeing with Hermippus (an "always careful researcher"), argues that Pythagoras, when speaking of the Deity, followed Jewish books.

For the Greek reader, all three claims were more or less identical. For Aristobulus, however, and for his Jewish readers it was a fact of capital importance that Pythagoras had learned from the Hebrews and not, say, from the Thracians. "Pan-Hebraism" made the Jews, in their own eyes, the equals of the Egyptians or the Babylonians. Every Greek knew that the Greek alphabet had developed from the Phoenician, but the Jews knew that the Phoenicians themselves had been taught by Moses.

Actually the claims of Aristobulus and his fellows were modest in comparison with the pan-Egyptian theory developed by Egyptian priests before 300 B.C.E. or with the later pan-Phoenician doctrine of Philo of Byblus. According to these, Enoch, who was assumed to be the inventor of astral lore, was not a Jew, and Abraham only transmitted Babylonian science of the West. Jewish and later Christian propagandists, by comparison, conceded to Orpheus the glory of being an apostle of monotheism.

In fact the Egyptian intellectuals, who represented a great and antique nation, easily found Greek advocates of their cause, such as Hecataeus of Abdera. Even the great Poseidonios in the first century B.C.E. innocently repeated the Phoenician claim that the theory of atoms had been invented by a Sidonian. But the Jews, at least before the Maccabean expansion, were an insignificant tribe; they had to sing their praises themselves. Only rarely, for instance under the pen of Hermippus, was their priority in religious thought acknowledged by a Greek scholar—and Hermippus mentioned the Thracians along with the Jews. It was Jewish superstition, not Jewish sapience, that impressed the Greek observer.

The Jewish literary works we have spoken of, even when written in Greek, were all parabiblical or at least related to Scripture. But two tales dealing with contemporary events have also come down to us: the success story of the Tobiads and the story of the unfortunate Heliodorus.

The arrogant aristocracy spoken of by Kohelet and Ben Sira was swept away by the Maccabean tempest because of its unorthodoxy. (The new leaders were no less rapacious, but more godly.) But the memory of the Tobiads, one of the foremost families of pre-Maccabean Jerusalem, has been preserved both in the literary tradition and on an architectural monument. Flavius Josephus, short of information about pre-Maccabean Jerusalem and never averse to speaking of Jews who had obtained royal favor, inserted in his work a panegyric, in Greek, of the Tobiads Joseph and his son Hyrcanus, obviously written at the time of Hyrcanus' grandeur.

Ancient biographers wrote about worthies in politics, literature, and art—from lawgivers to flute players—but the euologist of the Tobiads praises two tax gatherers. The narrator follows the Aristotelian idea (which largely influenced Greek biographical writers) that a man's actions are a constant expression of his true nature; little traits, Plutarch says, are often more revealing than great deeds. This conception presupposes man's character to be both monolithic and static. Theophrastus' Characters, the plays of the New Comedy, and Hellenistic art portray individuals according to this heuristic postulate as the braggart, the boor, the young lover, and other such types. To their biographer, the Tobiads exemplify cleverness.

The author introduces Joseph as a man who, despite his youth, was well known in Jerusalem for his uprightness *(dikaiosyne)*, dignity *(semnotes)*, and forethought. A royal officer bribed by Joseph admires the gravity *(semnon)*, kindness *(chrestotes)*, and loftiness *(eleutherion)* of his character, and describes him to the king as a good and honor-loving man. When Joseph puts the leaders of a tax strike to death, the king admires his "high spirit." Hyrcanus, too, when punishing his father's manager for refusing to deliver Joseph's money to him, is praised by the king for the loftiness of his soul.

As for the cleverness of his heroes, the author again and again indicates that their wit and witticisms were admired by everyone. Indeed, the whole panegyric is built on this motif. Unrelated facts such as the physical traits of the heroes are passed over, but an exchange of table jokes between Hyrcanus and a court fool is repeated in all its details. The prurient curiosity of the Hellenistic reader demanded a dose of gallantry in such biographical concoctions, and the author obliges here by telling of Joseph's passion for a dancing-girl—a passion which brings him into danger. Still, the episode is told only to emphasize, by contrast, the cleverness of Joseph's brother, who uses the deception practiced by Laban on Jacob to marry his daughter to Joseph. The name of the daughter, who became the mother of Hyrcanus, is not mentioned, but we do learn the name of her ingenious father.

By their wits Joseph and Hyrcanus win their fortunes. The necessary condition for this achievement is attained when Joseph is awarded the right to farm the taxes of the entire province. His wit guarantees his success: asked to name his sureties, he offers the Queen to the King and the King to the Queen. Cleverness is a tool capable of winning influential friends and insuring a large income. He is even contrasted with the parsimonious High Priest, who by his conduct endangered Jerusalem, for frugality is now a sign of dotage. Joseph and Hyrcanus are clever spendthrifts; they amass fortunes by throwing money around in gifts and bribes.

In an economy dominated by the royal court, social charm opens the way to success. The new hero, eager for goodwill and friendship, can adapt himself to the company of common men as well as to that of the court. Nevertheless, although affable and persuasive the new hero is also wily and shrewd. The Tobiads are successful businessmen in the acquisitive society of the Hellenistic age, in which even Socrates, in the pseudo-Platonic dialogue *Hipparchus,* comes to the conclusion that all gains are good because all men are greedy for gain. (We have treated this topic in *Four Strange Books of the Bible.*)

Yet Joseph and Hyrcanus were neither robber barons nor manipulators who used the financial expedients of the kind approvingly described in the second book of the pseudo-Aristotelian *Oeconomica.* Indeed, the eulogist is rather discreet about describing the financial operations of the Tobiads; we never learn how these tax-farmers, who in principle were closely controlled by royal officials, were able to accumulate their riches.

They were probably no more or less unscrupulous and efficient than, for example, Zenon, the agent of Apollonios, vizier of Ptolemy II.

As is usual in the first stages of capital accumulation, pleasure, which distracts from work, is considered the enemy. For the Stoic, "good men" were not only pitiless, they were also austere and neither had an appetite for pleasure themselves nor tolerated this inclination in others. Joseph grew wealthy, as his eulogist clearly states, because of his industry and self-control. Like Zenon, Hyrcanus and his father must have been tireless workers; we are told that the brothers of Hyrcanus, who later opposed him, were lazy and lacked "the love of work." When Hyrcanus was later deprived of power and relegated to Transjordan he did not waste time there, either. He again started to amass wealth, this time by the most ancient of means—war and plunder.

The story of the Tobiads was obviously written in Palestine. Readers in Alexandria or Ascalon would hardly have been enthusiastic about a tax collector who cheated them. But Jerusalem was proud of these native sons who did so well and who, like other successful businessmen of the Hellenistic age, remembered their hometowns. Joseph, we are told, brought the Jewish people from poverty to a splendid economic situation. The publication of the biography of the Tobiads shows that among the contemporaries of Ben Sira there were many in Jerusalem who not only read Greek but also appreciated a book written to the Greek taste, one in which the only Jewish elements were the proper names of the heroes of the story.

The weakness of the Tobiads (and other men of the same ilk) lay in the fact that their business success depended upon royal favor. Friends of the Ptolemies, Joseph and Hyrcanus were friendless in Seleucid Palestine. Although Antiochus III did not seize their fortune, Antiochus IV finally did put an end to the *razzias* of Hyrcanus (now in Transjordan) against the neighboring Arab tribes. Fearing his coming punishment, Hyrcanus committed suicide and his property was confiscated by the king. His Transjordanian seat, still unfinished, was apparently abandoned, for which reason some remains of it have been preserved.

The site that was probably the family estate, now called "The Prince's Cliff" (Araq el-Emir), is situated twelve miles east of the Jordan and about ten miles northwest of Heshbon. "Tyrus" (probably from the Aramaic *tur*, "rock"), as the manor was called, consisted of several structures. Two tiers of chambers and corridors, approximately five hundred meters long and over twenty-five meters high, tunneled into a precipitous cliff, probably served as living quarters for Hyrcanus' retainers and as a place of refuge against the enemy. One of these cavelike chambers in the upper tier, accessible by a ramp, had a gallery about thirty meters long, six meters wide, and four meters high; used as a stable, it had mangers for more than one hundred horses. The name "Tobiah" is inscribed in Aramaic script to the right of the entrance to another cave, but the date of the inscription is uncertain; it is attributed now to the beginning of the fifth century B.C.E. although Josephus ascribes the tunneling of the cliff to Hyrcanus.

It was some six hundred meters to the south, however, that Hyrcanus built the edifice that Josephus describes so admiringly. In an artificial lake, fed by an aqueduct bringing water from a perennial stream high in the mountains, a raised earthen platform supported an oblong building (thirty-seven by eighteen and one-half meters) of enormous white stones. A stairway led to a tower. The entrance was adorned by a porch, in the latest Alexandrian fashion, of two Corinthian columns between two pilasters. A frieze of enormous lions (each animal three meters long and two meters high) carved in relief, ran below the cornice and across the facade of the building. The pillars in the interior bore capitals of eagles and bulls' heads in the Persian style. The remains of an enormous winged sphinx, which probably flanked the edifice, are further evidence of Graeco-Egyptian style. Josephus speaks of artificial landscaping, of terraces and gardens laid out around the central edifice. The conduit of water, consisting of stones in which a thirty-centimeter channel was cut, brought water to the park and to the deep, wide moat around the palace. A fountain with a stone lion for a water spout has been discovered on the east side of the edifice. This seigneurial residence reminds us of Kohelet, who built houses for himself and made gardens and orchards and pools of waters.

We do not know, and may never know, what really happened when Heliodorus, the vizier of Seleucus IV, came to Jerusalem to verify the Temple accounts and to seize the monetary reserves of the sacred treasury. Two stories circulated in Jerusalem offering explanations of his retreat, both of which are now combined in II Maccabees.

According to one version, when Heliodorus and his military escort penetrate the treasury chamber, a galloping horse with a terrible rider suddenly appears. The galloping horse strikes at Heliodorus with its forefeet and his attendants carry him away, more dead than alive. Heliodorus recognizes divine might and the Jews bless the Lord. As the author says, he is describing a "great manifestation" of the "Almighty Lord," which rendered the Temple famous. But, in fact, Greek popular literature in the Hellenistic age abounded in patriotic stories about city gods who miraculously protected their shrines against intruders. For instance, in 279, the priests of Delphi saw their Apollo, together with Athena and Artemis, leave the temple and shoot arrows at Celtic invaders. In 73, Athena left Ilion to defend the city of Cyzicus, besieged by Mithridates; she returned covered with sweat, her robe torn. Official letters from Cyzicus and a decree of Ilion perpetuated the memory of this epiphany.

Heliodorus' story is patterned after this Greek schema. Biblical angels do not ride horses, but the Macedonian kings and nobles were masters of equitation, and the orientals began to represent their own celestial beings as Macedonian horsemen. In II Maccabees, celestial riders on horseback intervene in a battle to protect Judah Maccabee and his men.

It is rather strange that in this Heliodorus story it is not the rider but his horse that acts; it is clear that the author embellished the epiphany with a feature borrowed from Greek patriotic art, which also liked to represent heroes on prancing horses. The mixture of motifs was not happy. On patriotic monuments, the horse tramples the enemy so that the rider can dispatch the fallen adversary with one stroke. But Heliodorus does not lose his life on the soil of the Temple.

According to the other story, two strong and handsome youths visible only to Heliodorus meet him in the treasure chamber and scourge him incessantly; he is thrown to the floor "by divine power." That a man can be lashed by spirits is well known in folklore, and the author of the story uses the motif to show that the Diety not only prevented Heliodorus from despoiling the Temple but, in addition, castigated the offender.

Heliodorus' attendants beseech the High Priest to save their master. While Onias is offering a sacrifice for him, the same young men appear again to their victim and tell him to publish to all men the Sovereign Majesty of the Lord of Zion. Heliodorus goes home and does indeed testify to all men about the deeds of the Great God that he had experienced; just as in the Daniel cycle, Nebuchadnezzar in a manifesto announces the wonders that the Most High God wrought against him. In order to be saved, both men had to acknowledge publicly their own humiliation.

In real life a penitent of Isis shouted, "for my sins my sight was taken from me." Penitential psalms are confessions of the same kind. The propaganda value of such acknowledgments of guilt and chastisement is obvious. One could have claimed, and some did, that Heliodorus had been deceived by a priestly trick. But if Heliodorus and Nebuchadnezzar bore witness themselves to their divine punishment, no doubt was really possible. "Tellers of the god's wonders" were attached to the temples of Isis and Sarapis. Did the Temple of Jerusalem have its own heralds of God's powers, and did they tell the second version of Heliodorus' story to pious pilgrims?

The second version actually seems to be an adaptation of the original story to the Greek taste; later, Josephus was to transform even the appearances of angels in the Bible into the subjective visions of those to whom they appeared. But whichever of these versions of Heliodorus' misfortune the pilgrims of Jerusalem heard and believed, they learned that in their own day and, so to speak, before their own eyes, the Lord had again intervened for His Temple and His people.

The papyrus on which the tale was written was still fresh and easily readable when, some fifteen years after Heliodorus' episode, the Temple was burned, innocent blood shed in the Sanctuary, and the "Abomination of Desolation" set up on the altar—all by Jewish hands.

TWENTY-THREE

New Values in the Dispersion

T HE postbiblical period of Jewish history is marked by a unique
and rewarding polarity: on the one hand, Jerusalem, and on the
other, the plurality of centers in the dispersion. The diaspora
turned to the Holy Land for guidance and, in turn, determined its destiny:
Zerubabel, Ezra, Nehemiah, and Hillel came to the Holy Land from
Babylonia and Susa. This counterpoise of historical forces was without
parallel in antiquity.

The sojourner in a foreign land naturally endeavored to retain ties
with his land of origin. In the third century B.C.E. an Egyptian from Iasos,
in Caria, who happened to be at Rhodes, dedicated a statue there to the
Egyptian gods Osiris-Hapi and Isis. The man's name, Dionysios, was
Greek, but the inscription was composed in Egyptian. Zenon of Citium
(Cyprus), the founder of Stoicism, taught in Athens but refused to accept
Athenian citizenship; his countrymen from Citium who lived in Sidon
honored the philosopher there. Phoenician communities in Greece used
their native language in their decrees (often alongside Greek in bilingual
inscriptions) and the Sidonians at Piraeus in Attica and the Egyptian
association at Delos employed their national calendars. In a decree in
Greek, voted about 150 B.C.E., the Tyrians at Delos called Tyre their
"fatherland." Yet in due time the offshoots lost their connection with
the main stock and were absorbed into the populations of their new
countries.

Foreign groups, as a rule, were organized into religious associations.
The *politeuma* of the Idumeans in Ptolemaic Memphis centered around
a temple of the Idumean gods, which was complete with priests and
sacred singers. But here the similarity between the synagogue and the
sacred places of polytheist immigrants ceased. The plurality of their gods
made it possible for the Egyptians in Greece, for example, to worship
Anubis in Smyrna and Isis in Eretria, but the same Deity, and no other,

was adored in every synagogue. On the other hand, the pagan cults in foreign lands were of the congregational type; the worshippers of the Egyptian god Sarapis in Athens could and did organize their cult differently from the devotees of the same god in Tomi. Praising Isis at Cumae, a certain Demetrios, a contemporary of the Maccabees, could copy (or pretend to copy) his hymn from an inscription at Memphis. But the Isis community at Cumae was independent of the sanctuary at Memphis; the latter might be holier and more renowned, but Isis was no less present at Cumae than at Memphis.

It was different with the Jews. The jealous Deity of Israel had commanded his worshippers not to serve other gods. Yet, paradoxically, although the Lord was present everywhere, the Jew could not sacrifice to Him anywhere other than on the altar of Jerusalem. What we call monotheism in practice meant monolatry. We have already stressed the capital importance of this fact for the diaspora, in our discussion of the Jews in the Babylonian exile.

Sacrifice was not only the core of the public cult for Jews and gentiles alike, it was also and above all a necessary part of everyday private life, from the cradle to the grave and beyond—even the dead received offerings. Before making an important decision, or returning from a voyage, or entertaining a guest, the ancients offered a sacrifice. The lighting of a lamp was accompanied by a libation. The ironical inference of a Greek unbeliever, "if altars exist, gods must exist," only caricatured the most obvious aspect of ancient religions. But although the Jew in Jerusalem could and sometimes was obliged to sacrifice to the Lord, the Jew in the diaspora, except as a pilgrim in Jerusalem, was deprived of both the right and the duty of sacrificial communion with his God. He was an anomaly, who must have appeared boorish and arrogant to his gentile neighbors. To understand his plight let us remember that, driven by missionary zeal, the rabbis permitted gentiles to erect altars to God everywhere and to offer thereon whatever sacrifices to Heaven they wished. Thus two centuries after the destruction of the Temple in Jerusalem, a famous rabbi even arranged to have an animal sacrificed to God in Persia on behalf of a Sassanian queen. Otherwise, gentiles ready to revere the Lord, but offended by intransigent missionaries, would become indifferent or even hostile to the Jews' religion. For the same reason, as early as 139 B.C.E. Jews who were endeavoring to transmit their worship to the Romans erected altars in the streets of Rome. But for the Jews, wherever they might be, their only Temple was in Jerusalem. And it was this fact, that sacrifices could be offered to the Lord only in Jerusalem, that made it impossible for pagan cities to receive the God of Jerusalem into their pantheons.

Furthermore, a unique altar in Jerusalem produced a single, unified clergy. An Egyptian or an Idumean priest who emigrated could take his gods with him and establish a fully legitimate cult wherever he might settle. Apollonios, for instance, an Egyptian priest from Memphis, migrated to Delos about the middle of the third century B.C.E. and founded a shrine of Sarapis there; for three generations his descendants continued to officiate at this shrine. In this way, the Delian worship of Sarapis came to be fully independent of the "mother church," although the priests in Memphis probably looked down on any clergy or any worship outside the holy land of Horus. In Judaism, however, an Aaronite outside Zion had no sacral functions to perform; he could officiate neither at Delos nor at Alexandria.

Still, in a world where the delivery of a letter from the Jordan to the Nile took two weeks at least, centrifugal forces necessarily strained the diaspora's ties to Zion. Under the Persian kings, the Jews at Elephantine offered sacrifices to God in their local shrine, and sacrificial temples of the same kind may have existed elsewhere. Shortly after 162 B.C.E. a temple was built at Leontopolis in Egypt, probably as a center for another Jewish military settlement. The rabbis recorded that sacrifices to God were offered in this temple (which for a short time survived the destruction of Zion) and recognized the legitimacy of its priests.

The temple at Leontopolis was established with the approval of the Ptolemies, illustrating the importance of political factors in the spiritual cohesion of the diaspora. Gentile governments as a rule, however, disapproved of religious innovations as likely to lead to political disturbances. Thus the traditional authority of Zion was upheld by the Macedonian sovereigns and orthodoxy dominated the Jewish communities of the dispersion—a state of affairs that in turn helped to preserve a more or less uniform standard of religious behavior among the faithful. Indeed Ptolemy II, about 260 B.C.E., cemented the unity of world Jewry by giving it the Greek Torah, whose possession was yet another factor that distinguished the religion of the diaspora.

Each oriental religion had its sacred books, but none possessed a Scripture. The sacred books of the oriental religions were part of the apparatus of worship and were accessible to no one but the clergy, whose duty it was to preserve the hereditary knowledge of the sacred tongues, the sacred writings, and the sacred objects. Thus the chief priests of Egypt were required to learn twenty "volumes" dealing with gods, laws, and sacred acts, out of the forty-two rolls written by Thoth, the divine scribe of heaven. These secret writings were, of course, never rendered into the unhallowed language of the Greek conqueror. In the third century B.C.E. there were innumerable scrolls in Greek bearing the name of Zoroaster, but no Persian Magian ever translated a hymn of Zoroaster from Avestan into Greek. Even in a foreign land, a sacred text, as a matter of principle, had to be read in its original language. That is why, in the Greek city of Priene, an Egyptian was engaged to serve the Egyptian deities. As late as the middle of the second century c.e., in a Persian temple at Hierocaesarea (Lydia), the official recited his litanies in Persian. Because the cult of the Great Mother came to Rome from Greek Asia Minor, the office of that goddess in Rome was read in Greek. For the same reason, until the last decades of the fourth century c.e. the liturgical language of the Christian church in Rome was Greek.

Yet, in order to conquer the Western mind, all oriental religions, those of Isis and the Dea Syria no less than that of the true God, had to speak Greek. But the sacred books of the pagan East, left untranslated, remained unknown to the Greek worshipper, protected from his curiosity by the foreign script (as Apuleius says of a liturgical book in Egyptian hieroglyphs); the religious tracts of Isis or of the Syrian goddess that were published in Greek were virtually devoid of native elements. The result was that when Greek converts in due course adopted an oriental cult, the god lost its originality and individuality. In the Greek temples of Egyptian gods, unless the priest was an Egyptian, nothing but some decorative detail, such as sphinxes, and some formulas spoken in Egyptian reminded the devotees of the pharaonic land. As Lucian says, Mithra, the Persian god, never learned Greek. Conversely, the God of the Septuagint, although speaking in Greek, always remained the God of Abraham, Isaac, and Jacob. The Greek version of the Torah made it possible for both the Jew who had lost the sacred tongue and the convert who had never known it to feel in unison with coreligionists everywhere, even with the officiating priests on Zion. In possession of God's own words, a Jew in Ethiopia was no less Moses' disciple than the High Priest himself.

The Septuagint also solved the problem of liturgical language in the diaspora. Private prayer, dissociated from the sacrificial service, could of course be uttered in any language—assuming one's deity was familiar with it. A later rabbi ventured to opine that the angels (who transmit prayers to God) do not understand Aramaic, but no one, it seems, doubted the value and validity of private devotion uttered in Greek: The confession of faith (the Shema) could be recited in Greek in the Holy Land itself. Thus the synagogal service in the diaspora was conducted in Greek. One could, of course, also pray in Hebrew.

The cohesive importance of Scripture in the history of the dispersion, and then of the Church, is obvious. Men who believed in Isis or Mithra had a faith as pure and as abiding, although perhaps misplaced, as that of the Jews, but each local group of worshippers was unconnected to any other. Lucius (in Apuleius' *Metamorphoses*), initiated into the mysteries of Isis at Corinth, was invited to repeat the sacramental action by the Isis community in Rome. The dispersed Jews, however, directed their eyes to Zion from all points of the compass. God was One, the Temple was one, and to the Oneness of God and His altar corresponded the unity of the "Hebrew race," as Josephus says. Yet it was this unity that created problems and tensions for diaspora Jews—in relation to their worship, to the lands of their sojourn, and to the gentile world around them— that were unknown to the pagan immigrant in a Greek city.

Deprived of an altar, the Jew in the dispersion had no channel of daily communication with his Maker and Father other than prayer. In Nineveh, Tobit enjoined his son to "bless the Lord thy God" always, but he could not enjoin upon him the duty of sacrifice. In Ecbatana, when Tobias and Sarah had been found alive, Raguel, forbidden to slaughter a thank offering outside the Temple, poured his heart out in a hymn of praise to God, Who had been merciful to His children. Many centuries before the end of sacrificial worship in Jerusalem, there was, in the diaspora, sup-plication instead of incense and a lifting up of the hands as a bloodless oblation.

The newly acquired importance of prayer is evident in the literature of the diaspora, in which, from Tobit to Esther and Asenet, the turning point of a story is brought about by a personal petition to God. The liking for orison is such that the authors revive old liturgical texts in order to reemploy them in modern settings. Jerome notes that the prayer of Azariah in a Greek recension of the story of the Three Youths is inappropriate to the occasion. In fact, the text is an ancient supplication composed during the Exile, when there was no place to sacrifice. The song (an imitation of Psalm 148), uttered by the children in the story, was probably popular in the synagogal service; under the name of the "Benedicite" it became a part of the Church liturgy.

Private devotion was performed in a traditional manner. In the dias-pora, as in the Holy Land, the worshipper turned his face toward Zion; if he happened to be under a roof, he prayed before an open window. The time for prayer became standardized: at the Persian court Daniel kneels three times a day to give thanks to his God.

Prayer meetings outside the Temple had undoubtedly existed in Israel long before the Exile. But in ancient societies an offering (or the promise of one) was the natural complement of a prayer, and the principle that no one should appear before the Deity empty-handed was universally accepted; even a widow had to bring her mite when coming into Herod's Temple. Nevertheless, although in the dispersion religious gatherings were compelled to do without sacrifice, permanent and regular com-munity worship paralleling the Temple service of Jerusalem is not attested before the Hellenistic period. We have noted that as early as the middle of the third century B.C.E. houses of prayer existed even in the villages of Ptolemaic Egypt. And despite the fact that no evidence about prayer houses outside Egypt in the pre-Maccabean period has yet come to light, it is difficult to believe that in Antioch, for instance, where a synagogue is attested around 150 B.C.E., none had existed a century before.

Gradually houses of prayer came to be thought of as holy in the minds of those who worshipped in them, as well as in the minds of their pagan rulers. As pagans expressed their loyalty by dedicating their temples to the king, so, too, the Jews in Egypt consecrated their prayer houses on behalf of the Ptolemies; and when in the second century B.C.E. pagan temples in Egypt began to obtain the right of asylum, the same privilege was granted by the Ptolemies to some synagogues. In the late Hellenistic period the Jews of the diaspora even liked to call their synagogues "temples" and quarreled about the preeminence of some of these meeting places. Yet, in Jewish sacral law the synagogue building was never considered to be a holy place.

The liturgy of the pre-Maccabean synagogue remains unknown; we cannot even say whether a service was performed daily. Still, because in the Septuagint a special introduction precedes the exhortation "Hear, O Israel," we can assume that before 250 B.C.E. the Shema was already accepted as the confession of faith. We may also assume that the synagogue liturgy included a prayer for the sovereign.

From the diaspora, public prayer without sacrifice came in turn to Jerusalem. In the story of Heliodorus, the priests, during a "general supplication," prostrate themselves before the altar of the Temple and the people hold out their hands toward heaven and call upon the Almighty. In 162 B.C.E., in expiation of a sin committed by his fallen soldiers, Judah Maccabee and his men pray to God on the field of battle—although an offering is sent to the Temple as well. Ablutions, fasts, sexual abstention, and perseverance in prayer combined with belief in its power of intercession all became components of the Jewish religion before 200 B.C.E. Belief in the atoning efficacy of prayer to save the dead came soon afterward.

Today, for a Jew as well as for a Christian and a Muslim, a House of God is a place of communal prayer; the sacrificial cult has disappeared. Two historical accidents brought about the change. Neither King Josiah, when he limited sacrificial worship to Zion, nor the Emperor Titus, who almost seven hundred years later burned the Temple, suspected that they were preparing the doom of sacrificial religion. But if Jews and Christians could worship the Godhead without bloody victims after 70 C.E. it was because, long before that, prayer had become the sole normal expression of devotion for the greatest number of His worshippers. The roots of modern religious feeling took hold in the soil of the Jewish dispersion. A passage in pseudo-Aristeas is almost symbolic in this respect: when the envoys from Jerusalem banquet with Ptolemy II, the king dispenses with the usual pagan sacrifice before the meal and the guests, Jews and gentiles together, sanctify the food by a grace recited by a Jew.

On the other hand, an immigrant not only brought the gods of his native land with him, he also served the gods of his new country. In Persian Egypt a Syrian, Anan, son of Elisha, became a priest of Isis (probably for a Syrian colony) and in Ptolemaic Egypt there was a "chief priest" of the Egyptian god Ammon "in the Ashur [Syrian] settlement." No reference, of course, is required to prove that the Greeks everywhere piously worshipped the local deities—even crocodiles. In a polytheistic society, to refuse worship to a deity was madness. A god represented a force that, although invisible and perhaps at this moment latent, might in the very next moment prove either useful or dangerous.

The Jews alone—with their Samaritan brothers—were monotheists; the rest of the whole inhabited earth was polytheist. It was this religious separatism that prevented the Jews from sanctifying the soil of any of the idolatrous countries in which they lived. For the descendants of Macedonians who had settled in an Egyptian district, the district was their "fatherland" because the twelve Egyptian gods worshipped there had become their own "ancestral deities." For the Jews in Egypt, the ram-headed god of the terrible face, Harsaphes, patron deity of the Egyptian Heracleopolis, was an abomination, if not an object of scorn. Yet the land of the Nile, where they and their fathers had been born, the Egypt of animal gods, was, as Philo remarks, also *their* "fatherland."

Repelled by the idols of the land, the Jews pathetically tried to hallow their dwelling place by inventing Jewish memories. That is the historical significance of the tales about Jeremiah's bones being transferred to Alexandria, of Noah's ark coming to rest in the vicinity of Phrygian Apamea, and of Abraham's sojourning at Damascus. It is a pity that we are unable to date these inventions exactly, although the tradition that attributed a Damascene origin to Abraham is in any case pre-Roman.

In fact, the attempt to remain in communion with the Jews in Jerusalem could become a liability in the divided world of the Hellenistic age. The pharaoh of the Exodus, according to the Bible, was afraid that in a war the children of Israel might join his enemies; in Jubilees this pharaoh initiates the persecution of the Jews because "their hearts and faces are towards the land of Canaan." The author of Tobit finds it natural for Sennacherib to take vengeance on the Jews of Nineveh for his defeat at Jerusalem. We, too, may well understand that Artaxerxes Ochus, for instance, could take measures against the Sidonians in his empire when their city revolted against Persian rule.

Tobit, however, was legally only "sojourning" in Nineveh, Sennacherib's capital, in the same way that a Tyrian in Heliopolis was considered only to be "residing" in this Egyptian city. The problem of dual allegiance did not appear until later, particularly under Roman rule, when the Jews claimed citizenship in Greek cities. In the third century B.C.E. no one expected an immigrant to feel any attachment to his new country. In Ptolemaic Egypt the newcomer, whether from Jerusalem or Athens, entered into royal service; fealty to the king was all that was demanded. Indeed, a passage in the Torah (later changed in the traditional Hebrew text) should have appeased even the most scrupulous conscience. God, it said, had fixed the borders of the peoples according to the numbers of His angels. Each nation had its celestial patron—except Israel, which remained God's own portion. This schema corresponds to the Assyrian and Persian administrative organization. Later, in Daniel, Michael contends for the Chosen People. Because, in this view, heathen kingdoms also served to fulfill the divine plan, a Jew's fidelity to his heathen sovereign could not be regarded as derogatory to the Divine Majesty.

The Jews rightly insisted on their loyalty to the Macedonian sovereign. They pointed out that their religion, by rendering their oath of fealty inviolable, made them particularly loyal subjects. Because Greeks forswore with ease, the Jewish arguments must have seemed convincing; as we have seen, Antiochus III even alludes to the subject. In effect, however, to love one's king (*philobasileus*) was an imperative for all foreign settlers in Hellenistic monarchies, for the king alone protected them from the hatred of the exploited natives. As members of the class of "Hellenes," and therefore separated from and raised above the natives, foreigners knew that they would all have to hang together or they would all hang separately; accordingly, to be "philhellene" was an attitude required of a royal official in Egypt. The Jews in the diaspora were consequently from the beginning sincerely "graecophile."

Nevertheless, the superficial unity of all "Hellenes," created by the king's order and held together by fear of a native revolt, only lightly concealed the traditional as well as newly contrived rivalries among peoples, groups, and gods. Sojourners in alien lands were scorned, as Tobit says and as the demotic Wisdom Book echoes. In a world where virtually every act had religious connotations and was viewed in relation to divine forces, it was necessary for self-preservation, as we have repeatedly noted, that each particular group demonstrate the power and superiority of its celestial protectors. In an Egyptian village, in about 200 B.C.E., the private shrine of the Syrian goddess Atargatis was damaged by intruders who were devotees of the rival Phrygian goddess. Both parties in the dispute were Greeks. On the other hand, in 261, a poor Greek copied a hymn on a potsherd in praise of the healing god Amenothes, an Egyptian deity, so that men might know "the power of this god." Four years later, a servant of the god Sarapis wrote to convince Apollonios, the royal vizier, of the superiority of Sarapis, who he said had the power to make the favorite "much greater with the king." The rivalry between different clergies made engaging in religious propaganda a duty of the faithful: "Every Hellene should revere Imouthes, son of Ptah."

Although the rivalry of cults was not new, under the Macedonian kings the hodgepodge of peoples, the cosmopolitanism of the age, and the existence of two common languages, Aramaic and Greek, in the Near East, intensified the competition of gods and made it international. The Jews entered into the game with zest, opposing the sole true and living God to the dead idols of all the other nations and all the other clergies. Toward the end of the Persian era Tobit admonished his brethren to declare God's greatness before the gentiles, and the stories in the Book of Daniel convincingly proved to readers that the Lord of Zion protected His votaries. At the end of four out of five Daniel stories, a pagan king, overwhelmed by a miracle, publicly acknowledges to the Jews that their God is in truth the Lord of kingdoms and the God of gods. In the fifth story, Belshazzar, who had not heeded these testimonies, was swiftly overtaken by divine wrath: "In that night Belshazzar, the king of the Chaldeans, was slain, and Darius the Mede received the kingdom." Later, Heliodorus, vizier of Seleucus IV, punished for his sacrilegious arrogance, also testified about "the wondrous works of the Great God, which he had seen with his own eyes."

Although these stories were probably read only by Jews, in a religious world in which miracles were rarely doubted, even by adherents of other religions, the stories of a Heliodorus or a Daniel enabled Jews to glorify their faith before the gentiles and to confirm its value in their own eyes. For some Jews, praising their God in a foreign land gave meaning to the Captivity in the Providential plan: "Confess Him before the gentiles . . . for He has scattered us among them." Then, in the Lord's own day, "a bright light shall shine unto all the ends of the earth" and many nations from afar will worship the Name of the Lord. Tobit, like Isaiah, expects the divine miracle of conversion. In the meantime, since the believers are only a minority, if they behave well God will be glorified among the gentiles through them, but if they do evil God will be dishonored among the nations.

The Jew in the dispersion needed such consolation. In every Greek city, from Alexandria to Athens to Seleucia-on-the-Tigris, the burgesses looked down upon a sojourner. A patriot ought to live and die in his own city, as pseudo-Aristeas says, adding that residence abroad brings contempt on the poor man and brings on the rich one suspicion of having been exiled from his own country. In the tightly knit world of the *polis*, the foreigner had to know and keep his place; he had to be neither burdensome nor obnoxious, as Aeschylus says. Two centuries later, in Hellenistic Cos, he was still advised to remember his place and "to shudder before the least of the commoners" of the city. Pseudo-Aristeas, toward the end of the second century B.C.E., echoes the advice: Be humble when you are abroad, for God protects the lowly man. And the Seventy, mistranslating the dire words announcing the punishment destined to fall upon unfaithful Israel, say: "You shall go against your foes on one way, and flee seven ways before them. You will be a dispersion among all the kingdoms of the earth." It is this feeling of homelessness, common to all aliens settled in a city not their own, that often colors the voice of Jews of the diaspora. To quote King Solomon, they often felt as "a bird fallen out of its nest" (Prov. 27:8).

The stripes received at the hands of the angels convinced Heliodorus, as their chastisements convinced Nebuchadnezzar and Darius the Mede in the Book of Daniel, that the Most High of Israel was above all other gods. Men who shared this salutary belief often accepted certain Jewish practices, such as not eating pork or not wearing shoes on the Day of Atonement; such people were later called "Fearers of Heaven." But Nebuchadnezzar, even in legend, did not become a monotheist; he only added a new deity to his pantheon, in the same way that those who revered Anubis particularly did not abandon the worship of other gods. The rabbis said that Jethro, the Midianite priest, after witnessing the miracle of the Exodus, acknowledged that the Lord was greater than all gods, but nonetheless continued to worship idols. Naaman of Damascus, however, recognized that there is no other God but that of Israel.

It appears that Naaman found few imitators in the pre-Maccabean era. In the Testaments of the Twelve Patriarchs, Potiphar's wife promised to abandon idols, to convert her husband, and to walk with him in the Law of Joseph's God. Instead, under the pretext of obtaining instruction in the word of God, she importuned the chaste Joseph. Although it was natural for her to want to know something about the tenets of her future faith, neither this Joseph nor any other hero produced by the Jewish imagination of the pre-Maccabean age made a single convert. Nor did they preach salvation to the gentiles. Ironically, Antiochus Epiphanes, the Persecutor, is the first Greek convert named in our sources. Stricken by a horrible disease, he promised to become a Jew. The tardy conversion was of no avail, but his example inspired other tormentors of the Chosen People. Murdered in his slumber, Holofernes had no time for a change of heart, and the gallows waited for Haman, but Achior, Holofernes' general in the Book of Judith, entered into the covenant of Abraham, and the would-be persecutors in the time of Esther also "turned Jews."

The terminology in Esther is significant. An Egyptian woman who, like Potiphar's wife in the edifying story, began to worship the Lord no more became a Jew than she would have become an Athenian by beginning to worship Athena. The Ptolemaic government punished an arbitrary change of status with death. By abandoning their idols, individuals would make their situation in pagan society impossible, but they still would not acquire the legal status of "Jew." A legal conversion would have involved not only a change of religion, but also a change of communal allegiance. This seems to be the meaning of the statement in Esther that "many from among the peoples of the land became Jews; for the fear of the Jews was fallen upon them."

Christian critics of Esther do not understand that in a polytheistic world, and perhaps even today, deference to a deity is correlated with the might of his worshippers. As Philo says, should the Jews become powerful again all the world will be converted. It was in the Hasmonean period, in which Esther was written, that mass conversion to the true faith began, but it was only after, or perhaps under, Hasmonean rule, probably in connection with Hasmonean legislation, that the word *proselytos* acquired a religious meaning and came to describe persons who, as Philo puts it, "ran way" from idols to serve the true God.

Besides the minority who were prepared in varying degrees to reverence the Lord of Zion, the immense majority of the people of the world among whom the dispersed Jews sojourned remained hostile or indifferent to the appeals of truth. Was a Jew obliged to condemn these idolaters, to throw down the images and break the altars of the false gods? Since that would have been suicidal, the dispersion took a more tolerant attitude toward gentile superstition.

The Greek Torah was enriched by a divine commandment that would have surprised Isaiah and Jeremiah: "You should not abuse [the] gods." Philo and Josephus explain that the Law forbids insult to gods that other cities revere and, indeed, no Jewish hero in the Hellenistic period strikes idols or tries to convert the worshippers of foreign gods. Abraham alone is an exception, and he sets fire only to his father's idols and preaches only to his own family. Only when provoked, like Daniel in the story of Bel, are diaspora Jews driven to prove that there is no god beside the Lord of Zion.

This tolerance was facilitated in everyday life by the resemblances between the prayers, rites, and thinking of both Jews and gentiles. For instance, for the Greeks, as for the Jews, childbirth ritually defiled the mother and rendered unclean all who approached her. Yet the ritual strictness of the gentiles in this matter left the Jew cool, since for the Jew the defilement was not produced by the physical condition of the mother but was created by the Law. As the Jew saw it, a pagan who stood outside the covenant could be neither clean nor unclean in terms of Jewish ritual purity. That burden, like the joy of Torah, was reserved for the covenanted people alone.

Nonetheless, the Jews knew from the Torah that their gentile neighbors were, like them, Noah's descendants and that in the name of Noah rules had been formulated that were binding upon all his progeny. The list of injunctions varies in our sources, but they always include the common principles upon which every human society must be based. As Noah says when giving these laws in Jubilees, fornication, iniquity, and impurity were three causes of the Flood. Note that in this list—the oldest list of Noachic commandments—there is no prohibition of idolatry. Rabbinic authorities were the first to claim that idolatry was forbidden to Noah's descendants, thus completely changing the meaning of the Noachic rules. Originally the laws of Noah had paralleled the common rules of decency and comity accepted by the gentiles themselves: the Greek commandments demanded that one revere gods, parents, and guests, and the Egyptian contemporaries of the author of Jubilees continued to repeat the millennial confessions of their ancestors, maintaining that they had not committed murder, theft, sacrilege, adultery, or numerous other outrages. The original conception of the Noachic laws thus consecrated pagan morality in the eyes of the orthodox Jew; a law-abiding gentile, although an idolater, might be in an exterior ring but remained nevertheless within a ring of divine legislation and grace. And because Israel was not a church, it did not exclude pagans from the possibility of salvation. Philo, somewhat arrogantly—but in the logic of monotheism—pretended that the Jews were the priests of mankind.

Actually, the expanded list caused problems for Jews in their relations with their gentile neighbors in two other areas beside that of idolatry: food and marriage. Particular dietary restrictions often separated peoples and sects in the Hellenistic age, with the Egyptians outdoing everyone else in this respect; according to their place of origin, some Egyptians abstained from beans, some from lentils, and some from still other things— each group at odds with its neighbors. Still, because crabs, winged insects, and other such items forbidden to the Jew were only rarely to be found on a gentile table, and because the separation between meat and milk utensils was a later rabbinic innovation, it would seem that it was only the prohibition against eating meat containing blood that separated Jews from their pagan neighbors at table. But since the Greeks were rather sparing in their everyday consumption of meat, this dietary restriction would not have completely excluded common meals with gentiles either.

In fact, it was the religious use of food that disqualified the pagan table for the Jew. The Law prohibits the consumption of anything that has been offered as a sacrifice to idols. But at that time a meal was inseparable from cult: any meat that was available usually came from an animal that had been sacrificed; the first fruits of field and tree were offered by Jews to the Lord but by pagans to false gods, thus consecrating the entire crop; a cake made of the same dough as the bread on the table had been presented to the domestic spirits, and the wine served for libations. Moreover, a grace was said before every meal. Therefore there was no way that Jews who partook of a heathen meal could avoid exposing themselves to the germs of idolatrous impurity.

Accordingly, Tobit, toward the end of the Persian period, was already avoiding "the bread of the gentiles" altogether. Pagan oil was refused by the Jews as early as the period around 300 B.C.E., while toward the end of the second century B.C.E. Judith brings not only wine but even bread and figs to Holofernes' tent and has her meals prepared by her Jewish maid. Thus the precept ascribed to Abraham in Jubilees, not to eat with the gentiles, must already have been followed by the Jews in the third century B.C.E. In this way, as Tacitus says, the Jews became "separated at table." The Syrians might refuse to taste fish (and were ridiculed for it by the Greeks), the white cock might be forbidden to the adepts of Mazdaism, and the diet of Egyptian priests might be saltless, but only the Jews cut themselves completely off from the circle of their neighbors, whose society was created and sustained by the pleasures of the table.

The primary question, however, is how many Jews in the pre-Maccabean diaspora followed the pious examples of Tobit and Judith. This question must remain without answer, although it is probable that Paul's somewhat disingenuous advice, "Whatsoever is set before you, eat, asking no questions for conscience," was followed by a goodly number of Jews in the diaspora long before Saul's conversion.

The connubial question was more complicated. Mosaic law prohibited marital alliances only with the seven peoples of Canaan, but based on this rule, Ezra coerced the Jews in Jersualem into repudiating all foreign women. In the same period endogamy was also imposed in Rome and Athens. In all three societies at that time civil status conditioned the legitimacy of a marriage: a Jew might not marry a Canaanite woman even if she worshipped the Lord, but union with foreign women captured in war was expressly permitted. In the Hellenistic period, however, the old prohibitions with regard to intermarriage were generally considered obsolete: in a Greek play, a man of Syracuse marries a girl from Epidauros without any legal hindrance. All the same, some political and emotional restrictions remained. The laws of Naucratis, for instance, continued to prohibit intermarriage with Egyptians, and in Cyprus, where Greeks and Phoenicans labored to preserve their national individuality, a father could oppose the marriage of his daughter to a suitor "because of the shame of his Phoenician origin." But an Alexandrian poet of about 275 B.C.E. who treats this subject takes the side of the lovers.

No rule of Scripture prevented a Jew from entering into marriage with a Phoenician, Greek, or Egyptian woman. Although in the Testament of Levi, about 200 B.C.E., priests are warned against marrying foreign women—which extended to all the sons of Levi a prohibition that, in the Law, concerns the High Priest alone—this innovation implicitly admits the possibility of an alliance between a layman and an alien woman. When Tobit advises his son against a mixed marriage, his reason is purely social: to take a foreign girl is to display disdain for one's own people. Only in Jubilees is foreign marriage generally damned. But this is an erratic book. In fact, according to rabbinic tradition, it was "the law court *(beth-din)* of the Hasmoneans" that had prohibited cohabitation with a foreign *(goy)* woman. Without being aware of it, the Maccabean legists duplicated the Athenian norm of the fourth century B.C.E. referred to above concerning intercourse between aliens and citizens of either sex.

This endogamic rule of the Maccabees soon came to be understood in the religious rather than the civil sense. The poet Theodotus, who wrote before 80 B.C.E., has Jacob say, in a paraphrase of Dinah's story, that the "Hebrews" are not allowed to take sons-in-law except "from a kindred race" and that they required the men of Shechem to be circumcised and to "follow the custom of the Jews." Theodotus is thus our earliest witness to a rule later to become generally acknowledged among Jews: legitimate marriages with foreigners required the conversion of the non-Jewish partner. Philo and Josephus present this rule as self-evident, although rabbinic authorities were aware of its non-Scriptural origin. The Church afterward followed the Synagogue in prohibiting the union of believers and infidels, "since there cannot be any companionship between faithful and infidel."

Jacob, as seen by Theodotus, insists on the conversion of his future son-in-law in order to preserve the religion of his daughter, since a wife was expected to practice the faith of her husband. Ancient moralists disapproved of a wife who worshipped different deities from those of her husband. Yet women were particularly sensitive to the appeal of alien cults, from Jezebel to the women of Damascus, who, in 66 C.E., followed Jewish practices in great number.

Indeed, this is a point of Judeo-pagan perplexity. From the point of view of a gentile, his wife's worship of the Lord of Jerusalem, or of the Egyptian Isis, would be an outlandish suspect expression of an otherwise legitimate faith, but no more. To a Jew, however, foreign worship was not just a superstition, but an abomination. The Puritans regarded the idea of religious toleration as a device of Satan. For a Jew the idea that idolatry should be tolerated would have appeared inane, as though one were being asked to tolerate the opinion that two and two equal three. The flippant Greek might pretend that, concerning the gods, no one knows the truth. The Jew, however, knew the truth. Unfortunately, possession of the truth makes one intolerant of error, and idolatry, as Maimonides states, is the greatest of errors.

The truth, alas, is also a burden. In a society where not only feast days but virtually every aspect of daily life, at home as well as in public, was shaped by its appropriate ritual, common worship tended to foster friendship among men of various origins, as an ancient geographer noted. But the Jew, forbidden to worship other gods, excluded himself from this "mark of fellowship." A Jewess leaving her house became conspicuous because, unlike everyone else, she neither prayed to Hecate, whose idol protected her neighbor's door, nor threw a little offering on one of the small altars so ubiquitous in the streets. The unwillingness to do as other people did was an act of unsociability that might have been condoned, on the grounds that the Jews were merely following the ways of their ancestors, but it was surely never understood. Thus the Jews felt themselves, and were felt by others, to be strangers on this idolatrous earth, even if they in turn conceded that the gentiles were not to be blamed for their foolishness. After all, they too were simply following in the ways of their fathers.

But many of the Jews of the diaspora, forced to mingle with the *goyim* daily, were led by these everyday contacts, in the words of the Psalmist, to learn their works and to serve their idols. In order to live in a Greek world, a Jewish boy had to learn Greek letters, and learn them under the eyes of the heathen Muses; a boy who was truant because he "hated" these august sisters was appropriately flogged before their images. Religious processions punctuated the school calendar and hymns to the gods were learned in the schoolroom; Homer was the first schoolbook. Nor could one attain a state of advanced hellenization without taking part in gymnastic training, and no Jewish ephebe could avoid participation in the rites of the gods of the *gymnasium,* whose idols adorned the *palaestra.*

His Greek education finished, the Jew still could not escape the grasp of heathenism. When the patron saint of the city had his or her festival, the entire population was invited to wear wreaths, to free their slaves from work, and in other diverse ways to celebrate the occasion. Was the Jew to be an eyesore? A benefactor often distributed meat or oil to the citizens, or even to all inhabitants, of the city. Jews needed to be a steadfast indeed to relinquish their share.

Then there were the duties and amenities of neighborliness. Invited to a gentile wedding feast, Jews shared in idolatry unwittingly—"in cleanness," as a charitable rabbi of the second century C.E. said—even if they brought their own food. The tractate on alien worship in the Mishna and Tertullian's pamphlet on idolatry show how complex must have been the task of keeping the monotheist faith unspotted in an idolatrous world. Even in death Jews remained in contact with gentiles: they were buried among them.

The compulsion to relinquish their separatist manners and customs was particularly felt at the extremes of the social ladder. Jews who worked and lived in an Egyptian village and who were unable to sign their names in Greek naturally spoke Egyptian and adapted themselves to native ways of life. In a document of the second or first century B.C.E. from an Egyptian village, Sabbataios, son of Horus, is a business partner of Paous, son of Sabbataios; the name attesting the observance and veneration of the Sabbath alternates in two Jewish families with the names of Egyptian gods. In the upper strata, Jews at the courts were daily enticed into breaking the ritual laws and were in no position to respect the Sabbath rest. Daniel's refusal to use his portion of the king's dainties is presented as an act of exceptional merit, worthy of miraculous reward. Philo's complaint that the successful Jews of Alexandria had abandoned their ancestral customs was no doubt already true in the third century B.C.E. Even minor functionaries in royal service, who were able to stay away from work on the Sabbath, had to close their offices on Isis' feast.

Jews in a Greek city could not hope to elude the heathen gods even if they withdrew completely into the sanctuary of their homes. There were taxes and public charges that they were required to pay and that implicated them in the maintenance of idolatrous worship. When Jews, whether citizens of a Greek city or just resident aliens (who, as pseudo-Aristeas says, had to live humbly), were approached for contributions to a pagan festival, could they refuse? Nicetas, son of Jason, the Jerusalemite, who lived as a sojourner at Iasus in Caria, subscribed one hundred drachmas to the festival of Dionysus. Perhaps he thought, along with his contemporary Jesus, son of Sirach, the Jerusalemite, "What does an offering profit an idol?"

He might, however, have actually believed in Dionysus. It is a monotheistic habit of thought to formulate religious statements alternatively: either-or. In a polytheistic world, however, the religious attitude was normally one of addition, not exclusion. Gods lurked everywhere and help was sought by worshippers from any god to whom they might rightfully appeal. The Jews were no less credulous than their pagan neighbors. A Jew might believe that the gods of the nations were daimons, as the Psalmist says in Greek, but such a belief in itself indicates some degree of recognition that idols were forces to be reckoned with and appeased. Despite Turgot's epigram on the invention of the lightning rod, the use of Franklin's device does not negate Providence. We have seen that some of the puritan soliders of Judah Maccabee carried as charms objects taken from a pagan temple that they had burned.

This most insidious form of polytheism never disappeared from Jewish thought. The amulets with pagan gods and images engraved on them, like the talisman showing the head of Medusa found in a Jewish grave, come from Roman times, but a Greek inscription of the first half of the third century B.C.E. illustrates how early the contagion of Greek superstition had taken hold. There was a famous shrine of the oracular god Amphiarus at Oropus, in Boetia. No wonder, as we also saw above, that a Jewish slave in the city of Oropus saw Amphiarus (along with Hygeia, the goddess of health) in a dream! And how could he refuse credence to his vision? Jewish wisdom and Greek philosophy both believed in premonitory dreams. Therefore, "Moschion, son of Moschion, a Jew," liberated by his master, placed a slab near the pagan altar announcing the fulfillment of the god's command that had been revealed to him in his dream. We may surmise that there were in the diaspora many Jews like Moschion, ready to acknowledge some pagan deity in addition to the Lord (although probably set somewhere below Him), just as many gentiles wanted to sacrifice to the God of Jerusalem. Such syncretism, or *shituf*, as the rabbis called this recognition of plural divine control of the cosmos, was widespread in the polytheist world.

Credulity sometimes led to faith. Juvenal speaks of superstitious Romans who began with Sabbath observance and ended as full converts to Judaism. R. Akiba, Juvenal's younger contemporary, knew that healings in pagan temples impressed Jews. He did not deny the reality of these miraculous cures, but rationalized them by a theory of predestination. He was a sage and a saint who knew that idolatry "has nothing in it," but he also knew that the evil impulse might well urge a Jew to worship idols, and that the Jew might well succumb to such urging. If such behavior was possible in Palestine, under rabbinic ferule, it is likely that the pre-Maccabean Jews of the dispersion were even more susceptible to the attraction of foreign gods.

The Septuagint Deuteronomy contains, for instance, an injunction that is lacking in the Hebrew original: "There shall be no *telesphoros* among the daughters of Israel, neither shall there be a *teliskomenos* among the sons of Israel." Later, the Greek translator of Hosea understood the prophet to be condemning sacrifices with *tetelismenoi*. Again, in the Greek text of Kings we find that Asa did right by removing idols and *teletai* from the land. The conventional explantion of the Hebrew texts of these passages is that they refer to the consecrated persons (*kedesh, kedeshah*) of Canaanite worship, that is, to temple prostitution. But the Greek terms show that the Greek translators were thinking not of Canaanite rites but of Greek, particularly Dionysiac, mysteries. Originally the devotees of Dionysus had been ecstatic women, but in the third and second centuries B.C.E. men also became initiates, although the leader of each group (*thiasos*) continued to be a woman. This transitional stage of Dionysiac religion is reflected in the Septuagint formulation of the Deuteronomic interdiction.

Various data evidence the spread and importance of the Greek mysteries, particularly of the secret Dionysiac rites, in the third century B.C.E. Ptolemy IV (221–204 B.C.E.) was himself a fervent worshipper of Dionysus, and a Jewish legend, already popular a century after his death, attributed to him a decree requiring the Jews of Egypt to become devotees of Dionysus, too. The author of III Maccabees believes that many Jews in Alexandria readily obeyed this call. A contemporary of Philo warns the Jews against the Dionysiac revels. Philo, too, denounces the Greek mysteries, although at the same time he imitates their religious language in his pious tracts; an imitation that testifies to the attraction exercised by the mysteries on the Jews of Alexandria. Whereas the holy ibises and sacred crocodiles of the Egyptians provoked the scorn of hellenized Jews, the Greek mysteries seduced them, because they were secret—indeed, because they were Greek secrets. To quote III Maccabees again, by participating in Greek mysteries, the Jews shared in their prestige. Above all, however, the mysteries compensated for a horrifying deficiency that was common to the official worship of both Greece and Israel. The ultimate purpose of all Greek mysteries was to secure for the initiate a chosen lot in the world to come, to give him the hope of individual survival. The fear of death, which "troubles human life to its inmost depth," was the impelling force behind the Greek mystical current in the early Hellenistic world. The achievement of the Pharisees was to channel this current into the mainstream of Jewish tradition.

The essential fact, which we have so often mentioned but which must be stressed again and again, is that sharing in the Greek mysteries or in any other kind of polytheistic worship did not demand conversion. A Jew was free to continue to pray to God of Jerusalem; he was not required to give up the faith of his ancestors. Pagan cults relied only on practice, not on conversion. In order to describe an apostate, the author of III Maccabees must use the significant circumlocution "changing the practices and estranged from ancestral doctrines." In other words, for the Jew, apostasy meant the abandonment of religious separatism.

For the same reason, a Jew seduced by polytheism was not legally excluded from the rest of Jewry. Of course, as III Maccabees tells us, stalwart Jews might boycott a backsliding brother and despise him, but legally he remained a Jew, even if his father had neglected to circumcise him and even if he did not observe his ancestral rites but followed Dionysian ceremonies. Conversely, an Egyptian or an Athenian who followed the way of the Lord did not legally become a Jew. Only by a purely political act, the performance of which did not depend on his decision alone—that is, only by obtaining citizenship in a Greek city or by gaining entrance to a non-Jewish ethnic community—could a backsliding Jew legally break away from the Chosen People. Thus, in III Maccabees, the king promises Alexandrian citizenship to Jews who are initiated into the mysteries. Dositheus, the apostate named in the same book, is probably identical with the priest of Alexander and the deified Ptolemies known to us from a papyrus written in 222 B.C.E. Yet in 217, at the time of the events narrated in III Maccabees, he had no other legal status than as a Jew.

Despite widespread laxity, there was no schism. Despite backsliding Jews who combined synagogal worship and pagan rites, and despite the wide diversity in the diaspora with regard to the strict fulfillment of the commandments, heathen pressure could not endanger the Jewish faith. In the autonomous congregations of paganism, lacking a standard of orthodox faith, contact with and contagion by a foreign cult could transform their worship; for instance, sacred prostitution invaded the precincts of the Persian goddess Anahita in the Persian diaspora. And because the Alexandrians never let a day pass without laughing at sacred animals, the Egyptian Isis in the Greek world was no longer represented as cow-headed; in the temples outside Egypt her image and ideology became Greek. She became the embodiment of progress, having initiated, it was now claimed, the advance of civilization.

The Jewish cult was imageless and synagogues were just places in which to pray. But, although the Torah scroll on which the diaspora necessarily lavished its affection was only a book, the Godhead and the divine commandments were enshrined in it. It was the same everywhere, from the Caspian Sea to the cataracts of the Nile; no one could change one jot or tittle in this scroll, and nowhere but in Jerusalem could the Holy Scripture be interpreted authoritatively. Judaism was a catholic and universal religion, presided over and directed by the Pontiff in the Holy City. As long as Jerusalem remained orthodox, pagan impact on the diaspora might produce individual or local additions or deletions, but it would never affect the general practice and doctrine of Judaism.

This situation explains the emphasis and direction of Jewish apologetics in the Hellenistic age. The apologist was addressing his wavering brother in the diaspora, which before the Hasmonean monarchy began almost at the gates of Jerusalem and in which coercion was difficult if not impossible. Nevertheless, although the apologist, and those who listened, agreed that the Torah was God's word and that Mosaic precepts were good and valid, the reflective religion of the Hellenistic age was no longer satisfied with the recognition of the Deity in the traditional sense. Gods and men now demanded *pistis*, acts of faith based on conviction. It was now thought that if Jews did not know why they should not eat pork or should observe the Sabbath, they were more liable to temptation. Thus the apologist endeavored to prove the harmony of thought between the Torah and Greek wisdom. His object was to show that Jews, although educated in the Greek manner, ought to follow the ancestral laws into which they had been born and according to which they had been bred.

This task is common to all defenders of religious minorities. But the fact that in this case it was the minority, and not the majority, that was exclusive and intolerant made the defense particularly difficult. An obstinate sense of alienation was required to fight gods and to reject neighbors who were well disposed toward you and who were always ready to see you in their temples and at their tables—ready even to accept your own Deity into the common pantheon. Philo proudly remarks that although every nation shows an aversion to foreign institutions, every country honors those of the Jews. Why, then, should the Jews not honor the gods of the country in which they lived? The endless, monotonous, and unjustified attacks on idolatry in virtually every Jewish book of the Hellenistic age could hardly have offended or persuaded a Greek; the Greeks eagerly repeated stories about clever foreigners laughing at Greek idolatry. These attacks were needed, rather, to bolster the faith of those Jews who through too much contact with Greeks might be persuaded to transgress the divine commandments. They are not simply restatements of biblical warnings: they are new answers to the ever-present danger of polytheism. *Credere non potest, nisi volens,* as Augustine said.

The Jews of the diaspora, who lived in a world that did not seek their conversion—indeed, a world in which conversion would have been legally difficult—needed the passions of contempt and hatred for the religion of their neighbors to protect their faith from the daily allure of paganism. "For the lips of a strange woman drop honey, and her mouth is smoother than oil."

TWENTY-FOUR

Old and New in Religion

N ANCIENT society was a political body and an established religious body at one and the same time. In Greece and Rome the absence of a priestly caste made this coalescence particularly conspicuous: any citizen could be chosen to do a priest's duty and all citizens had to worship the gods of the city, aliens being excluded from the public altars. When, for instance, the Athenians accepted the Thracian god Bendis into their pantheon, public worship of Bendis by the citizens of Athens was separate from the cult of Bendis carried on by Thracian settlers in Athens. But even in Jerusalem, where the sons of Aaron were clearly marked off from the rest of the population, civil and ecclesiastic were aspects of the same interwoven whole.

This interpenetration of two activities that for us are essentially different makes understanding ancient religions, whether of Athens or of Jerusalem, difficult. For us, religion is essentially expressed in the feelings and acts of the believer; it is *religio animae,* to use a formula of Augustine's; or, to speak with Lactantius, another Christian author, the whole of religion is in the soul of the individual worshipper. But, as we have said, this Christian view would have been seen as a kind of philosophy by the pagans, rather than as religion. The essential reason for the persecution of the Christians in the Roman Empire was that they confounded cult and philosophy. We also accept the individual, and sometimes capricious, opinions expressed by ancient thinkers about theological questions as testimony about their own religion, or even about the nature of paganism itself. But what these thinkers are expressing is only their philosophy; they take the real texture of their religious life—the daily rites, gestures, and words—for granted.

Origen made the same mistake—or, rather, used the idea for his own apologetical purposes—when he asked rhetorically how the wise Socrates could offer prayers to Artemis as if she were God. Socrates' religion was not realized in his discourses, but in his silent faith in ancestral ritual (to use Lactantius' definition of paganism): in going as a child with his father to the local shrine, or later in consulting the oracle of Apollo, or in remembering, before his execution, the sacrifice promised to Asclepius. Likewise, Cotta, in Cicero's treatise *On the Nature of God* states that religion consists of rites and ceremonies, and that with regard to the service of the gods he follows his ancestors unquestioningly. On the other hand, he continues, if philosophers want to discuss religion, he is ready to deal with their arguments, and then proceeds, in spite of his being a patrician and a member of the board of Roman *pontifices,* to demolish the Stoic argument for the providential government of the world.

For the Jews, similarly, the Temple cult was their religion; only under the impact of Greek philosophy did they begin to philosophize about their faith. Consequently, in trying to understand the religion of Jerusalem in the early Hellenistic age, we too are compelled to describe the "philosophical" or "theological" views of the Jewish thinkers of the period. First, because the real faith of the Jews was expressed in traditional gestures and actions, it too was silent and spoken of only indirectly: God will answer the prayer of a son who respects his father, Ben Sira says (3:5—a reminder, incidentally, that there were many irreverent sons in the seemingly stable patriarchal society of ancient Jerusalem). Second, because the traditional cultic acts have already been competently described in numerous works on the Temple service, we will note in the present work only recognizable changes in the cult, although our evidence even for these changes is accidental and therefore insufficient.

We learn from a talmudic tradition, for instance, that the High Priest Yohanan, that is, John Hyrcanus I (134–104 B.C.E.), in all probability modified the biblical rules with regard to tithing agricultural produce because the landowners of his time were generally disregarding this duty. May we infer from his decree that earlier, say around 200 B.C.E., Jewish farmers separated the tithes faithfully? Ben Sira's admonitions show that even in his time the neglect of tithes was already well known. Did neglect of tithing become particularly acute under the pious Hasmonean rulers? Again, we do not know. In the present state of our ignorance, we can only rehearse the facts, if we are lucky enough to know any, and attempt some guesses about the causality of these alleged facts.

The historical problem, thus, is how to ascertain the religion of the average Jew in early Hellenistic Judea. At the very least, the existing evidence allows us some clues. As a starting point we have a saying of the High Priest Simon II, who officiated toward the end of the third century B.C.E. Eulogized by Ben Sira and regarded by the Pharisees as a link between Moses and Hillel, Simon may be considered a good witness to the state of mind of his people and his time. In his saying, preserved by the Pharisees, Simon states that "this age" rests upon three pillars: *ha-Torah*, *ha-Avodah*, and *Gemilut Hasadim*. Let us use these three concepts as signposts in the mental landscape of the men of Jerusalem of around 200 B.C.E.

In the postexilic usage followed by the High Priest, *ha-Torah* meant the whole Law given by Moses, that which we call the Five Books of Moses. Because this huge scroll contained the rule of life for the Chosen People, Moses was classified by Greek students of comparative religion—along with Zoroaster, Zalmoxis, Minos, Lycurgus, Zaleukos, and Numa—as one of the clever lawgivers who attributed their commandments to divine inspiration in order to impress their respective peoples.

This Greek rationalist position throws light on two particular features of the Torah. First, the gods of the ancient Near East did not enact laws. Neither Marduk nor Thoth inspired a lawbook. Hammurabi and other kings, invested by the gods with the duty of proclaiming and upholding eternal justice, legislated by virtue of their royal vocation. Direct divine— that is, oracular—authorship of laws appears outside the traditional monarchic structure of society. It was because neither Moses nor Lycurgus could claim constitutional authority to proclaim laws that their laws were said to be of divine origin. It is interesting to note that Xerxes speaks of the law established by Ahuramazda, and that Artaxerxes speaks of the law *(dat)* of the God of Heaven, without mentioning Moses (Ezra 7:12), while the Chronicler calls Ezra the scribe of the Torah of Moses, which the Lord has given (Ezra 7:6).

Second, the Torah is not just a law book. It is a history of the relationship between the Chosen People and their God, from Adam to the death of Moses. As R. Isaac remarked in the third or fourth century C.E., if the Torah were just a code, Moses' book would have commenced with the twelfth chapter of Exodus. In fact, even the ordinances of the Passover in this chapter, like many other legal rules in the Torah, are proclaimed with respect to or on the occasion of some particular historical event. A number of the rules refer to future historical events: "When you shall come into the land . . . " Law and history are inseparable parts of the same record; both are manifestations of God's benevolent might. The Torah narrates the wonders of the One, True, and Living God, and at the same time lays down the rule of life, the *nomos*, of God's people.

The solidarity between a people and its gods was self-evident in ancient society; it was inconceivable that Rome or, say, Sidon could exist without its gods, or that a god could exist without its people: "Has a nation changed gods?" (Jer. 2:11). But in the sacred history related in the Bible, both God and man are free agents. On the one hand, Israel can turn to and serve other gods. On the other, although Esau is Jacob's brother, God can choose to love only Jacob (Mal. 1:2). God can even say to

Jacob's progeny: "You are not My people, and I will not be with you" (Hos. 1:9). Surely out of stones God can raise children unto Abraham. Therefore, in the sacred history the Absolute God condescends to treat with His creatures, to bind them to Himself and Himself to them by a Covenant; as Ben Sira says, the Torah is "the book of the Covenant of the Most High God." The laws of the Torah result from the Covenant. The Torah tells of all the good things that await those who fulfill the Covenant and all the evil things that must befall those who breach it. The Torah becomes a witness against Israel, as Moses says (Deut. 31:26), mutually obligating the Chosen People and its dread Sovereign. After the destruction of the Temple, Josephus will say, "We are deprived of wealth, of cities, of all advantages; yet the Law for us remains immortal." The term *ha-Torah* in Simon's saying refers to this unique relationship between God and the covenanted people.

The covenantal relationship was unique because it bound Israel to the one and only God. "There is no other God than Thee," proclaims Ben Sira in a prayer, and he stresses that God, Who lives forever, has created all things. This was a traditional and thus a self-evident truth. Only when addressing the heathens did a Jew need to insist that "there is one God, sole ruler, ineffable, dwelling in the sky, self-begotten, invisible, Who Himself alone sees all things." It is worth noticing that on the eve of the great apostasy under Antiochus IV the oneness of God remained an unchallenged and unchallengeable truth in Jerusalem.

Although particular aspects of the Supreme Being were mentioned only incidentally, the Jews of the time, following biblical usage, would have agreed that God is just, truthful, merciful, good, and everlasting. For many, it is true, these terms were considered to be merely figures of speech and were used prudently. We have seen how the author of Jubilees eliminated theophanies in his retelling of Genesis; only Abraham and Moses communicate with the Deity directly. In this respect, this ultra-orthodox author was in agreement with the Orphic poem written by a Greek-thinking Jewish contemporary that we have discussed above.

But for others of the faithful, anthropomorphic phraseology happily continued to steady their belief. For instance, Ben Sira speaks freely of God's wrath, anger, and loathing; he mentions God's eyes and voice and speaks of His hands stretching out the heavens. In contrast to lifeless idols, but also differing from the abstract deity of the philosophers and savants, the God of Abraham, Isaac, and Jacob was personal: "Vengeance is Mine and recompense." Quoting these words from the Torah, the author of the Epistle to the Hebrews, writing in the first century C.E. before the destruction of the Temple, exclaims: "It is a fearful thing to fall into the hands of the Living God." The contemporaries of the High Priest Simon were probably less reflective, but for them, too, the immediacy of the Omnipotent God was an awesome reality: "Say not, 'I shall hide from the Lord, and who shall remember me from on high?' "

Yet, in this and similar passages in Ben Sira, traditional language clothes a new attitude. To experience the awesome closeness of God had been the lot of only the elect—priests, prophets, and devotees chosen to be holy. For the Psalmist, the eye of the Lord was upon those who fear Him and the wicked could only hope that the Lord would not see their misdeeds (Ps. 94:7). "Who sees us?" they ask in Isaiah (29:15). But Ben Sira insists that no thought escapes the Most High and that not one word is hidden from Him. God was now at man's elbow, keeping watch on his evil inclination, as Gad says in the Testaments. From Reuben's testament we learn that when he sinned with Bilhah, his father's concubine, an angel of the Lord "immediately" informed Jacob of the misdeed. Joseph, according to Jubilees, did not surrender to Potiphar's wife, among other reasons, for fear that the sin would be recorded against him in the celestial account books in which the good and evil deeds of each person were entered.

How did the average Jew feel under the eternally watchful eye of this *deus curiosus et plenus negotii,* of whom Cicero speaks? Susanna refused to commit an offense that would not remain hidden from the Lord, and in a Christian work, the Pseudo-Clementine Homilies, we learn that a woman who does not fear God would also not fear her husband. In the same work, a Jew-baiter sneers that Jewish women are virtuous only because they are afraid of their all-seeing God. Nevertheless, in the Roman period the rabbis were still trying to convince the wicked of God's omniscience.

We are virtually ignorant of the state of religious thinking in the Hellenistic Levant outside Judea. The Aramaic records have not come down to us, cuneiform tablets deal mainly with omens, and hieroglyphic inscriptions are stilted imitations of ancient texts. But the Greeks of the same age felt divine immanence no less forcefully than the Jews. Of course, although the more or less vague idea that Zeus sees everything was a natural part of implicit faith, in the Classical period the average Greek, in agreement with common sense, held that "the gods partly know and partly do not know." In 307, however, the Athenian hymn to the deified king Demetrius, in an Isaiah-like vein, contemptuously refers to the gods of wood and stone who pay no heed to their worshippers. At the end of the fourth century, the Athenian who feared his gods lived in a constant state of pusillanimity with regard to them and their interference in his private actions.

Neither the fervor of Epicurus in proclaiming that the gods are not concerned with us nor the liberating effect that this discovery had on people's minds, however, is understandable except against the background of the general feeling that the gods indeed knew all that happened on the earth. Zeus also had his ivory tablets (or leather scrolls) on which the good and evil actions of men were recorded. Of course, the Greek gods had their own frailties. Zeus, "mad after women," as Theocritus says, could understand an eager lover, and the grave and deeply religious Plutarch, a contemporary of Akiba, could still believe that gods save sinners who are handsome.

The Lord of Jerusalem, however, was above and beyond all mythology. The Greek may have lived in fear of the chastisement of the gods, but no Greek could know the consciousness of guilt that the Jew felt before the Lord. From the Decalogue, the Jew knew that God punishes those who "hate" Him. Still, represented by its king, Israel also knew that it could cry to God, "Thou art my Father" (Ps. 89:26). Hellenistic Jews, as Ben Sira shows, took this idea even further; they individualized this cry, and in their trouble appealed to God as they would to their own fathers. In the Bible, God is often called the Shepherd of Israel and of the godly men in Israel. Ben Sira, boldly using this biblical figure of speech, says that God cares for each individual sheep, and even brings the sinner back to the fold, "as a shepherd does his flock" (Ben Sira 18:13). Indeed, it would seem that the Jews did not live in total and abject fear of their sinless Deity; instead the Lord Who governed with divine mercy, so often spoken of in Scripture, was deemed even more worthy of the absolute confidence of those who believed that His eyes were fixed on them day and night.

Another marked change in the attitude of the new age to the ancient revelation was the progressive disuse of the proper name of the Deity, YHWH (disclosed to Moses in the burning bush), and the adoption of various circumlocutions to denote the God of Jerusalem. The change is postexilic; thanks to Persian documents, we can date it exactly. When Cyrus invited the Jews of the Captivity to return to Jerusalem, he spoke of "YHWH, the God of Heaven," and of "YHWH, the God of Israel." That was in 539 B.C.E. But beginning with Darius I, some twenty years later, the proper name of the Deity disappears from Persian records referring to the Temple of Jerusalem; the Deity of Zion is now called the "God of Jerusalem," the "God of Israel," the "Great God," or, most often, the "God of Heaven." This means that from 520 B.C.E., that is, from the time of the Restoration of the Temple, the authorities of Jerusalem refused to use the proper name of their Deity in dealing with pagan authorities. The reason for this reluctance is made clear to us in the Elephantine documents we have discussed.

We saw in those documents that the Jews of Elephantine, provincial and unsophisticated, speak at the same time and, as it were, in the same vein of "the temple of YHW, the God who dwells in the fortress of

Elephantine" and of "the priests of the god Khnub [a ram-headed idol of the Egyptians], who dwells in the fortress of Elephantine." As long as the God of Jerusalem could be designated by a personal name, he could appear to be on a level with Khnub, or Nergal, or any of the vanities of the heathen. It is worthy of notice that, in contrast, the Persian governors of Judah and Samaria, answering the letters from Elephantine, speak only of the "God of Heaven." Yet, translated into Greek (or Latin), this designation of the Lord was somewhat equivocal; "the God of Heaven" could seem to refer to the sky and therefore, to the cosmic deity of the philosophers. In fact, Greek savants perpetuated this interpretation of the God of Jerusalem; it still appears under the pen of Juvenal and even in Celsus' critiques of the Christian faith. Even worse, with the advancing influence of astrological ideas, the "God of Heaven" began to appear to be involved in the doctrinal tenets of this pseudo-science and pseudo-religion. Philo was obliged to stress the difference between the faith of Abraham and the belief of the "Chaldeans" (that is, the astrologers) with regard to the divinity of heavenly bodies.

The result was that—certainly at the insistence of Jewish authorities—the Lord of Zion is never called "Heaven" or "the Lord of Heaven" in Greek and Roman official acts. Thus, in the Greek documents of the third century B.C.E. the Lord of Jerusalem became the Deity in the abstract. When Antiochus III mentions him, he speaks simply of "Theos," a term which, used absolutely, had rather a predicative force, meaning something like "divine power." The Jews accepted this formula. As late as 124 B.C.E. the official message of the Jews of Jerusalem to the Jews in Egypt referred to the Deity as "Ho Theos" in the Greek version, which means that in the original the Lord was called "Elohim" or "El."

Another device to avoid the use of the proper name of the Deity was to call Him the "Most High" (Hypsistos), the equivalent of the Hebrew title "El Elyon," used in the Bible from Genesis 14 on, almost always in poetical passages. In Aramaic stories about Nebuchadnezzar (Dan. 3–4) the Babylonian king and the Jewish prophet call the Lord "the Most High" when miracles confirm His unique greatness. The term is very popular in the early Hellenistic age—the periphrase was used by Egyptian Jews, for instance, and often by Ben Sira writing in Jerusalem—and this title became the official designation of the Lord of Jerusalem in Greek, and later in Roman, documents and in Hasmonean terminology as well.

We have dealt first with official nomenclature because its changes are datable. To trace the evolution of the style of nomenclature in more general use is more complicated. In the last months of the First Temple, the writers of the Lachish ostraca did not pen even trivial memos without mentioning YHWH; that was the sole divine name they invoked. The Exile changed all that. In the Holy Land, at least, the name was no longer written. Neither was it uttered, except in the Temple service; for as R. Shimon b. Azzai acutely observed, the Torah calls the Deity YHWH in the sacrificial context. The name also continued to be pronounced in adjurations and oaths, as we learn from a rabbinic rule stating that all the oaths prescribed in the Torah are by the Name.

Yet the Tetragrammaton is written some six thousand times in Scripture. The authors who after the Restoration chose to retell the deeds of their forefathers and the prophets who followed in the steps of Isaiah and Jeremiah could not avoid mentioning YHWH. In the fifth century B.C.E. Jonah speaks of YHWH, the God of Heaven, who made the sea and the dry land. How long public taste tolerated this usage we are unable to say, inasmuch as the earlier parabiblical books, such as the Enochic works, have come down to use in translation only. But although in the narration of pre-exilic history in Chronicles the Tetragrammaton is written 446 times, it is used only 31 times in Ezra-Nehemiah, a record of contemporary events. Ezra and Nehemiah, in their respective memoirs, call on YHWH only in solemn formulas of blessing or adjuration (Ezra 8:28, 9:15, and 10:11; Neh. 1:5 and 5:13). The Ineffable Name is never used in the stories about Daniel, and Daniel himself appeals to YHWH only in his prayer for enlightenment about the future of the Chosen People.

The Masada scroll of Ecclesiasticus shows that toward the end of the third century Ben Sira did not use the Tetragrammaton but substituted for it the terms "Adonai," "El," and particularly "Elyon." Nor does the Ineffable Name appear in the Aramaic Genesis Apocryphon, or in the works authored by the Covenanters of the Dead Sea, except for quotations from Scripture. In the works of the Covenanters, even the angels who glorify the Creator call him "El" or "Elohim," whereas the Covenanters themselves use the term "Adonai." But it is even more significant that the Greek word *kyrios,* which became the most common substitute for the Tetragrammaton in Greek, was avoided in III Maccabees (written around 100 B.C.E.), in IV Maccabees, in Josephus, and in Jewish inscriptions in Greek.

Although the use of the Tetragrammaton was avoided in written works because it might be pronounced by inexperienced readers (the ancients read aloud), nevertheless the intrinsic holiness of the Ineffable Name required its appearance in scrolls deemed to be holy. In the third century CE, Origen still saw old and accurate copies of the Greek Bible in which the Name was marked in Hebrew letters, and in some Hebrew manuscripts written in modern ("square") characters, the Name was inserted in the antiquated ("Phoenician") script. In both cases the aim was to emphasize the holiness of the Name and at the same time, by the use of foreign characters, warn the reader not to utter it.

Written as "YHWH," the Name was perhaps at first pronounced

"Elohim." Some also said "the Holy One," or "the Name *(ha-Shem),*" as the Samaritans still do, but the custom of pronouncing YHWH as "Adonai" was, as we have noted, popular from the end of the third century B.C.E. on. In an Isaiah scroll from Qumran copied in the second century B.C.E., the scribe used YHWH and Adonai interchangeably, and the sectarians of the Dead Sea forbade swearing not only by "Aleph Dalet" (Adonai), but by the use of the "Most Honored Name" as well.

In Hebrew and Aramaic, *Adonai* means "my Lord" and was used as a mark of respect when speaking to or of a superior person. Accordingly, in the second century Greek-speaking Jews, as Aristobulus and pseudo-Aristeas attest, used the Greek isogloss *kyrios* with reference to YHWH. But in Greek, *kyrios* was attributive, as in "Kyrios Zeus," or was used in the vocative *(kyrie)* as a polite form of address, like "sir" in English. Used absolutely, as a divine name, the term *Kyrios* was a Hebraism. Yet in later Septuagint manuscripts the word was substituted for the YHWH of the original.

The term "Elohim" also continued in use, without reluctance, in the pre-Maccabean period, as Kohelet, Ben Sira, and the books written in or translated into Greek attest. It seems that only under the Hasmoneans did people begin to avoid the extra-Scriptural use of "Elohim." It never occurs in I Maccabees, which speaks rather of "Heaven," and if the rabbinic memory of the sayings of first Pharisaic sages is exact on this point, as early as approximately 180 B.C.E., Antigonus of Socho spoke of the "Fear of Heaven."

There were other circumlocutions to designate God as well, "Father" and "King of Kings" among them. The multiplication of divine epithets belonged to a style of piety shared by Jews and pagans alike. Although the polyonomy on occasion could lead a pagan to believe that "Sabaoth" and "Adonai" were separate beings, it still permitted the worshipper to stress now one, now another, aspect of the Supreme Being. The new and various metonymies opened new ways to God, as it were, and new means for the individualization of devotion. The essential fact, however, is that the Lord of Jerusalem, who had so many epithets, lacked a personal name in the Hellenistic age—and afterward.

But in the Greek world, full of gods who were individuals and who bore personal names, a distinctive name was an asset for a celestial being. A nameless deity was felt to be imperfect: it was an exception, to be explained away by learned men, that the founder of the city of Messina in Sicily was not called upon by name to accept a sacrifice offered to him. And although it was right to say to the Greeks, as the Jews do in the Alexander Romance, that no man can apprehend their God, it was annoying to have to speak of Him as "God," without being able to state His name. Josephus, although himself a Jewish priest, tells his Greek readers that Moses besought the Deity not to deny him the knowledge of the Divine Name, so that he might invoke his presence at sacred sites. Nevertheless, in 166 B.C.E. the Samaritans officially acknowledged that their God, who was also the God of Jerusalem, was an anonymous deity. The prohibition against uttering the Ineffable Name outside the Temple of Jerusalem, like the prohibition against sacrificing outside Zion, concentrated the divine force on the sacred mountain, strengthened its uniqueness for the Chosen People, and, last but not least, helped to concentrate the emotional force of the dispersed nation on the Holy City and its sanctuary.

It was impossible, of course, to prevent the misuse of the Tetragrammaton, particularly in witchcraft. In the second century B.C.E. a Jewish author imagined that it was by uttering the Name that Moses had overpowered the Pharaoh, and as late as the fourth century C.E. Jewish hags were still swearing by the Tetragrammaton. It was also appropriated by international craftsmen of the magical arts and written on amulets. Yet transcriptions show that these magicians spoke the name inexactly (as "Iu," for instance) and therefore inefficiently. The Aaronides succeeded in keeping the pronunciation of the Tetragrammaton secret, and the Name has remained ineffable until today.

Unable as we are to describe the Deity except in anthropomorphic imagery, so we are unable to speak of His government except in the simile of terrestrial power: the heavenly Sovereign, too, must have His court. In Judaism, however, whether they are called "Members of the Divine Order" *(benei Elohim)* or "Holy Beings" *(kadoshim)* or *seraphim,* these ministers have no separate existence as minor deities; they are merely God's messengers *(malakhim;* in Greek, *angeloi,* from which we derive "angel"), instruments of God's will.

When Jerusalem became part of the great Persian and Hellenistic empires, it was naturally thought that the Lord of Kings needed an even more complicated administrative apparatus than did a Darius or a Ptolemy. There was the Host of Heaven, God's "force," from which celestial soldiers were sent to intervene in human affairs; the heavenly horseman in Heliodorus's story had the appearance of a Macedonian cavalry officer. God had His bodyguard, the "Watchers" who flanked the Deity at the theophany. The seven holy archangels, the Angels of the Presence, who go in and out before the glory of God, were similar to the seven Persian grandees who alone had unrestricted access to the Shah. Four of these superior angels became individualized as Michael, Gabriel, Raphael, and Uriel. R. Shimon ben Eleazar (ca. 200 C.E.) noted that the names of these individualized angels had been brought by the Jews from the Babylonian exile.

Angels were thought to be spirits who were able to assume human form when necessary. Some people speculated about their nature and inquired when they were created and whether they were circumcised or observed the Sabbath. From tradition the Jew knew that the Heavenly Host waited on the Lord and praised the Creator; some thought that the movement of the luminaries, or of the winds, must be regulated by the angels. But ordinary people, interested in themselves and their fellows, thought of the heavenly messengers as intermediaries between themselves and the Deity. Angels presented the prayers of men and women to God; they interceded on behalf of the righteous and descended to help them. God heard the voice of innocent Susanna and sent an angel down to rescue her. Levi asked the angel to reveal his name so that he might appeal to him in trouble (T. Levi 5:5). There is, however, no evidence for the worship of angels in the sources of the Hellenistic period.

The myriads of angels that comprised the Heavenly Host did not make God transcendent; the meaning of angelology was to bring God nearer to people in need. A character in Menander says: "The world has one thousand cities and each of them thirty thousand inhabitants. How can you expect that the Deity should find time for each of us?" Lost in the limitless spaces of Hellenistic empires, however, ordinary men and women did expect that Heaven would take care of them, and Hellenistic philosophers taught the existence of innumerable intermediate beings between their pantheistic Supreme Being and humankind. Philo already identified the "daimons" of the philosophers with the angels of the "sacred records" and compared them to the famous "ears and eyes" of the Persian king, that is, the inspectors who oversaw the carrying out of royal orders.

In the sacred history, only great figures, such as Abraham or Moses, received direct assistance from God. Now, however, Tobit, an average man in a faraway Mesopotamian city sending his son on a trivial business trip, confidently expects that God's angel will keep him company. In the Susanna story Daniel tells the vicious elders that the angel of God will punish them immediately. The angels now record every action of every man on heavenly tablets, while every man has his own guardian angel, or "daimon." The existence of these angels overcame Menander's argument and guaranteed providential care to everyone. Angelology served to democratize Heavenly protection.

Furthermore, although in the Bible envoys of God at His command inflict punishment on men, by the early Hellenistic age these avenging angels have become a separate division of God's ministers who dwell in the lowest heaven of the sky. At the head of this corps is Satan, the "Adversary," who, as in Zechariah (3:1), induces men to sin and accuses them before God. This Prince, also called Belial, or Mastema, had his own troops, the "sons of Belial," who in accordance with Hellenistic technological trends were specialized; there were spirits of pride, of avidity, of fornication, and of a host of other sins. In the same way, the Greek philosophers of the period classified daimons as good, neutral, or malevolent. In Athens, and in Jerusalem as well, the supposed existence of evil spirits served to explain the existence of evil in a world governed by Providence. Thus it was the spirit of jealousy that excited Dan against Joseph and the spirit of anger that counseled him to murder his brother. In Jubilees, Abraham prays to God to deliver him from the evil spirits who lead him away from the Creator. The author of the Book of Noah, quoted in Enoch, even attributed diseases to the actions of evil spirits, an idea that is singular in Hellenistic sources, but that in Roman times became popular in both the Synagogue and the Church.

The Greek philosophers of the Hellenistic age, rather, placed the origin of sin within the human soul. They postulated that two daimons dwell in each man from birth, one urging him to goodness, the other enticing him to wickedness. This psychological and agonistic conception also appears in the Testaments of the Twelve Patriarchs—alongside the theory that evil spirits act from the outside to corrupt people. The Greek conception later prevailed, however, and the doctrine of the good and evil inclination *(yezer)* dominated rabbinic psychology. Still, even in Hellenistic Jerusalem the idea of personal responsibility came to be important: God gave humankind both the Law and understanding in order to turn it away from temptation.

This intellectualist approach to the problem of sin agrees perfectly with the spirit of the Greek age. For the Greeks, however, philosophy took the place of the Torah: follow the right teaching and you will conquer your impulse, not the impulse you. Or, as Ben Sira put it: God left men and women in the hands of their own volition. In vain the Egyptian woman tries to seduce Joseph; the disposition of his soul admitted no evil thought. In his testament, having completed his instructions to his children, Levi says: "You have heard all. Choose yourself either the light or the darkness, either the Law of God or the work of Belial." Of course, such freedom of choice had been already stressed in Deuteronomy (30:19) and Jeremiah (21:8). On this point the popular philosophy of the Greeks agreed with the Torah: two ways are open to human choice, the hard path of righteousness or the easy road of evil.

The choice of the right path was facilitated by the existence of paragons of goodness, such as Herakles, hero of the Greek allegory of the two ways. The idea of imitation, foreign to the world of the Bible, entered Jewish consciousness in the Hellenistic age. The Testaments of the Twelve Patriarchs were written for this purpose; in his testament Benjamin advises his children to imitate "the good and holy man" Joseph. Even the idea that the wicked imitate the spirits of deceit while the godly imitate the Lord appears at this time, and convenient lists of vices to avoid (a device of Greek rationalism) were already circulating in Jerusalem around 200 B.C.E. Accordingly, as in contemporary Greek philosophy, there was no pity for the sinner, for God, as Kohelet (7:29) states, made men upright. Therefore, grace was a necessity in the battle to conquer sin. In Jubilees, Abraham's farewell to Jacob ends on this note: "May the Most High God, my God and thy God, strengthen thee to do His will." That sounds almost Augustinian, but a Greek contemporary of the author of Jubilees, the Stoic Cleanthes, also prays to Zeus, the "Father," to rescue his children from the ignorance that leads them into error.

For a Greek philosopher, the choice of evil was a mistake. For the pious, however—whether in Jerusalem or Athens—it was a transgression. Still, although God would punish the transgressor, He could also pardon a penitent. Prayer accompanied by fasting and other external signs of contrition were in Ben Sira's time the usual practices of a penitent. It is perhaps worthwhile emphasizing that fasting in this context is but a means of pressure, a hunger strike, as it were. Rachel prayed and fasted to obtain children and Joseph did the same to escape the wiles of Potiphar's wife.

The beginning of repentance is the confession of sin. In Mosaic law, individual confession is tied to the sacrifices prescribed for certain ritual offenses. On the other hand, the visible signs of heavenly displeasure—sickness, for example—may force the sinner to acknowledge hidden transgressions. This avowal, along with the necessary rites and actions, purge guilt. The sequence is secret sin, chastisement, confession, pardon. This formula for purging sin occurs the world over and is well represented in the Psalter: "Have pity on me . . . against Thee have I sinned . . . let the bones which Thou has crushed rejoice" (Ps. 51).

The inward response of the heart to chastisement was, of course, known to all ancient peoples (note, however, that Job's heart did not condemn him despite the thunders of heaven). In early Hellenistic Jerusalem, however, conscience came to be recognized as an independent and fair judge, capable of reproving wrongdoing even when there was no accuser. As Ben Sira says, "Blessed is the man whom his soul does not convict."

Deepening self-analysis led to the conclusion that simplicity of soul equaled all the other virtues combined. Belial works on the imagination, but the net of deceit cannot ensnare an artless man, a *vir integer*. We have seen that guilelessness was dear to the author of the Testaments of the Twelve Patriarchs, a pious Jew. It was also important to the worshippers of the god Men, a divinity in Asia Minor who was, as a Greek inscription says, "merciful" to those who served him "with a simple soul." A pure mind was now valued for itself; it produced inner peace.

The men and women of Jerusalem, following Plato, learned that hatred is ruinous to those who hate because it fills them with evil. Vengeance should be left to God. Ben Sira (28:2) says that if you forgive your neighbor, your own sins will be pardoned—a concept later expressed by both Jesus and the rabbis.

Repentance also began to acquire its own cathartic value, independent of its religious function. It healed the soul, an idea that explains the literary form of the Testaments of the Twelve Patriarchs: at the approach of death, each son of Jacob publicly avows his secret sin. Reuben, for instance, tells us that, having been forgiven by God, he still did not dare to look his father in the face, nor even to speak to his brothers: "Even until now my conscience causes me anguish on account of my impiety." Or, as Judah puts it, the sinner is burned up by his own heart. In a Greek comedy written in the third century, a young man says that it is easier to fight in a war than to face your friends after you have injured them. It is noteworthy that confessions were made in public: the sons of Jacob confess to their own sons. Later, Philo asserts that in order to be forgiven by God apostates should first recognize their transgressions in their own consciences and then confess them publicly. Public avowal of sins served as a warning and an encouragement to those who heard it. The confessions of the twelve patriarchs are followed by exhortations to their sons. *Discite iustitiam moniti et non temnere divos.*

God was merciful, but He was also just. He was loved, but also feared. Unlike human justice, however, heavenly justice was inexorably fair, for it adhered to the rule of measure for measure, abandoned by earthly courts. Greek and Jewish moralists of the Hellenistic age delighted in describing the exact correlation between a crime and divine punishment. Since Gad's "liver" was set against his brother, God brought upon him a disease of the liver.

Punishing the children of a wrongdoer had ceased in Jerusalem after Deuteronomy (24:16), that is, after 622 B.C.E., and in Athens after the sixth century. Yet Greeks, Jews, and, later, Christians stubbornly continued to cling to the principle that divine punishment was visited on the children of sinners to the third and fourth generation (Exodus 20:5). Plutarch, who preached kindness to animals, insists that divine retribution intended for the wicked is meted out to their progeny if the sinners escape. In the third century B.C.E. rare minds such as the Cynic Bion protested against this doctrine, but his voice was not heard in Jerusalem.

Insistence upon collective responsibility for the sins of individuals was also felt to be a feature of divine justice. A grave sin, like an infection, contaminated the whole community: the plague decimated Thebes because of the sins of Oedipus. Indeed, in order to defend itself against this kind of celestial vengeance, society had to eliminate the source of pollution as expeditiously as possible. When the Epicurians were expelled from Messene as enemies of the gods, the city and its shrines were purified to eliminate any remaining contagion. Likewise, the culprit caught in the flagrant crime of sacrilege could be put to death immediately, without recourse to the ordinary rules of procedure: an alien entering Herod's Temple could be killed by the outraged witnesses of his deed.

Jewish authors of the early Hellenistic age, remembering the collective contaminations in the Torah, grimly emphasized that the whole nation would be judged for the uncleanness of one man. On the other hand, it was also pointed out that an individual could be held liable for the transgressions of the nation. When Tobit became blind, he knew he was being punished not only for his own sins but also for the sins of the fathers who had not kept the divine commandments—a manner of thinking that seemed both strange and dismaying in the century of progress and individualism, from 1815 to 1914.

Rewards were measured on the other side of the providential balance. Greeks, Romans, and Jews in the third century B.C.E. agreed, with Theocritus, that men who care for immortals are really better off; or, as Ben Sira said, fear of the Lord leads to joy and long life. Hence, Levi's advice to his sons: "Sow good things in your soul, that you may find them in your life" (T. Levi 13:6).

Moreover, just as people accepted the doctrine of corporate retribution, so they also trusted the doctrine of corporate merit. It was a concept not completely unknown to the Greeks. Trying to refute objections to the idea of the providential government of the world, the Stoics argued that the gods sometimes spared the wicked because of their ancestors, sometimes even for the sake of their still unborn descendants (but this was casuistry). In Jerusalem, however, the concept of the Merit of the Patriarchs was an article of faith that helped preserve confidence in the salvation of the chosen, but faithless, nation. Thus Levi warns his sons: "If you were not to receive mercy through Abraham, Isaac, and Jacob, our Fathers, not one of our seed should be left on earth" (T. Levi 15:4).

Yet death comes to the righteous and the wicked alike; all arise from the dust and all return to dust again. Although the conventional view was that the spirit returns to God who gave it (Tob. 3:6; Koh. 12:7), the Jews continued to cling to the primeval belief in the continuous existence of the departed in their graves as long as their bones remained there. The tomb was man's eternal home, as Kohelet (12:5) said. Offerings of food, generally bread and wine, were commonly brought to the grave in ancient Israel, the Lawgiver having forbidden only the offering of consecrated food to the dead (Deut. 26:14). Tobit advises his son to scatter bread on the graves of the just, but not on the graves of sinners (Tob. 4:17). The Psalmist (106:28), however, identifies such gifts with heathenism and the author of Jubilees repeats this condemnation. Ben Sira, a sophisticated traditionalist, regards food placed on the grave for the use of the dead as wasted. At any rate, there was no worship of the dead, which in paganism was necessary to secure the survival of the departed.

Although sleeping in their tombs, the dead also belonged to the common realm of the nether world. There in the depths of the earth was Sheol, where the shades of the dead had no portion of anything under the sun. The Psalmist repeatedly states that in this pit the dead were cut off from God (Ps. 6:5; 30:9, 88:10, 115:17; and Isa. 38:18). In Ben Sira's version of this idea, the dead cannot praise the Most High (17:27).

Isaiah (14:9) and Ezekiel (32:21) could imagine that at least the shades of mighty kings were distinguishable in Sheol and able to stir up that nether region, but in the early Hellenistic age ordinary people, too, began to desire the privilege of distinctive survival in Sheol. About 200 B.C.E. some people, as we learn from the Testament of Judah, demanded to have their corpses embalmed, "as the kings do"; but this Egyptian custom was, it seems, rarely followed in Jerusalem. Instead, opulent families began to erect funerary monuments above the ground. The mausoleum built by Simon Maccabee for his parents and his brothers around 140 B.C.E. was hardly the first construction of this kind in Judea. Some of the funerary monuments built under the Hasmonean rulers still stand in the valley of Kidron, while the "Tomb of Jason," probably erected around 100 B.C.E., can be seen on a street in Rehaviah in modern Jerusalem.

The essential difference between these buildings and biblical burials (as well as postbiblical burials of the same kind) was that in the subterranean family chambers the individuality of the deceased vanished, just as it did in Sheol. The dead were put into the grave in their clothing, a soldier in his panoply (Ezek. 32:27), for instance; there were no coffins; nothing isolated one corpse from another. When a Hebrew was gathered to his fathers, as a common biblical expression has it, he really did join them, lying on a bench in the same grave, the common resting place of his extended family—together in life, and even after death.

In the mausoleum of Simon Maccabee, however, seven pyramids set in a row indicated seven individual burials. Such a sepulchral marker was called a *nefesh*, that is, a "person," and it expressed the idea of individual survival in the grave. For instance, the so-called Tomb of Saint James in the Kidron valley is, as its inscription states, the "grave and personal memorial" (*nefesh* is rendered in Greek as "memorial" in Palmyrene bilingual funerary inscriptions) of the priestly family of Hezir. Four generations were buried there, and the Hebrew inscription cut into the monument names each and every person committed to this tomb. The *nefesh* no longer descended to Sheol, but somehow was attached to the funerary monument and would last as long as that massive structure. The *nefashot* (singular *nefesh*) of the *benei Hezir* still stand in the valley of Kidron.

Not everyone could erect a mausoleum, but the less affluent at least could carve separate niches in the traditional burial chamber and further isolate these niches from each other by sealing them with slabs of stone. Each such niche could then serve for a single corpse or for the corpses of a nuclear family of parents and children, as in the Maccabean mausoleum. The "Tomb of Jason" had ten separate compartments of this kind.

Unfortunately, even in these *kokim* (singular *kok*), as such sections were called, the corpses decomposed—and the dead felt this disgrace (Isa. 66:24). Because after about a year only the bones remained, in ancient Israel "bones" came to be a synonym for a person: "All my bones shall say, Lord, who is like Thee?" (Ps. 35:10). As long as the solid framework of the body, or at least the skull, remained, the individual could not disappear completely. In the traditional family subterranean chamber, each person's bones were gathered into a little pile in some corner.

By the Hellenistic age, however, and, perhaps even earlier, the bones of the deceased were being placed in a wooden box, which was then stored in a separate bone chamber within the large burial cave. Jason's tomb illustrates this practice. The wooden boxes also rotted away in the course of time, but one of them, preserved by chance, has been found in a tomb at Nahal David in the Judean desert. The new custom is already attested around 200 B.C.E. in the Testaments of the Twelve Patriarchs. According to this book, the bones of each son of Jacob were carried to Hebron from Egypt. Indeed, the practice of gathering bones in individual receptacles seems so natural to the author of the Testaments that he even disregards the biblical passage (Gen. 50:26) about the embalming of Joseph's corpse. It must be noted, however, that the secondary burial of the bones was a custom peculiar to the Jews in Palestine and was unknown in the diaspora. From about 100 B.C.E. the wooden receptacles were replaced by ossuaries of stone on which were carved the name(s) of the person(s) whose remains were preserved in it. Of course, the bones could be reburied without either a wooden box or a stone ossuary.

After two thousand years of belief (originally Pharisaic) in the doctrine of immortality, it is somewhat difficult to realize that no hope of heavenly bliss ever cheered either Ben Sira or the Maccabees or the *benei Hezir*. In the third or second century B.C.E. there were few people in the Hellenistic world who held such comforting hope. Even Egyptian belief in immortality had become stale, and the Praises of Isis, composed in Greek under the Ptolemies, gives no hint that it could be won by converts. All the Greek philosophical schools of Ben Sira's time had discarded the idea of a future life, and funerary inscriptions from Athens attest that sorrowful resignation was the rule. As Ben Sira puts it: "Yesterday for me and today for thee." With Kohelet and the author of a Greek inscription in Jason's tomb, the men and women of Jerusalem could only repeat the advice of the sinners of old: "Let us eat and drink, for tomorrow we shall die" (Isa. 22:13).

Men of valor, however, like kings, could hope to escape oblivion in Sheol if their deeds were remembered. Of the fathers of old, Ben Sira says both that their bodies were buried in peace and that their names would live throughout all the generations. Speaking of the twelve prophets, he exclaims: "May their bones flourish again from the ground where they lie" (49:10). We can now understand the survival value of the ossuaries inscribed with the names of the deceased. Alas, average individuals could not hope to leave a name to be commemorated through the generations. They belonged to the mass of unremembered dead, of whom Ben Sira says, "[They] have become as though they had not been born" (44:9). Still, as the wise Diotima says in Plato's *Symposium*, the share in immortality conceded to mortal creatures lies in the children they leave behind. Without reading Plato, the Jews agreed with him. In the Testaments of the Twelve Patriarchs, we read that if the children of Potiphar's wife had perished because of her contemplated suicide, she would herself have destroyed her memorial on earth.

Inevitably, the insoluble question of survival in the hereafter became connected with the no less insoluble question of providential justice. People of all faiths and races often believed that after death they would be either recompensed or punished in accordance with their deserts. In Plato's *Republic* the wise Kephalos, thinking of his approaching death, is frightened at the thought of posthumous punishment in Hades. Participants in some mysteries, the initiates at Eleusis, for instance, relied on some form of bond with the divine force in order to escape Hades (but they were not interested in the postmortem destiny of the noninitiated). Similarly, Isaiah 26 promises that the (godly) dead shall live, but that the shades of the wicked shall not arise. Again, a Psalmist (Ps. 49) opposes those who are destined for Sheol to himself, who will be rescued from its power.

The idea of the posthumous chastisement of an offender from whom the ordinary person could not exact retribution pleased the imagination of every sufferer of injustice, whether real or fancied. Moreover, the fear of infernal punishment was useful to the powerful: Polybius thought that this superstition helped bridle the masses. In Greece, the division of souls into two classes based on the vice or virtue of the departed already appears in Pindar's second Olympian ode, written in 476 B.C.E. Here, righteous conduct brings about blessedness after the grave, whereas wickedness is punished by the eternal torments of Hades. Yet Greek intellectuals tended to avoid the subject, in the same way that they generally disregarded the vulgar conceptions of common men—their belief in magical arts, for example.

In Hebrew thought (and in Zoroastrian doctrine as well) the judgment of the dead is postponed until the advent of God's kingdom, although no such general judgment is ever described in the Bible. In the early Hellenistic period, the idea of a final retribution meted out by God to all the dead does appear in the Testament of Benjamin, but is presented without much ado: some will rise into glory and some into dishonor. In the testaments of Judah and Zebulon, the Patriarchs speak only of the resurrection of the just, although Zebulon also adds that the Lord will punish the impious with eternal fire. In Jubilees, God instructs Moses that the spirits of the righteous will rejoice forever and see the fulfillment of all their curses against their enemies.

It is, rather, in the Enochic writings, that is, in the books ascribed to the biblical Enoch—written by members of a sect whose motto, as it seems, was "uprightness" (Aramaic *qsht*) and who obviously regarded themselves, and only themselves, as "the upright"—that the Last Judgment becomes important. In the Book of the Watchers, probably written in the third century B.C.E., the thoughtful author divides the dead into three classes: the righteous, the sinners who were not punished in their lifetime, and the sinners who were punished while they were alive. The spirits of the godly will be blessed, the spirits of the godless will be tormented forever, and the spirits of the men of the third category will not be afflicted, but will remain in Sheol.

The Epistle of Enoch, written sometime between approximately 300 and 100 B.C.E., probably before Antiochus' persecution, is an attack against those who sin and flourish. Like Kohelet (9:2), it claims that the same fate awaits all, both the righteous and the wicked who die in prosperity and honor. The author comforts the righteous, however, by telling them that on the Day of Judgment the souls of the wicked will be thrown into the burning flames. His charges against his enemies are vague, for the most part: they pervert the Covenant, lead people astray, and commit other sins. They are also mighty and rich and oppress the poor, which reminds us of Psalm 49. But the core of the accusation is specific: the masters and enemies of the righteous (who are "wise" and "pious," in opposition to the "fools") persecute them, make them few, and do not accept their petitions. The righteous cry for vengeance and, alluding to Deuteronomy 28:13, pseudo-Enoch gives voice to their (psychologically remarkable) grievance: we have toiled and labored in vain; "we have hoped to be the head, and have become the tail." Pseudo-

Enoch, who was writing for the men of his fraternity, did not need to explain the substance of the conflict between the fraternity and the authorities of Jerusalem, nor why the upright were being persecuted; for him, the refusal of the "fools" to listen to the words of the "wise" was a sufficient reason for indignation.

However agreeable the vision of flourishing sinners receiving their just punishment at the great judgment, pseudo-Enoch understood that the righteous also needed to know what blessings awaited them. At this point he discloses the secret that he, the heavenly scribe, had learned from the Tablets of Heaven: the souls of the righteous will not perish, but will shine like the lights of heaven.

The secret revealed by Enoch was a Greek one, that of stellar immortality. In Greek mythology several heroes, as a reward for their merits, are spared from death and instead translated to the heavens to become brilliant stars—the Dioscuri and Andromeda, for instance. In the Hellenistic period this lot came to be reserved by the Greeks for those rulers who deserve apotheosis. If we believe the poet Callimachus, Arsinoë II, sister and spouse of Ptolemy II, ascended into the constellations at her death in 270 B.C.E. Twenty-five years later, Berenice III vowed a lock of her hair to the gods for the safe return of her husband, Ptolemy III, from the war against Syria, but it disappeared from the sanctuary. It was the gallant astronomer Conon who discovered that the gods had carried off Berenice's hair and had placed it—transformed into a group of brilliant stars—in the sky. Callimachus celebrated this event, too, in a poem, and a constellation between the Great Bear and the Virgin bears the name "The Lock of Berenice" even today. What pseudo-Enoch was promising his fellow sectarians was that one day they, too, would shine in the midst of the stars.

Writing around 167 B.C.E., amid Epiphanes' persecution of the Jews faithful to the traditional cult, pseudo-Enoch promises not only that God will deliver Israel in a short time, but also that at that time many of the dead will awaken—some to everlasting life, some to everlasting "abhorrence," and some, the wise men who turned the many to righteousness, to shine as the stars for ever and ever (Dan. 12:2–3). It is not strange that the author of Daniel here uses an early Greek idea of stellar immortality or, at least, an early Greek metaphor for blissful afterlife. He and the Maccabees were defending their faith, not fighting Greek civilization.

Ordinary people in early Hellenistic Jerusalem probably thought of retribution in the nether world only on exceptional occasions. We learn from II Maccabees that in 162 BCE, after his victory over Gorgias, Judah Maccabee discovered pagan amulets on the corpses of his fallen soldiers. His response was to sacrifice a sin offering and to offer a prayer in order to blot out the wrong committed by the dead. The pharisaic author of

II Maccabees attributed to his hero a belief in resurrection, but this anachronistic inference misses the point. Judah clearly believed that punishment awaited the sinners in the world of the dead, and that the intercession of the living might deliver the spirits of his dead comrades from their pains in Sheol.

Traditional prepharisaic Judaism could accept the idea of compensatory justice in the afterlife for the man who had done wrong on earth, but the concept of the eternal felicity of the blessed infringed upon the privilege of heavenly beings. Neither rites nor merit could make a mortal man godlike; only a miracle, brought about by God, could translate Enoch and Elijah to heaven alive. Alien to the esoteric hopes of Enoch and Daniel, and still far removed from the paradoxical credo of bodily resurrection later taught by the Pharisees, the ordinary Jews of the early Hellenistic age probably believed, with Ben Sira (39:33), that all the works of the Lord were good and that evil was only a temporary accident in His creation. Evil had a beginning: the origin of sin and death was traced by Ben Sira to Eve; others accused the Fallen Angels; and some thought that the ineptitude or malice of the celestial bureaucracy was to blame for the imperfections of the world.

In fact, the moral conduct of the average inhabitant of Jerusalem, and of Athens, too, was guided by the utilitarian principle that rewards and punishments were meted out by providence in this life. The Stoics reproached the Epicureans for their denial of providence, a position that, for the Stoics, overthrew the basis of social life. This optimistic faith in the ultimate justice of life on earth must have been a great motivation for good. One who believed that "the blessing of the Lord was the reward of the godly" (Ben Sira 11:22) was probably a better person than one who was assailed by fears of punishment in the afterlife. The optimistic credo of the Psalmist (37:25), repeated by Ben Sira (2:10), was probably believed in early Hellenistic Jerusalem: "Look at the generations of old and see. Was anyone who put his trust in the Lord ever disappointed?" Two thousand years later, John Bunyan, although reared in the belief of a future life and firmly accepting that belief, was saved from despair by reading these reassuring words in Ecclesiasticus.

The Psalmist and Ben Sira prospered and, as Aristotle says, prosperous men tend to be devout. On the other hand, as another Greek author observed, in calamity men forsake piety. The Jew, however, even in calamity was comforted by the biblical hope that, in time, there would be a new heaven and a new earth. Ben Sira himself composed a passionate prayer for the deliverance of Israel (36:1–17). The details of the coming golden age varied according to the taste and the imagination of each writer. Isaiah (65:20) promised that in the Kingdom of God a man would still be young at one hundred years of age. An Enochic author promised that men would live to one thousand years without getting old and that all their days would be blessed. The promise in the Testament of Levi is no less attractive: the saints will eat of the Tree of Life. Another visionary was no less sure that under the direct rule of God pious men would each beget thousands of children.

All, however, agreed that sin would disappear from among the sons of men and thus that the evil on this earth was only episodic and the reign of justice just around the corner. As intimated by the prophets, the transformation would come suddenly. An Enochic author wrote that the earth would open its mouth and swallow the enemies of Israel. Others imagined that the future would reverse the past. The sins of Jerusalem had caused the Exile and because the evildoers of the present are even worse than those of the past, they would certainly provoke God's wrath and the final calamities. But this time, at the end, God would establish His own reign. This schema explains the absolute condemnation of the present in apocalyptic literature, and modern scholars vainly strive to discover historical allusions in these standard descriptions of man's depravity.

The apocalyptic writers, like the prophets before them, expected that God Himself would initiate the new eon. Some of them, however, imagined that a deputy of God, that is, an angel or a "Son of Man," as Daniel says, would be entrusted with waging the war against the powers of darkness. In accord with Deuteronomy 18:15, some believed that Moses would return. Another opinion, agreeing with the expectations of Zechariah (4:14), was that two anointed beings, a Priest and a King, would preside over the happy Israel of the future. However, according to the extant evidence, there was still no belief in a Messiah, a single anointed one, a human being destined to become the savior of the Chosen People. Although the prophets spoke of the return of the scion of David, and although the Davidic covenant was dutifully referred to, the legitimist idea became a force only toward the end of the Hasmonean dynasty, and then in opposition to it. At that time the term "Anointed" began to be used as the distinctive title of the future savior, the "Messiah." It is first attested in this sense in the Psalms of Solomon, composed around 60 B.C.E.

The preceding remarks may seem to be haphazard, but no organized body of religious doctrine was taught in pre-Maccabean Jerusalem. Theological casuistry, such as the distinction between fearing God and loving Him, came later, as an offshoot of Greek dialectics; R. Akiba, in the second century C.E., was more influenced by Greek thought than Ben Sira had been three centuries before. Nor can we discuss here the influence of foreign religions on Judaism, a favorite topic of modern theologians. The plain fact is that although we know only a very few things about the ideology of early Hellenistic Jerusalem, we know still less about contemporary religious developments in Alexandria, or Antioch, or among the Iranians. Yet modern scholars happily discover marks of Persian influence in the religion of the Hellenistic Jews. The later Babylonian faith became astral, and the idea of stellar immortality was a force among the Greeks of the later Hellenistic age, but the ritual texts in cuneiform copied and used in Hellenistic Babylonia offer no hint of star worship, to say nothing of an afterlife. The latter subject is not referred to in astrological texts, either. The Epistle of Jeremiah, directed against the gods of Babylonia, does not mention astrolatry and astrology; its author was obviously not concerned with those features of Babylonian religion that seem to a modern scholar to be the most important.

Pseudo-Jeremiah was not mistaken. Let us stress again that ancient piety was expressed in acts, not in theological speculations. Deities demanded worship and sacrifices. The Pharisees tithed dill, rue, cumin, and mint, and Greek fishermen offered fish, a cup of wine, and a crust of dry bread, "a poor man's sacrifice," to the deity who filled their nets. A weary wayfarer did not relieve his thirst at a spring without an offering to Pan and the Nymphs. From the cock's crow, which banished the nightly demons, to the prayer that ended the day, gestures and words of worship were integral parts of life. The unbelievers had no need to sneer at dogmas; instead they feasted on unlucky days and mocked those who sought oracles. Opinions about the divine were of little importance as long as worship was performed according to the laws and customs of the place. Belief will follow if performance is honored.

Accordingly, the High Priest Simon named *ha-Avodah,* the sacrificial worship of the Temple, as the second pillar of this world. The homage due from the covenanted people to its lawful Sovereign, Who was enthroned on Zion, was the correlative of the God-given Torah. We have already dealt with daily worship in the Temple and have seen that in the days of the high Priest Simon, the traditional ceremony, at least on festival days, was enriched by a new rite.

Sacrifice, like every action, exercises influence in and of itself, even if a verbal formula is required to direct the action. A story that circulated in Hellenistic Jerusalem described how Nehemiah, having recovered the holy fire of the Solomonic Temple, offered a sacrifice; while it was being consumed, the priests, on behalf of Israel, asked God to accept the offering, to gather in the diaspora, and to afflict the oppressors of the Holy City. But there is no hint in the Bible or in later sources that statutory sacrifices in the Temple were ever accompanied by any prayer other than a request for the gracious acceptance of the offering. Instead, it was the silence of the priests during the sacrificial operation that impressed the observer; the offering itself was sufficient to conciliate heaven. With regard to public prayers spoken in the Temple precinct—and our information concerns only the Herodian Temple—they were uttered in a place separate from the area in which the statutory sacrifices took place. The only exception was in the case of the sin offering.

Yet, as we have noted, Ben Sira, a contemporary and admirer of the High Priest Simon, describing the pontifical service of his time, mentions a collective supplication offered after the sacrifice and libation but before the priestly blessing. The people, in prayer, besought Him Who is merciful. Some fifty years later, the Hasmonean High Priest Jonathan wrote to the Spartans that the Jews remember them unremittingly "in the sacrifices which we offer and in prayer." It is this collective prayer, to which both Ben Sira and Jonathan refer, offered by and in behalf of the nation, that became the nucleus of the *Amidah* of the Synagogue, the sole traditional request for the well-being of the community in the Jewish liturgy. Just as the Greeks in their cities prayed for health, food, and peace, the Jews of Jerusalem besought "the Lord our God" to heal them from disease, to bless the year with every kind of produce, and to be compassionate "toward us and toward Jerusalem."

The addition of this civic prayer to the sacrificial ritual of Jerusalem betrays a new feeling that offerings alone did not suffice to unite God and His covenanted people. Nobody doubted the value or the meaning of the statutory national sacrifices in effecting a reconciliation under the covenantal system, but a fuller apprehension of their unworthiness led postexilic Jews to intensify their worship. The civic prayer was now needed to supplement sacrifice, because the unfaithfulness of Israel had impaired her legitimate place under the Covenant.

Before the Exile, the king had not only furnished the regular daily sacrifice in the Temple, but he had also prayed for the nation to "the God of his Fathers" when Israel had offended the Lord or when an enemy had threatened the Holy City. Only in a postexilic, kingless Jerusalem, under Persian and Greek rule, could the idea that the nation should pray for itself take hold. Nevertheless, even in the Second Temple, the laity were only mute spectators of the sacerdotal performance; the Temple liturgy remained the exclusive office of the clergy. The civic prayer was an anomaly in this context.

When the Second Temple was being built, the elders of the Jews had explained to the Persian authorities that "our fathers had provoked the God of heaven." Now the remnant "that had escaped" felt itself responsible for the fulfillment of the Law. The High Priest could not substitute for the Davidic King: he represented God and not God's people. The situation demanded an insistent prayer with which the nation could supplement the continuous sacrifice. And who could offer this supplication better than the nation itself? "The Lord is good, and His mercy for Israel endures forever" (Ezra 3:11).

This feeling of unworthiness, which in the Hellenistic age naturally coexisted with the optimistic hope that the sins of Israel had been cleansed, explains another significant departure in Jewish liturgy. Biblically, the Hebrews clearly distinguished between a petition addressed to God and a benediction: one either requested God's help for the future (Gen. 24:12) or blessed the God of Abraham who had already provided help (Gen. 24:27). As a matter of fact, a blessing is not a prayer but a ritual formula that increases the potency of the blessed. Thus, Jacob stole Esau's blessing. Nevertheless, a benediction for God and a blessing bestowed upon a human being were both formally and functionally different. A person was addressed directly, as in "The Lord bless thee," and the formula anticipated the future. God was blessed in the third person for His past deeds: "Blessed is YHWH who delivered you from the hand of the Egyptians" (Exod. 18:10). Thus, an individual who "blessed" God in fact uttered praise of Him. But although praise, naturally, can also be used to introduce a request, biblical hymns of praise contain no petition, except by implication. After the Exile, however, the Jews began to bless God for His deeds in order that He might be prevailed upon to act again in the present and future as the protector of the Chosen People. Ezra's prayer (Neh. 9) contains a survey of the sacred history, and a prayer in Chronicles (I Chron. 29) is the earliest attested instance of a petition introduced by a benediction: "Blessed be the Lord, God of Israel." This particular text became a model for later liturgists. The civic prayer for Jerusalem was also introduced by a blessing.

The yearly rhythm of worship was determined by the liturgical calendar, which itself was determined by the agricultural calendar: Passover had to coincide with the time when the barley was in the ear (Deut. 16:1). Consequently the religious calendar would not always agree with the civil one, which was regulated by the fixed Babylonian scheme of intercalation. The complaints in pseudo-Enoch and in Jubilees that the use of the moon for determining the dates of feasts disturbed the seasons indicates both the importance and the irregularity of the year's arrangement by the priests of Jerusalem, who from time to time had to intercalate a month to make the calendar year correspond to the agricultural year. The only fixed astronomical rule, as Aristobulus attests about 175 B.C.E., was that Passover should be celebrated after the spring equinox. We may also suppose that around 200 B.C.E., and later in the Herodian Temple, the religious calendar was set from month to month, following the appearance of the new crescent. Some bold minds, like the author of Jubilees, proposed abandoning the solar-lunar year altogether and introduced a fixed year of 52 weeks and 364 days. The Hasmoneans and perhaps the High Priests before them used to send a special letter to announce the future dates of festivals. The jubilee year was no longer observed, but the Hasmoneans did renew the sabbatical cycle in 163–162. We do not know whether the biblical rule of the seventh-year fallow had been, or even could be, observed in Ptolemaic and Seleucid Judea without disturbing the entire taxation system of the Macedonian overlords.

In a society that, by custom and training easily expressed thoughts and emotions in religious language, solemn or even simply insistent assertions or negations often took the form of oaths. Scriptural authors attack oaths by false gods and Deuteronomy specifically reminds Jews to swear by the Name of the Lord. After the Exile, Jews in the diaspora still in some cases called upon a foreign deity as the guarantor of an oath, but in the third century B.C.E. the real danger was that the Jew invoked the name of the true God too often and in vain. The trend away from pronouncing the divine name, however, also led to the use of substitutes in oaths. Toward the end of the fourth century, according to Theophrastus (in Josephus, *C.Ap.* 1.166-167), the Jews in Tyre were already swearing by the *korban,* the oblation to God in the Temple; rabbinic sources show that this expression came to be the usual substitute for the Divine Name in oaths taken in Jerusalem. It seems, however, that in the judicial oath prescribed in the Law, the awesome Name of God continued in use for a long time.

The vow, like the oath, was a device intended to unite sacred and profane elements for the benefit of the devotee. As Plato put it, when people are sick or in difficulty and do not know what to do, or even when some of them become prosperous, they vow to sacrifice to a deity upon the fulfillment of certain conditions. Josephus explains the popularity of the nazirite vow among the Jews of his time in almost the same terms. When a person, male or female, promised to abstain from wine and from cutting his or her hair for a short period, say, thirty days, such a person immediately became "consecrated" to the Deity for this period. As a result, heaven was compelled to take care of the one who made the vow for whatever period of time had been specified, since he or she now belonged to the Lord. No wonder that the High Priest Simon the Just did not favor this easy way to blessedness.

In times of danger, sickness, or other need, Jews also continued to resort to prayer and propitiatory sacrifices (the sin offering) in order to purge themselves and to make themselves worthy of heavenly mercy. In the early Hellenistic period, however, prayer, even separate from sacrifice, came to be thought of as potent enough to persuade heaven. According to the Testaments of the Twelve Patriarchs, the wife of Potiphar had a son as a result of Joseph's prayer, and Judah Maccabee assembled his men at Mizpah because it formerly had been a praying-place for Israel. When Ben Sira was on the brink of the grave, he sent up a prayer from the earth and was rescued. Indeed, the ascending importance of prayer led to its association with rites originally belonging to sacrifice. Washing now preceded devotion and even sexual purity began to be regarded as necessary for personal supplication.

The consecration of food before eating is attested by pseudo-Aristeas and the grace after eating is mentioned by Ben Sira and described in Jubilees (22:8). The prerabbinic *Birkat ha-Mazon* was tripartite. The first section consisted of an affirmation of thankfulness for the food itself. (It is remarkable that this formula was universalist: one thanked God for nourishing all the world.) The second section consisted of an affirmation of thankfulness for life and health. And the third section was (originally) a prayer for the safety of Jerusalem and the Temple. Thus, prayer at table was essentially a home variant of the civic prayer for the Holy City.

Except for these prayers related to food, the religious practices of the Jews at home remain unknown. Did they affix the *mezuzah* to the door-posts of their dwellings? Ben Sira (6:30) seems to allude to the tassels prescribed in Numbers 15:38. From I Maccabees we know that there were Torah scrolls in private possession, but how many laymen in pre-Maccabean Jerusalem could afford to enjoy such expensive manuscripts? Although Ben Sira insists on the study of wisdom, that is, the Law, he never mentions private readings of the Torah.

As Yehuda Halevi noted, it is not easy to abstain from idolatrous practices in a world full of idols and their worshippers. Yet there is a surprising lack of evidence about superstitious practices in early Hellenistic Jerusalem. Daniel was represented as an exorcist in the Prayer of Nabonidus—even the canonical Book of Daniel makes him the head of the Babylonian magicians—and Dardanus of Phoenicia, whose works on magic were said to have been found in his grave, may be identical with the biblical Darda. We have seen that the first Jew mentioned in Greek sources was a miracle worker. Moreover, we may surmise that Jewish women used love potions no less than Potiphar's wife did in the Testament of Joseph. Nor is it likely that the arts of spells, counterspells, and collecting herbs for witchcraft, all taught by the Fallen Angels, were forgotten in Hellenistic Jerusalem. But the grave authors whose books we read, with the exception of Tobit, disdained mentioning these practices (only by chance do we learn about the Maccabean soldiers who used the idolatrous amulets). It seems, rather, that in the early Hellenistic age occult disciplines, in Jerusalem as well as among Greeks, were primarily practiced by the lower classes. Only much later did superstition invade polite society: both the Roman emperor Tiberius and his subjects who wrote the Dead Sea Scrolls believed in astrology and we find Jewish elements very conspicuous in the magical papyri of the third and fourth centuries C.E.

As the book of Ben Sira shows, law-abiding Jerusalem felt secure under the wings of the Covenant. The Pontiff of Jerusalem, however, disturbed this complacent attitude. He said that *Torah* and *Avodah,* while necessary, are not sufficient: God's abundant grace demands more, namely, *Gemilut Hasadim.* As the rabbis already saw, what Simon the Just was demanding were works of supererogation that go beyond one's legal duties. Although by adding a third requirement to the original two that had traditionally supported Israel, *Torah* and *Avodah,* the Pontiff was making a true innovation, it was an innovation that was based on *Torah* (which in turn is the foundation of *Avodah*). In his pithy saying, Simon the Just does not state explicitly what he demands from the Chosen People in terms of *Gemilut Hasadim,* nor is this formula recorded before him; when it is used in later talmudic sources it is always employed with implicit reference to Simon's saying. However, the meaning of both components of his formula can be elucidated.

In biblical Hebrew, *hesed* means "favor," that is, some service or benefit rendered without present recompense. The essential quality of *hesed* is that it is a voluntary act, and not a covenanted or contractual obligation—in contradistinction to the duties imposed by the Torah or the service rendered in the Temple. The first mention of the term in the Bible is in Genesis 20:13: Sarah performs an act of *hesed* for Abraham by passing herself off as his sister in order to save him from death. In the latest books of the Bible, we find that it is an act of *hesed* for the keeper of the royal harem to promote Esther (2:9) and that it is an act of *hesed* for Nehemiah (Neh. 13:14) to have done good deeds for the Temple.

But *hesed* is not only a social quality, it is above all a divine atribute: The whole earth is full of God's *hesed* (Ps. 33:5). Moreover, it is impossible to make a conceptual distinction between heavenly and human *hesed:* although an unimaginable distance separates man's faint efforts from divine omnipotence, both are part of the providential government of the world. *Hesed* is an act of goodwill, and Greek translations of the Hebrew term show that it was understood as such in the days of Simon the Just. The Hebrew term is mainly rendered as *eleos,* that is, an act of kindness, but also as *charis,* "favor," *eusebeia,* "piety," or even *dikaiosyne,* "right conduct," as in Genesis 20:13, where Abraham, speaking to Abimelech, king of Gerar, justifies Sarah's lie. As Jeremiah (9:24) suggests, human beings, like God, should practice *hesed* and justice.

As to the term *gemilut* (*gemilot* in the Bible), cognate words (*gemul, gemilah, tagmul*) indicate the idea of reciprocation: *reddo vicem.* For instance, in Isaiah 50:18, the *gemul* of God corresponds to the just deserts of human beings. Accordingly, in the Septuagint the words of this group are rendered by *antapodounai*, that is, "to repay" *(antapodosis* and *antapodoma),* except when the translator paraphrases for the sake of clarity.

Reciprocity of favors, although not obligatory, is expected. One good turn deserves another, and as Hesiod, a contemporary of the earliest prophets of Israel, had already stated, we give only to those who also give. This social rule was even transferred to the heavenly sphere: Socrates (Xen. *Mem.* IV, 3, 16) and the Psalmist (116:12) agree that people are required to repay the bounties they receive from heaven. Likewise, the beneficiary of a *hesed* done by a fellow man was expected to requite the favor. In any case one who has shown *hesed* to another could confidently expect God to grant His *hesed* to him. Ruth had shown *hesed* to the family of her first husband and, by virtue of God's *hesed*, she married Boaz (Ruth 1:8, 2:10).

The question is why the High Priest Simon added the exchange of favors to the concepts of Torah and Temple Service, as the third pillar supporting Israel. The answer is that in the early Hellenistic age obedience to the Law and the cult was no longer sufficient to hold the Chosen People to the ways of their fathers.

Philo already stressed that Moses had filled virtually the whole body of the Law with precepts enjoining pity and kindness. A religiously motivated conscience was a feature of the ancient Orient; there was an accepted reciprocity between wealth and poverty that served to stabilize society. Humility on the one side corresponded, at least ideally, to benevolence on the other. Bow down before a magnate, says Ben Sira, but also receive the greetings of the poor without arrogance. In Ptolemaic Egypt, natives asking an influential Greek for redress speak as if they had a natural claim on his assistance. By placing duty to the poor among the other religious obligations imposed upon the Jew, the Hebrew Lawgiver had on one hand raised social responsibility to the level of a sacred duty and on the other protected the self-esteem of the needy. Gleaning the fields was a hallowed perquisite of the poor in Israel.

In Hellenistic Jerusalem, however, this balance between the rights of the group over the individual and the rights of the individual to his share in the community weakened. Tribal organization had virtually disappeared. Tribal designations had given way to personal names; even kinship, which is still important in Tobit, does not count for much. Ben Sira speaks of a man's duties to his servants, to his cattle, to priests, and to the poor, but he limits family ties to the nuclear family consisting of parents and children. Even brothers are mentioned only exceptionally, and he feels he must warn against refusing a gift and against turning away the face of a kinsman (41:10, 21). Friendship, the elective relationship, is now the foundation of mutual benevolence. Friendship, however, does not mean the sharing of sweet emotions, but the bond of mutual aid. Epicurus himself, for whom friendship was the greatest of blessings, soberly stated that the origin of friendship is need. Kohelet echoes him: "Woe to him who is alone and falls with no companion to raise him" (4:9). Ben Sira, too, illustrates the practical aspects of friendship by speaking of friends who sit at your table in good times but who are nowhere to be seen when they are needed (6:10), and of a fool who complains about friends who eat his bread, but, forgetting his *hesed* (*charis*, "favor" in Greek), speak ill of him (20:16).

Moreover, empathy should extend even beyond family and friendship. In the Testaments of the Twelve Patriarchs, Benjamin brings together two commandments widely separated in the Torah: to fear the Lord and to love one's neighbor (Deut. 6:13; Lev. 19:18). Issachar not only shares his bread with the poor, he also grieves with sufferers, and Zebulon teaches his children to show *hesed* (*eleos* in the Greek version) to his neighbor and compassion to all men—even to animals. (In the third century B.C.E. funerary inscriptions for pets became fashionable in Greek society).

We are reminded of *philanthropia* (not to be confused with philanthropy), an egalitarian benevolence to fellow beings that was the most prized social quality of a good man in the Hellenistic city. The High Priest Simon the Just wants to use *Gemilut Hasadim*, the Jewish version of the Greek *philanthropia*, as a means of firmly uniting the Jewish people in a period when the limitless greed of the new acquisitive society nurtured by the Ptolemies threatened their moral stability. "All labor and skillful enterprise come from envy of each other—another futility and pursuit of wind," Kohelet complains (4:4). If people would follow the principle of *Gemilut Hasadim* and repay favors done for them by their fellow human beings, and above all favors done for them by the Deity, the reign of fair play would return. Do *hesed*, says Zebulun in his testament and, as you do to your neighbor, God will do to you. Ben Sira stresses the moral duty of *Gemilut Hasadim*: A person who neglects *tagmul hesed* (an expression rendered in Greek as *eucharisteia*, "return of thanks") is a skinflint, whereas doing good to a godly person will be repaid by the Most High. Sacrifices are commanded in the Torah and therefore should be offered, Ben Sira says, but the repayment of *hesed* (again, *charis* in the Greek) equals the offering of fine flour, and an act of righteous benevolence (*zedakah; eleemosyne* in Greek) equals a praise offering (35:2); here he is equating the value of two private, voluntary sacrifices to that of two voluntary acts of kindness to others.

The High Priest Simon names *Torah, Avodah*, and *Gemilut Hasadim* as pillars upon which *ha-olam* stands. By the word *ha-olam* Simon means "the present age." The word *olam* is used here as an independent noun, just as in Psalm 145:13 and in Kohelet 11:10, where the Preacher says that everything that appears to be new has already happened in the ages (*olamim*) before us. The idea of the succession of world empires taught the Jews the importance of historical periodization. By speaking of "this age" in his adage, the High Priest is implying not only that the next age, the Day of the Lord, may not be far away, but that God's wrath can and would strike again soon if Israel did not adhere to the virtues of *Torah*, *Avodah*, and *Gemilut Hasadim*.

Following the prophetic tradition, the High Priest saw injustice and inequality as the primary menaces to the future of the Chosen People. In the end, however, it was not *Gemilut Hasadim* that failed to protect Israel, but *Torah* and *Avodah*. Jason, a younger son of Simon the Just, and other scions of the priestly aristocracy—and not the oppressed— brought down the House of Israel because its traditions and obligations appeared ugly to them. They wanted to live in the Greek manner and in 175 B.C.E. asked Antiochus IV to allow them to observe the ordinances of the gentiles. As usual, it was the patricians and not the needy plebians who started a revolution.

TWENTY-FIVE

Faith and History

E ARE SO accustomed to speaking of the People of the Book that it is difficult for us to realize that the ordinary Jew of the early Hellenistic age hardly read the Torah; even in the synagogal service only isolated sentences of Scripture were quoted. There was no Torah reading in the Temple and there were no religious schools. Only specialists, such as Ben Sira and his pupils, seeking wisdom, studied the Covenant-Book of the Most High God. The common Jew learned something about the Torah from the oral traditions of his family and from religious practice, just as a good Christian did in the Middle Ages, who had no access to the Latin Bible.

But from the time of Alexander's conquest, the Jews from the Nile to the Indus lived in the Greek world and were exposed to the Greek spirit of rational research. Jewish intellectuals who knew the Torah could not escape the influence of Greek curiosity and started to ask and answer questions in the Greek style. For instance, from Genesis the Jew learned that in the beginning men consorted with the sole Maker and Ruler of the Universe (Noah was privileged to be God's companion), but that Abraham's fathers had turned to serve other gods. The return to the true Deity did not come about until Abraham, Isaac, and Jacob. Consequently, in the spirit of Greek science some Jewish writers of the Hellenistic age began to ask when and why the apostasy had occurred. In Jubilees, for some obscure reason the corruption of mankind is ascribed to the generation of Serug, that is, to the fourth generation before Abraham. Other scholars, whose views were followed in later sources, preferred to hold Enosh, Seth's son, or Nimrod, grandson of Ham, responsible for the beginning of idolatry. An Enochic writer thought that the Fallen Angels had led men to sacrifice to idols.

Idols were of course things of nought and, according to Judith, no Jew any longer worshipped gods made by the hands of men. Still, the author of Jubilees, following Deuteronomy 32:17, asserted that behind the wood and the stone lurked potent and malicious evil spirits, and two Enochic writers, the writer of the Epistle of Enoch and the writer of the Visions of Enoch, followed the biblical view. Generally speaking, however, it seems the Jews did not pay serious attention to the problem of idolatry. It is noteworthy that two remarkable passages of Deuteronomy were neglected in the discussion of heathenism: 32:8, which states that "the sons of God" are the protectors of the other peoples, whereas Israel is the Lord's portion; and 4:19, which states that the Lord allotted the worship of the hosts of heaven to all the nations except Israel. It is true that Ben Sira (17:17) refers to the first passage, but only in order to stress the uniqueness of the Chosen People. As for the worship of the stars, it was alien to the Greeks, and Plato hoped in vain that his astral deities would be worshipped in Athens. Babylonian priests may later have developed an astral religion, but the Jews did not care for the "barbarians" and the Babylonian Bel was for them only a manmade and ridiculous idol.

Having learned from the Greeks the historical approach to religion, the Jews also began to ventilate a question in the air among their Greek neighbors: How did the Deity first come to be known? The faithful knew that Abraham was the founder of the true religion. But although in the biblical account God chooses the Patriarch, in Jubilees God's call to Abraham is turned into Abraham's quest for God: "Thee and Thy dominion have I chosen" (12:19). Abraham is viewed as a self-taught convert who comes to the truth when, observing the stars in order to foretell the coming of rain, he realizes that God alone gives and withholds rain. The esoteric Jewish writer here follows a theory of Plato's and Aristotle's, which continued to be popular in the Hellenistic age, that the sight of the starry heavens led men to recognize the existence of the gods. Astronomy, rather than leading to atheism, upheld faith, and Abraham, like Plato, deduced the Designer from the Design. It is interesting to note that it was the steady circular movement of the heavenly bodies that, for Plato, proved it was God who caused this motion. The author of Jubilees, however, writing for a less sophisticated audience, made rain and its prognostication the source of Abraham's discovery. We may remember the prayer for rain in the Jewish liturgy, which calls upon Him "Who gives rain upon the earth" (Job 5:10).

The idea of Abraham as a stargazer fascinated the Jews of the Hellenistic age. The Jewish philosopher Aristobulus already quotes the Jewish poet (whom we have met above) who, writing in Greek and pretending to be the legendary Orpheus, tells his readers that no mortal being had seen the Creator save Abraham who was skilled in astronomy and who (according to this pseudo-Orpheus) had anticipated the Greek theory of the uniform movement of superimposed concentric spheres in the heavens. A generation later, another Jewish (or Samaritan) writer proposed that Abraham had taught the science of the stars, discovered by Enoch, to the Phoenicians and Egyptians. For Philo, Abraham progressed from idolatry to stargazing, and thence, by virtue of his own reasoning, to the discovery that the body of universe was governed by an intelligence. Abraham's departure from Chaldea symbolizes his abandonment of astral worship.

Josephus, or more probably a source he uses, updates and corrects the astronomical explanation of Abraham's conversion. The Platonic argument from the perfect revolution of the heavens, used by the Jewish pseudo-Orpheus, had been rendered useless by the acquisition of a greater knowledge of celestial mechanics. (Philo relegates the question of celestial mechanics to the class of those that cannot be answered with certainty.) Accordingly, Josephus now asserts that it was the irregularity of stellar motion that demonstrated to Abraham the subjection of the stars to a higher power. The rabbis, however—who, like the worshippers of Isis, also insisted that their Deity was above the power of the stars—accepted the idea, already advanced by Philo, that Abraham had discovered God by reasoning alone. Nevertheless, some of them understood God's words to Abraham, "Number the stars" (Genesis 15:5), as meaning that He revealed the paths of the stars to the Patriarch, and a painting in the Dura synagogue from around 260 c.e. shows Abraham as a stargazer. In this manner Hellenistic Jews could assert that astronomy was created by their ancestor and at the same time stress that astral worship was only a step in the direction of the true religion, that is, the religion of Abraham and his descendants.

The idea of perfect order in the world of nature pleased preachers, who could use it to contrast a law-abiding universe to lawless man. Jeremiah (8:7) already complained that although migratory birds keep the time of their coming, Israel does not observe the commandments of God. In the same spirit, Plato insisted that man must learn to regulate the lawlessness of his soul by observing the unchanging motion of the luminaries. In the early Hellenistic age, Greek and Jewish moralists continued to use the same argument. The Stoic Cleanthes asserted that the perfection of the cosmos is marred by the work of the wicked in their folly, while in Jerusalem Kohelet stressed the regularity of natural phenomena and Ben Sira noted that God had so ordered His luminaries that they would never shrink from their duties nor ever interfere one with the other. The Enochic compiler of the Book of Watchers, opposing the lasting order of nature to the disorder among men, warns his hearers that if they do not follow the commandments of the Lord they will find no mercy. Naphtali, in his testament, reminds his sons that the sun, the moon, and the stars do not transgress their appointed order, and that it is greedy human beings who alter the divine law. In the beginning of the second century B.C.E. the philosopher Aristobulus stresses that the sky does not encroach upon the earth. Later, the hymnodist of the Dead Sea Sect and the author of the Pseudo-Solomonic Psalms repeat that the luminaries respect their divinely established order and Philo of Alexandria gravely explains that whereas other lawgivers used fables to inculcate obedience in their peoples, Moses began with the cosmogony in order to demonstrate the harmony between his law and that of the universe. The reassuring periodicity of nature is a perpetual marvel and a permanent source of thankful amazement.

Yet, although the heavens declared the glory of the Creator to Jews and Greeks alike, the Jews and the Greeks understood the message differently. The Greeks saw the universe as a *polis:* the Maker of the world was the *demiourgos,* that is, a craftsman in public service, and the relations between the elements, like the relations between the inhabitants of a *polis*, were governed by justice. Consequently, Pythagoras of Samos, a contemporary of Second Isaiah who was both a prophetic figure and a scientist—and who, we are told, was the first to call the heavens *cosmos,* that is, the ordered universe—also announced to the Greeks that the study of numbers, that is, mathematics, could disclose the secret of the visible order in the universe. Scientists from his time onward—from the Greek astronomers to Newton and Einstein—applied his seminal idea to the study of the heavens.

In the Jewish view the world was governed by an absolute monarch Who, in His goodness, sustained the work of Creation, just as He kept His promises to the Patriarchs. The author of the Epistle of Jeremiah opposes the powerless idols to the God to Whom the luminaries are obedient and Who commands the lightning, the winds, and the clouds. The difference between this perspective of the universe and the mechanistic theory of Greek science may be well illustrated by a passage in the apologetic work of Aristobulus mentioned earlier. Speaking of the Creation, Aristobulus cautions his Greek readers that although God has established the order of nature forever, it does not mean that He, as some believe, is now idle. Far from ceasing to act, God, having arranged the universe, now holds it together.

Some three hundred and fifty years after Aristobulus, the famous Greek physician Galen, roughly a contemporary of R. Judah, the compiler of the Mishnah, clearly recognizes the difference between the two world views. The Jew believes that for God everything is possible, while the Greek philosopher argues that God neither attempts to nor can interfere with the working of the mechanism He created.

The disagreement between Jew and Greek is neither accidental nor a part of the warfare between science and theology. The philosopher was, for the most part, religious in the manner of the Greeks—that is, he observed the religious practices of his city; the rabbis, who believed in miracles, prepared calendars that presupposed the regular movement of the luminaries. But as Hegel, following Philo and the Church Fathers, observed, in paganism nature takes precedence over the gods, whereas in Hebrew monotheism it is degraded to a mere creature of the Deity. As the heroic mother in II Maccabees explains, God did not create the world out of things existent: nothing exists unless it was wrought by God and nothing takes place unless it is determined by God. Man is not a cog in the mechanism of the universe, but a separate creature made by the Master. Israel and nature are parallel manifestations of God's design, and man's duty of obedience to God is derived from the Torah, which preceeds Creation. Similarly, nature must obey God: Enoch saw seven stars bound for ten thousand years at the end of heaven and earth for not having come forth at their appointed times. In paganism, as Plato, quoting an Orphic saying, states, God is the beginning, middle, and end; for the Jews, the Lord is before the beginning and beyond the end.

Exhorting the people of God to obedience, the moralists added an argument from history to their cosmological inference. The doctrine that God's choice of Abraham's posterity, though abiding, was dependent on Israel's fulfillment of the Torah, was explicitly or implicitly admitted by all pious writers of the Hellenistic age. This idea was neither new nor peculiar to the Chosen People. Every people in antiquity regarded themselves as chosen, because only they worshipped the true gods. The Egyptians, the Athenians, and the Romans, no less than the Jews, believed themselves the most pious—or even the only pious—race, and attributed their triumphs to the blessings of their gods. Disrespect for the gods was the sole failure that could be charged collectively to a nation that had lapsed into disobedience or had been stricken with calamity.

In the Decalogue, however, the declaration of true faith is followed by moral precepts—and the Hebrew prophets threatened the Chosen People with doom for moral transgressions as well as for the worship of foreign gods. For a pious Jew of the early Hellenistic age, therefore, immorality came to be identified with idolatry and was seen as a vice, like fornication or avarice. Quoting the authority of Enoch, the Testament of Naphtali explains that the Captivity was brought upon the Jews because they had separated from the Lord and had acted according to all the lawlessness of the gentiles and the wickedness of Sodom. It was this concept that gave the Jews their arrogant self-righteousness: they might be sinners under the Law, but outside the Law there was nothing but sin.

Heathens could be honest and follow the Noachic commandments, but if so, it was despite their abominable faith. Jews could be honest because of the Law and in obedience to the Revelation. On the other hand, even the private sins of the Jew endangered the status of Israel as an elected people, for if fornication is like idolatry, it too becomes a moral sin. Indeed, the sins of the people of God had already brought about the fall of Jerusalem.

Discussion of the fall of Jerusalem in 586 B.C.E. was no antiquarian pastime even as late as 200 B.C.E., four centuries later. The stiff-necked people who mistreated Jeremiah—and in this way, as some believed, caused the destruction of the Holy City—continued to pay the penalty for the transgressions of ancestors whose bones had already turned to dust. The people of God was still scattered, the restored Jerusalem was forced to obey a pagan sovereign, and Israel, God's own portion, still waited for the Lord to exalt it.

Some people believed that disobedience to Levi had been the primary transgression of Israel. The priesthood, they believed, was more exalted than the kings, and priests should be approached in humbleness of heart. When, in an allegory, the "ship of Israel" is broken by mighty waves, Judah and Levi remain on it together and bring it back to land, while Joseph (the ancestor of the Samaritans) escapes in a small boat and the rest of Jacob's sons are scattered to the ends of the earth. Thus from this point of view the diaspora and Samaria should bow down before Jerusalem, in which pride of place is awarded to the clergy. Nor is this just an example of clericalism.

In the allegory from the Testament of Levi just quoted the Patriarch warns that his descendants will teach commandments contrary to divine law, steal offerings, eat sacrifices in the company of harlots, defile women, and marry the daughters of gentiles. Puffed up because of their exalted rank they will provoke God's anger, and because of their uncleanness the Temple will be laid waste. In context the prediction refers to the First Temple, but the author and his readers would certainly have had the contemporary clergy of the Second Temple in mind.

In traditional thought we find the idea that there is an immutable and perfect order in the world, and that if the order is violated a "re-forming," a return to the pristine condition, is needed. The ancient Egyptians, for whom the accession of a new pharaoh meant the restoration of the true and eternal order by which the gods live; the Greeks, who clamored for the return to the ancestral constitution; and Luther, who pretended to "reform" the apostolic church, all shared this salutary belief. It is this belief that explains the respect paid to primeval revelation in all ancient societies. The founding fathers of the United States were the first who consciously opened a *novus ordo saeculorum* and announced that their pyramid was unfinished.

Yet the Torah itself denied the antiquity of Mosaic law. Abraham, the founder of the true faith, had preceded Moses by centuries, and had served meat and milk together to the Lord himself. As soon as Jews learned something of Greek and something of the Greeks, they could not help comparing Moses to Lycurgus and Zoroaster or the other inspired lawgivers of the nations. Unknown at the beginning of the world and the beginning of the nation, Mosaic law, however useful and necessary for the conquest and establishment of the commonwealth, could not have eternal value. Moreover, some statements in Scripture itself gave those who wished to find one a handle against the authority of the Torah. After the destruction of the Temple by the Romans, some people, quoting Jeremiah 7:22, asserted that the sacrificial commandments were no part of the genuine Torah.

Ungodly men and women who violated and even attacked inconvenient commandments had existed at all times. It would be naïve to imagine that Jerusalem under the High Priest Simon the Just was peopled only by the pious. Ben Sira, a rather placid preacher, thunders: "Woe be unto you, impious men, who have abandoned the Law of the Most High" (41:8). We should not confuse the Jews of the Hellenistic age with medieval Jews. When the world was dominated by Christian and Muslim clergies, the Jews lived under the ferule of the rabbis; but the Greek Jews had no clergy. In Hellenistic Jerusalem the staunch defenders of the faith had no other recourse but to assert that the truly pious from Adam onward had fulfilled the ceremonial law: Adam had offered a sacrifice of incense; Noah had made his burnt offering in strict accordance with Mosaic law; the law of purification after childbirth had been given to Eve, the first mother; Asher had known that the hare was unclean; Rachel had presented the mandrakes to the priest of the Most High "who was at that time"; and Abraham had celebrated the Passover.

This reinterpretation of the history of the Patriarchs appears not only in Jubilees, written to establish the everlasting value of the Torah, but also in the Testaments of the Twelve Patriarchs, a moralizing historical novel. In the latter, Jacob and his sons again and again refer to the Law of the Lord and admonish their descendants to keep it. The author of Jubilees was more systematic: he told his readers that the revelation on Sinai was but the codification of precepts that had been given gradually, from the beginning, and that the Law of Moses was a copy of an eternal text inscribed on "Tablets in Heaven." A Jewish poet spoke in Greek hexameters of Abraham, who pleased God by living in agreement with the primal commandments. In Solomon's Proverbs, personified Wisdom is said to have been created from the beginning. Quoting these words, Ben Sira not only adds, significantly, that wisdom will not fail to the end of time, but also goes on to explain that the wisdom he praises is the Law which Moses commanded. Somewhat later, Aristobulus, writing in Greek, quotes the same passages of Proverbs as Ben Sira to prove that *sophia* (wisdom) existed before heaven and earth. Existing from the beginning, the Law is therefore valid in perpetuity. The orthodox Ben Sira, the somewhat wild author of Jubilees (who believed that the angels themselves were circumcised), the novelist who wrote the Testaments of the Twelve Patriarchs, the epic poet Philo, and even the philosopher Aristobulus at the Alexandrian court, all agree on this point.

Such heartening unanimity among the pious writers in Hebrew and Greek around 200 B.C.E. demonstrates the weight and impact of the antinomian argument that the Law, because new, was by definition transient. A generation after Ben Sira the "sons of Belial," as I Maccabees calls them, persuaded many in Jerusalem when they claimed that ever since Israel had separated itself from its neighbors, evils "have overtaken us." This argument, advanced by the reformers in the days of Antiochus Epiphanes, presupposes that the separatist rules of Moses, which fenced Israel in, were unknown to the Patriarchs, and for this reason not perpetually binding upon the Chosen People.

Pious Jews, however, despite the insidious arguments of the "sons of Belial," continued to believe in the impending salvation of God's peculiar people. Ben Sira prayed to Him for mercy for the people called by His Name and adjured the Almighty to "make the time short." He must have been thinking of those who were losing patience and who were almost ready to listen to the arguments of the "sons of Belial," for he exclaims: "Let Thy prophets be found faithful."

Couched in biblical terms, Ben Sira's hope was really the same as the hope that sustained the Greek patriots of his time: the liberation of their sacred cities from the Macedonian yoke. It was a deliberate insult to these dreamers when a disciple of Epicurus dared to proclaim that eating and drinking mattered more than talking about saving the Greeks. Liberty was no less sweet to a burgess of Sidon or to a priest in Memphis than to a priest in Jerusalem or to a citizen of Athens. Under Macedonian domination the Egyptians cheered the memory of the last pharaoh, Nectanebus, and read prophecies (which had also been translated into Greek for the nationalists of Greek education) that announced the coming expulsion of the impious foreigners, the destruction of Alexandria, and the coming of the new pharaoh—who would be installed by Isis and who would be a "giver of blessings." The woes of the past would be forgotten, and those who survived the calamities of the final war, which would end all wars, will wish that those who had perished might rise to enjoy the new eon. In Babylon, behind the closed doors of the sanctuary, a secret prayer went up to Bel, Lord of Babylon, to have pity on his city, to turn his face to the temple, and to establish the liberty of his servants, the children of Babylon.

In the meantime Roman might was coming into view against the western sky. To the Greeks in Europe, who had just experienced the horrors of the Roman conquest, an oracle that circulated in 188 B.C.E. promised revenge: the heavy horses of the Seleucids would land in Italy and the Seleucid army would burn cities, fill the rivers with blood, and impose merciless servitude on Rome—vain hopes all.

In Seleucid Jerusalem, however, the prayers of Ben Sira and his disciples appealed to God to act against the Seleucids: "Crush the heads of the rulers of the enemy." Their prayers were heard; soon, in the cities conquered by the Hasmonean rulers, other men supplicated other gods to pour out their wrath upon the new masters of Palestine and upon the godless nation of the Jews who, by force, had converted the pagans to the only true faith.

The force and the danger of the myth of the new eon is obvious. Yet the religious hope for redemption can be also a source of quietism. The Lord will surely renew the signs and repeat the wonders of old and a truly trusting man will abstain from trying foolishly to force God's hand. Orthodox Jews still fast in expiation of the patriotic murder of Gedaliah, who was the first Babylonian governor of Judea, twenty-six centuries ago.

As a matter of fact, from Gedaliah to Herod, as long as the priestly aristocracy determined the spirit of the nation there was messianic hope in Jerusalem, but no messianic movement. Sometimes, when the fates seemed to indicate that the end might be at hand, apocalyptic calculations and expectations became more urgent, as happened during the persecution of Epiphanes. But it was only when the Pharisees had succeeded in weakening the prestige of the High Priest that the Zealots could open the age of the Messiahs.

Toward the beginning of the second century B.C.E. the authority of the traditional leaders was paramount. They knew well that the Fourth Empire of which they read in the Daniel stories meant peace and, as well, the security of their own power in Jerusalem. Imperial protection shielded Zion from the Arabs beyond the Jordan, from the Idumeans in the south, from "aliens" of all kinds on the seacoast, and from the envy of Samaria and the brotherly hatred of Gerizim. Shielded by foreign overlords, the Jews were nevertheless sure, just as were, say, the Zoroastrians, and as later the Christian Church was to be, that no salvation was possible outside the fold and that the nations had gone astray in worshipping idols. Like the Greek philosophers of their time, the Jewish intellectuals sharply divided mankind into fools, whether pagans or strayed Jews, and the elect. Exactly like the Greek philosophers, they awaited the conversion—or the damnation—of the infidel fools.

On the topic of the fate of the infidels, opinions naturally varied. The Enochic writers wanted to see idolaters and other sinners thrown into the eternal fire, while the more hopeful author of Tobit just expected them to bury their idols. Ben Sira also prayed to God for the conversion of the nations. Idolaters had only to learn that there is no deity but the Lord, a pagan had only to embrace the true faith—for in the Lord there is no distinction between Jew and Greek. But until their conversion, they would be condemned by God and His people. As the Stoics used to say, a blind man is still blind, even if a minute later he regains his sight. Thus Tobit and Ben Sira hoped simultaneously for both the conversion and the punishment of the nations. As a matter of fact, the future of the gentiles, a topic that arouses the curiosity of modern scholars, was dealt with only perfunctorily in Jewish or, say, Egyptian messianic dreams. Even the apocalyptic visionaries were more interested in the destruction of their godless brethren than in the salvation or damnation of other nations.

Trusting in the mercy of God forever and ever and awaiting the advent of the Messiah, the Jerusalem of Ben Sira and of the High Priest Simon the Just was passably pleased with the present eon. The foreign overlord upheld the Torah and paid the expenses of the sacrifices, and when a Ptolemaic or a Seleucid king did happen to overstep his rights—as in the case of Ptolemy IV and Heliodorus, the vizier of Seleucus IV—God abated his arrogance.

TWENTY-SIX

A Retrospect

WE HAVE surveyed the evidence pertaining to the pre-Maccabean period. It is necessary to stress again, and emphatically, the peculiar limitations of our knowledge. The works, extracts of works, and even the names of authors, real or fictitious, that we have dealt with have not been preserved by capricious chance, nor for reasons of their historical or literary quality, but simply because their subjects were parabiblical. These works feature biblical heroes, or are allegedly written by persons named in the Torah, or are set in the biblical period, or imitate biblical works. The first Jewish book we know of in which the author introduces himself to the reader, that of Jesus, the son of Sirach, of Jerusalem, is an imitation of Proverbs. But books unrelated to Scripture have been lost—for instance, "the writings of men of old" who were founders of the Therapeutic group described by Philo—because the channel of transmission of Jewish postbiblical books, with some exceptions, was the Church and the Church was only interested in a Jewish book if it was related to Scripture, whether it was a book of stories about Daniel or a novel like the Testaments of the Twelve Patriarchs. Without the discovery of the settlement of the New Covenanters at the Dead Sea, we should have remained ignorant of the books they produced, although their library contained no less than seven Aramaic copies of Enochic books that were known to us previously only in Greek translation. Of course, many parabiblical books, such as the so-called Genesis Apocryphon found at Qumran, that for some reason were not popular among the Jews in the Roman age, might never have been known to the Church or might have been disregarded by Christian copyists for reasons unknown to us. The only non-parabiblical tracts that have survived, the story of Heliodorus and that of the tax-farmer Joseph, were preserved as elements of larger works glorifying the Chosen People.

Thus, everything that we have was chosen by devout hands. We have nothing of belles-lettres, scientific works, historiography, or rhetoric written by the Jews of the early Hellenistic age, whether in Hebrew, Aramaic, or Greek. (We hear by chance of two men, called Agathobouloi, who were teachers of the philosopher Aristobulus and who dealt with the Jewish calendar, but these Agathobouloi, like Aristobulus, or like the anonymous predecessors of Philo to whom he sometimes refers, also dealt with sacred studies.) Therefore, if we want to understand Enoch, Jubilees, and the rest as reflections of the ideas and the historical movements of the period, we must never forget that these books reflect only a chosen and limited sector of the Jewish life and the Jewish mind of the time. Our sources, almost without exception, permit us to see their authors and the era only from a religious perspective. But the Jewishness of even devout Jews was only one aspect of their lives and thought-worlds. They worked and rested, traveled and paid taxes, judged their spouses and neighbors, were treated in sickness, and enjoyed their dinners, not as abstract and eternal members of the Jewish people, but as human beings living in the third century B.C.E. And let us remember further that even the Jewishness represented in these books is not only uniform but completely one-sided. We hear only the voice of the side that triumphed with the Maccabees. Nothing has been preserved of the writings of the "sinners" condemned by Ben Sira, Enoch, the author of Jubilees, and others. But these nonconformists were Jews, too, and according to their own fashion, God-fearing Jews.

We have, nevertheless, no other medium of information for those years. In examining books of the pre-Maccabean age we have endeavored to recognize signs of spiritual change, but we have mostly avoided pinpointing the reasons for them. We have often contrasted Hebrew and Greek thought, using these terms as indications of modes of thinking characteristic of classical Israel and classical Hellas, but we have rarely pointed to Greek influences.

In the first place, Jerusalem was no more unchanging than Athens. Many unexpected traits that appear to be un-Jewish, that is, outside the ideal line that in our imaginations links the last prophets and the first rabbis, may result from changes within the Jewish organism itself. Historians of the Chosen People still consider the topic from the standpoint of *Pirke Abot:* "Moses received the Torah from Sinai and handed it on to Joshua . . . Hillel and Shammai took over from them." It is hardly an improvement when John the Baptist and Jesus are substituted for Hillel and Shammai. The Jews of the Hellenistic age did not suspect that they lived in the "intertestamental" period, nor did they see themselves merely as the descendants of the Patriarchs and the ancestors of the rabbis. They were people of their own times, and Hellenistic civilization offered them an almost endless variety of experiences.

In addition, let us also emphasize again the existence of an unknown force of the first magnitude that disturbs any calculation of influences. Although the Aramaic world which began at "the River of Egypt" and extended as far as the Caspian Sea and beyond the Indus, remains barely discernible, and although we know next to nothing about its varieties and variations—for example, we only dimly perceive native Egyptians behind the rows of "Hellenes" in the Ptolemaic kingdom—a common Levantine civilization stubbornly persisted under the Macedonian rulers. Written Aramaic was a common bond between the Buddhist emperor Asoka and the contemporary High Priest of Jerusalem as well as between a Parthian tax collector and a Jewish scribe. Around 200 B.C.E. a leading man in Seleucid Uruk (Erech) bore both a Babylonian and a Greek name, Anuballit-Nephalon, but he also had a long Aramaic inscription placed in the Babylonian temple he had restored. Northern Syria was made into a second Macedonia by the Seleucids, but the nicknames given them by the populace were Aramaic; the coins of the Persian dynasts, vassals of the Seleucids, carried Aramaic legends; and in Jerusalem even the voice from the Holy of the Holies spoke Aramaic to the High Priest Simon the Just.

The Levant, from Alexander to Muhammad, possessed two channels of communication: Greek and Aramaic. Babylonian legends entombed in cuneiform script became known to the Greeks through Greek or Aramaic translations and even reached Ovid in Augustan Rome. Aramaic was also a vehicle for the religious propaganda of the Persian Magi in the West; even their enemy Mani wrote in Aramaic and knew the Book of Enoch, written in Aramaic by a Jew some six hundred years earlier.

It was international, that is, Greek and Aramaic elements, in a perpetual interchange with local forces, that molded the spirit of the Hellenistic East. We have seen the similarities between Jewish and Greek stories of divine help, and there are similarities between Asoka's solicitude for man's salvation and the *philanthropia* of the Hellenistic kings to whom the Buddhist ruler of India sent his missionaries. Indeed, Asoka's inscriptions in the western part of his realm, Afghanistan, were also published in Greek and Aramaic. How are we, then, to disentangle Greek, Aramaic, and Indian threads in these historical webs?

The complexity of the Levantine civilization of the early Hellenistic age appears clearly in Phoenicia. From 270 B.C.E. on, Phoenicians are listed among the victors in Greek athletic contests. Yet when Phoenician cities obtained minting privileges from Antiochus IV, champion of Hellenism, their coins exhibited symbols of native gods and the legends on them were in Phoenician or in Phoenician and Greek. From about the same time, we have a portrait of a Phoenician priest, and although the inscription on the portrait is in Phoenician, the vestment is Egyptian. A century later, across the Jordan in Gadara, a city that boasted of its Atticism, the Greek greeting *"chaire"* and the Phoenician (or Aramaic) greeting *"salam"* were both on the lips of the people.

But let us return to Jerusalem. In Naphtali's testament, a ship is used as a symbol of Israel. The ship of state was a natural allegory for the Greeks and was used in their literature from around 600 B.C.E. onward. But a galley with a square sail furled was also the standard ship represented on Sidonian coins and rabbinic opinion on maritime law followed Phoenician custom. Again, when Kohelet insisted that one should drink and eat and enjoy life before it is too late, was he repeating the words of Greek poets or the admonitions of ancient Egyptian songs (which were still recited in his day), or was he simply echoing the hedonist wisdom of ancient Israel: "Let us eat and drink, for tomorrow we die" (Isa. 22:13)?

Greek civilization was, however, the civilization of the conquerors and masters of the Levant; the weight of the Macedonian spear put the advantage on the Greek side. But in contrast to the modern system of colonization no bar separated the conquered from the conquerors: the laic Greek civilization was open to everyone and graecism was in the air breathed by all.

Nevertheless, it would be unwise to overestimate the force of the Greek impact. We are inclined to imagine hellenization as similar to the modern Europeanization of the East. But the European impact on the culture of the Orient became overwhelming only when it was concomitant with an industrial revolution. The Greeks did not bring steamboats and miracle drugs with them. The Macedonian *sarissa* was longer than the spear of the Persian guard, but both were weapons of the same kind. The Greek masters gave to the East a more efficient and perhaps a somewhat more honest administration; an improved bureaucratic machinery, operating by means of hierarchical written orders; the Greek rule of law; and more peace and more order; but they neither wished to, nor would they have been able to plough up the deeper layers of life. The Macedonian state just did not have enough horses or runners or officers or money to do more than keep order and collect taxes. One new element that Greek domination did create in the social life of the East, however, was an increase in the strength and importance of the middle class—a result of their economic policies and particularly of the addition of large numbers of hellenized natives to the lower ranks of government service. In this way, too, they created a new pool of native leadership.

The ability to speak and write Greek fluently and in the prevailing fashion was a requisite for advancement in the army, in the administration, in business, and above all in social standing. A man in Zenon's service complains that he has not received his wages because he does not have a proper command of Greek. In a Greek play written in the third century B.C.E. a gentleman is praised for his moral qualities. One of the qualities listed is the "simplicity" *(haplotes)* that is so highly appreciated in the Testaments of the Twelve Patriarchs, but also listed are the facts that he is faithful to the king *(philobasileus)* and "fond of the Greeks" *(philhellen)*.

Still, the masses of the indigenous population did not need to learn Greek or love the Greeks. Hor (Horus in Greek), a priest of the Ibis, a sacred bird, could send his dream-oracles to Ptolemy Philometor even though his Greek was poor, because his Egyptian letters were certainly translated into Greek by bilingual scribes. Likewise, the Greeks had no particular reason to learn the languages of the Orient, since the scribes were ubiquitous. Indeed, the scribes were probably the most important element of the new indigenous middle class.

The indigenous populations grouped themselves around their sanctuaries, which were inaccessible to foreigners. Just as in the case of the Temple of Jerusalem, entry to Egyptian temples was forbidden to aliens, who sometimes are specified: Asiatics, Bedouin, Phoenicians—and Greeks. Protected by the sanctity of their temples and by Greek ignorance of the sacred languages of the Orient, some dreamers—Egyptian, Babylonian, Jewish, and probably also Phoenician—composed tracts predicting the end of Greek rule. Others sided with the Macedonian rulers. The Horus mentioned above assured his Ptolemaic masters that Isis, the divine protector of Egypt, loved and favored them.

The essential fact is that contact between Greeks and Orientals was, so to speak, tangential, connection taking place only at the point marked "government." Rulers and their tax collectors changed; soldiers came, usually accompanied by looting and exaction, and went; wars devastated the country. But these intrusions were like the plagues of locusts: they ravaged the land but did not change its basic way of life.

The real hellenization of the Seleucid Empire, outside Asia Minor, began only after the end of Seleucid domination, when the hellenizing process was taken over by the native rulers. It is no accident that the Arsacids, the Hasmoneans, and other oriental princes of the later Hellenistic age called themselves "philhellene"; they needed to adopt Greek civilization in order to play a role in international politics. Moreover, in order to survive, these new native rulers were obliged to diffuse Greek techniques among their subjects. The officer corps and the higher ranks of the civil service of the Seleucids were, for the most part, Greek. Under the Hasmoneans the personnel was Jewish, but keeping the bureaucratic machinery and the military going required that the new staff learn, and know well, the ways of the Greeks. Cosmopolitanism was the price of independence.

In examining the process of cultural diffusion we have to distinguish between those who received a Greek education and those who did not. Because a Jewish educational system did not exist in the pre-Maccabean period, Jews—and particularly Jews in the dispersion—who received a Greek education, or who simply lived among the Greeks, necessarily became alienated from the civilization of their ancestors. The Greek Torah and the Greek synagogal service were the sole links, beside family tradition, between such Jews and the nation of their forefathers. The Jewishness of the poets and philosophers who dealt with Jewish subjects—Aristobulus, Ezechiel, Theodotus, and others—was bookish: the peculiarity of the Chosen People does not actually affect them any longer. Aristobulus, living at the Ptolemaic court, can state in his *Explanation of the Mosaic Scripture:* "All philosophers agree that thoughts concerning the Deity should be pure, and this is exceedingly well encouraged by our school." And although the poet Ezechiel writes of the Exodus and the poet Philo deals with Abraham and Joseph, the manner of their treatment of these subjects is Greek. From their choice of rare words to their choice of—for the Greeks—exotic topics, these Jewish poets represent the taste of Alexandria. The pagan reader who had learned enough to appreciate the obscurity of Philo's verses could enjoy the miraculous appearance of a ram during the offering of Isaac in the same way that he could read with pleasure some exotic episode in Apollonius of Rhodes. Josephus, and later the Christian compilers, were right in principle when they classed this Philo among pagan writers. Why shouldn't a pagan Greek also choose Abraham as the subject of a poem?

The system of education in the ancient world did not include foreign languages; were it not for the Septuagint, the poet Philo and the philosopher Philo as well, neither of whom knew Hebrew, would have known hardly anything about their ancestral faith. On the other hand, Greek ideas did percolate down to the Jews in Judea, even to those who lacked the advantages of a Greek education. Although in an isolated and fragmentary manner, and without asking how such newfangled notions could be reconciled with their general worldview, the Jews drew upon new insights, adopting those elements of Greek culture that appeared to them useful or stimulating and neglecting the rest. For instance, the author of the Testaments of the Twelve Patriarchs, making use of the traditional metaphor of the potter molding clay, adds that God made the body after the likeness of the spirit and gave man a soul according to the capacity of the body. The idea is Aristotelian. Moreover, the author capped his argumentation with the general formula, again of Greek origin, that Creation was accomplished according to weight, measure, and rule. Yet he hardly knew, and surely would never have understood, the idea of formal cause, the distinction between *hyle* and *morphe,* or any of the other components of the Aristotelian system. As we all do, he merely picked up some bits and pieces of foreign thought that seemed useful for his purpose.

Similarly, the very nationalist author of Jubilees states that in the division of the earth among Noah's sons the lot of Shem was the best, inasmuch as his lands were less cold than the territory of Japhet and less hot than the region of Ham. The idea that the middle belt enjoys the best climate and accordingly produces the best men was popular among the Greeks from the middle of the fifth century B.C.E. This geographic determinism should have made the natives of Asia Minor as strong and spirited as the Hellenes, but nationalism is no servant of logic and the Greeks limited the praise to themselves. The author of Jubilees had apparently heard of the Greek theory and appropriated it for the glorification of Israel; for him it is Zion, facing Sinai and the Garden of Eden, that is the navel of the earth. A Hermetic writer applied the theory of the golden mean of climate to his own country, Egypt.

These examples show that discoveries of borrowings and influences have only a modest heuristic value unless we can learn why and to what purpose the new motif was woven into the traditional design. Darwinism was one of the main forces in the formation of the worldview prevalent between 1870 and 1918, but in Europe it acted as a solvent whereas in America the same ideology worked cohesively. In the New World the notion of the survival of the fittest both justified and ennobled the aggressive businessman who never gives a sucker an even break and at the same time cheered the poor newcomer to the land of unlimited possibilities. On both continents people converted bits and pieces of a complex ideological system to their own purposes, indifferent to the general meaning and value of the theories they so used.

The purpose of this retrospective chapter is to warn the reader that the foundations upon which our historical construction is built are weak. Our sources are not only fragmentary, but one-sided as well. Documents, papyri, and inscriptions mention Jews, but as a rule do not say anything about their Jewishness. The Jewish literary sources that have survived were selected by sectarians and therefore as a rule reflect only the religious aspects of Jewish life in the early Hellenistic age.

Because the sources that are available place the Jews in the framework of Greek civilization, they compel the investigator to formulate historical questions only as alternatives—Jewish or Greek—without being able to take into account all the other elements of the Levantine civilization of the time. Again, our sources sometimes allow us to take notice of intellectual changes, but do not allow us to discover the reasons for these changes. Yet, as Vico observed more than two centuries ago, people accept only the ideas for which their previous development has prepared their minds, and which, let us add, appear to be useful to them.

Nevertheless, even if we do not as yet know the answers, we shall never obtain them if we do not ask the questions. The present author hopes that this book will allow the reader to ask why. As Seneca says: *Plurimum ad inveniendum contulit qui speravit posse reperiri.*

Bibliographical Note
Bibliography
Index

Abbreviations

AASOR	Annual, American Schools of Oriental Research
AC	L'antiquité classique
AJP	American Journal of Papyrology
BA	Biblical Archaeologist
BAR	Biblical Archaeology Review
BJRL	Bulletin of the John Rylands Library
CBQ	Catholic Biblical Quarterly
CRAI	Comptes rendus de l'Académie des Inscriptions et Belles-Lettres
HTR	Harvard Theological Review
HUCA	Hebrew Union College Annual
IEJ	Israel Exploration Journal
JBL	Journal of Biblical Literature
JJS	Journal of Jewish Studies
JQR	Jewish Quarterly Review
JSJ	Journal for the Study of Judaism in the Persian, Hellenistic, and Roman Period
JSS	Journal of Semitic Studies
JTS	Journal of Theological Studies
NTS	New Testament Studies
PAAJR	Proceedings of the American Academy of Jewish Research
PEQ	Palestine Exploration Quarterly
RB	Revue biblique
REJ	Revue des études juives
RHR	Revue de l'histoire des religions
RQ	Revue de Qumran
SH	Scripta Hierosolymitana
VT	Vetus Testamentum
ZAW	Zeitschrift für die alttestamentliche Wissenschaft

Bibliographical Note

A. I. Baumgarten

This book is appearing in print many years after it was first completed and seven years after its author's death. A few words of explanation therefore seem appropriate. Professor Elias Bickerman completed the initial version of the work in 1963 and expected it to be published fairly soon thereafter. In the preface to *Four Strange Books of the Bible* (1967), he referred to his forthcoming "History of the Jews in the Greek Age." For whatever reason, these hopes were not realized and the manuscript remained unpublished. Bickerman continued to work on the topic, and a number of his later articles were studies directly resulting from research connected with this book.

At some point Bickerman decided on a fundamental change in format. Originally, the volume had been planned as a book with full scholarly apparatus, including copious notes (which I helped edit and check in 1963–64). Bickerman concluded that the task of bringing the notes up to date was hopeless, and elected to have the text alone published. The typescript of the notes seems to have been destroyed.

Bickerman himself did, however, revise the text. That revision, which is the basis of this book, can be dated with certainty. Bickerman regularly typed lecture notes or corrected pages of works in progress on the backs of letters or memos he had received. This book is no exception; additions and changes in the final typescript are inserted on the backs of dated correspondence. I noted one letter from March 31, 1978, and a few dated 1979; the overwhelming majority of the letters, however, are from the academic year 1980–81, the latest date being April 2, 1981. These dates indicate that Bickerman prepared the final revision during the last years of his life, with most of the work done in the months before setting off for Israel in the summer of 1981, a trip from which he was not to return.

This book therefore represents Bickerman's statement on the subject as of 1980–81, not 1963. As one illustration of this point, I would note that the discussion of Ezra and of the involvement of the Persians in fixing Jewish law reflects the ideas presented at what must have been Bickerman's last academic appearance, the paper he delivered at the 1981 World Congress of Jewish Studies in Jerusalem just weeks before his death.

The decision to drop the notes was significant. The book now appears with only minimal mention of the primary sources on which the argument is based, and with no references to the views of scholars with whom the author agreed or disagreed. This situation is unfortunate because this work, aside from presenting and analyzing the history of the period it covers, also argues an important thesis whose significance may be obscured because of the lack of notes.

Bickerman's greatest contribution to Jewish History is universally acknowledged to be his *Gott der Makkabäer,* which appeared in Berlin in 1937, and in English translation in 1979. In this work Bickerman proposed the revolutionary notion that the instigators of the persecutions of Antiochus Epiphanes were the Jewish Hellenists of Jerusalem, under the leadership of Menelaos. Antiochus IV, according to Bickerman, persecuted the Jews at the urging of the Jewish authorities. Bickerman was convinced that this interpretation of Antiochus's policy would explain aspects which he believed to be otherwise unintelligible.

Response to *Der Gott der Makkabäer* at the time of its initial appearance showed great respect for its author's learning and refutation of previously accepted hypotheses, but little inclination to adopt the book's suggestion that Jewish reformers inspired Antiochus' decrees. Of the various criticisms written, the most trenchant was by I. Heinemann, in *Monatschrift für Geschichte und Wissenschaft des Judentums,* 82 (1938), 145–172. Bickerman himself admitted the force of Heinemann's review, and even referred the reader to it in the preface to the English translation of his work (p. xii). Nevertheless, Bickerman continued to hold to the interpretation he had proposed, writing several pages in defense of his views in the preface to the English edition (pp. xii–xiii) and a long note at the end of the same volume (pp. 113–114). It will be obvious to the reader of the present book that Bickerman did not change his mind. Scattered throughout this volume are remarks that make it clear that the author continued to see the Jewish reformers as having inspired Antiochus IV.

Of the various points Heinemann made against Bickerman, one in particular is essential to appreciating the present work. There is a section in *Der Gott der Makkabäer* in which Bickerman tries to understand what inspired the reformers to take the steps he attributed to them (pp. 83–92 in the English translation). In writing these pages, he assumed that the reformers were familiar with ideas current in the contemporary Hellenistic world. Heinemann asked, very pointedly, whether it was reasonable to ascribe such ideas to Jews in Jerusalem toward the end of the first half of the second century B.C.E. The hellenization of orientals at the time, in the Seleucid Empire in general and in a provincial backwater town such as Jerusalem in particular, would have been very superficial, according to Heinemann. This lack of extensive hellenization, Heinemann concluded, made Bickerman's hypothesis implausible (Heinemann, pp. 157–159). The issue of the extent of hellenization in pre-Maccabean Jerusalem has been of much interest to scholars since the publication of Heinemann's review; contributions on this important question have been made by Victor Tcherikover, Martin Hengel, and Arnaldo Momigliano, to mention but three of the distinguished participants in this scholarly discussion.

This posthumous book is Bickerman's fully nuanced response. He concedes a few vital points: the really thorough hellenization of the Jews first took place after Hasmonean independence. He admits how little we know, how scanty and one-sided the evidence is, and the existence of numerous unknown factors that impair our ability to draw firm conclusions. Nevertheless, he argues for sufficient change prior to the Maccabees to support his interpretation in *Der Gott der Makkabäer*. Thus he elaborates the arguments against the antiquity of the Law, which he believes he hears echoed in the writings of pious authors of the period. He specifically connects that antinomian argument with the program of reforms in the days of Antiochus IV. Similarly, he discusses the selective nature of the surviving evidence and the fact that nothing has survived of the writings of the "sinners" condemned by Ben Sira and others. But these nonconformists, he reminds us, were Jews; if we knew their beliefs they would help us draw a less one-sided picture of Judaism in the period and thus teach us about changes that had taken place. Finally, I am sure Bickerman had Menelaos and the other reformers (as he understood them) in mind when, on the last page of the book, he makes the remark based on Vico that people accept only those ideas for which they are ready, and which they find useful.

Bibliography

Hellenistic History and Civilization

Bevan, E. R. *The House of Ptolemy.* 1968.
—— *The House of Seleucus.* 1902.
Bouché-Leclerq, A. *Histoire des Séleucides.* 1913–14.
Hadas, M. *Hellenistic Culture: Fusion and Diffusion.* 1959.
Preaux, C. *Le monde hellénistique.* 1978.
Tarn, W. W., and E. Griffiths. *Hellenistic Civilization.* 1952.
Will, E. *Histoire politique du monde hellénistique,* vols. I–II. 1966–67.

Hellenistic Civilization and the Jews

Charlesworth, J., ed. *The Old Testament Pseudepigrapha,* vols. I–II. 1983–1985.
Goldstein, J. "Jewish Acceptance and Rejection of Hellenism," in *Jewish and Christian Self-Definition,* vol. II: *Aspects of Judaism in the Graeco-Roman Period,* ed. E. P. Sanders et al., pp. 64–87, 318–326. 1981.
Guttman, J. *The Beginnings of Hellenistic Jewish Literature,* vols. I–II (in Hebrew). 1958–1963.
Hengel, M. *Jews, Greeks, and Barbarians.* 1980.
—— *Judaism and Hellenism,* vols. I–II. 1974.
Millar, F. "The Background to the Maccabean Revolution: Reflections on Martin Hengel's *Judaism and Hellenism.*" *JJS,* 29 (1978), 1–21.
Momigliano, A. *Alien Wisdom.* 1975.
Schurer, E., G. Vermes, and F. Millar. *History of the Jews in the Age of Jesus Christ,* vols. II–III. 1979–1986.
Stern, M. *Greek and Latin Authors on Jews and Judaism,* vols. I–III. 1976–1984.
—— and U. Rapaport. *The History of Eretz Israel: The Hellenistic Period and the Hasmonean State* (in Hebrew). 1981.
Stone, M., ed. *Jewish Writings of the Second Temple Period: The Literature of the Jewish People in the Period of the Second Temple and the Talmud.* 1984.

—— *Scriptures, Sects, and Visions.* 1980.
Tcherikover, V. *Hellenistic Civilization and the Jews.* 1959.

Alexander the Great

Cohen, S. J. D. "Alexander the Great and Jaddus the High Priest According to Josephus." *AJS Review,* 7–8 (1982–83), 41–68.
Delling, G. "Alexander der Grosse als Bekenner des jüdischen Gottesglaubens." *JSJ,* 12 (1981), 1–51.
Golan, D. "Josephus, Alexander's Visit to Jerusalem, and Modern Historiography," in *Josephus Flavius, Historian of Eretz Israel in the Hellenistic Roman Period,* ed. U. Rappaport, pp. 29–56 (in Hebrew). 1982.
Kasher, A. "Alexander of Macedon's Campaign in Palestine" (in Hebrew). *Beth Miqra,* 20 (1975), 187–208.
Marcus, R. "Alexander the Great and the Jews," in Josephus, *Jewish Antiquities Books IX-XI* (LCL Translation), vol. VI, pp. 512–532.
Momigliano, A. "Flavius Josephus and Alexander's Visit to Jerusalem." *Athenaeum,* 57 (1979), 442–448.
Pacella, D. "Alessandro e gli ebrei nella testimonianza della Ps. Callistene." *Annali della Scuola Normale Superiore di Pisa,* 12 (1982), 1255–1269.

Insurrection against Darius I

Bickerman, E. "Darius, Ps. Smerdis, and the Magi," in *Religions and Politics in the Hellenistic and Roman Periods,* pp. 617–641. 1985.
—— "En marge de l'écriture," in *Studies in Jewish and Christian History,* vol. III, pp. 331–336. 1976–1986.

Samaritans

Bickerman, E. "Un document relatif a la persécution d'Antiochus IV Epiphane," in *Studies,* vol. II, pp. 105–135.
Cross, F. M. "Aspects of Samaritan and Jewish History in late Persian and Hellenistic Times." *HTR,* 59 (1966), 201–211.
——"Papyri of the Fourth Century B.C. from Daliyeh, " in *New Directions in Biblical Archaeology,* ed. D. N. Freedman and J. C. Greenfield, pp. 45–69. 1969.
Dexinger, F. "Limits of Tolerance in Judaism: The Samaritan Example," in *Jewish and Christian Self-Definition,* vol. II: *Aspects of Judaism in the Graeco-Roman Period,* ed. E. P. Sanders et al., pp. 88–114, 327–338. 1981.
Kippenberg, H. G. *Garizim und Synagoge.* 1971.
Lapp, P., and N. Lapp, eds. *Discoveries in the Wadi ed-Daliyeh (AASOR 41).* 1974.
Mor, M. "Samaritans and Jews in the Ptolemaic Period and the Beginning of Seleucid Rule in Palestine" (in Hebrew). *Studies in the History of the Jewish People and the Land of Israel,* 5 (1980), 71–81.

Purvis, D. J. *The Samaritan Pentateuch and the Origins of the Samaritan Sect.* 1968.

Rowley, H. H. "Sanballat and the Samaritan Temple." *BJRL*, 38 (1955), 166–198.

Schiffman, L. H. "The Samaritans in Tannaitic Halakhah." *JQR*, 75 (1985), 323–350.

Wright, G. E. "The Samaritans at Schechem." *HTR*, 55 (1962), 357–366.

Greeks and Jews

Feldman, L. "The Jews in Greek and Latin Literature," in *The Diaspora in the Hellenistic Roman World*, ed. M. Stern, pp. 238–264 (in Hebrew). 1983.

Gager, J. *Moses in Greco-Roman Paganism.* 1972.

Guttman, J. *The Beginnings of Jewish Hellenistic Literature,* vols. I–II (in Hebrew). 1958–1963.

Sevenester, J. N. *The Roots of Pagan Anti-Semitism in the Ancient World.* 1975.

Stern, M. *Greek and Latin Authors on Jews and Judaism,* vols. I–III. 1976–1984.

—— "Hellenistic Jewish Literature," in *The Diaspora in the Hellenistic Roman World*, ed. M. Stern, pp. 208–237 (in Hebrew). 1983.

Daniel

Bickerman, E. *Four Strange Books of the Bible*, pp. 51–138. 1967.

Collins, J. *Daniel.* 1984.

Delcor, M. *Le Livre de Daniel.* 1971.

Ginsberg, H. L. *Studies in Daniel.* 1948.

Grabbe, L. L. "Chronology in Hellenistic Jewish Literature." *SBL Seminar Papers*, 17 (1979), 43–68.

Hartman, L. E., and A. Dilella. *The Book of Daniel.* 1978.

Koch, K. *Das Buch Daniel.* 1980.

Lacocque, A. *The Book of Daniel.* 1979.

Cyrus' Proclamation of Restoration

Bickerman, E. "The Edict of Cyrus in Ezra I," in *Studies*, vol. I, pp. 72–122.

Eilers, W. "Der Keilschrifttext des Kyros-Zylinders." *Festgabe deutscher Iranisten zur 2500 Jahrfeier Irans*, pp. 156–166. 1971.

Tadmor, H. "The Historical Context of Cyrus's Proclamation," in *David Ben Gurion Jubilee Volume*, pp. 450–473 (in Hebrew). 1964.

Ezra and Nehemiah

Smith, M. *Palestinian Parties and Politics That Shaped the Old Testament*, pp. 99–147. 1971.

The Jewish Periphery

Abel, F. M. _Géographie de la Palestine_, vols. I–II. 1933–1938.
Avi-Yonah, M. "Historical Geography" in _The Jewish People in the First Century_, ed. S. Safrai and M. Stern, vol. I, pp. 78–85. 1974.
———— _The Historical Geography of Palestine_ (in Hebrew). 1962.
Vogel, E. K. "Bibliography of Holy Land Sites." _HUCA_, 42 (1971), 1–96.

Lachish

Aharoni, Y. _Investigations at Lachish: The Sanctuary and the Residency (Lachish V)_, pp. 3–11. 1975.
———— "Trial Excavations at the 'Solar Shrine' at Lachish, Preliminary Report." _IEJ_, 18 (1968), 157–169.
Campbell, E. F. "Jewish Shrines of the Hellenistic and Persian Periods," in _Symposia Celebrating the Seventy-Fifth Anniversary of the American Schools of Oriental Research_, ed. F. M. Cross, pp. 159–167. 1979.

The Diaspora

Collins, J. _Between Athens and Jerusalem_. 1982.
Radin, M. _The Jews among Greeks and Romans_. 1915.
Schürer, E. _The History of the Jewish People in the Age of Jesus Christ_, rev. and ed. by G. Vermes, F. Millar, and M. Black, vol. III, pp. 1–177. 1973–1986.
Stern, M., ed. _The Diaspora in the Hellenistic Roman World_ (in Hebrew). 1983.

The Jews at Elephantine

Bresciani, E. "Egypt, Persian Satrapy" _CHJ_, 1 (1984), 358–372.
Muffs, Y. _Studies in the Aramaic Legal Papyri from Elephantine_. 1969.
Porten, B. _Archives from Elephantine_. 1968.
Yaron, Y. _Introduction to the Law of the Aramaic Papyri_. 1961.

Murashu Archives

Bickerman, E. "The Babylonian Captivity." _CHJ_, 1 (1984), 342–357.
———— "The Generation of Ezra and Nehemiah," in _Studies_, vol. III, pp. 299–326.
Zadok, R. _The Jews in Babylonia in the Chaldean and Achaemenid Periods in the Light of Babylonian Archives_ (in Hebrew). 1976.

Tobit

Deslaers, P. _Das Buch Tobit_. 1982.
Greenfield, J. C. "Ahiqar in the Book of Tobit," in _De la Torah au Méssie: Mélanges H. Cazelles_, ed. M. Carrez et al., pp. 329–336. 1981.
Lebram, J. "Die Weltreiche in der jüdischen Apokalyptik: Bemerkungen zu Tobit 14:4–7." _ZAW_, 76 (1964), 329–331.

Milik, J. T. "La patrie de Tobit." *RB*, 73 (1966), 522–530.
Perdue, L. "Liminality as a Social Setting for Wisdom Instructions." *ZAW*, 93 (1981), 114–126.
Schürer et al. *History of the Jewish People*, vol. III, pp. 222–231.
Thomas, J. D. "The Greek Text of Tobit." *JBL*, 91 (1972), 463–471.

Aramaic

Greenfield, J. C. "Aramaic and Its Dialects" and "The Language of Palestine, 200 B.C.E.–200 C.E.," in *Jewish Languages: Themes and Variations*, ed. H. H. Paper, pp. 29–43, 143–154. 1978.
Kutscher, E. Y. "Aramaic." *Hebrew and Aramaic Studies* (1977), 90–155.
Schürer et al. *History of the Jewish People*, vol. II, pp. 1–28.

Pesher

Brooke, G. J. "Qumran Pesher: Towards the Redefinition of a Genre." *RQ*, 10 (1981), 483–503.
Fishbane, M. "The Qumran Pesher and Traits of Ancient Hermeneutics." *Proceedings of the Sixth World Congress of Jewish Studies*, 6 (1977), 97–114.
Horgan, P. M. *Pesharim: Qumran Interpretations of Biblical Books*. 1979.
Patte, D. *Early Jewish Hermeneutic in Palestine*. 1975.
Rabinowitz, I. "Pesher/Pittaron: Its Biblical Meaning and Its Significance in the Qumran Literature." *RQ*, 8 (1973), 219–232.

Jewish Response to Pagan Cults

Frey, J. B. *Corpus Inscriptionum Iudaicarum*, with prolegomenon by B. Lifshitz, p. 82. 1975.
Lewis, D. M. "The First Greek Jew." *JSS*, 2 (1957), 264–266.

Ptolemaic Palestine

Bagnall, R. S. *The Administration of Ptolemaic Possessions outside Egypt*. 1976.
Shalit, A. "Koile Syria from the Mid-Fourth Century to the Beginning of the Third Century, B.C." *SH*, 1 (1954), 64–77.
Schürer et al. *History of the Jewish People*, vol. III, pp. 38–62.
Tcherikover, A., and A. Fuks. *Corpus Papyrorum Iudaicarum*, vol. I, pp. 1–47, 115–130. 1957.
Westermann, W. L. "Enslaved Persons Who Are Free." *AJP*, 59 (1938), 1–30.

Ptolemaic Diaspora

Fraser, P. M. *Ptolemaic Alexandria*. 1972.
Kasher, A. "The First Jewish Military Units in Ptolemaic Egypt." *JSJ*, 9 (1978), 57–67.
——— *The Jews in Hellenistic and Roman Egypt*. 1985.

Smallwood, E. M. *Philonis Alexandrini Legatio ad Gaium.* 1961.
Tcherikover, A. "The Third Book of Maccabees as a Historical Source." *SH*, 7 (1961), 1–26.
——— and A. Fuks. *Corpus Papyrorum Iudaicarum,* vol. I, pp. 131–257. 1957.

Seleucid Dispersion

Kraeling, C. H. "The Jewish Community at Antioch." *JBL*, 51 (1932), 130–160.
Schürer et al. *History of the Jewish People,* vol. III, pp. 5–38.
Wilken, R., and W. Meeks. *Jews and Christians at Antioch.* 1978.

Susanna, Bel, and Dragon

Delcor, M. *Le Livre de Daniel.* 1971.
Milik, J. T. "Daniel et Susanne à Qumran," in *De la Torah au Méssie: Mélanges H. Cazelles,* ed. M. Carrez et al., pp. 337–359. 1981.
Moore, C. A. *Daniel, Esther, and Jeremiah: The Additions.* 1977.
Schürer et al. *History of the Jewish People,* vol. III, pp. 730–734.

Epistle of Jeremiah

Moore, C. A. *Daniel, Esther, and Jeremiah: The Additions.* 1977.
Roth, W. "For Life He Appeals to Death." *CBQ*, 37 (1975), 21–47.
Schürer et al. *History of the Jewish People,* vol. III, pp. 743–745.

Septuagint

Bickerman, E. "The Septuagint as a Translation," in *Studies,* vol. I, pp. 167–200.
Dodd, C. H. *The Bible and the Greeks,* pp. 3–98. 1935.
Frankel, Z. *Über den Einfluss der palästinischen Exegese auf die alexandrinische Hermeneutik.* 1851.
——— *Vorstudien zu der Septuaginta.* 1841.
Orlinsky, H. "The Septuagint as Holy Writ and the Philosophy of the Translators." *HUCA*, 46 (1975), 89–114.
Schürer et al. *History of the Jewish People,* vol. III, pp. 474–493.
Tov, E. "The Rabbinic Tradition Concerning the Alterations Inserted into the Greek Pentateuch and Their Relation to the Original Text of the LXX." *JSJ*, 15 (1984), 65–89.

Aristobulus

Collins, A. Y. "Aristobulus," in *The Old Testament Pseudepigrapha,* ed. J. H. Charlesworth, vol. II, pp. 831–842.
Schürer et al. *History of the Jewish People,* vol. III, pp. 579–587.
Walter, N. "Anfänge alexandrisch-jüdischer Bibelauslegung bei Aristobulos." *Helikon*, 3 (1969), 353–372.
——— *Der Thoraausleger Aristobulos.* 1964.

Letter of Aristeas

Bickerman, E. "Zur Datierung des Pseudo-Aristeas," in *Studies,* vol. I, pp. 123–136.
Cohen, N. "The Names of the Translators in the Letter of Aristeas: A Study in the Dynamics of Cultural Transition." *JSJ,* 15 (1984), pp. 32–64.
Gooding, D. W. "Aristeas and Septuagint Origins." *VT,* 13 (1963), 357–379.
Hadas, M. *Aristeas to Philocrates.* 1951.
Howard, G. E. "The Letter of Aristeas and Diaspora Judaism." *JTS,* 22 (1971), 337–348.
Jellicoe, S. "The Occasion and Purpose of the Letter of Aristeas: A Reexamination." *NTS,* 12 (1966), 144–150.
Pelletier, A. *Lettre d'Aristée à Philocrate.* 1962.
Schwartz, D. R. "The Priests in Ep. Arist. 310." *JBL,* 97 (1978), 567–571.
Shutt, R. J. "Letter of Aristeas," in *Old Testament Pseudepigrapha,* vol. II, pp. 7–34.
Schürer et al. *History of the Jewish People,* vol. III, pp. 677–687.
Tcherikover, A. "The Ideology of the Letter of Aristeas." *HTR,* 51 (1958), 59–85.

Seleucid Conquest

Bar-Kochva, B. "The Battle of Raphia (217 B.C.E.)" (in Hebrew). *Studies in the History of the Jewish People and the Land of Israel,* 4 (1978), 41–58.
Bickerman, E. "La charte Séleucide de Jérusalem" and "Héliodore au Temple de Jérusalem," in *Studies,* vol. II, pp. 44–85, 159–191.
Fischer, T. "Zur Seleukideninschrift von Hepzibah." *Zeitschrift für Papyrologie und Epigraphik,* 33 (1979), 131–138.
Galili, E. "Raphia 217 B.C.E. Revisited." *Scripta Classica Israelica,* 3 (1976–1977), 52–126.
Landau, Y. H. "A Greek Inscription Found near Hepzibah." *IEJ,* 16 (1966), 54–70.
Taeubler, E. "Jerusalem 201–199 B.C.E." *JQR,* 37 (1946–1947), 1–30, 125–137, 240–263.

Gerousia

Mantel, H. *Studies in the History of the Sanhedrin.* 1961.
Rivkin, H. "Beth Din, Boule, Sanhedrin: A Tragedy of Errors." *HUCA,* 46 (1975), 181–199.

High Priest

Mantel, H. "The Development of the Oral Law," in *The World History of the Jewish People: Society and Religion in the Second Temple Period,* ed. M. Avi-Yonah and Z. Baras, pp. 42–43, 1977.
Schwartz, D. R. "The Priests in Ep. Arist. 310." *JBL,* 97 (1978), 567–571.

Temple

Bickerman, E. "The Civic Prayer for Jerusalem" and "Une proclamation Séleucide relative au Temple de Jérusalem," in *Studies*, vol. II, pp. 209–312, 86–104.
Liver, J. "The Half Sheqel Offering in Biblical and Post-Biblical Literature." *HTR*, 56 (1963), 173–198.

Delos

Frey, J. B. *Corpus Inscriptionum Iudaicarum*, with prolegomenon by B. Lifshitz, no. 725, pp. 523–525. 1975.

Priests and Levites

Cody, A. *A History of Old Testament Priesthood*, pp. 175–196. 1969.
Liver, J. *Chapters in the History of the Priests and Levites* (in Hebrew). 1968.

Pharisees

Bickerman, E. "La chaîne de la tradition pharisienne," in *Studies*, vol. II, pp. 256–269.
Herr, M. D. "Continuum in the Chain of Torah Transmission" (in Hebrew). *Zion*, 44 (1979), 43–56.
Neusner, J. *The Rabbinic Traditions about the Pharisees before 70*, vols. I–III. 1971.

Economic Life

Bickerman, E. *Four Strange Books of the Bible*, pp. 158–167. 1967.
——— "The Maxim of Antigonus of Socho," in *Studies*, vol. II, pp. 270–289.
Rostovtzeff, M. *Social and Economic History of the Hellenistic World*, vols. I–III. 1941.

Scribes and Sages

Drazin, N. *History of Jewish Education from 515 B.C.E. to 226 C.E.* 1940.
Ebner, E. *Elementary Education in Ancient Israel*. 1956.
Goodblatt, D. "The Talmudic Sources on the Origins of Organized Jewish Education" (in Hebrew). *Studies in the History of the Jewish People and the Land of Israel*, 5 (1980), 83–108.
Urbach, E. E. "The Derasha as a Basis of the Halacha and the Problem of the Soferim." *Tarbiz*, 27 (1958), 166–182.

Ben Sira

Academy of the Hebrew Language. *The Book of Ben Sira: Text, Concordance, and an Analysis of the Vocabulary* (in Hebrew). 1973.

Dilella, A. *The Hebrew Text of Sirach: A Text Critical and Historical Study.* 1966.

Haspecker, J. *Gottesfurcht bei Jesus Sirach.* 1967.

Jacob, E. "Wisdom and Religion in Sirach," in *Israelite Wisdom,* ed. J. G. Gammie, pp. 247–260. 1978.

O'Fearghail, F. "Sir. 50:5–21: Yom Kippur or the Daily Whole Offering?" *Biblica,* 59 (1978), 301–316.

Rüger, H. P. *Text und Textform im Hebräischen Sirach.* 1970.

Sanders, J. T. *Ben Sira and Demotic Wisdom.* 1983.

——— "Ben Sira's Ethic of Caution." *HUCA,* 50 (1979), 73–106.

Segal, M. *Sefer Ben Sira Hashalem.* 1958.

Stadelmann, H. *Ben Sira als Schriftgelehrter.* 1980.

Schürer et al. *History of the Jewish People,* vol. III, pp. 198–212.

Yadin, Y. *The Ben Sira Scroll from Massada.* 1965.

Theodotus Inscription

Lifshitz, B. *Donateurs et fondateurs dans les synagogues juives,* pp. 70–71. 1967.

Midrash

Bickerman, E. "Origines Gentium," in *Religions,* pp. 399–418.

Heinemann, I. *Darkhei Haggadah* (in Hebrew). 1970.

Lieberman, S. *Hellenism in Jewish Palestine.* 1962.

Porton, G. "Midrash: Palestinian Jews and the Hebrew Bible in the Greco-Roman Period," in *Aufstieg und Niedergang der römischen Welt,* ed. H. Temporini and W. Haase, vol. II, 19/2, pp. 103–138. 1979.

Pagan Mythology in Aggadah

Delcor, M. "Le mythe de la chute des anges." *RHR,* 190 (1976), 3–53.

Hanson, P. D. "Rebellion in Heaven." *JBL,* 96 (1979), 195–233.

Molenberg, C. "A Study of the Roles of Shemhaza and Asael in I Enoch 6–11." *JJS,* 35 (1984), 101–133.

Sperber, D. "Varia Midrashica." I, *REJ,* 129 (1970), 87–92; II, *REJ,* 131 (1972), 161–170; III, *REJ,* 134 (1975), 125–132; IV, *REJ,* 137 (1978), 149–157.

Spiegel, S. "Noah, Daniel, and Job," in *Louis Ginzberg Jubilee Volume,* ed. A. Marx, pp. 305–356. 1945.

Political Interpretation of Midrash

Finkelstein, L. "The Oldest Midrash: Pre-Rabbinic Ideals and Teaching in the Passover Haggadah," and "Pre-Maccabean Documents in the Passover Haggadah," in *Pharisaism in the Making,* pp. 13–40, 41–120. 1972.

Goldschmidt, D. *The Passover Haggadah* (in Hebrew). 1960.

Heinemann, J. *Aggadah and Its Development,* pp. 75–90 (in Hebrew). 1974.

Legal Reinterpretation

Bickerman, E. "Two Legal Interpretations of the Septuagint," in *Studies*, vol. I, pp. 201–224.

Halivni, D. W. *Midrash, Mishnah, and Gemara.* 1986.

Urbach, E. E. *The Halachah: Its Sources and Development* (in Hebrew). 1984.

Debt Slavery

Westerman, W. L. "Enslaved Persons Who Are Free." *AJP*, 59 (1938), 1–30.

Women

Gilbert, M. "Ben Sira et la femme." *Revue Theologique du Louvain*, 7 (1976), 426–442.

Trenchard, W. C. *Ben Sira's View of Women: A Literary Analysis.* 1982.

Pseudepigrapha

Bickerman, E. "Faux littéraires dans l'antiquité classique," in *Studies*, vol. III, pp. 196–211.

Charlesworth, J. *The Pseudepigrapha and Modern Research.* 1980.

Fritz, K. von. *Pseudepigrapha.* 1972.

Speyer, W. *Die literarische Fälschung im heidnischen und christlichen Altertum: Ein Versuch ihrer Deutung.* 1971.

Testaments of the Twelve Patriarchs

Becker, J. *Die Testamente der zwölf Patriarchen.* 1980.

Bickerman, E. "The Date of the Testaments of the Twelve Patriarchs," in *Studies*, vol. II, pp. 1–23.

Hollander, H. W. *The Testaments of the Twelve Patriarchs.* 1985.

Hultgard, A. *L'eschatologie des Testaments des Douze Patriarches.* 1977.

Kee, H. C. "The Ethical Dimension of the Testaments of the Twelve as a Clue to Provenance." *NTS*, 24 (1978), 259–270.

——— "Testaments of the Twelve Patriarchs," in Old Testament Pseudepigrapha, vol. I, pp. 775–828.

Philonenko, M. *Les interpolations chrétiennes des Testaments des Douze Patriarches et les manuscrits de Qoumran.* 1960.

Slingerland, H. *The Testaments of the Twelve Patriarchs: A Critical History of Research.* 1977.

Schürer et al. *History of the Jewish People*, vol. III, pp. 767–781.

Jubilees

Albeck, C. H. *Das Buch der Jubiläen und die Halacha.* 1930.

Davenport, G. L. *The Eschatology of the Book of Jubilees.* 1971.

Finkelstein, L. "The Book of Jubilees and Rabbinic Halaka." *HTR*, 16 (1923), 39–61.

Goldstein, J. "The Date of the Book of Jubilees." *PAAJR*, 50 (1983), 63–86.

Jaubert, A. "Le calendrier des Jubilés et de la secte de Qumran." *VT*, 3 (1953), 250–264.

Schürer et al. *History of the Jewish People*, vol. III, pp. 308–318.

Talmon, S. "The Calendar Reckoning of the Sect from the Judean Desert." *SH*, 4, (1965), 162–199.

Testuz, M. *Les idées réligieuses du livre de Jubilés*. 1960.

Vanderkam, J. *Textual and Historical Studies in the Book of Jubilees*. 1977.

Wintermute, O. S. "Jubilees," in *Old Testament Pseudepigrapha*, vol. II, pp. 35–142.

Kohelet

Bickerman, E. *Four Strange Books of the Bible*, pp. 139–168. 1967.

Braun, R. *Koheleth und die frühhellenistische Populärphilosophie*. 1973.

Whitley, C. *Koheleth*. 1979.

Oriental Historiography

Baumgarten, A. I. *The Phoenician History of Philo of Byblos: A Commentary*. 1981.

Bickerman, E. "Origines Gentium," in *Religions*, pp. 399–418.

Oden, R. "Philo of Byblos and Hellenistic Historiography." *PEQ*, 110 (1978), 115–126.

Demetrius

Bickerman, E. "The Jewish Historian Demetrius," in *Studies*, vol. II, pp. 347–358.

Gaster, M. "Demetrius und Seder Olam: Ein Problem der hellenistischen Literatur," in *Festkrift i anledning af Prof. David Simonsens 70-aarige fodelsdag*, ed. J. Fischer et. al., pp. 243–252. 1923.

Gutman, Jacob. *The Beginnings of Hellenistic Jewish Literature*, vol. I, pp. 132–147 (in Hebrew). 1958.

Holladay, C. R. "Demetrius the Chronographer as Historian and Apologist," in *Christian Teachings: Studies in Honor of Lemoine G. Lewis*, pp. 117–129. 1981.

——— *Fragments from Hellenistic Jewish Authors*, vol. I: *Historians*. 1983.

Hanson, J. "Demetrius the Chronographer," in *Old Testament Pseudepigrapha*, vol. II, pp. 843–854.

Schürer et al. *History of the Jewish People*, vol. III, pp. 513–517.

Mnaseas of Patra and Manetho

Stern, M. *Greek and Latin Authors on Jews and Judaism*, vol. I, pp. 62–86, 97–101. 1976.

Orphic Sacred Discourse

Lafargue, M. "Orphica," in *Old Testament Pseudepigrapha*, vol. II, pp. 795–801.
Schürer et al. *History of the Jewish People*, vol. III, pp. 661–671.
Walter, N. *Der Thoraausleger Aristobulos*, pp. 103–123, 202–261. 1964.
Zeegers-Vandervorst, N. "Les versions juives et chrétiennes du fr. 245–247 d'Orphée." *AC*, 39 (1970), 475–506.

Tobiads

Goldstein, J. "Tales of the Tobiads," in *Christianity, Judaism, and Other Greco-Roman Cults: Studies for Morton Smith at Sixty*, ed. J. Neusner, vol. III, pp. 85–123. 1975.
McCown, C. C. "The Araq el Amir and the Tobiads." *BA*, 20 (1957), 63–76.
Stern, M. "Notes on the Story of Joseph the Tobiad." (in Hebrew). *Tarbiz*, 32 (1963), 35–47.
Will, E. "L'Edifice dit Qasr el Abd à Araq al Amir." *CRAI* (Jan.–Mar. 1977), 69–85.

Diaspora Judaism

Bickerman, E. "The Altars of the Gentiles," in *Studies*, vol. II, pp. 324–346.
Lightstone, J. *The Commerce of the Sacred: Mediation of the Divine among Jews in the Graeco-Roman Diaspora*. 1984.
Smith, J. Z. *Map Is Not Territory*. 1978.

Fearers of Heaven

Feldman, L. "The Omnipresence of the God-Fearers." *BAR*, 12:5 (1986), 58–63, 64–69.
MacLennan, R. S., and A. T. Kraabel. "The God-Fearers—A Literary and Theological Invention." *BAR*, 12:5 (1986), 46–53, 64.
Stern, M. *Greek and Latin Authors on Jews and Judaism*, vol. II, pp. 103–106. 1980.
Schürer et al. *History of the Jewish People*, vol. III, pp. 150–176.
Tannenbaum, R. F. "Jews and God-Fearers in the Holy City of Aphrodite." *BAR*, 12:5 (1986), 54–57.

Conversion

Bamberger, B. J. *Proselytism in the Talmudic Period*. 1968.
Braude, W. G. *Jewish Proselytism in the First Five Centuries*. 1940.
Cohen, S. J. D. "The Origins of the Matrilineal Principle in Rabbinic Law." *AJS Review*, 10 (1985), 19–53.
Schiffman, L. H. "At the Crossroads: Tannaitic Perspectives on the Jewish-Christian Schism," in *Jewish and Christian Self-Definition*, vol. II: *Aspects of*

Judaism in the Graeco-Roman Period, ed. E. P. Sanders et al., pp. 115–156, 338–352. 1981.

Noachide Laws

Biberfeld, P. L. *Das noachidische Urrecht.* 1937.

Loewe, R. "Potentialities and Limitations of Universalism in the *Halakhah,*" in *Studies in Rationalism, Judaism, and Universalism in Memory of Leon Roth,* ed. R. Loewe, pp. 115–150. 1966.

Novak, D. *The Image of the Non-Jew in Judaism.* 1983.

Theodotus

Bull, R. J. "A Note on Theodotus's Description of Schechem." *HTR,* 60 (1967), 221–228.

Collins, J. J. "The Epic of Theodotus and the Hellenism of the Hasmoneans." *HTR,* 73 (1980) 91–104.

Fallon, F. "Theodotus" in *Old Testament Pseudepigrapha,* vol. II, pp. 785–794.

Guttman, J. *The Beginnings of Hellenistic Jewish Literature,* vol. II, pp. 245–261 (in Hebrew). 1963.

Pummer, R. "Genesis 34 in Jewish Writings of the Hellenistic and Roman Periods." *HTR,* 75 (1982), 177–188.

—— and M. Roussel. "A Note on Theodotus and Homer." *JSJ,* 13 (1982), 176–182.

Schürer et al. *History of the Jewish People,* vol. III, pp. 561–563.

III Maccabees

Hadas, M. *The Third and Fourth Books of Maccabees.* 1953.

Tcherikover, A. "The Third Book of Maccabees as a Historical Source." *SH,* 7 (1961), 1–26.

Old and New in Religion

Bickerman, E. "Couper une alliance," in *Studies,* vol. I, pp. 1–32.

Goldin, J. "The Three Pillars of Simon the Righteous." *PAAJR,* 27 (1958) 43–58.

Moore, G. F. "Simon the Righteous," in *Jewish Studies in Memory of Israel Abrahams,* ed. G. A. Kohut, pp. 348–364. 1927.

Sanders, E. P. *Paul and Palestinian Judaism.* 1977.

Divine Name

Baudissin, W. *Kyrios als Gottesname im Judentum und seine Stelle in die Religionsgeschichte,* vols. I–IV. 1926–1929.

Bickerman, E. "Anonymous Gods," in *Studies,* vol. III, pp. 270–281.

Finkelstein, L. "The Origins of the Pharisees." *Conservative Judaism*, 23 (1969), 25–35.

Marmorstein, A. *The Old Rabbinic Doctrine of God*, pp. 17–148. Reprinted 1968.

Spiegel, J. "The Employment of Palaeo-Hebrew Characters for the Divine Name at Qumran in the Light of Tannaitic Sources." *HUCA*, 42 (1971), 159–173.

Angels

Grant, R. M. *Les êtres Intermédiaires dans le judaisme tardif.* 1967.
Urbach, E. E. *The Sages*, vol. I, pp. 135–183. 1975.

Sin and Repentance

Büchler, A. *Studies in Sin and Atonement in the Rabbinic Literature of the First Century.* 1939.
Marmorstein, A. *The Doctrine of Merits in Old Rabbinical Literature.* 1920.
Urbach, E. E. *The Sages*, vol. I, pp. 420–523. 1975.

Death and Burial

Avigad, N. "The Necropolis of Jerusalem during the Second Temple Period," in *Sepher Yerushalayim*, ed. M. Avi-Yonah, pp. 320–348 (in Hebrew). 1956.
Figueras, P. *Decorated Jewish Ossuaries.* 1983.
Meyers, E. M. *Jewish Ossuaries: Reburial and Rebirth.* 1971.
——— "The Theological Implications of an Ancient Jewish Burial Custom." *JQR*, 62 (1971–1972), 95–119.
Rahmani, L. Y. "Jason's Tomb." *IEJ*, 17 (1967), 61–100.

Enoch

Beckwith, R. "The Earliest Enochic Literature and Its Calendar." *RQ*, 10 (1981), 365–403.
Black, M. *The Book of Enoch or First Enoch: A New English Edition with Commentary and Textual Notes.* 1985.
Greenfield, J., and M. Stone. "The Enochic Pentateuch and the Date of the Similitudes." *HTR*, 70 (1977), 51–65.
Hanson, P. D. *The Dawn of Apocalyptic.* 1975.
Hindley, J. C. "Towards a Date for the Similitudes of Enoch." *NTS*, 14 (1968), 551–565.
Isaac, E. "I Enoch," in *Old Testament Pseudepigrapha*, vol. I, pp. 5–89.
Knibb, M. *The Ethiopic Book of Enoch: A New Edition in the Light of the Aramaic Dead Sea Fragments.* 1978.
Milik, J. T. *The Book of Enoch: Aramaic Fragments of Qumran Cave 4.* 1976.
Russel, D. S. *The Method and Message of Jewish Apocalyptic.* 1964.
Schürer et al. *History of the Jewish People*, vol. III, pp. 250–269.

Prayer

Bickerman, E. "The Civic Prayer for Jerusalem" and "Bénédiction et prière," in *Studies,* vol. II, pp. 290–312, 313–323.

Elbogen, I. *Der jüdische Gottesdienst in seiner geschichtlichen Entwicklung.* 1913.

Heinemann, J. *Prayer in the Talmud.* 1977.

Petuchowski, J. "The Liturgy of the Synagogue: History, Structure, and Contents," in *Approaches to Ancient Judaism IV,* ed. W. S. Green, pp. 1–64. 1983.

Calendar

Herr, M. D. "The Calendar," in *The Jewish People in the First Century,* ed. S. Safrai and M. Stern, vol. II, pp. 834–864. 1976.

Vows and Oaths

Halivini, D. "On the Supposed Anti-Asceticism or Anti-Nazirism of Simon the Just." *JQR,* 58 (1967–1968), 243–252.

Lieberman, S. "Oaths and Vows," in *Greek in Jewish Palestine,* pp. 115–143. 1965.

Index

Entries in italic refer to headings in the Bibliography.